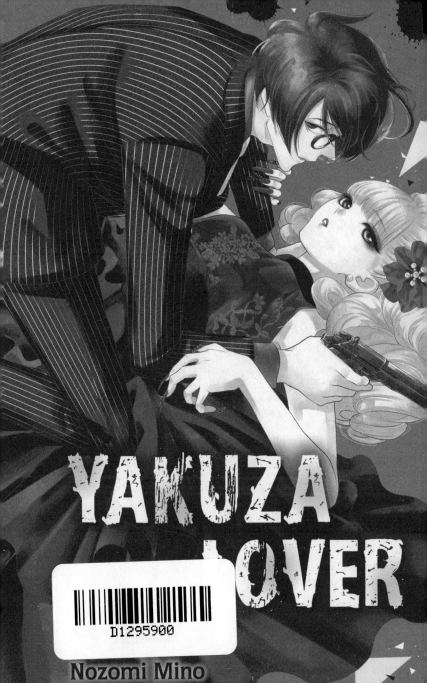

YAKUZA LOVER

Nozomi Mino

Contents

Characters

Toshiomi Oya
Underboss

Underboss of the Oya yakuza syndicate. He's a gentle man with a heart of gold—yet no mobster would dare defy him. He's drawn to Yuri's inner strength.

Yuri
College Student

A college student with a strong sense of integrity who cares deeply about her friends. After an assassination attempt against Oya, she realizes she's going to need to be stronger to survive as the lover of a yakuza.

Story

Feisty college student Yuri's life is turned upside down when drug dealers attack her at a party and Toshiomi Oya, the underboss of a yakuza syndicate, swoops in to save her.

Toshiomi lives life on the edge with no promise of tomorrow, and Yuri finds herself swept up in their passionate, all-consuming love affair. But after being attacked by Russion mob boss Semilio, Yuri vows to get stronger in order to not cause any more trouble for Oya.

Meanwhile, Shuichiro, Oya's father and the boss of the Oya syndicate, summons Yuri. He tells her to cut ties with the yakuza, but Yuri refuses. Later, Yuri and Oya's bond deepens after they spend a romance-filled Christmas together. But unbeknownst to them, a woman named Choko is hatching a scheme to make Oya hers...

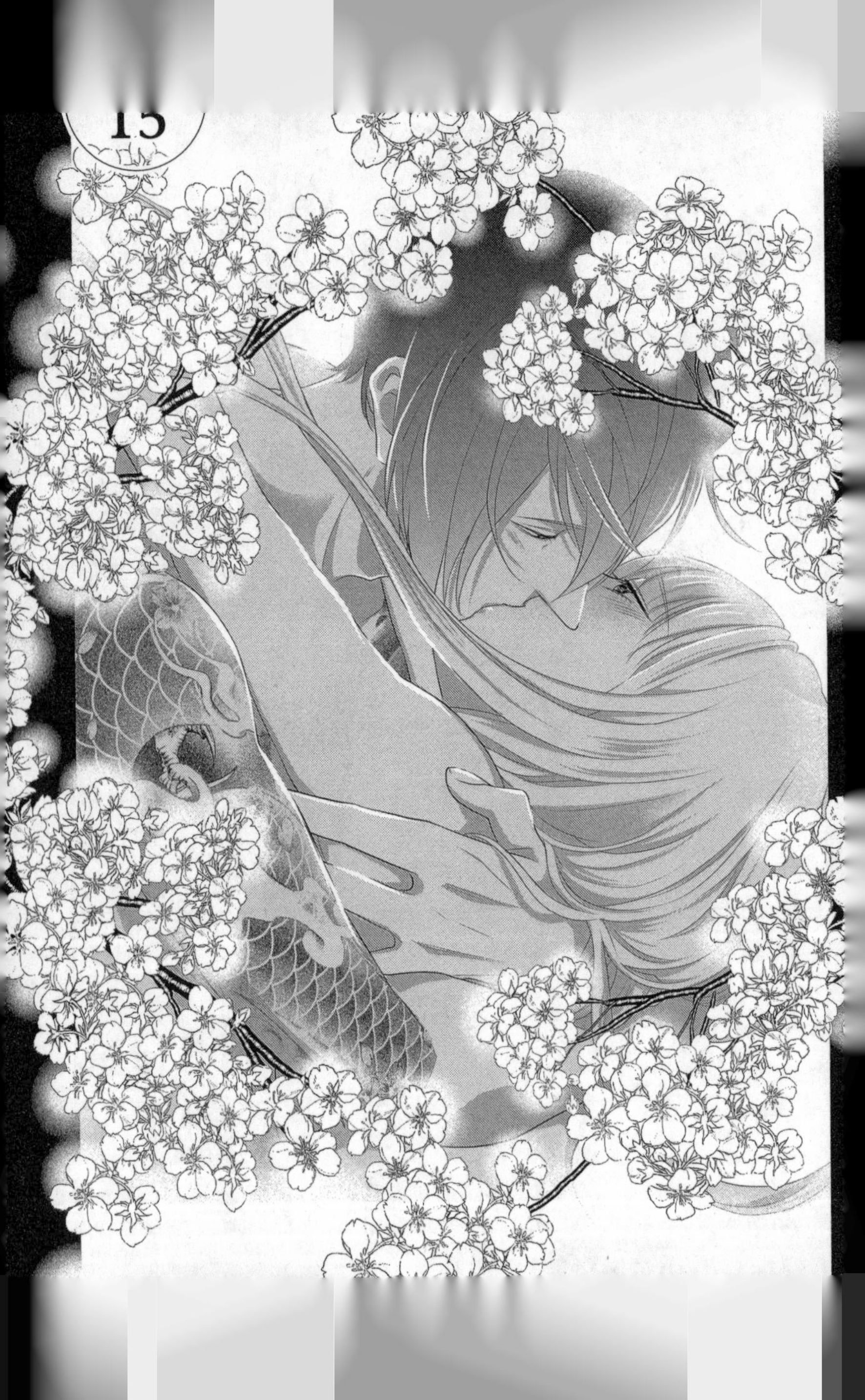
15

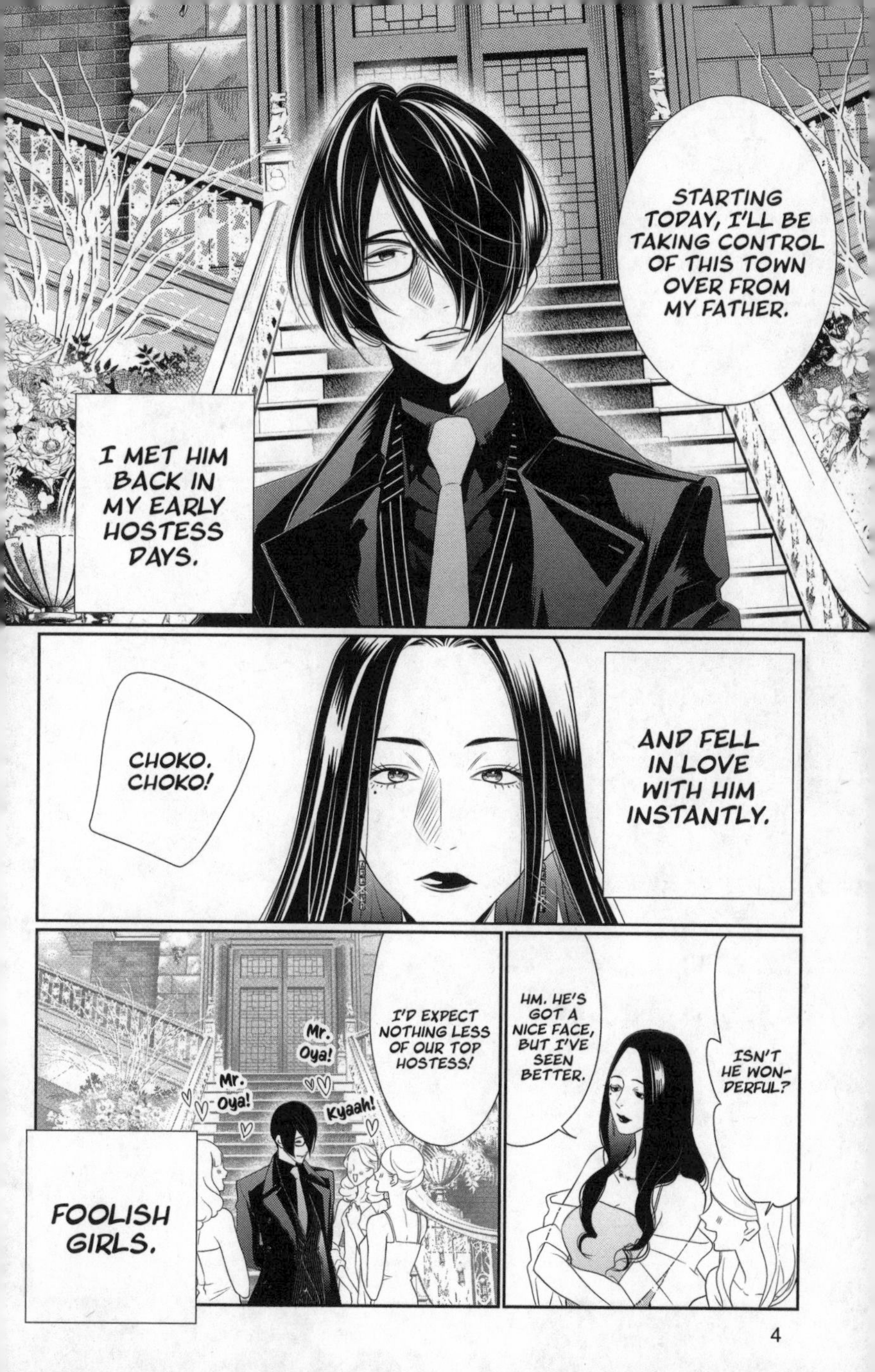
STARTING TODAY, I'LL BE TAKING CONTROL OF THIS TOWN OVER FROM MY FATHER.
I MET HIM BACK IN MY EARLY HOSTESS DAYS.
AND FELL IN LOVE WITH HIM INSTANTLY.
CHOKO. CHOKO!
ISN'T HE WON-DERFUL?
HM. HE'S GOT A NICE FACE, BUT I'VE SEEN BETTER.
I'D EXPECT NOTHING LESS OF OUR TOP HOSTESS!
Mr. Oya!
Kyaah!
Mr. Oya!
FOOLISH GIRLS.

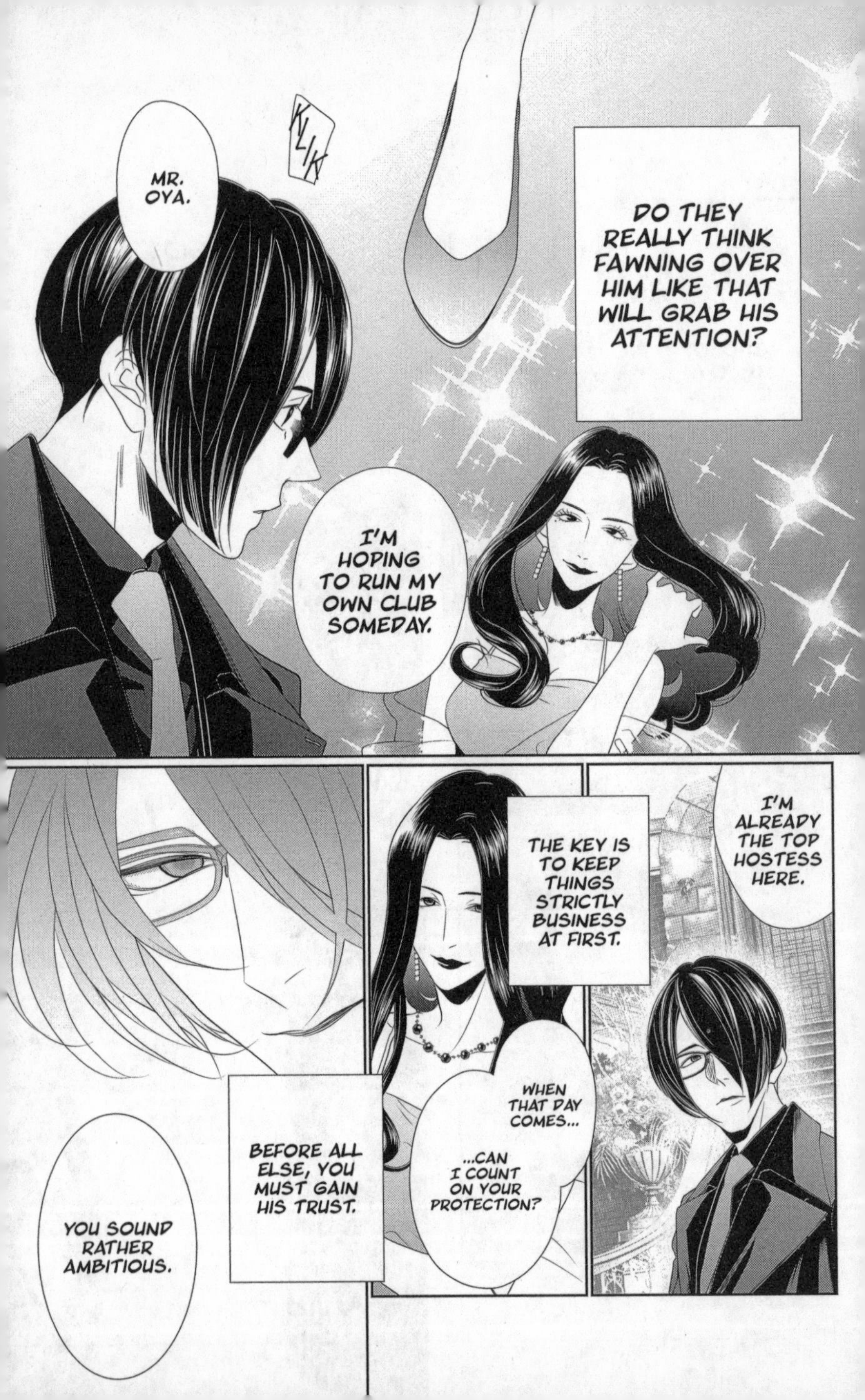
DO THEY REALLY THINK FAWNING OVER HIM LIKE THAT WILL GRAB HIS ATTENTION?
KLIK
MR. OYA.
I'M HOPING TO RUN MY OWN CLUB SOMEDAY.
I'M ALREADY THE TOP HOSTESS HERE.
WHEN THAT DAY COMES...
...CAN I COUNT ON YOUR PROTECTION?
THE KEY IS TO KEEP THINGS STRICTLY BUSINESS AT FIRST.
BEFORE ALL ELSE, YOU MUST GAIN HIS TRUST.
YOU SOUND RATHER AMBITIOUS.

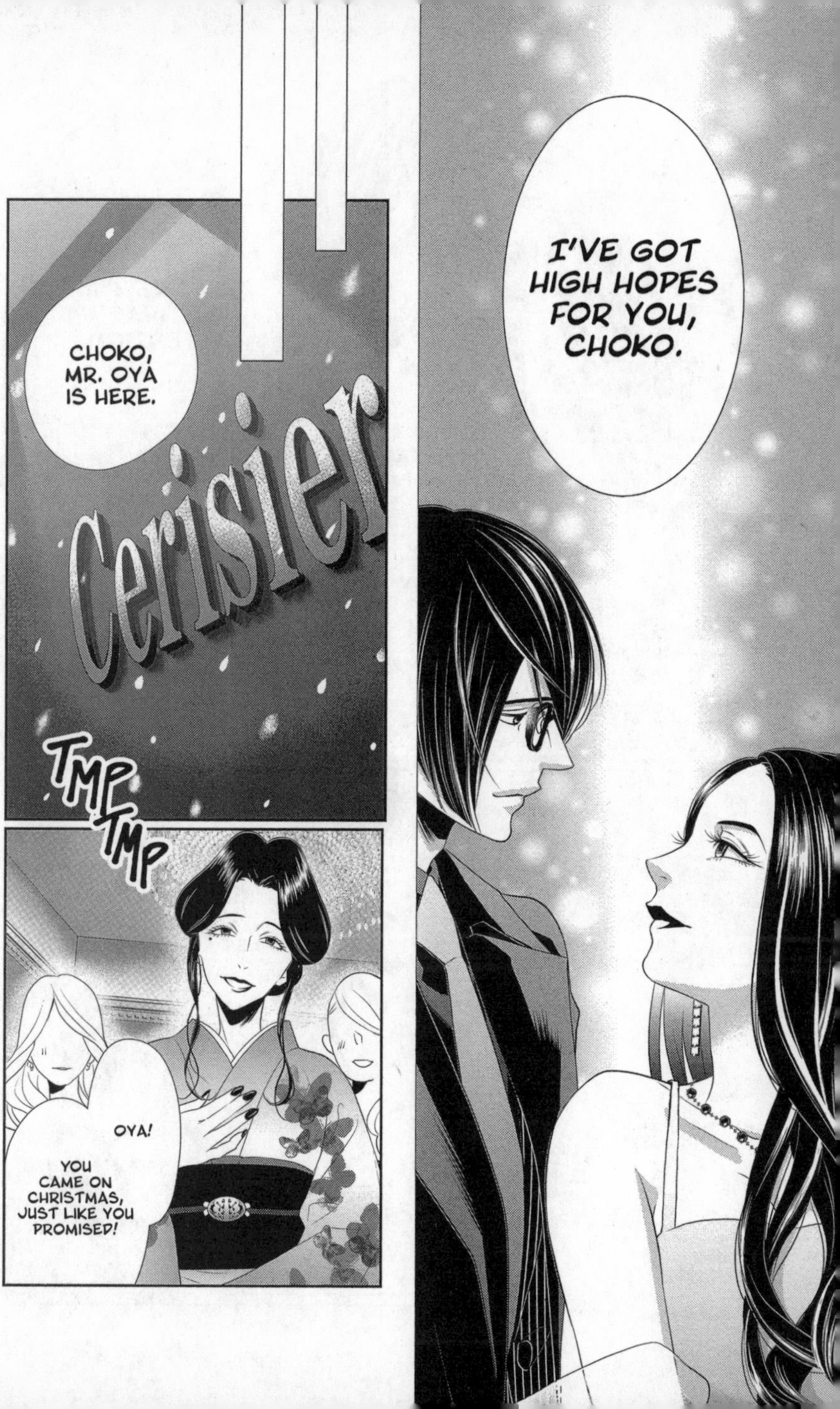
I'VE GOT HIGH HOPES FOR YOU, CHOKO.
CHOKO, MR. OYA IS HERE.
Cerisier
TMP TMP
OYA!
YOU CAME ON CHRISTMAS, JUST LIKE YOU PROMISED!

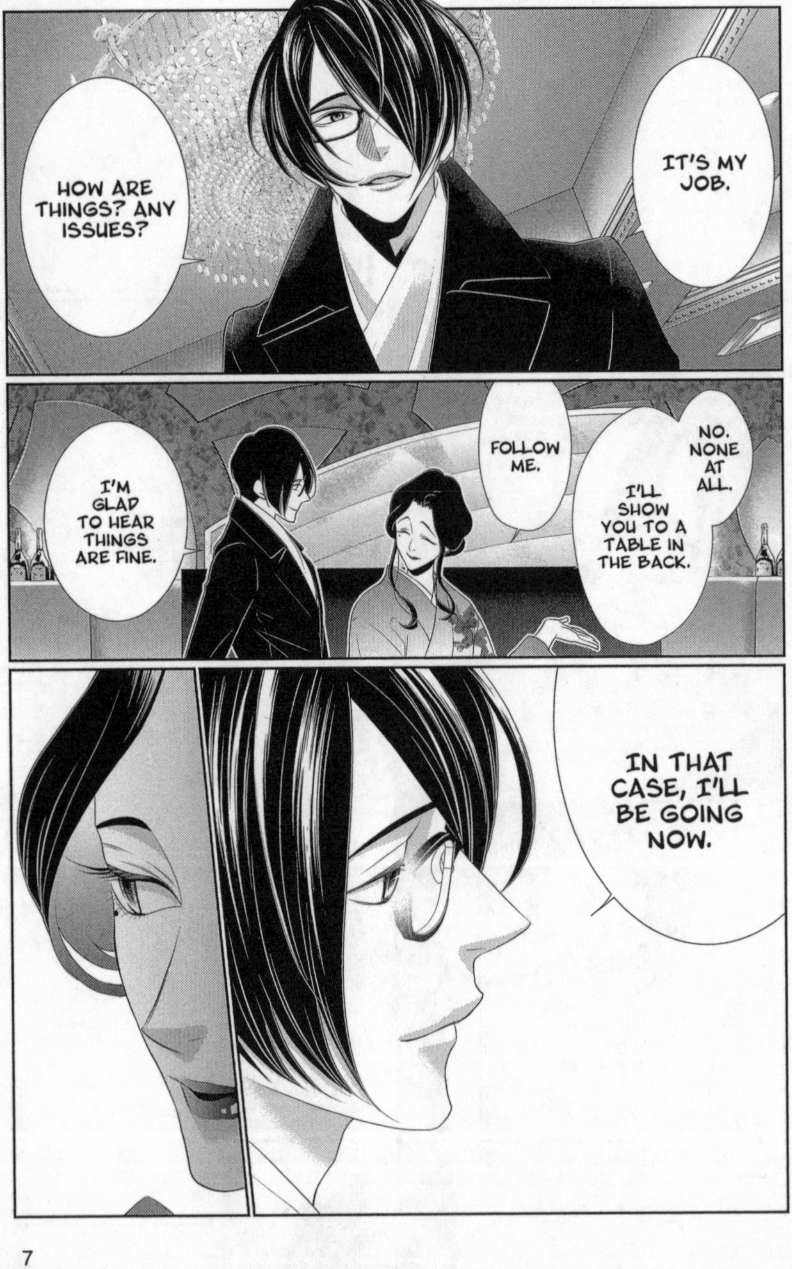
IT'S MY JOB.
HOW ARE THINGS? ANY ISSUES?
NO. NONE AT ALL.
I'LL SHOW YOU TO A TABLE IN THE BACK.
FOLLOW ME.
I'M GLAD TO HEAR THINGS ARE FINE.
IN THAT CASE, I'LL BE GOING NOW.

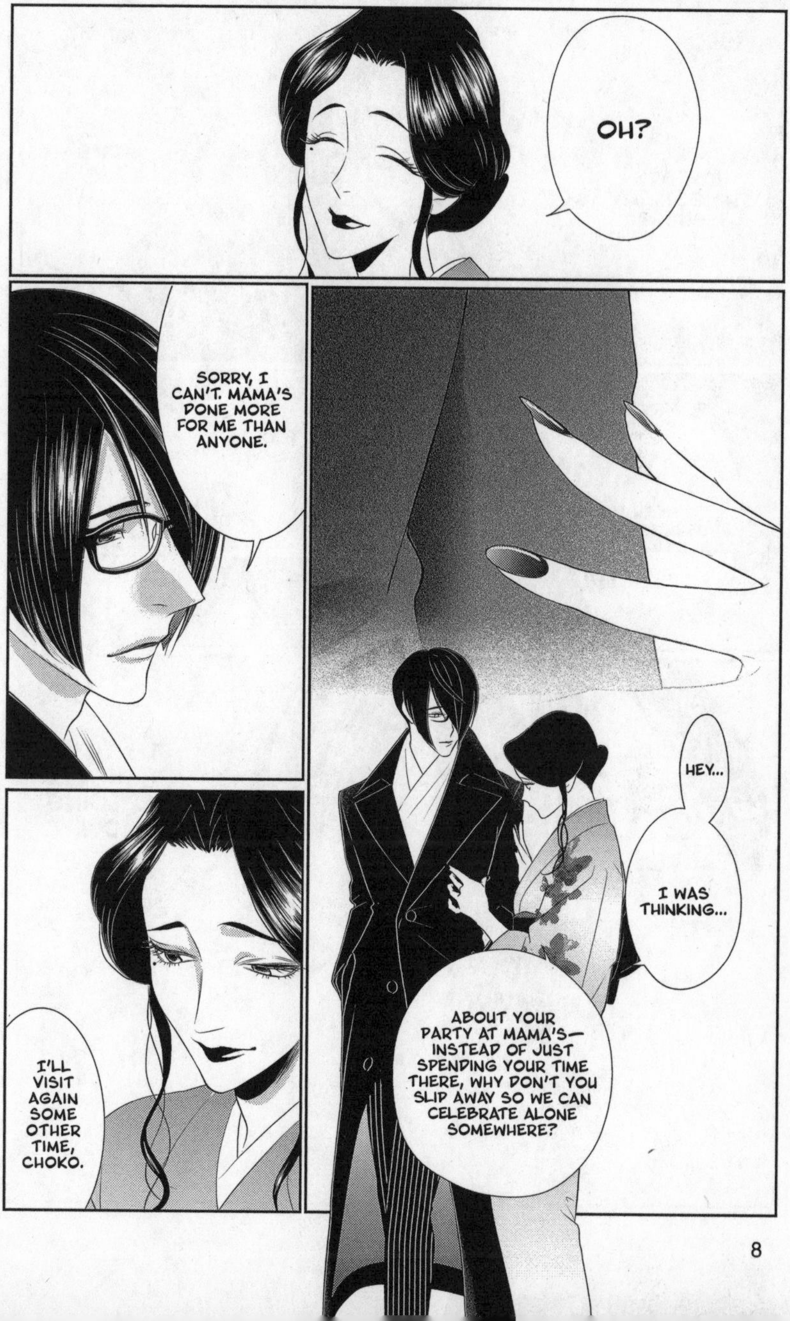
OH?
HEY...
I WAS THINKING...
ABOUT YOUR PARTY AT MAMA'S— INSTEAD OF JUST SPENDING YOUR TIME THERE, WHY DON'T YOU SLIP AWAY SO WE CAN CELEBRATE ALONE SOMEWHERE?
SORRY, I CAN'T. MAMA'S DONE MORE FOR ME THAN ANYONE.
I'LL VISIT AGAIN SOME OTHER TIME, CHOKO.

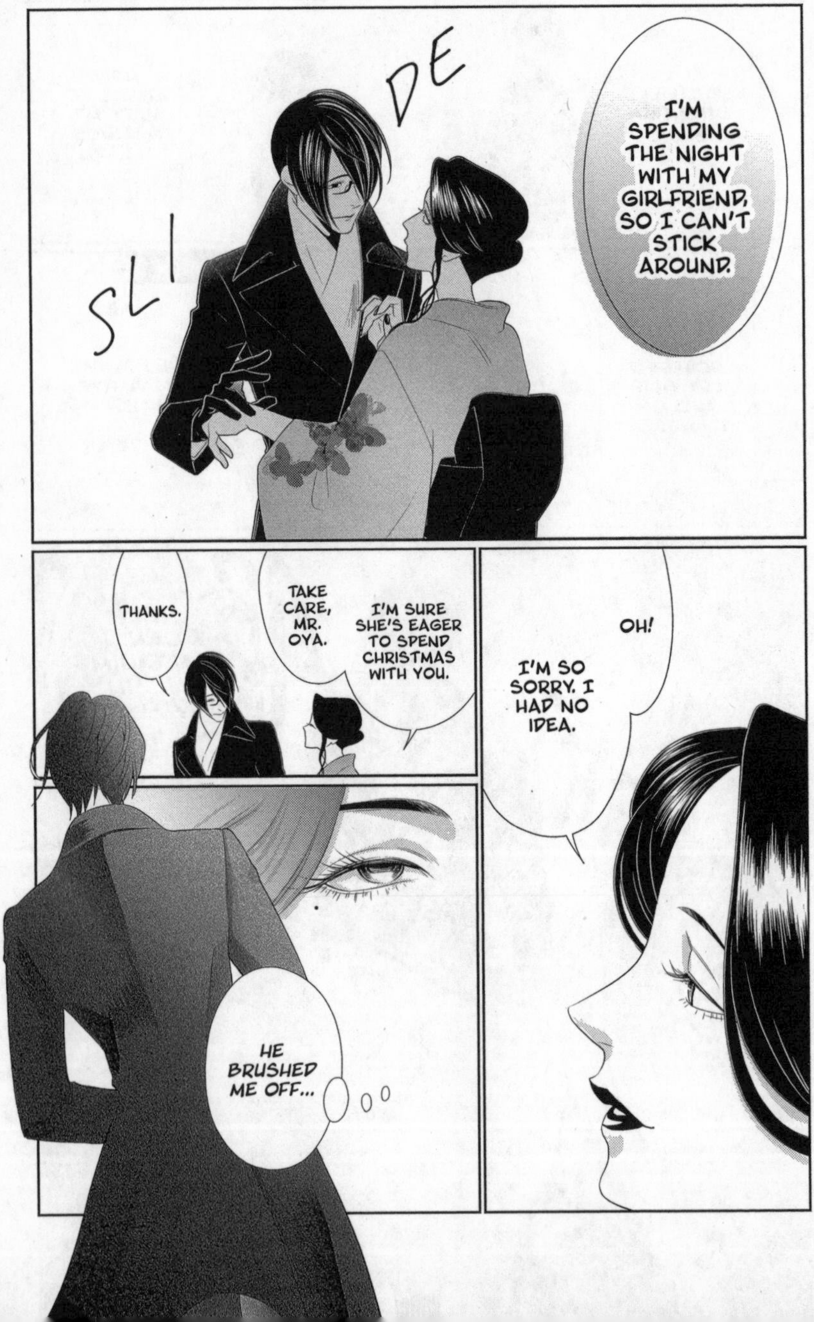
I'M SPENDING THE NIGHT WITH MY GIRLFRIEND, SO I CAN'T STICK AROUND.
SLIDE
OH!
I'M SO SORRY. I HAD NO IDEA.
TAKE CARE, MR. OYA.
I'M SURE SHE'S EAGER TO SPEND CHRISTMAS WITH YOU.
THANKS.
HE BRUSHED ME OFF...

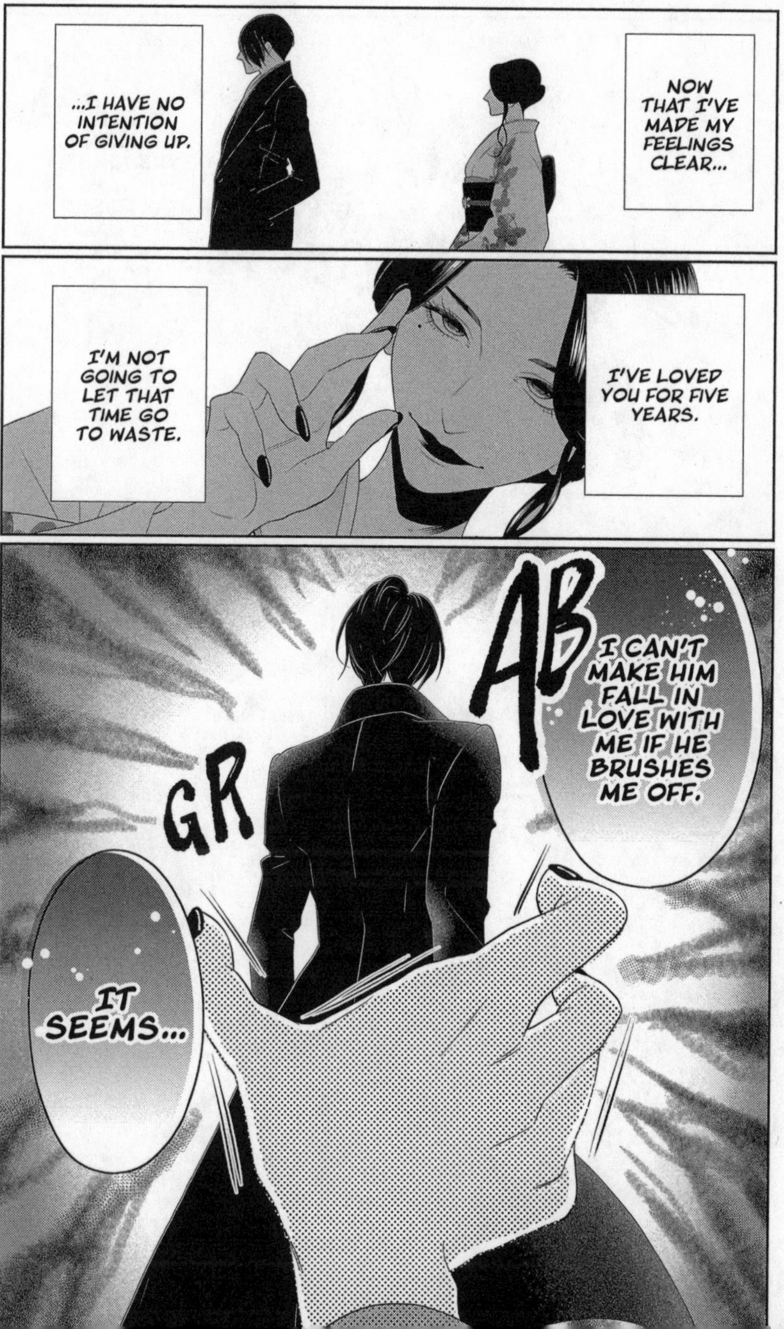
NOW THAT I'VE MADE MY FEELINGS CLEAR...
...I HAVE NO INTENTION OF GIVING UP.
I'VE LOVED YOU FOR FIVE YEARS.
I'M NOT GOING TO LET THAT TIME GO TO WASTE.
AB
I CAN'T MAKE HIM FALL IN LOVE WITH ME IF HE BRUSHES ME OFF.
GR
IT SEEMS...

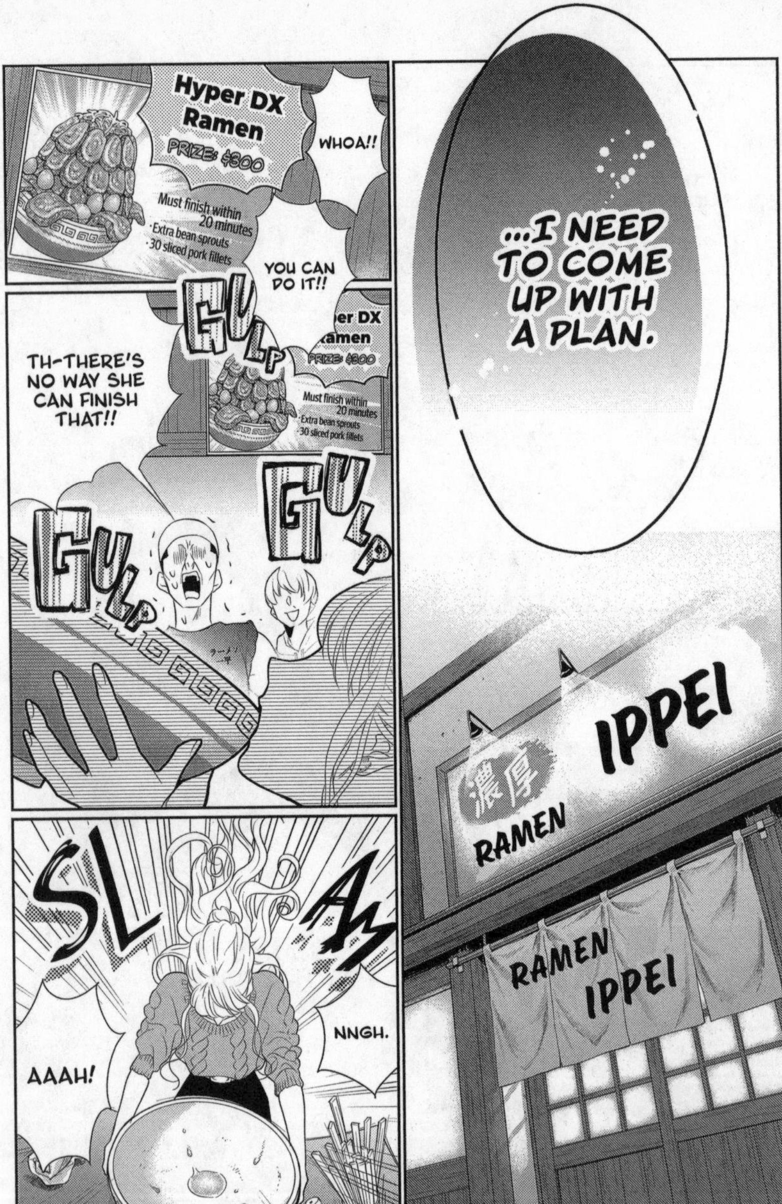
...I NEED TO COME UP WITH A PLAN.
濃厚
RAMEN
IPPEI
RAMEN
IPPEI
Hyper DX Ramen
PRIZE: $300
Must finish within 20 minutes
· Extra bean sprouts
· 30 sliced pork fillets
WHOA!!
YOU CAN DO IT!!
GULP
Hyper DX Ramen
PRIZE: $300
Must finish within 20 minutes
· Extra bean sprouts
· 30 sliced pork fillets
TH-THERE'S NO WAY SHE CAN FINISH THAT!!
GULP
GULP
SLAM
NNGH.
AAAH!

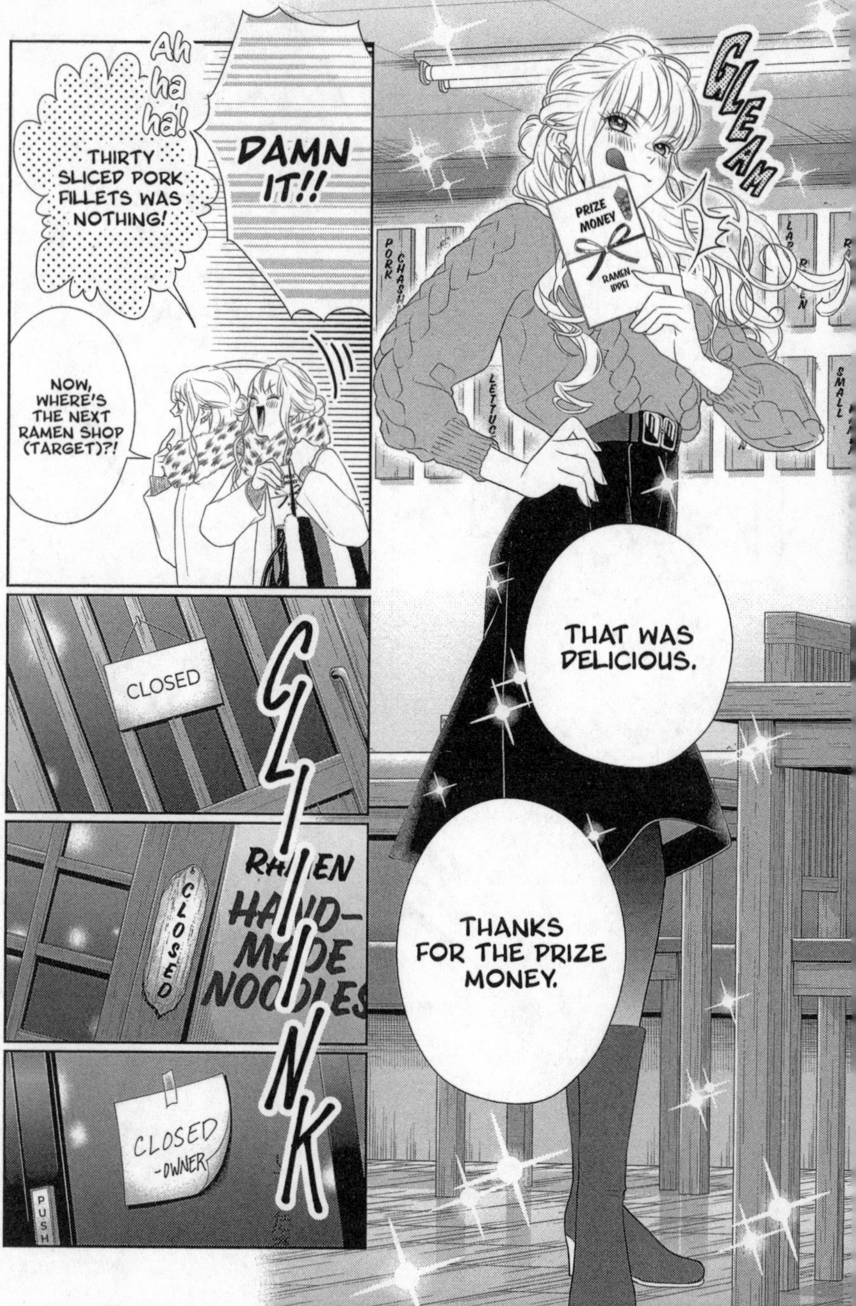
GLEAM
PRIZE MONEY
RAMEN IPPEI
THAT WAS DELICIOUS.
THANKS FOR THE PRIZE MONEY.
DAMN IT!!
Ah ha ha!
THIRTY SLICED PORK FILLETS WAS NOTHING!
NOW, WHERE'S THE NEXT RAMEN SHOP (TARGET)?!
CLOSED
RAMEN
HANDMADE NOODLES
CLOSED
CLOSED
-OWNER
PUSH
CLINK

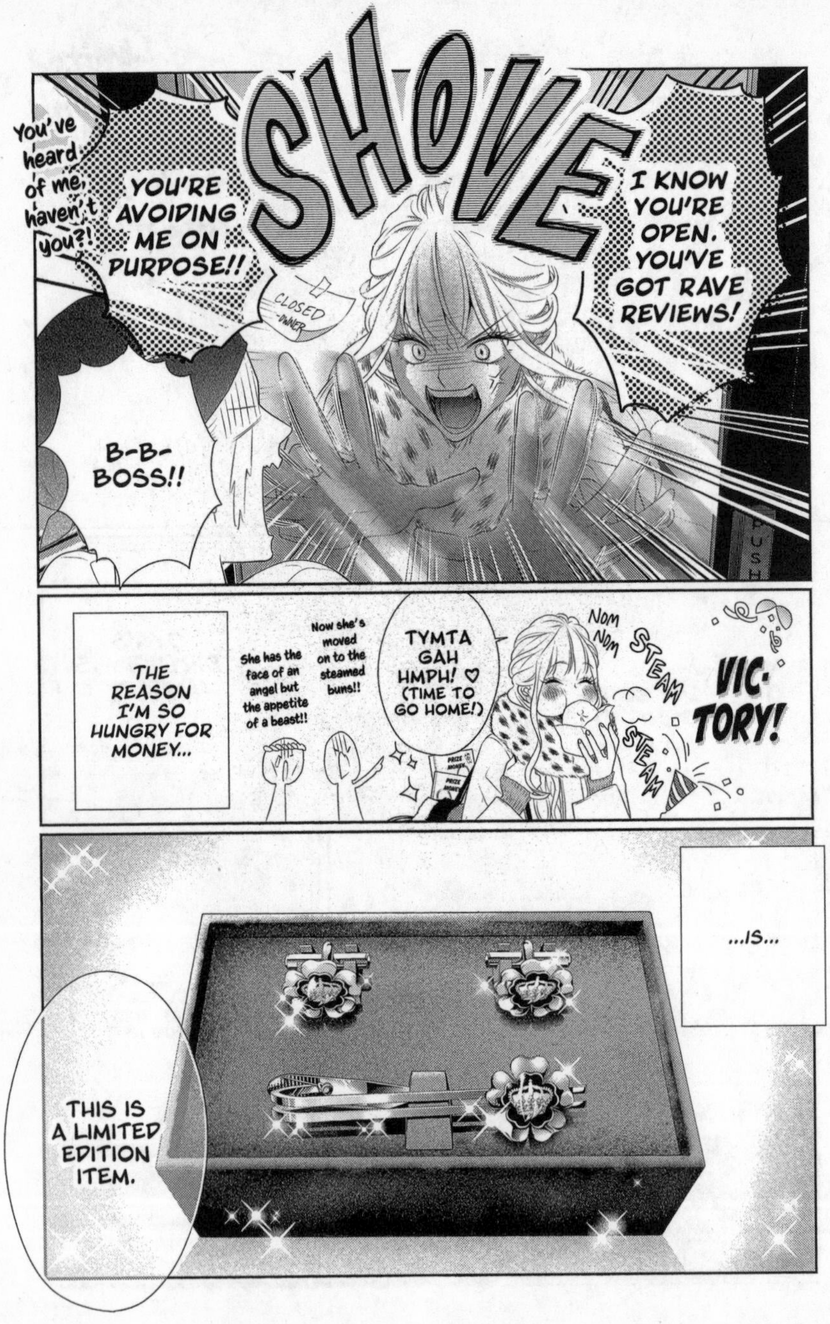
SHOVE
I KNOW YOU'RE OPEN. YOU'VE GOT RAVE REVIEWS!
YOU'RE AVOIDING ME ON PURPOSE!!
You've heard of me, haven't you?!
CLOSED
OWNER
B-B-BOSS!!
PUSH
VIC-TORY!
STEAM
STEAM
NOM NOM
TYMTA GAH HMPH! ♡ (TIME TO GO HOME!)
PRIZE MONEY
PRIZE MONEY
Now she's moved on to the steamed buns!!
She has the face of an angel but the appetite of a beast!!
THE REASON I'M SO HUNGRY FOR MONEY...
...IS...
THIS IS A LIMITED EDITION ITEM.

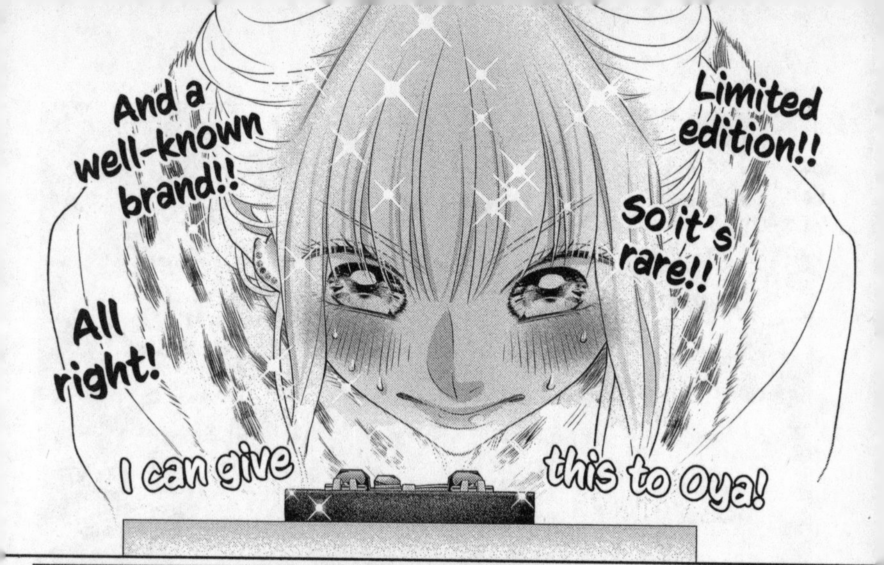
Limited edition!!
So it's rare!!
And a well-known brand!!
All right!
I can give
this to Oya!

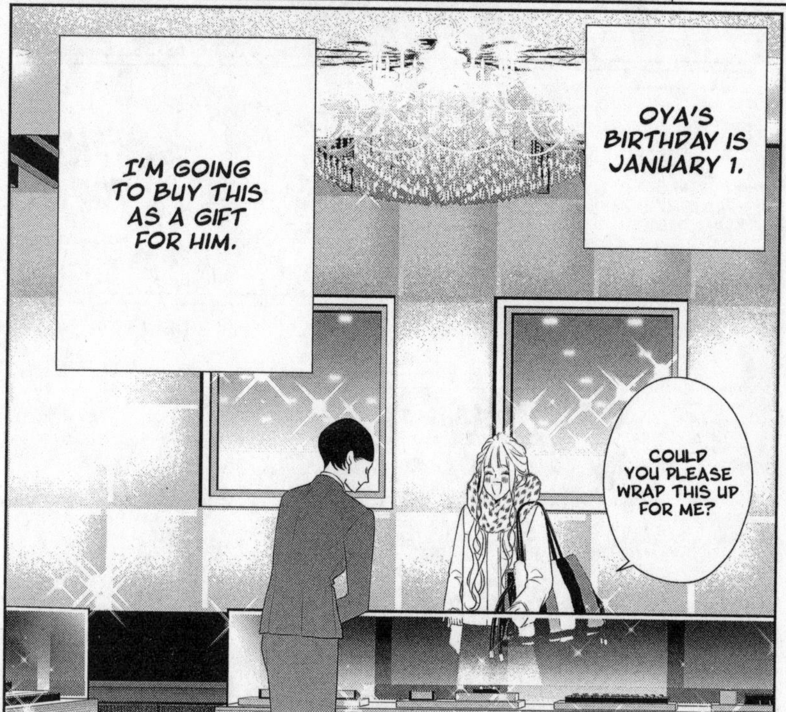
OYA'S BIRTHDAY IS JANUARY 1.
I'M GOING TO BUY THIS AS A GIFT FOR HIM.
COULD YOU PLEASE WRAP THIS UP FOR ME?

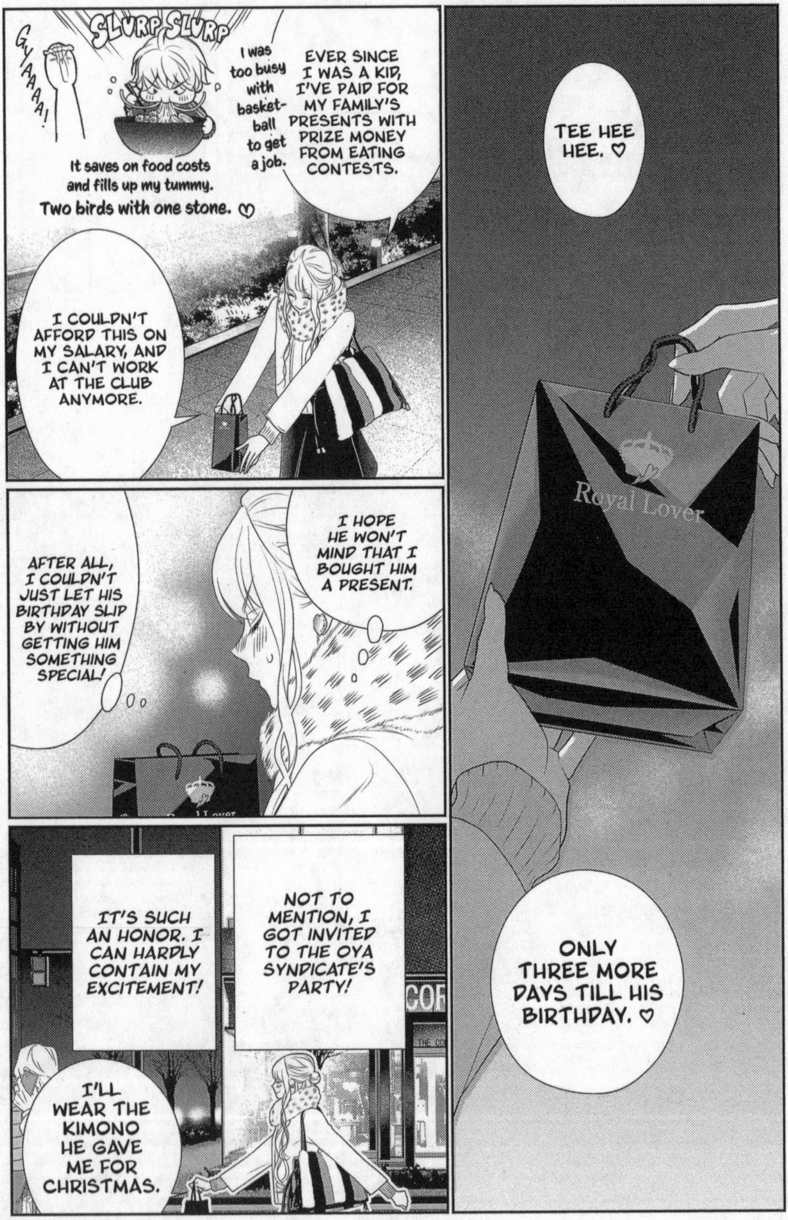
TEE HEE HEE. ♡
ONLY THREE MORE DAYS TILL HIS BIRTHDAY. ♡
Royal Lover
EVER SINCE I WAS A KID, I'VE PAID FOR MY FAMILY'S PRESENTS WITH PRIZE MONEY FROM EATING CONTESTS.
I was too busy with basket-ball to get a job.
SLURP SLURP
GYAAAA!
It saves on food costs and fills up my tummy.
Two birds with one stone. ♡
I COULDN'T AFFORD THIS ON MY SALARY, AND I CAN'T WORK AT THE CLUB ANYMORE.
I HOPE HE WON'T MIND THAT I BOUGHT HIM A PRESENT.
AFTER ALL, I COULDN'T JUST LET HIS BIRTHDAY SLIP BY WITHOUT GETTING HIM SOMETHING SPECIAL!
NOT TO MENTION, I GOT INVITED TO THE OYA SYNDICATE'S PARTY!
IT'S SUCH AN HONOR. I CAN HARDLY CONTAIN MY EXCITEMENT!
I'LL WEAR THE KIMONO HE GAVE ME FOR CHRISTMAS.

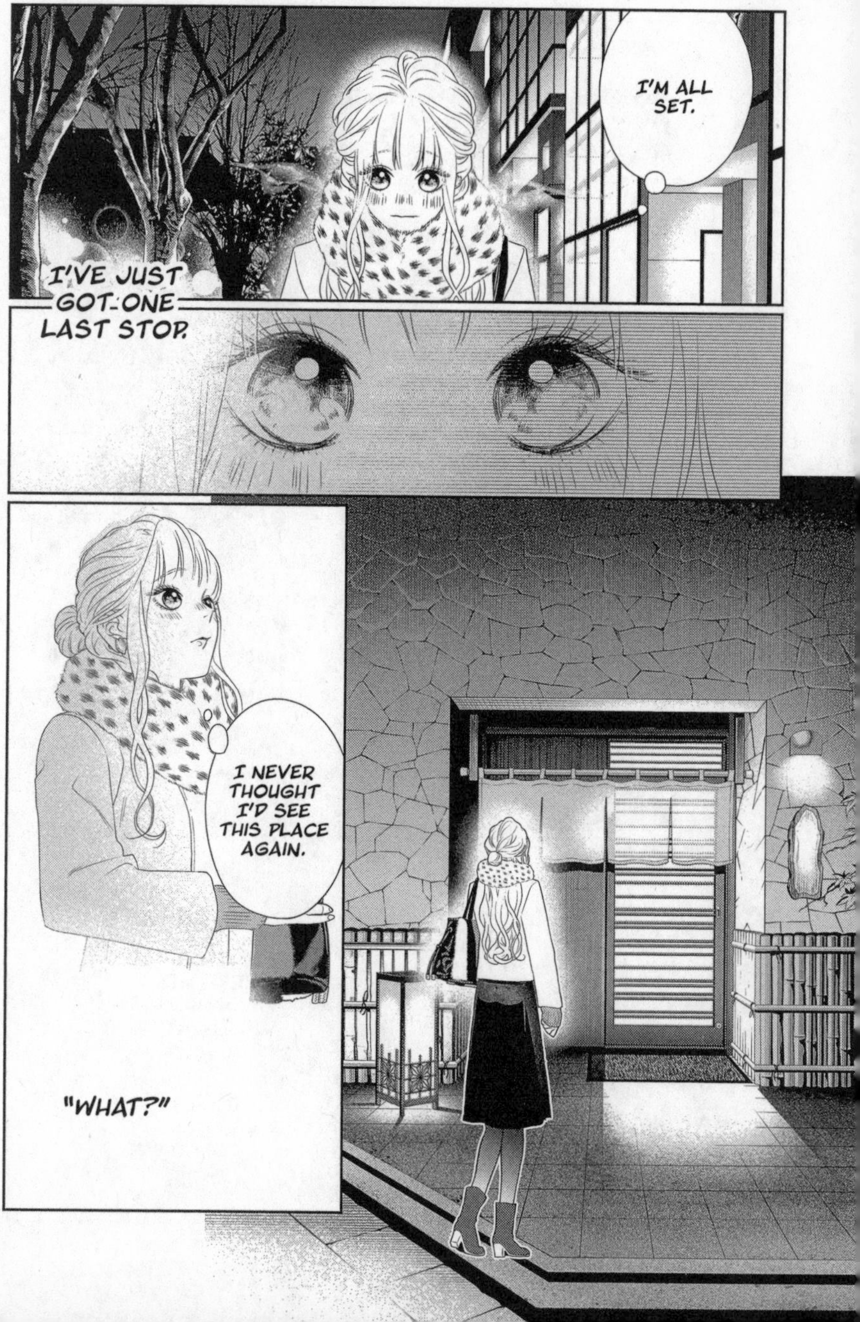
I'M ALL SET.
I'VE JUST GOT ONE LAST STOP.
I NEVER THOUGHT I'D SEE THIS PLACE AGAIN.
"WHAT?"

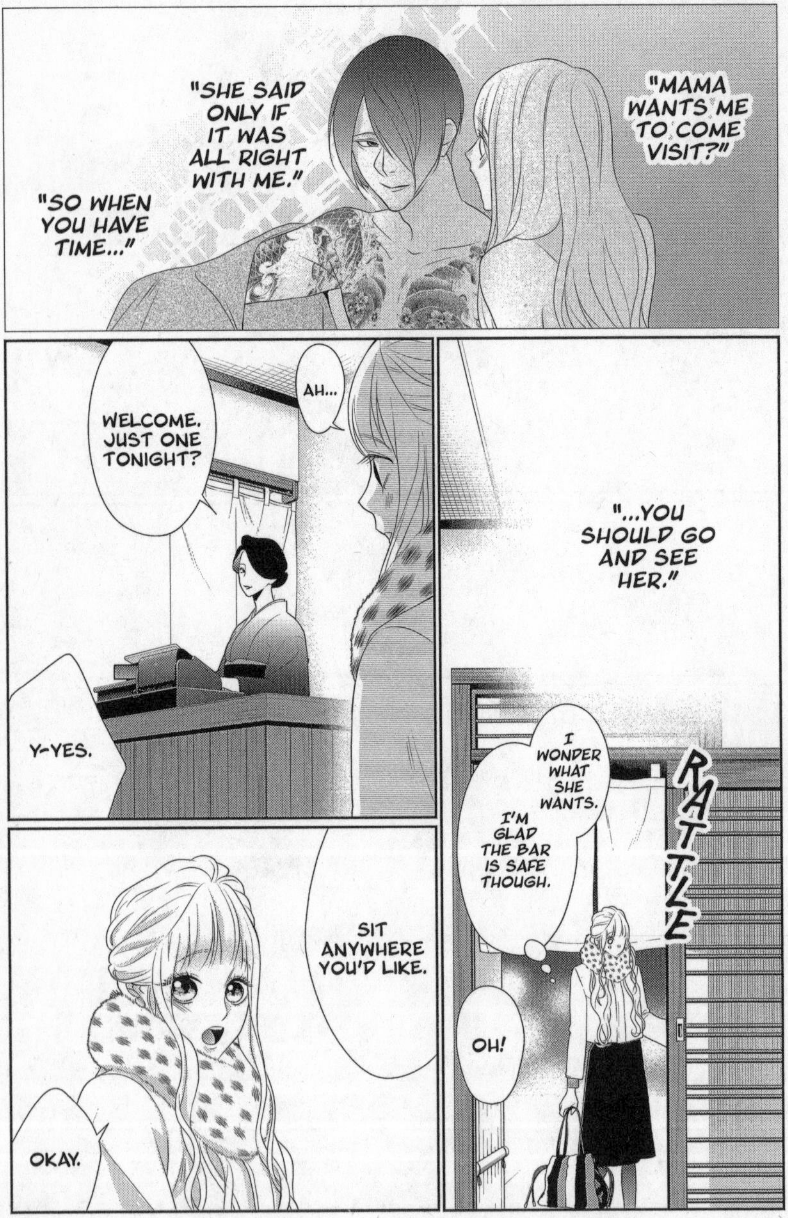
"MAMA WANTS ME TO COME VISIT?"
"SHE SAID ONLY IF IT WAS ALL RIGHT WITH ME."
"SO WHEN YOU HAVE TIME..."
"...YOU SHOULD GO AND SEE HER."
RATTLE
I WONDER WHAT SHE WANTS.
I'M GLAD THE BAR IS SAFE THOUGH.
OH!
AH...
WELCOME. JUST ONE TONIGHT?
Y-YES.
SIT ANYWHERE YOU'D LIKE.
OKAY.

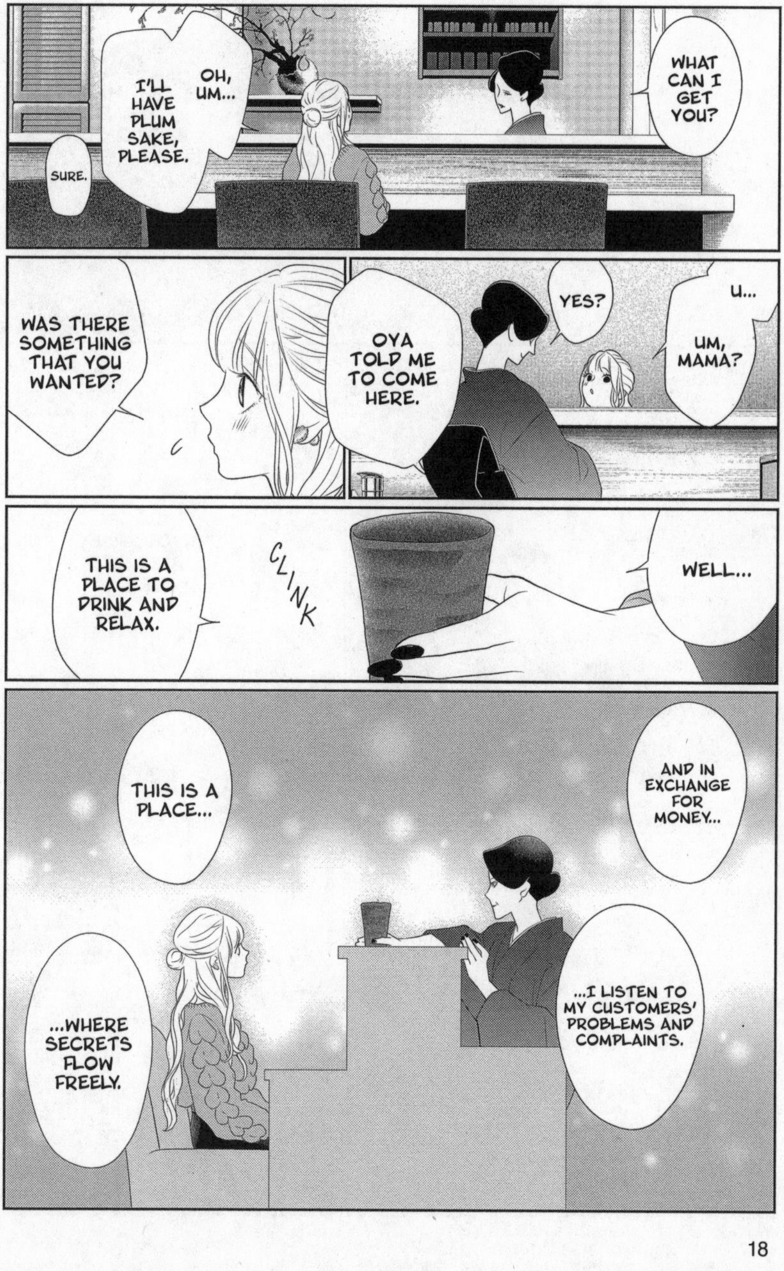
WHAT CAN I GET YOU?
OH, UM...
I'LL HAVE PLUM SAKE, PLEASE.
SURE.
U...
UM, MAMA?
YES?
OYA TOLD ME TO COME HERE.
WAS THERE SOMETHING THAT YOU WANTED?
WELL...
CLINK
THIS IS A PLACE TO DRINK AND RELAX.
AND IN EXCHANGE FOR MONEY...
THIS IS A PLACE...
...I LISTEN TO MY CUSTOMERS' PROBLEMS AND COMPLAINTS.
...WHERE SECRETS FLOW FREELY.

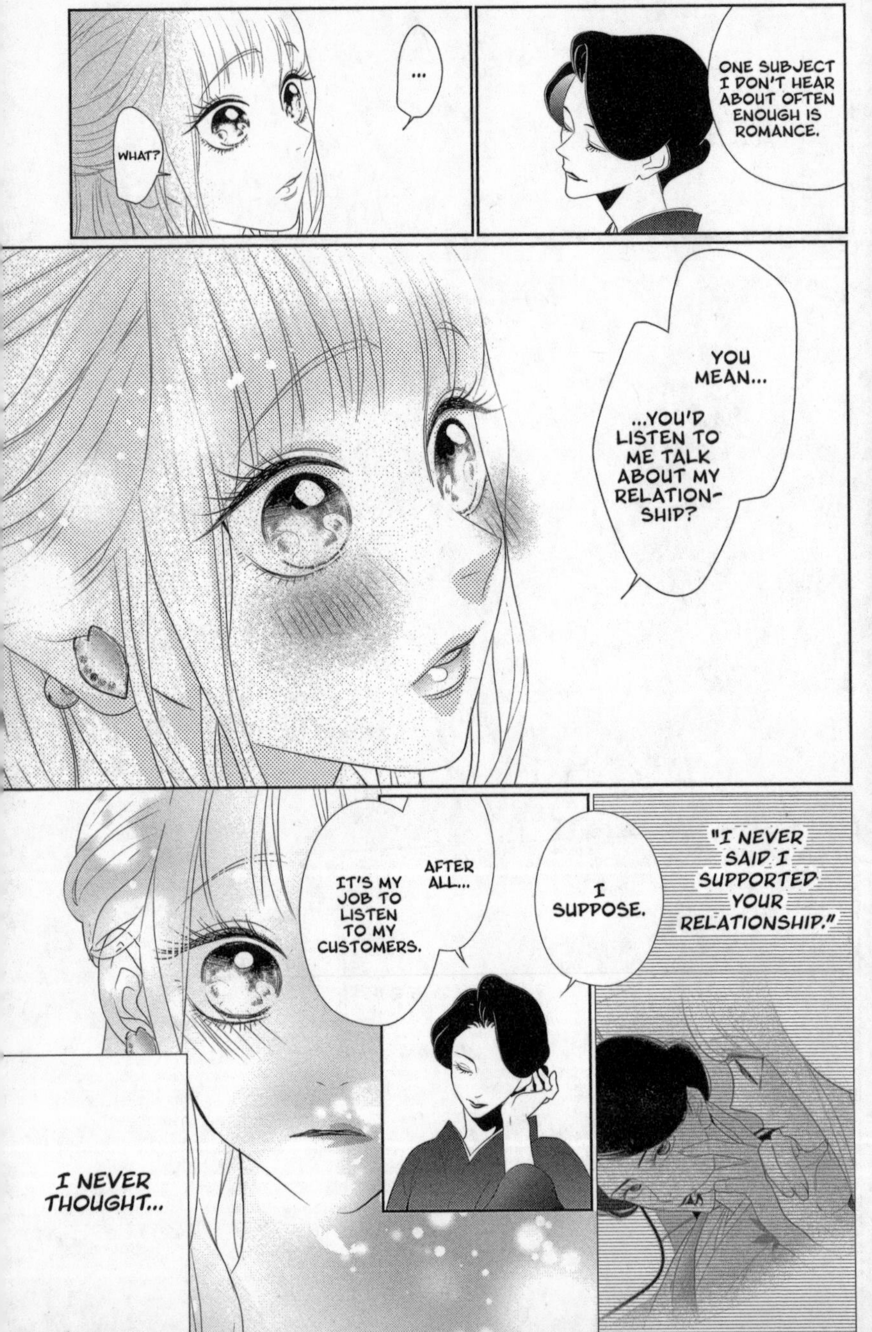
ONE SUBJECT I DON'T HEAR ABOUT OFTEN ENOUGH IS ROMANCE.
...
WHAT?
YOU MEAN...
...YOU'D LISTEN TO ME TALK ABOUT MY RELATION-SHIP?
"I NEVER SAID I SUPPORTED YOUR RELATIONSHIP."
I SUPPOSE.
AFTER ALL...
IT'S MY JOB TO LISTEN TO MY CUSTOMERS.
I NEVER THOUGHT...

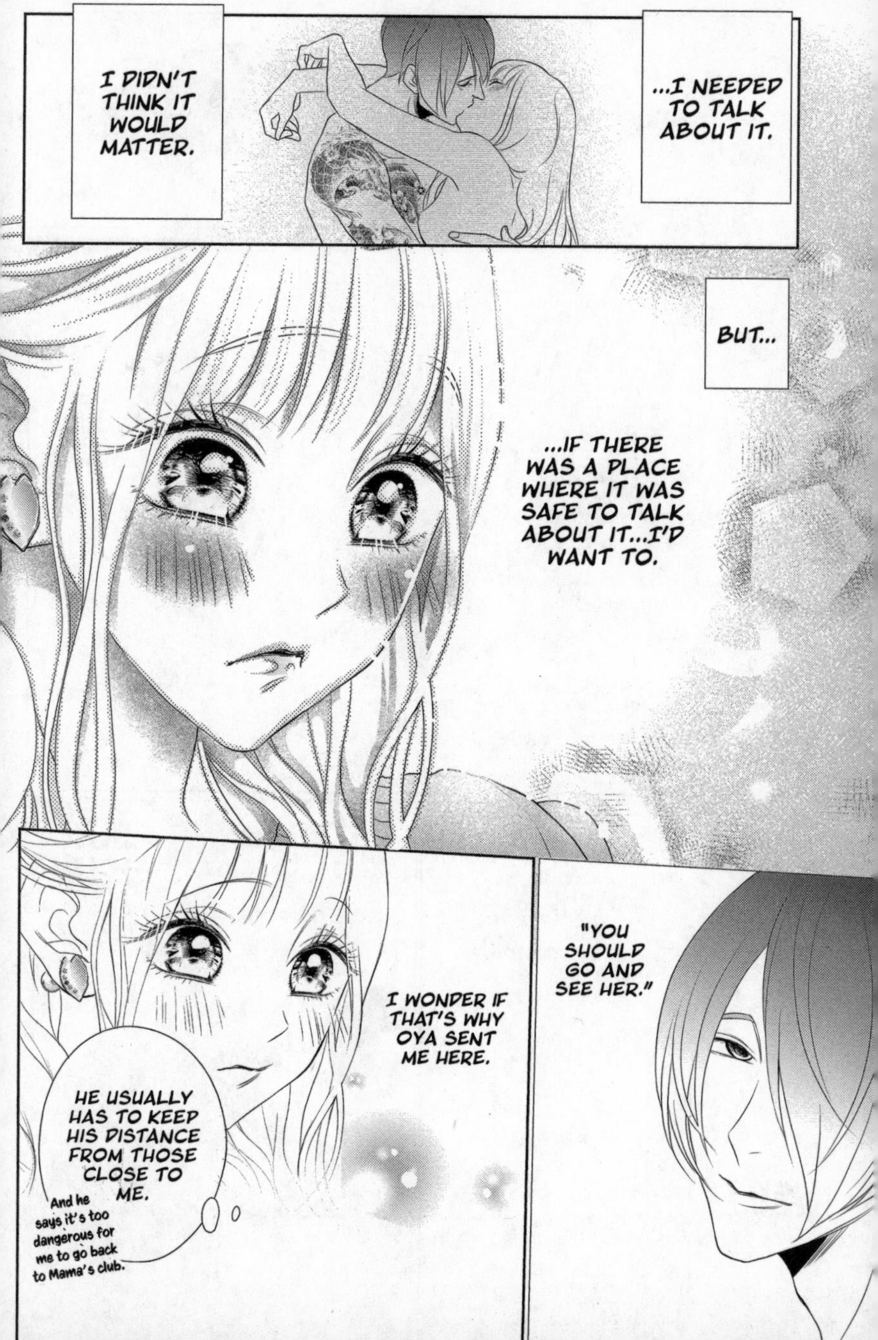
...I NEEDED TO TALK ABOUT IT.
I DIDN'T THINK IT WOULD MATTER.
BUT...
...IF THERE WAS A PLACE WHERE IT WAS SAFE TO TALK ABOUT IT...I'D WANT TO.
"YOU SHOULD GO AND SEE HER."
I WONDER IF THAT'S WHY OYA SENT ME HERE.
HE USUALLY HAS TO KEEP HIS DISTANCE FROM THOSE CLOSE TO ME.
And he says it's too dangerous for me to go back to Mama's club.

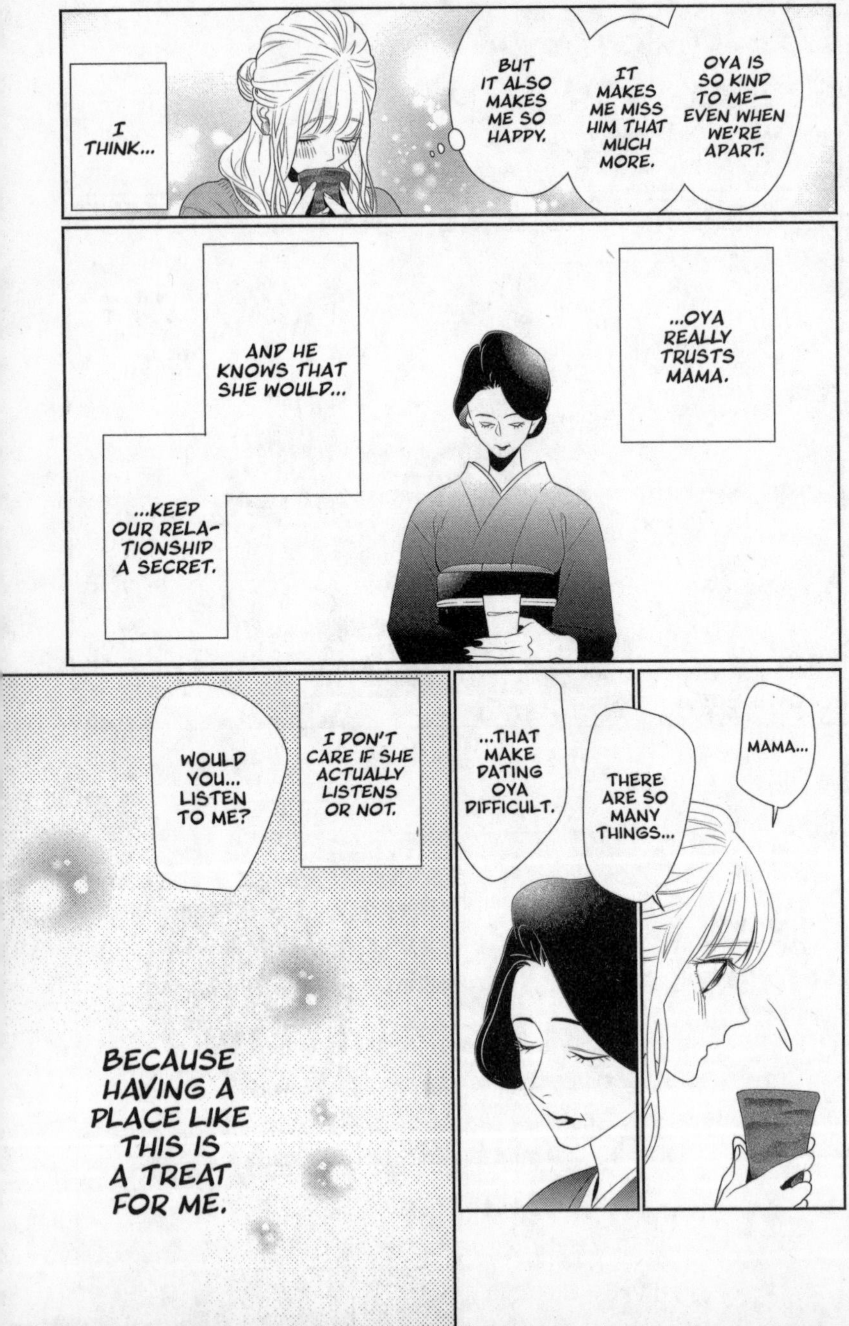
OYA IS SO KIND TO ME— EVEN WHEN WE'RE APART.
IT MAKES ME MISS HIM THAT MUCH MORE.
BUT IT ALSO MAKES ME SO HAPPY.
I THINK...
...OYA REALLY TRUSTS MAMA.
AND HE KNOWS THAT SHE WOULD...
...KEEP OUR RELA-TIONSHIP A SECRET.
MAMA...
THERE ARE SO MANY THINGS...
...THAT MAKE DATING OYA DIFFICULT.
I DON'T CARE IF SHE ACTUALLY LISTENS OR NOT.
WOULD YOU... LISTEN TO ME?
BECAUSE HAVING A PLACE LIKE THIS IS A TREAT FOR ME.

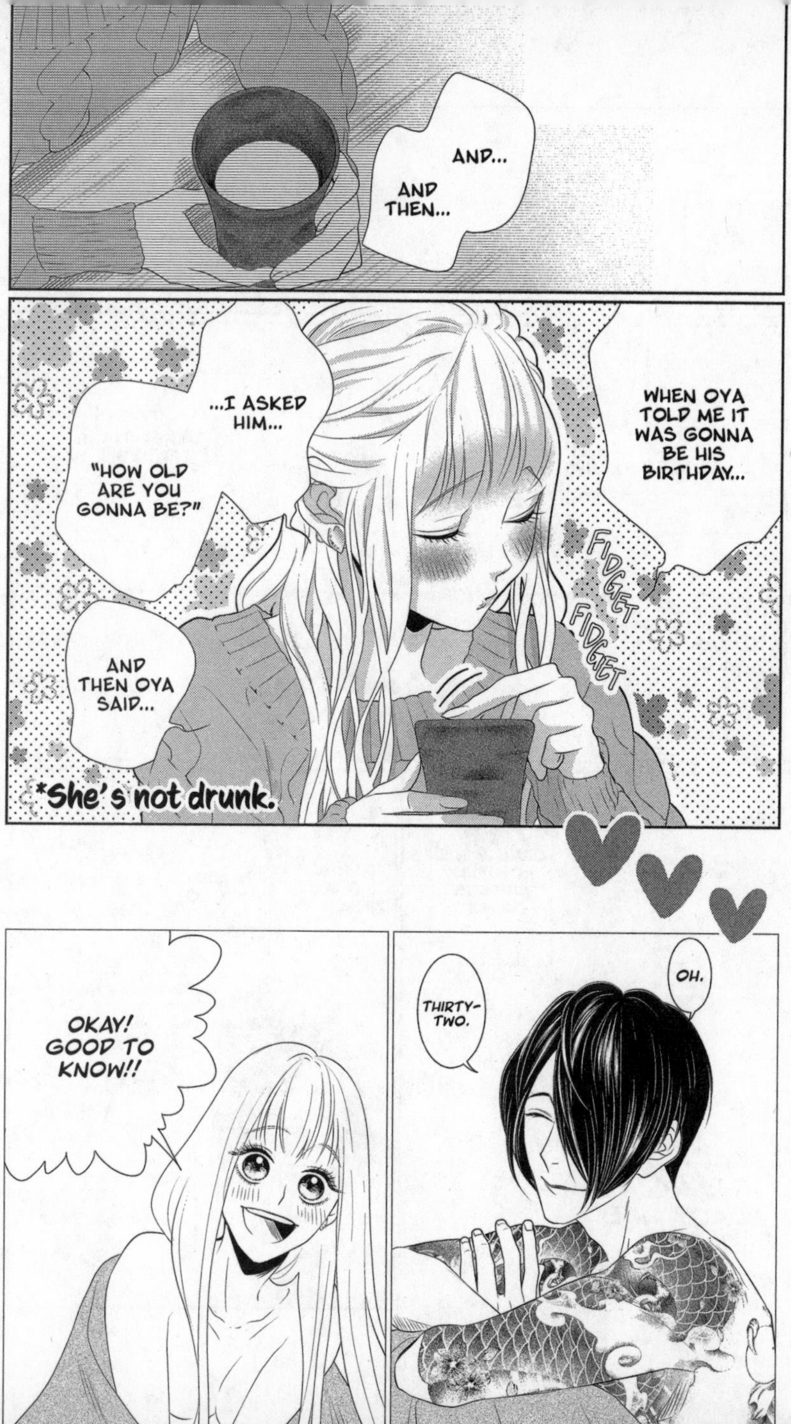
AND...
AND THEN...
WHEN OYA TOLD ME IT WAS GONNA BE HIS BIRTHDAY...
...I ASKED HIM...
"HOW OLD ARE YOU GONNA BE?"
FIDGET FIDGET
AND THEN OYA SAID...
*She's not drunk.
OH.
THIRTY-TWO.
OKAY! GOOD TO KNOW!!

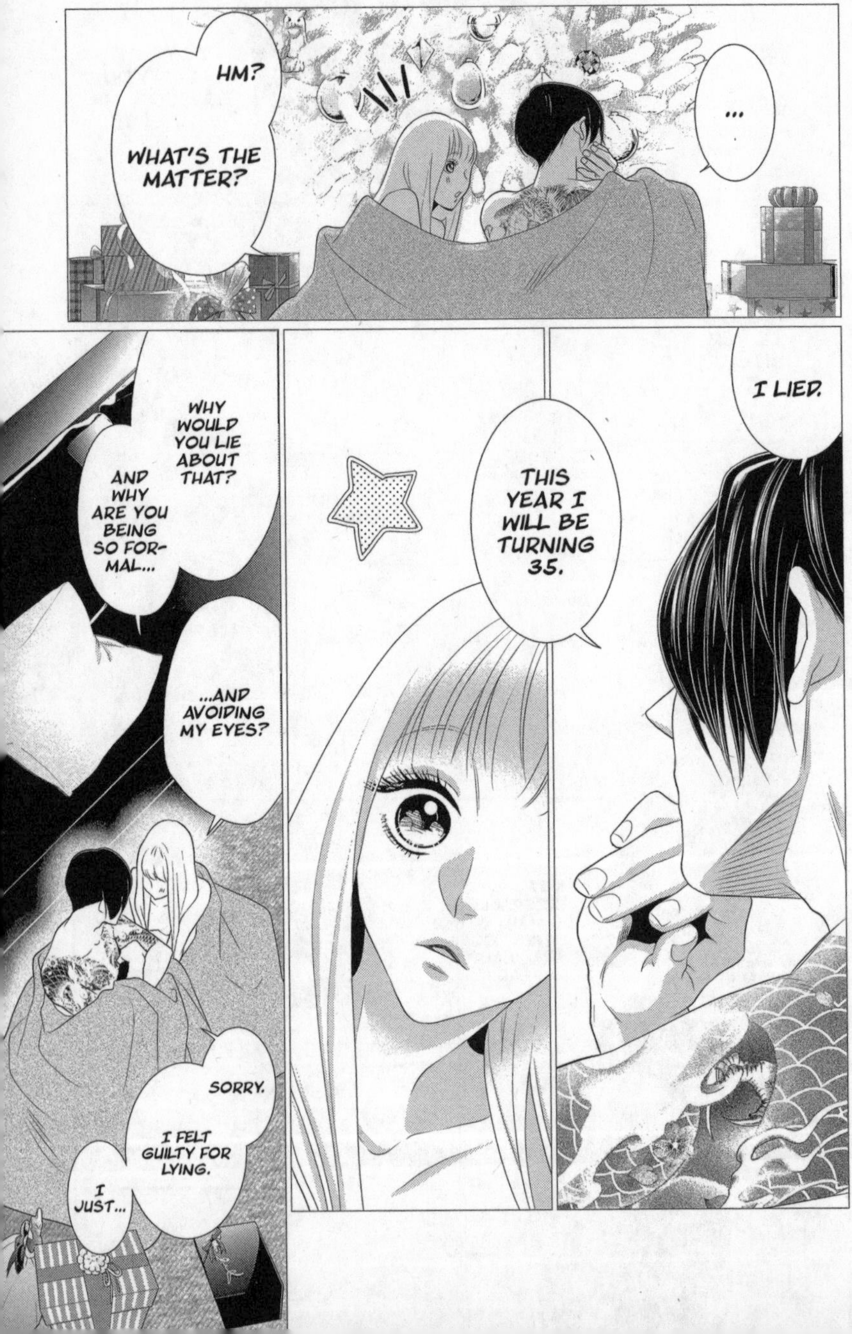
...
HM? WHAT'S THE MATTER?
I LIED.
THIS YEAR I WILL BE TURNING 35.
WHY WOULD YOU LIE ABOUT THAT?
AND WHY ARE YOU BEING SO FOR-MAL...
...AND AVOIDING MY EYES?
SORRY.
I FELT GUILTY FOR LYING.
I JUST...

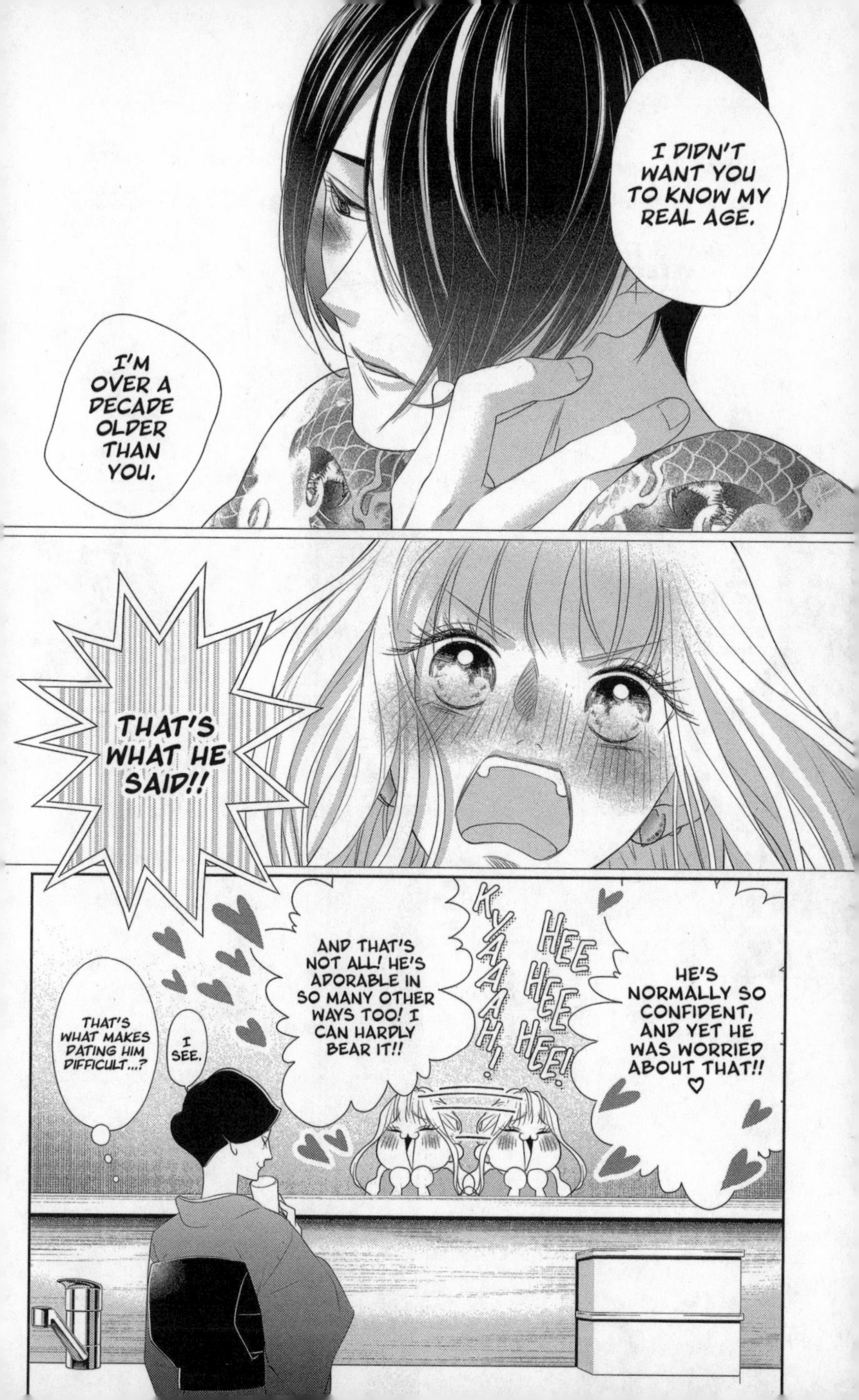
I DIDN'T WANT YOU TO KNOW MY REAL AGE.
I'M OVER A DECADE OLDER THAN YOU.
THAT'S WHAT HE SAID!!
HE'S NORMALLY SO CONFIDENT, AND YET HE WAS WORRIED ABOUT THAT!! ♡
HEE HEE HEE!
KYAAAAH!
AND THAT'S NOT ALL! HE'S ADORABLE IN SO MANY OTHER WAYS TOO! I CAN HARDLY BEAR IT!!
I SEE.
THAT'S WHAT MAKES DATING HIM DIFFICULT...?

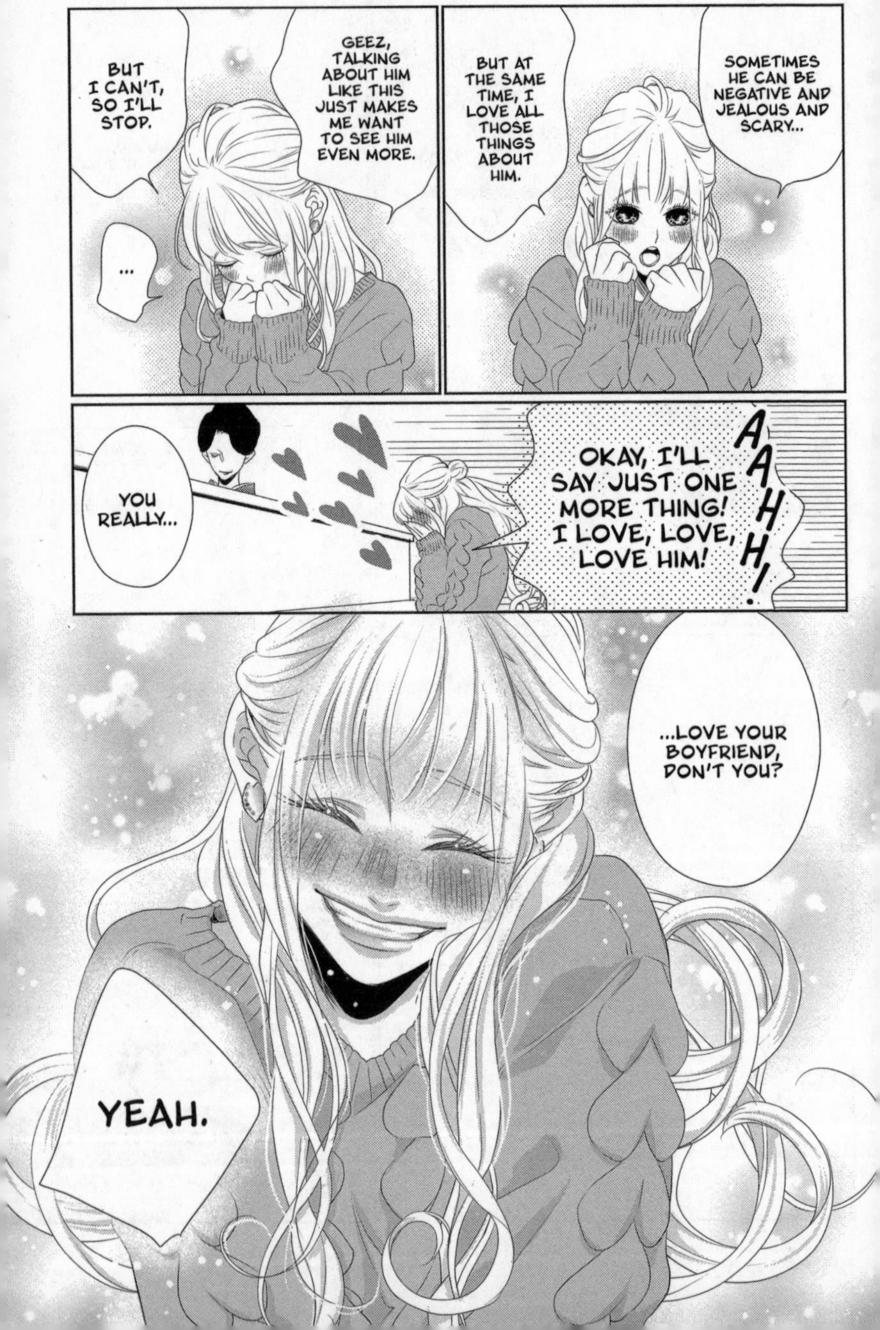
SOMETIMES HE CAN BE NEGATIVE AND JEALOUS AND SCARY...
BUT AT THE SAME TIME, I LOVE ALL THOSE THINGS ABOUT HIM.
GEEZ, TALKING ABOUT HIM LIKE THIS JUST MAKES ME WANT TO SEE HIM EVEN MORE.
BUT I CAN'T, SO I'LL STOP.
...
AAHH!
OKAY, I'LL SAY JUST ONE MORE THING! I LOVE, LOVE, LOVE HIM!
YOU REALLY...
...LOVE YOUR BOYFRIEND, DON'T YOU?
YEAH.

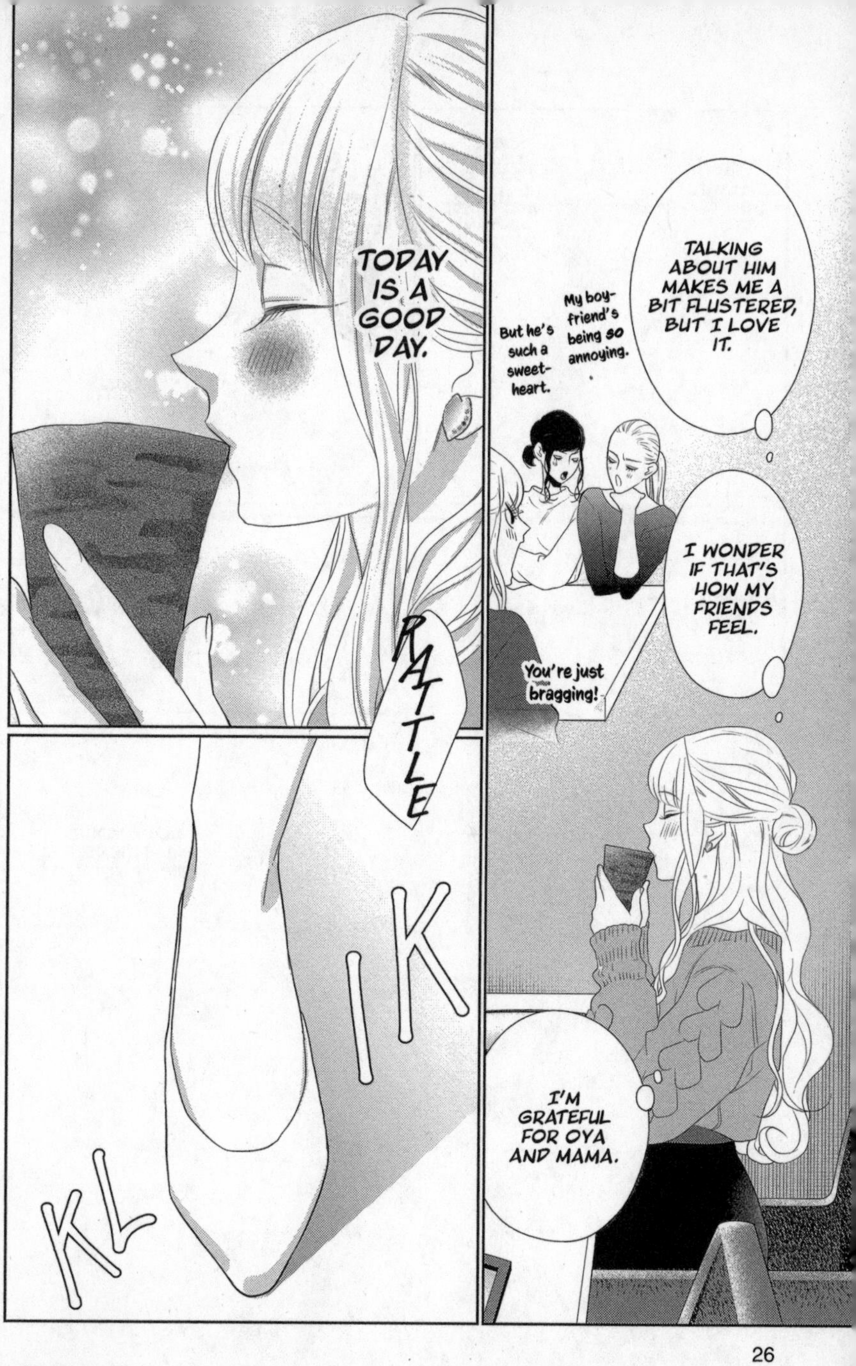
TALKING ABOUT HIM MAKES ME A BIT FLUSTERED, BUT I LOVE IT.
My boy-friend's being so annoying.
But he's such a sweet-heart.
I WONDER IF THAT'S HOW MY FRIENDS FEEL.
You're just bragging!
I'M GRATEFUL FOR OYA AND MAMA.
TODAY IS A GOOD DAY.
RATTLE
KLIK

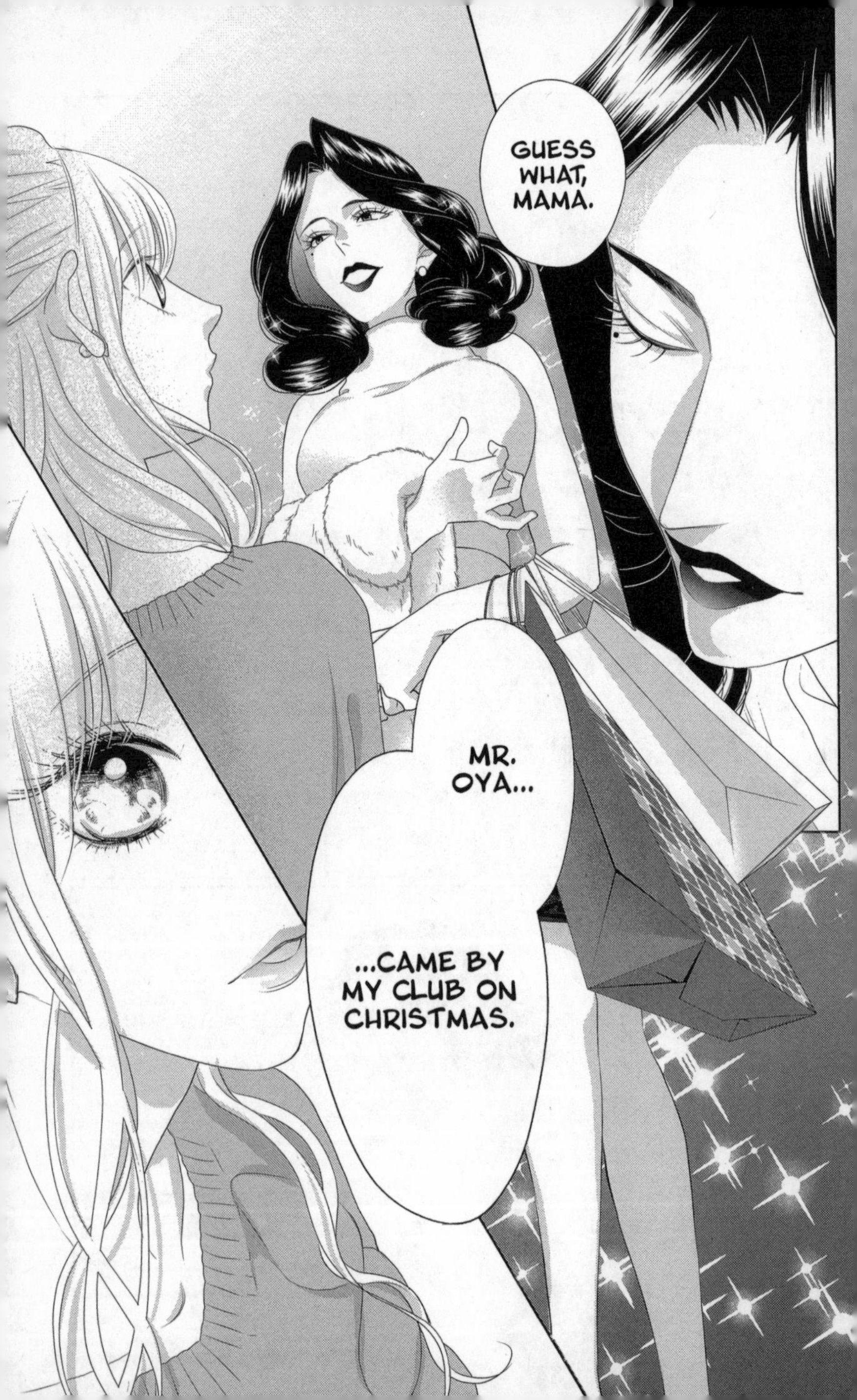
GUESS WHAT, MAMA.
MR. OYA...
...CAME BY MY CLUB ON CHRISTMAS.

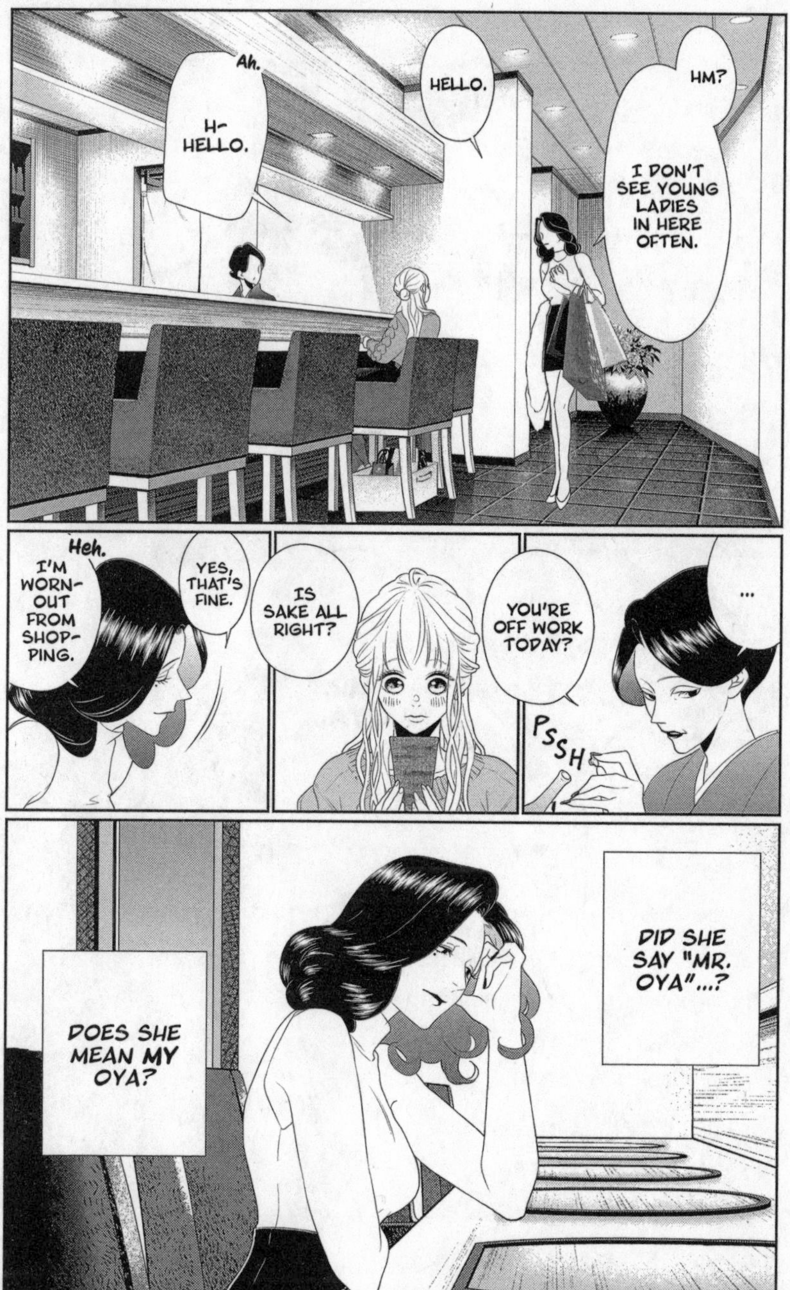
HM?
I DON'T SEE YOUNG LADIES IN HERE OFTEN.
HELLO.
Ah.
H-HELLO.
...
YOU'RE OFF WORK TODAY?
PSSH
IS SAKE ALL RIGHT?
YES, THAT'S FINE.
Heh.
I'M WORN-OUT FROM SHOP-PING.
DID SHE SAY "MR. OYA"...?
DOES SHE MEAN MY OYA?

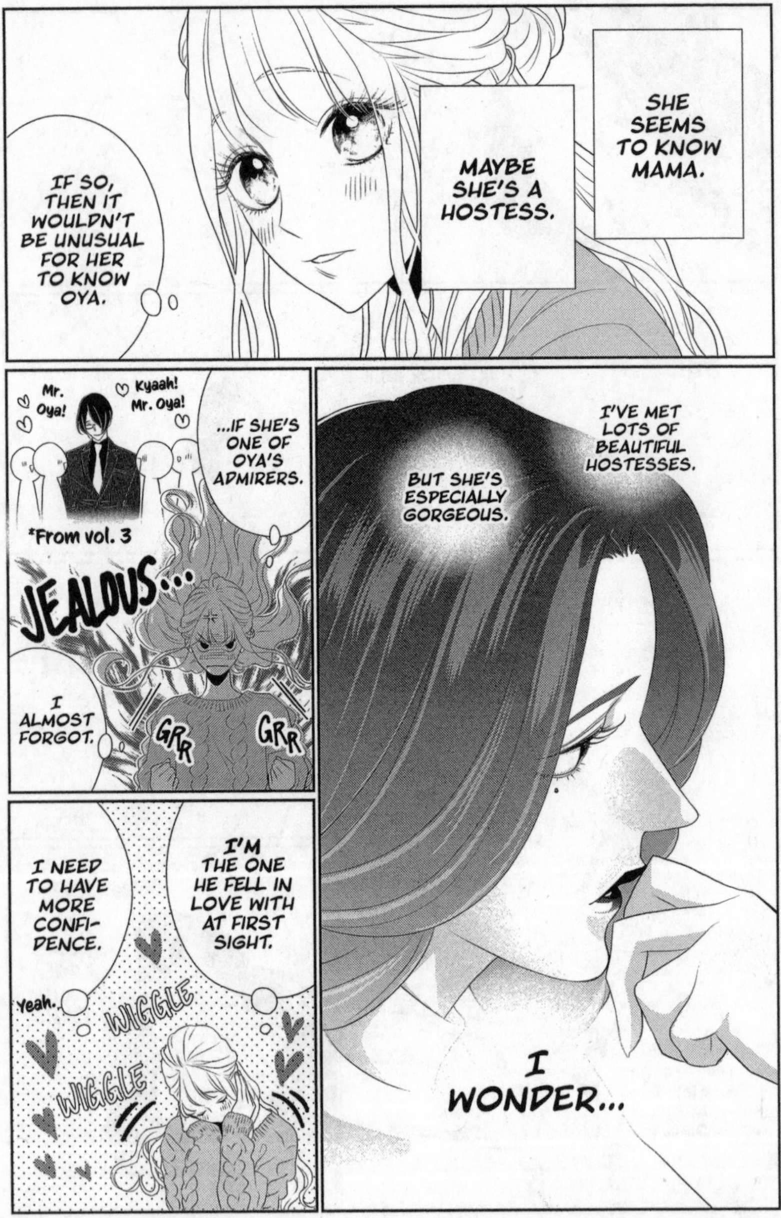
SHE SEEMS TO KNOW MAMA.
MAYBE SHE'S A HOSTESS.
IF SO, THEN IT WOULDN'T BE UNUSUAL FOR HER TO KNOW OYA.
I'VE MET LOTS OF BEAUTIFUL HOSTESSES.
BUT SHE'S ESPECIALLY GORGEOUS.
I WONDER...
...IF SHE'S ONE OF OYA'S ADMIRERS.
Kyaah! Mr. Oya!
Mr. Oya!
*From vol. 3
JEALOUS...
I ALMOST FORGOT.
GRR
GRR
I'M THE ONE HE FELL IN LOVE WITH AT FIRST SIGHT.
I NEED TO HAVE MORE CONFIDENCE.
Yeah.
WIGGLE
WIGGLE

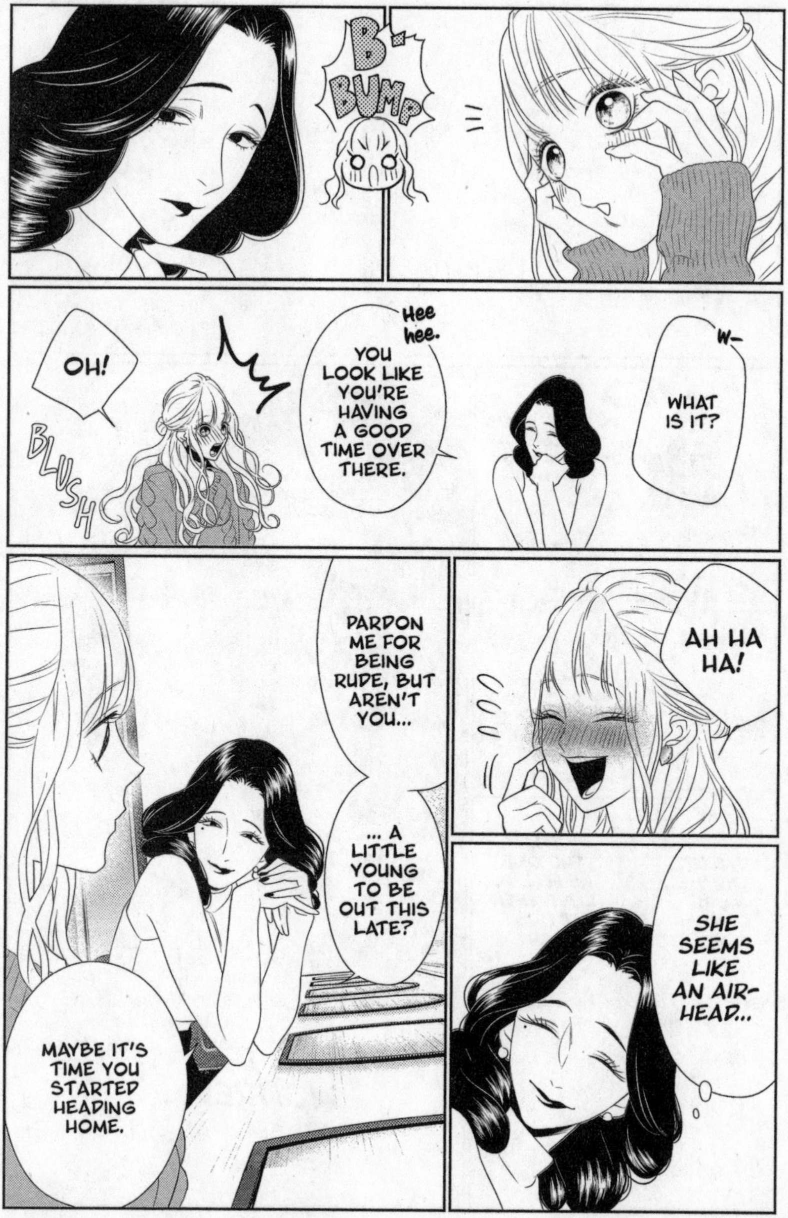
B-BUMP
W- WHAT IS IT?
Hee hee.
YOU LOOK LIKE YOU'RE HAVING A GOOD TIME OVER THERE.
OH!
BLUSH
AH HA HA!
SHE SEEMS LIKE AN AIR-HEAD...
PARDON ME FOR BEING RUDE, BUT AREN'T YOU...
... A LITTLE YOUNG TO BE OUT THIS LATE?
MAYBE IT'S TIME YOU STARTED HEADING HOME.

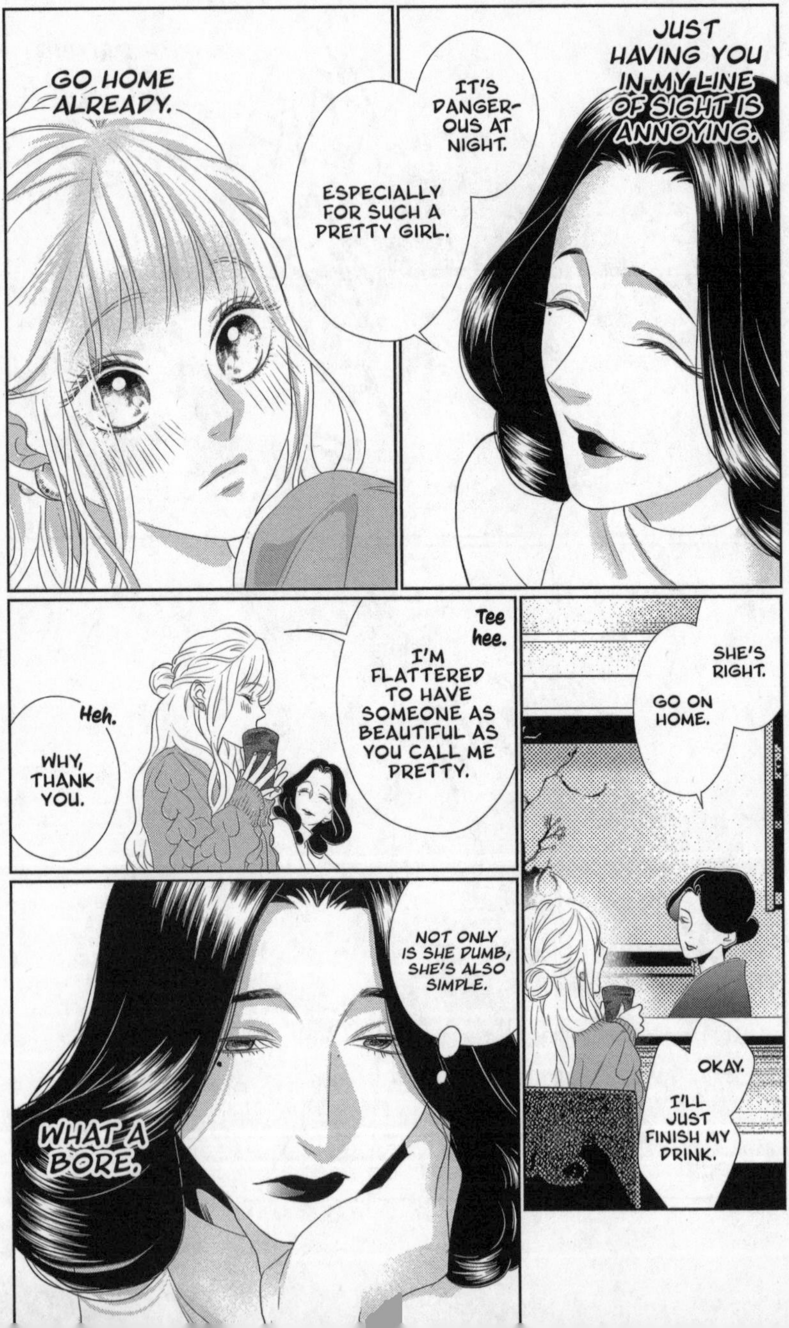
IT'S DANGEROUS AT NIGHT.
ESPECIALLY FOR SUCH A PRETTY GIRL.
JUST HAVING YOU IN MY LINE OF SIGHT IS ANNOYING.
GO HOME ALREADY.
SHE'S RIGHT.
GO ON HOME.
OKAY.
I'LL JUST FINISH MY DRINK.
Tee hee.
I'M FLATTERED TO HAVE SOMEONE AS BEAUTIFUL AS YOU CALL ME PRETTY.
Heh.
WHY, THANK YOU.
NOT ONLY IS SHE DUMB, SHE'S ALSO SIMPLE.
WHAT A BORE.

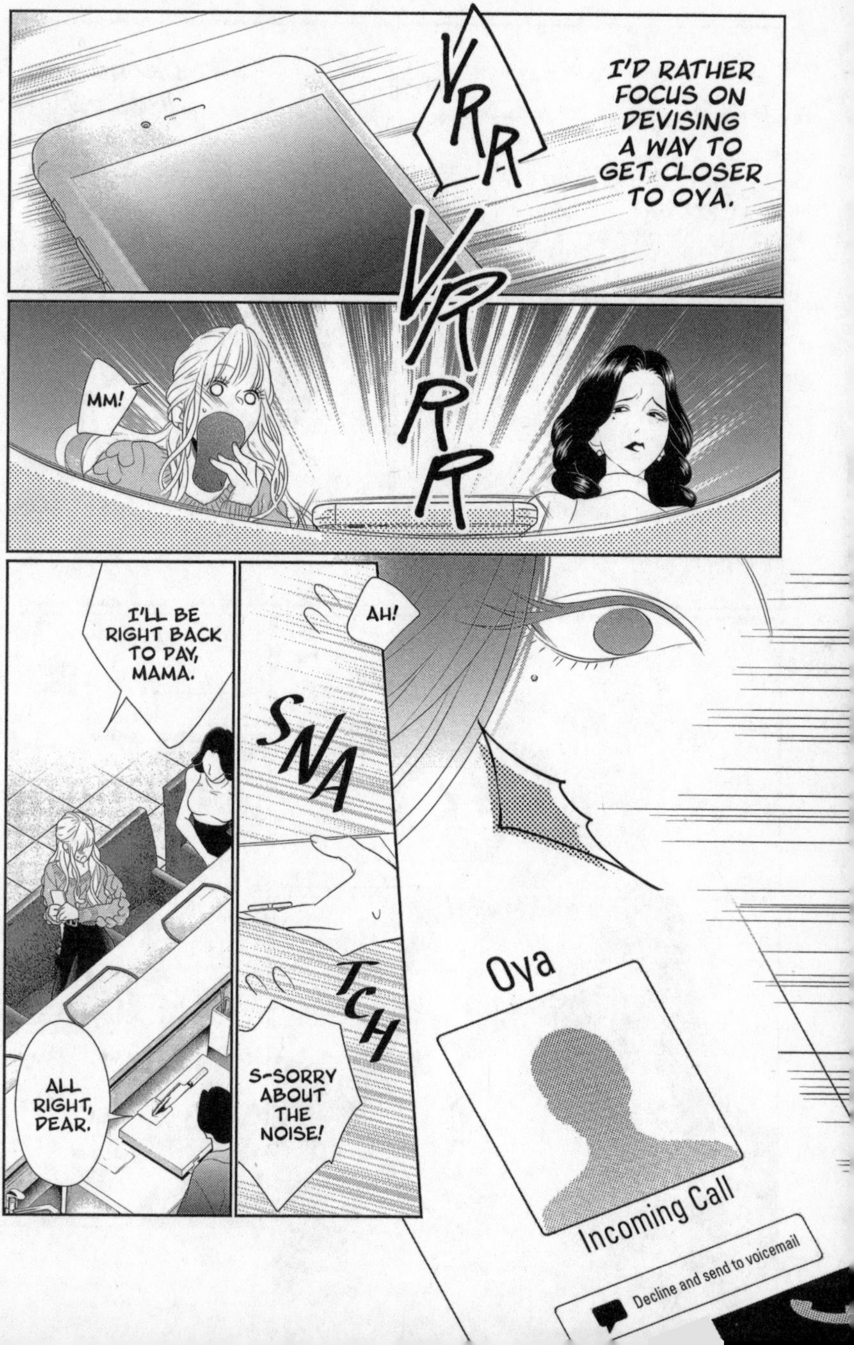
VRR
I'D RATHER FOCUS ON DEVISING A WAY TO GET CLOSER TO OYA.
VRRRR
MM!
Oya
Incoming Call
Decline and send to voicemail
AH!
SNATCH
S-SORRY ABOUT THE NOISE!
I'LL BE RIGHT BACK TO PAY, MAMA.
ALL RIGHT, DEAR.

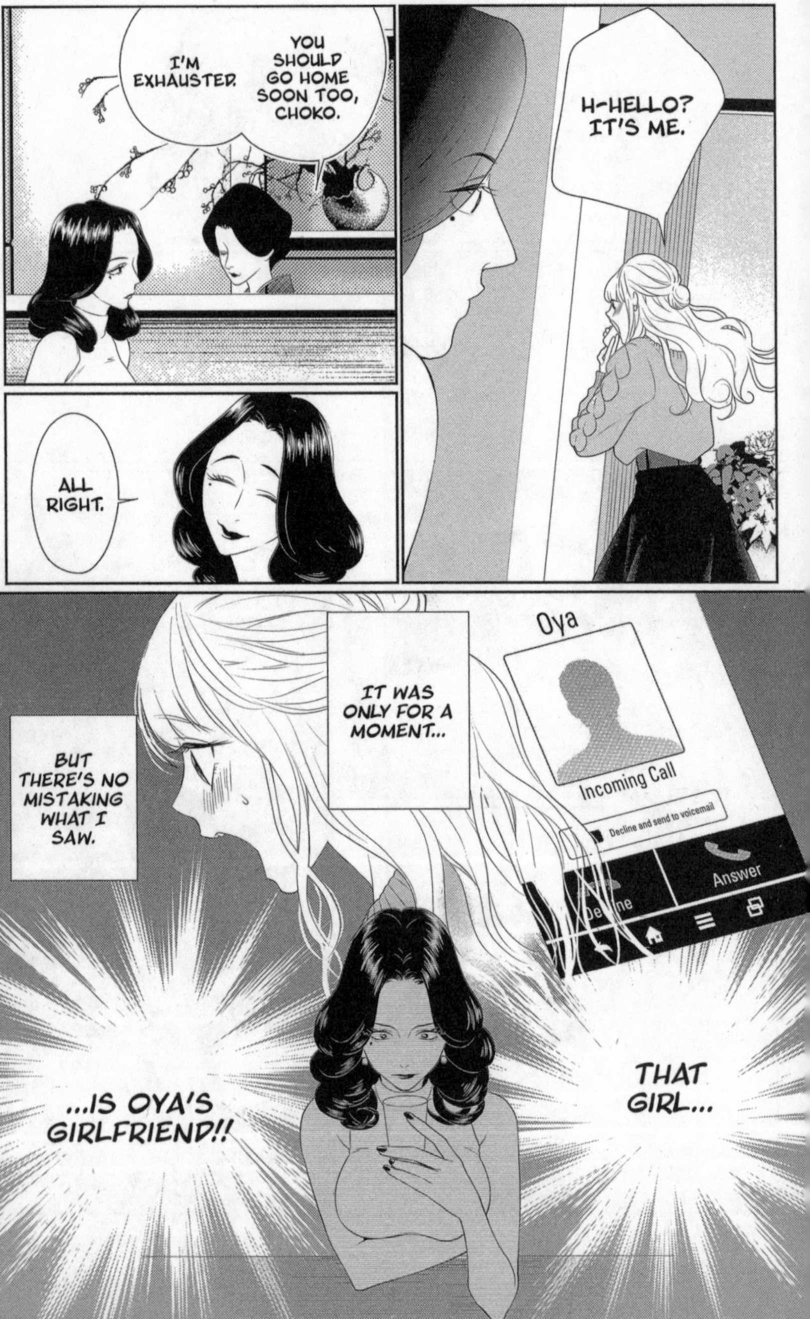
H-HELLO? IT'S ME.
I'M EXHAUSTED. YOU SHOULD GO HOME SOON TOO, CHOKO.
ALL RIGHT.
Oya
Incoming Call
Decline and send to voicemail
Answer
IT WAS ONLY FOR A MOMENT...
BUT THERE'S NO MISTAKING WHAT I SAW.
THAT GIRL...
...IS OYA'S GIRLFRIEND!!

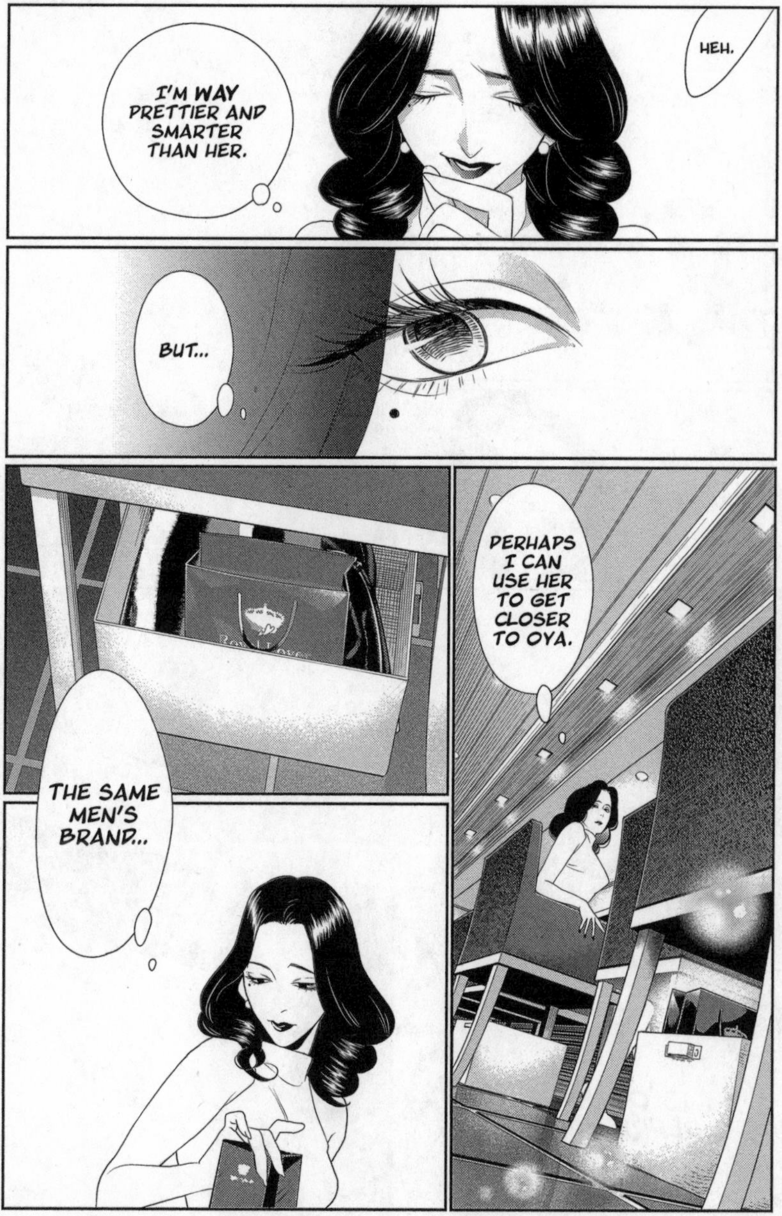
HEH.
I'M WAY PRETTIER AND SMARTER THAN HER.
BUT...
PERHAPS I CAN USE HER TO GET CLOSER TO OYA.
THE SAME MEN'S BRAND...

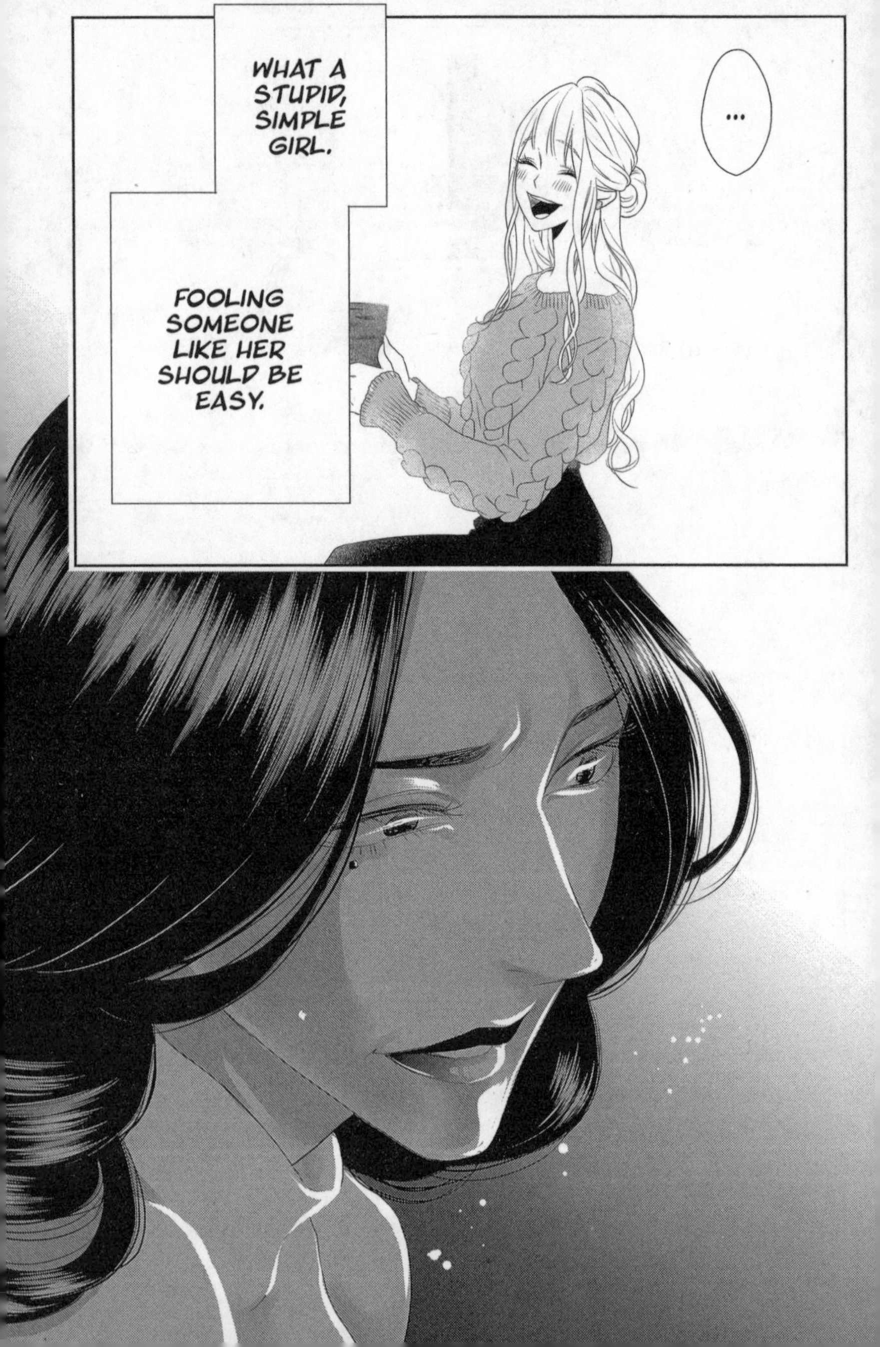
...
WHAT A STUPID, SIMPLE GIRL.
FOOLING SOMEONE LIKE HER SHOULD BE EASY.

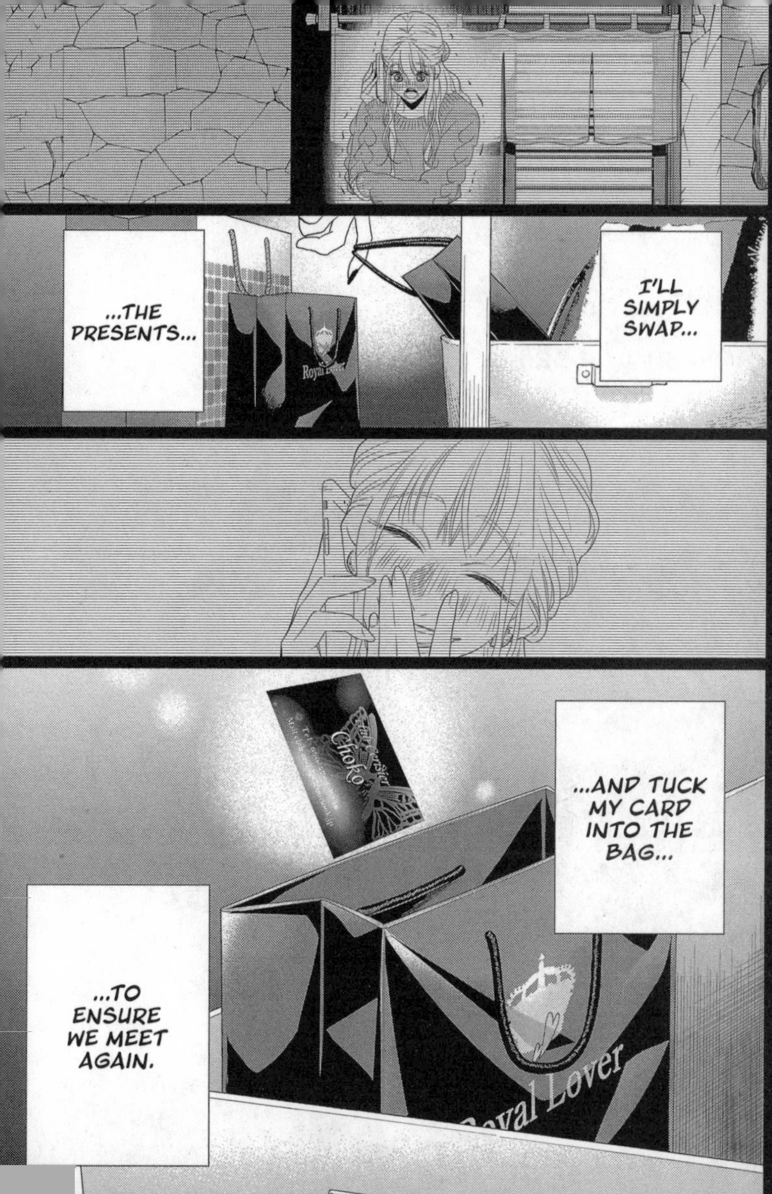
I'LL SIMPLY SWAP...
...THE PRESENTS...
...AND TUCK MY CARD INTO THE BAG...
...TO ENSURE WE MEET AGAIN.
Royal Lover

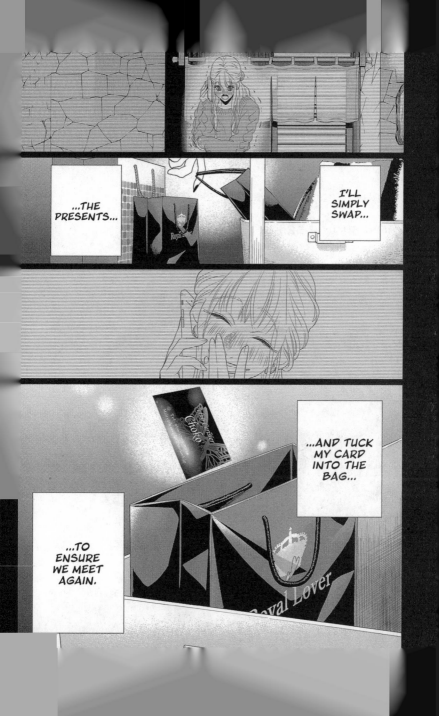

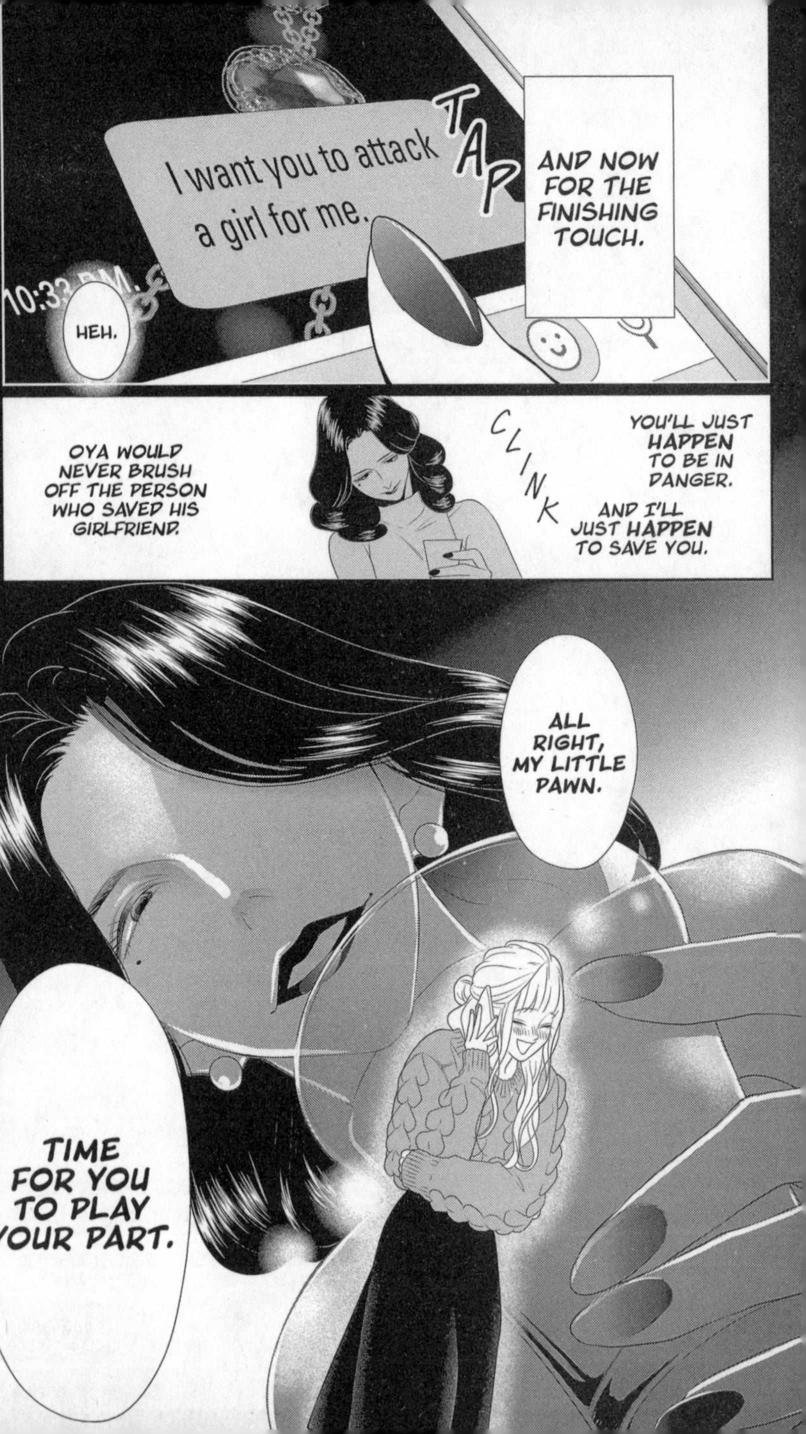
AND NOW FOR THE FINISHING TOUCH.
TAP
I want you to attack a girl for me.
HEH.
YOU'LL JUST HAPPEN TO BE IN DANGER.
AND I'LL JUST HAPPEN TO SAVE YOU.
CLINK
OYA WOULD NEVER BRUSH OFF THE PERSON WHO SAVED HIS GIRLFRIEND.
ALL RIGHT, MY LITTLE PAWN.
TIME FOR YOU TO PLAY YOUR PART.

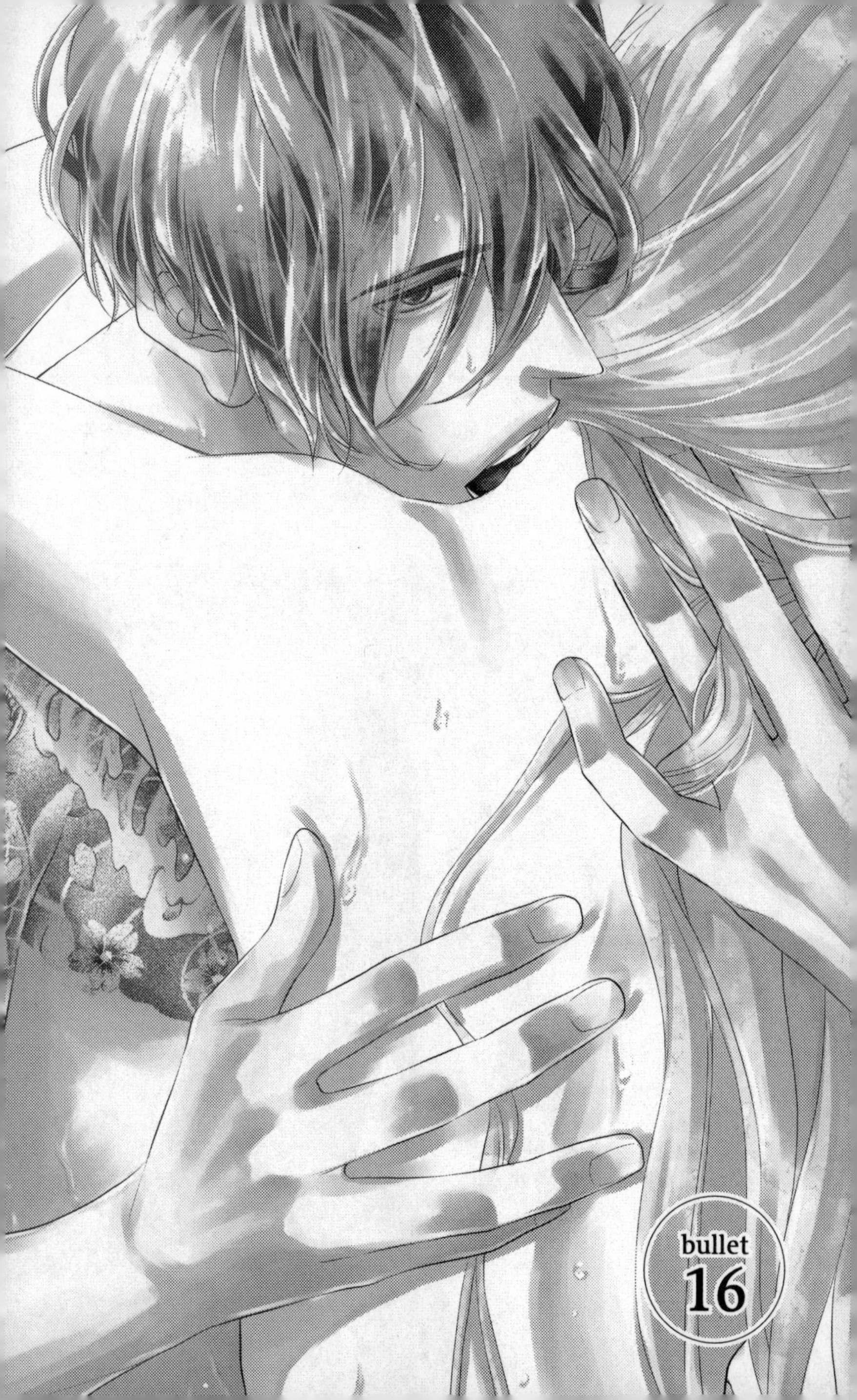
bullet
16

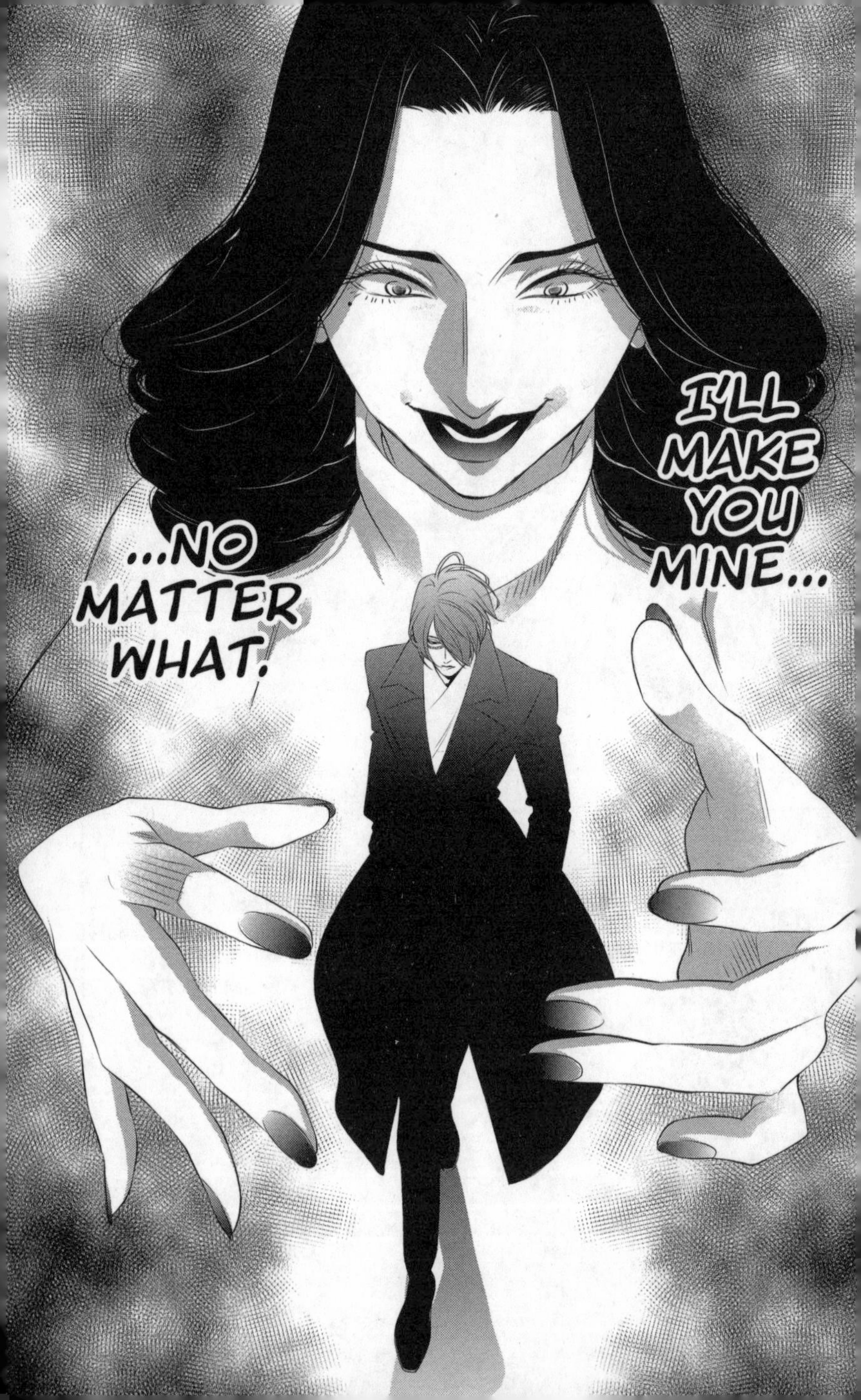
I'LL MAKE YOU MINE...
...NO MATTER WHAT.

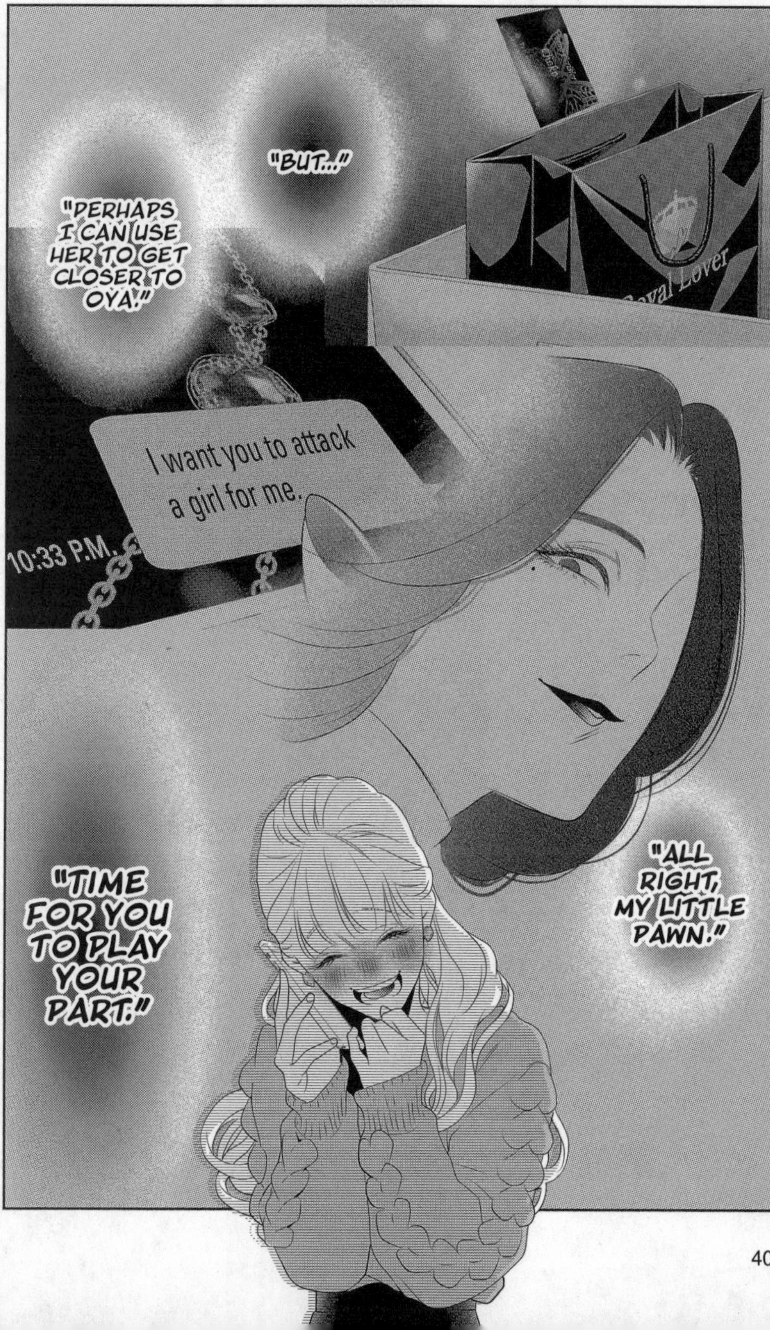
"BUT..."
"PERHAPS I CAN USE HER TO GET CLOSER TO OYA."
I want you to attack a girl for me.
10:33 P.M.
"ALL RIGHT, MY LITTLE PAWN."
"TIME FOR YOU TO PLAY YOUR PART."

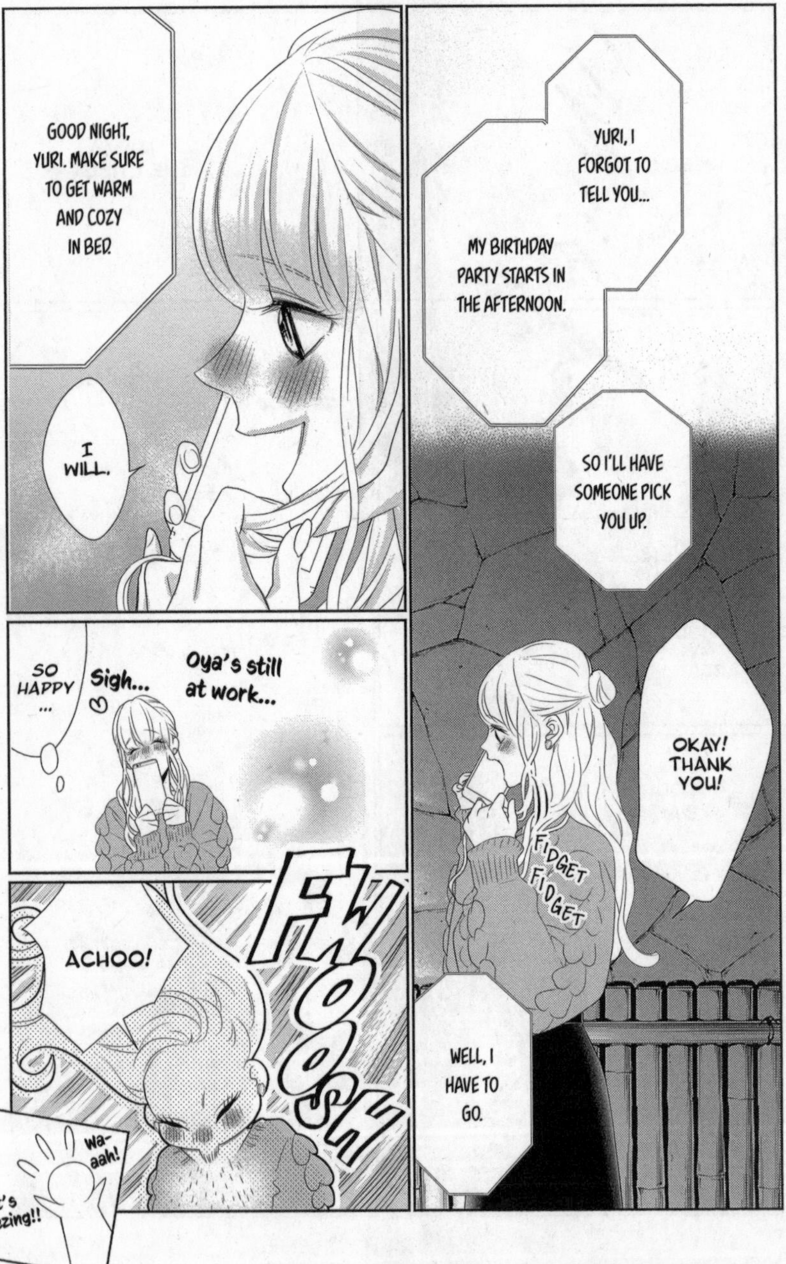
YURI, I FORGOT TO TELL YOU...
MY BIRTHDAY PARTY STARTS IN THE AFTERNOON.
SO I'LL HAVE SOMEONE PICK YOU UP.
OKAY! THANK YOU!
FIDGET FIDGET
WELL, I HAVE TO GO.
GOOD NIGHT, YURI. MAKE SURE TO GET WARM AND COZY IN BED.
I WILL.
Oya's still at work...
Sigh... ♡
SO HAPPY ...
FWOOSH
ACHOO!
Wa-aah!
It's freezing!!

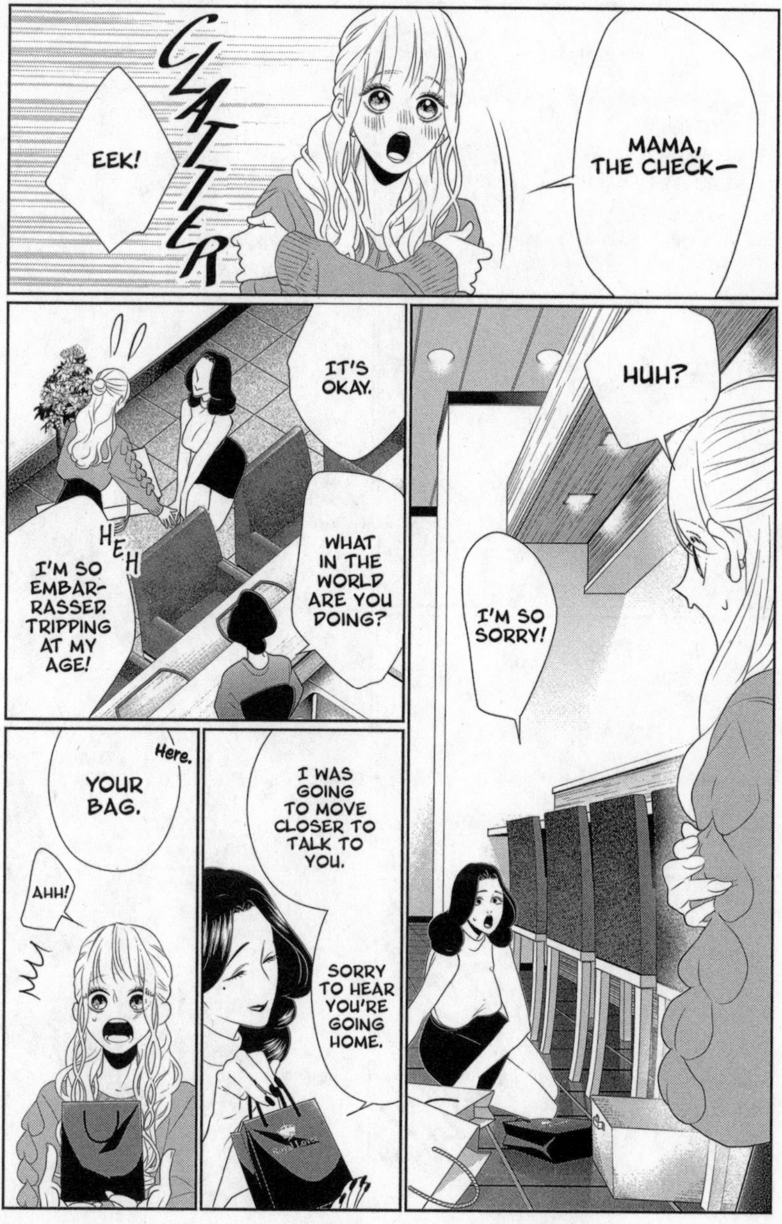
MAMA, THE CHECK—
CLATTER
EEK!
HUH?
I'M SO SORRY!
IT'S OKAY.
WHAT IN THE WORLD ARE YOU DOING?
HEH
I'M SO EMBARRASSED. TRIPPING AT MY AGE!
I WAS GOING TO MOVE CLOSER TO TALK TO YOU.
SORRY TO HEAR YOU'RE GOING HOME.
Here.
YOUR BAG.
AHH!

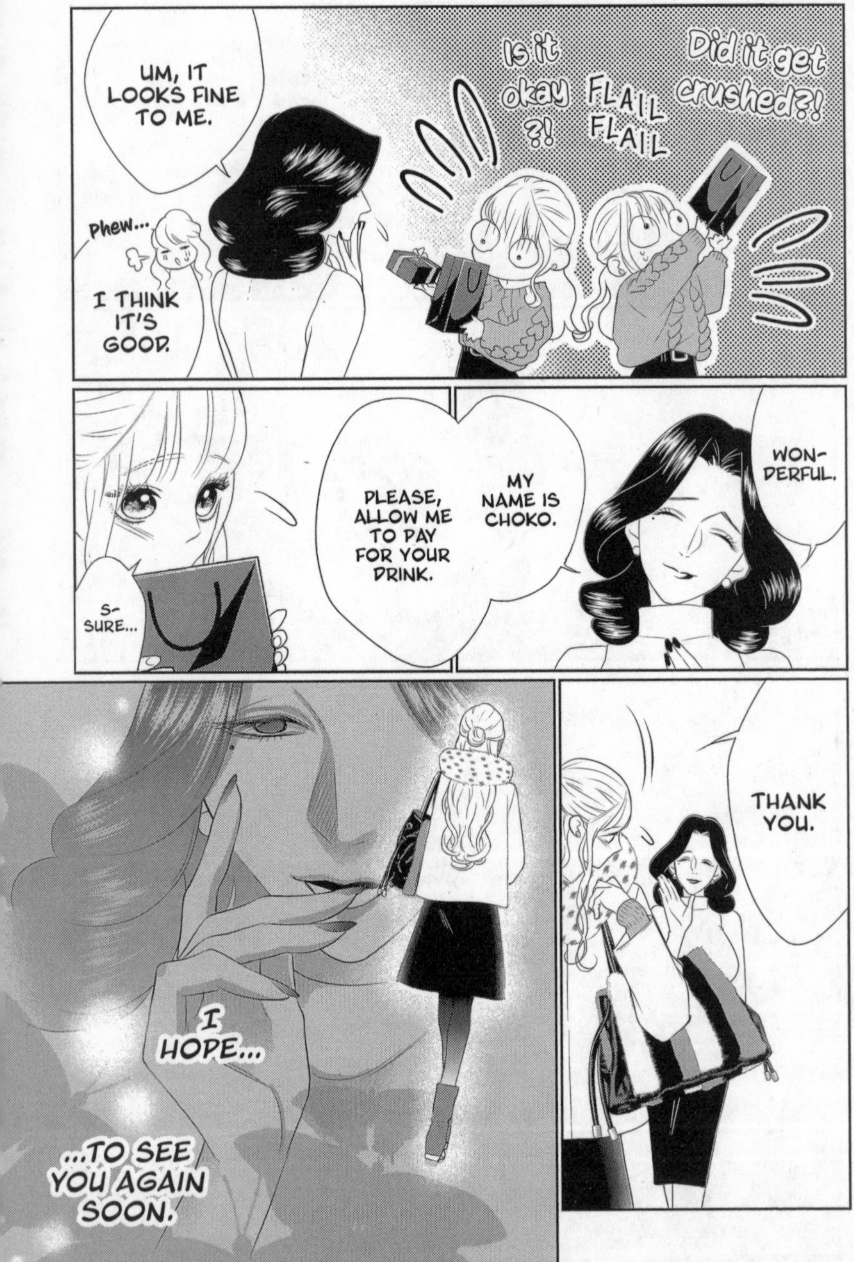
Did it get crushed?!
FLAIL FLAIL
Is it okay ?!
UM, IT LOOKS FINE TO ME.
Phew...
I THINK IT'S GOOD.
WON-DERFUL.
MY NAME IS CHOKO.
PLEASE, ALLOW ME TO PAY FOR YOUR DRINK.
S-SURE...
THANK YOU.
I HOPE...
...TO SEE YOU AGAIN SOON.

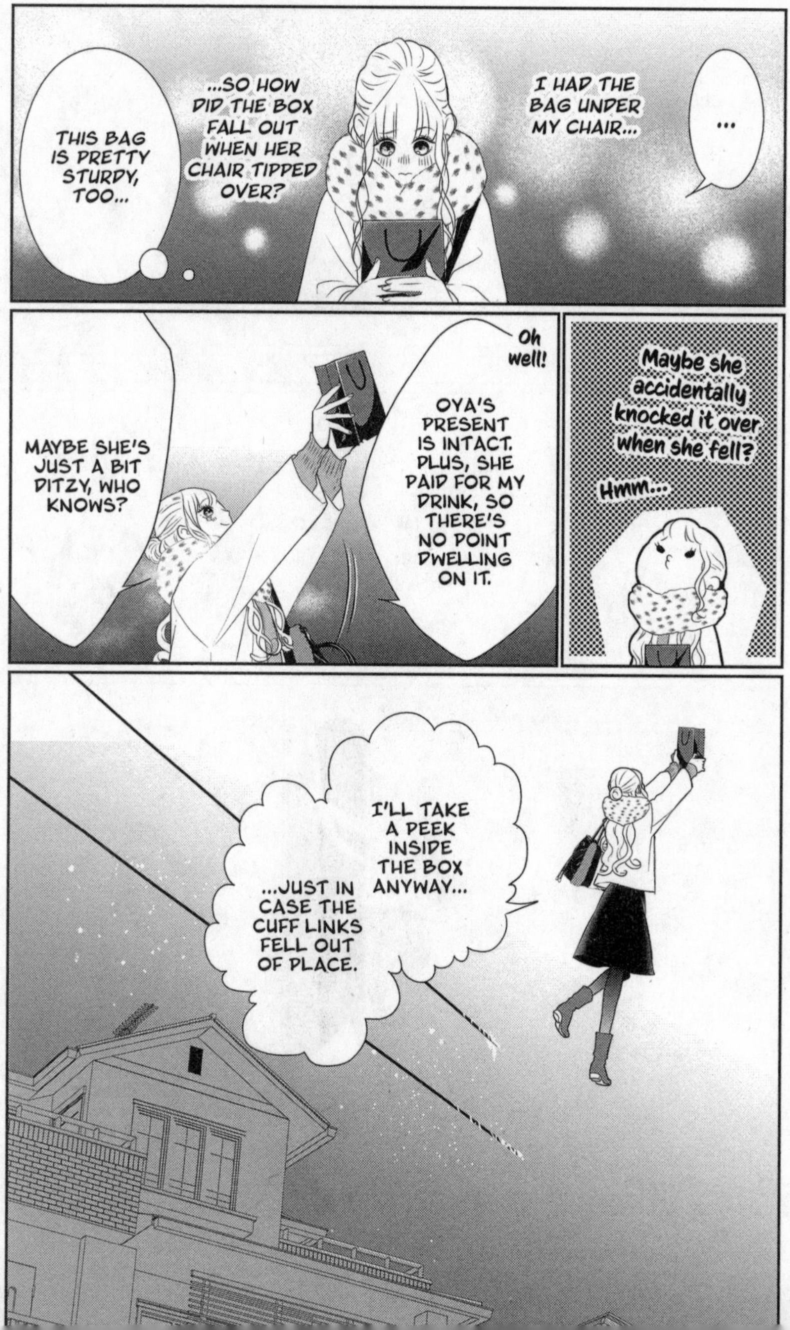
...
I HAD THE BAG UNDER MY CHAIR...
...SO HOW DID THE BOX FALL OUT WHEN HER CHAIR TIPPED OVER?
THIS BAG IS PRETTY STURDY, TOO...
Maybe she accidentally knocked it over when she fell?
Hmm...
Oh well!
OYA'S PRESENT IS INTACT. PLUS, SHE PAID FOR MY DRINK, SO THERE'S NO POINT DWELLING ON IT.
MAYBE SHE'S JUST A BIT DITZY, WHO KNOWS?
I'LL TAKE A PEEK INSIDE THE BOX ANYWAY...
...JUST IN CASE THE CUFF LINKS FELL OUT OF PLACE.

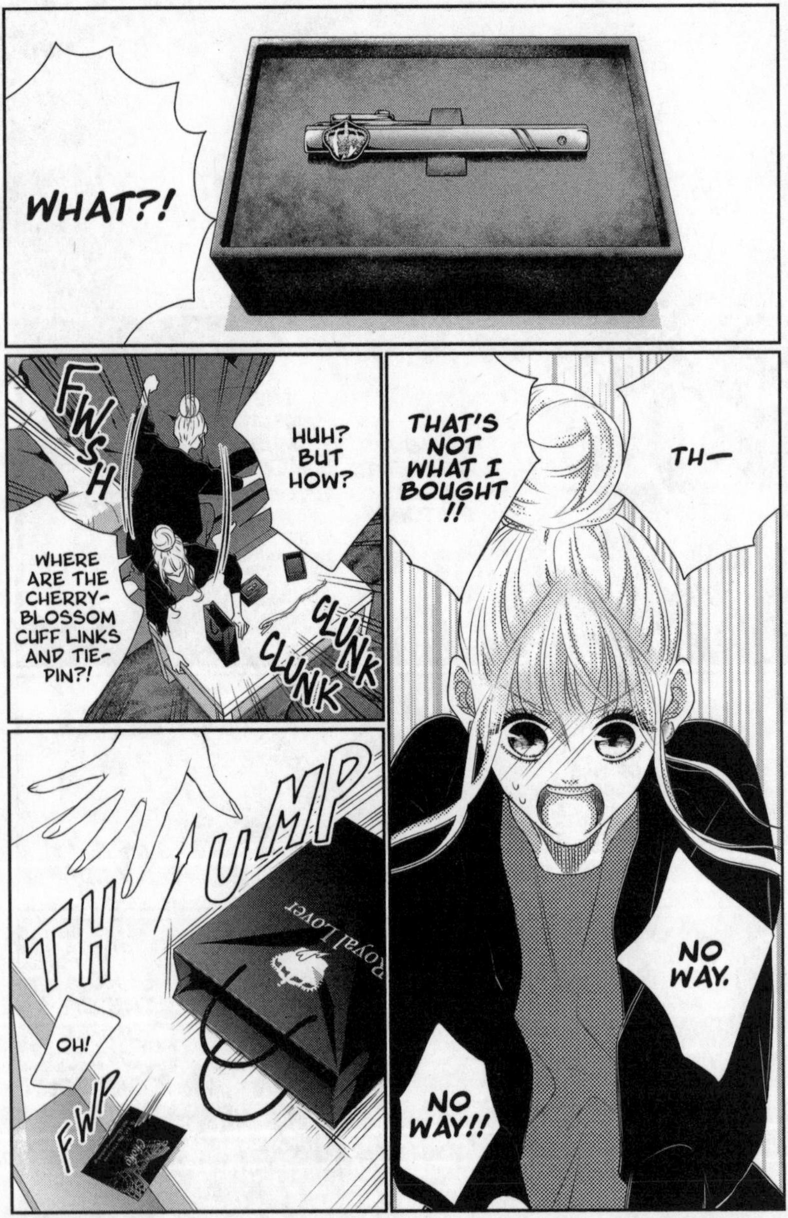
WHAT?!
TH—
THAT'S NOT WHAT I BOUGHT!!
NO WAY.
NO WAY!!
HUH? BUT HOW?
FWSH
WHERE ARE THE CHERRY-BLOSSOM CUFF LINKS AND TIE-PIN?!
CLUNK CLUNK
THUMP
Royal Lover
OH!
FWP

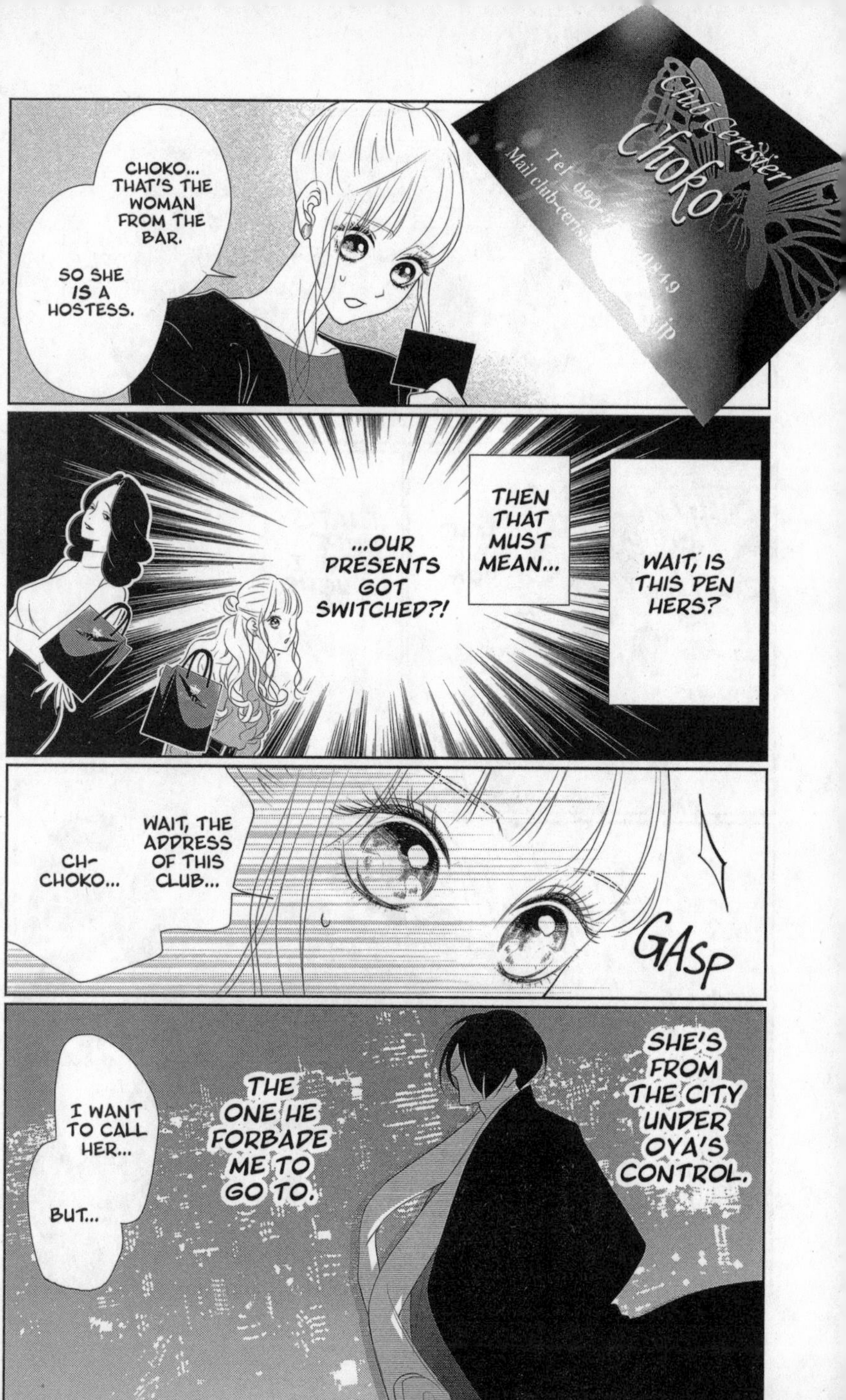
Club Cerisier
Choko
CHOKO... THAT'S THE WOMAN FROM THE BAR.
SO SHE IS A HOSTESS.
WAIT, IS THIS PEN HERS?
THEN THAT MUST MEAN...
...OUR PRESENTS GOT SWITCHED?!
GASP
WAIT, THE ADDRESS OF THIS CLUB...
CH-CHOKO...
SHE'S FROM THE CITY UNDER OYA'S CONTROL.
THE ONE HE FORBADE ME TO GO TO.
I WANT TO CALL HER...
BUT...

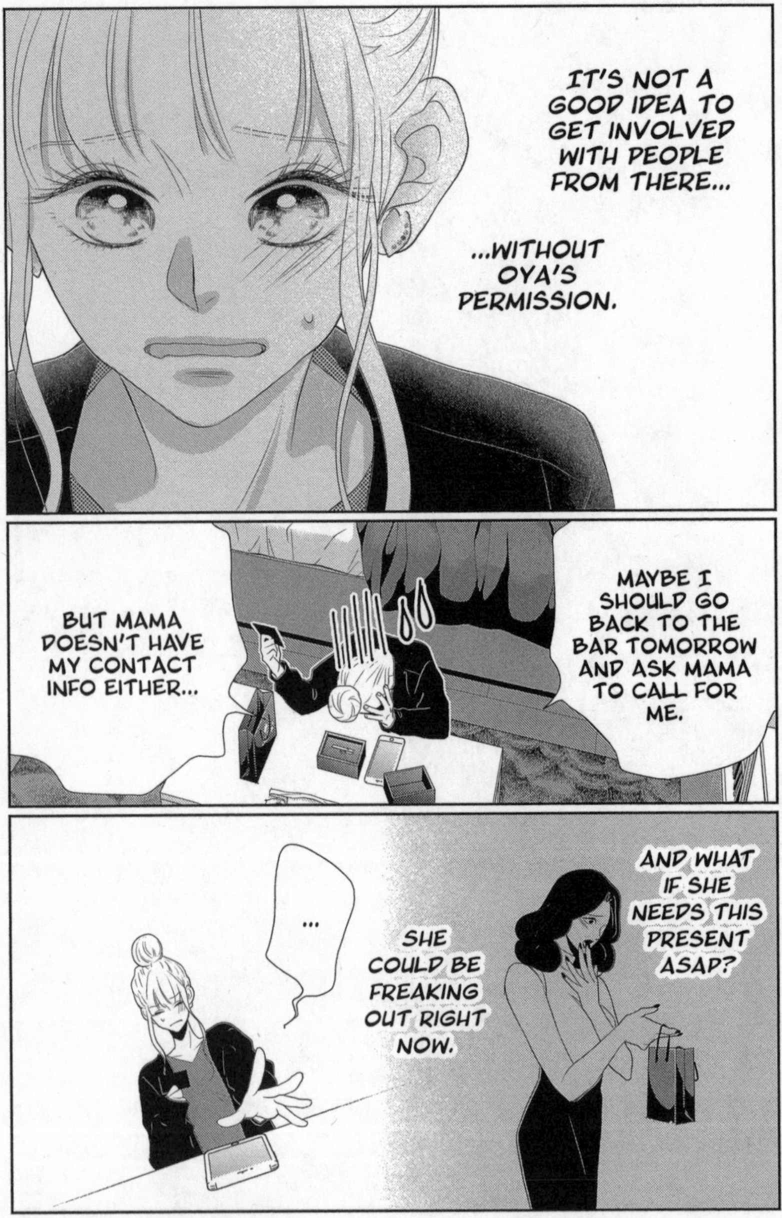
IT'S NOT A GOOD IDEA TO GET INVOLVED WITH PEOPLE FROM THERE...
...WITHOUT OYA'S PERMISSION.
MAYBE I SHOULD GO BACK TO THE BAR TOMORROW AND ASK MAMA TO CALL FOR ME.
BUT MAMA DOESN'T HAVE MY CONTACT INFO EITHER...
AND WHAT IF SHE NEEDS THIS PRESENT ASAP?
SHE COULD BE FREAKING OUT RIGHT NOW.
...

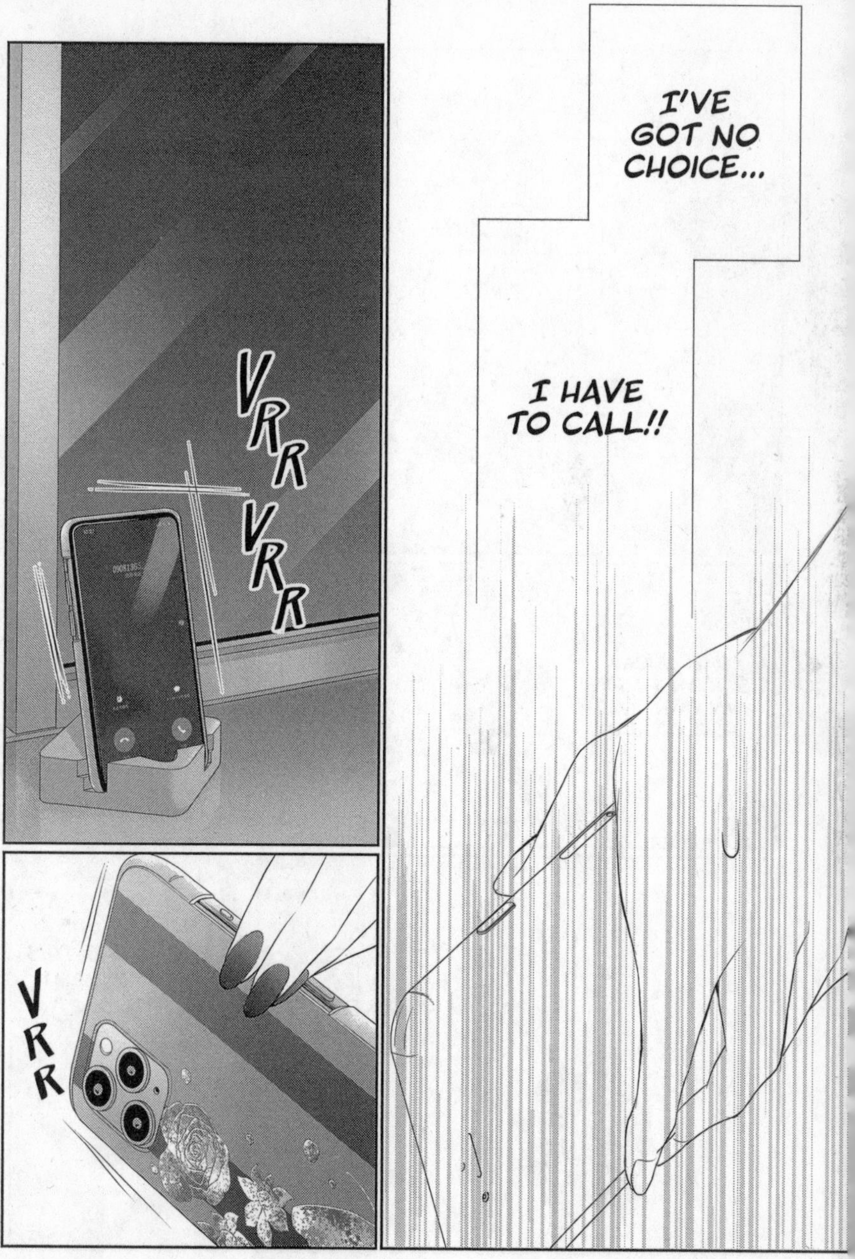
I'VE GOT NO CHOICE...
I HAVE TO CALL!!
VRR VRR
VRR

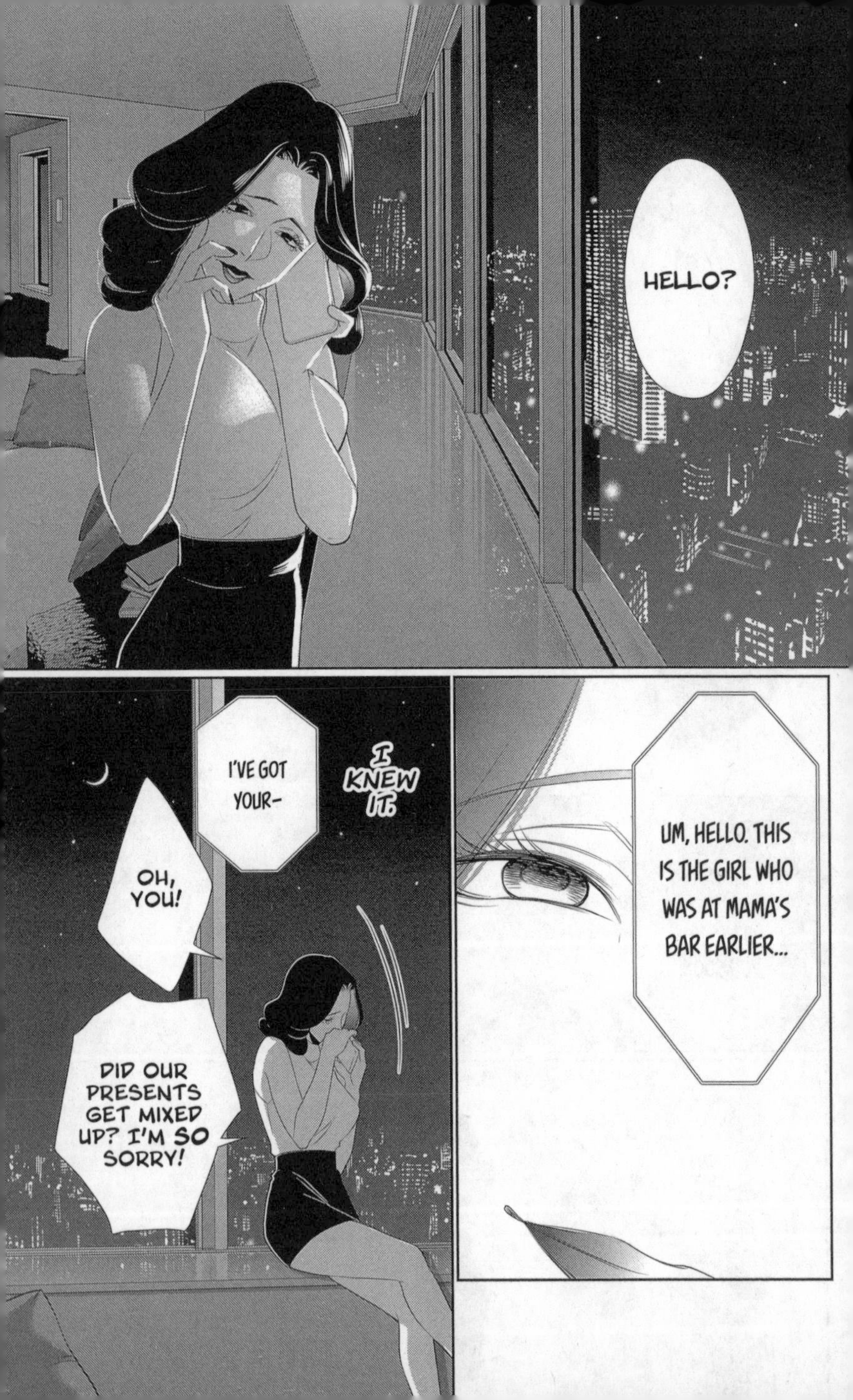
HELLO?
UM, HELLO. THIS IS THE GIRL WHO WAS AT MAMA'S BAR EARLIER...
I KNEW IT.
I'VE GOT YOUR-
OH, YOU!
DID OUR PRESENTS GET MIXED UP? I'M SO SORRY!

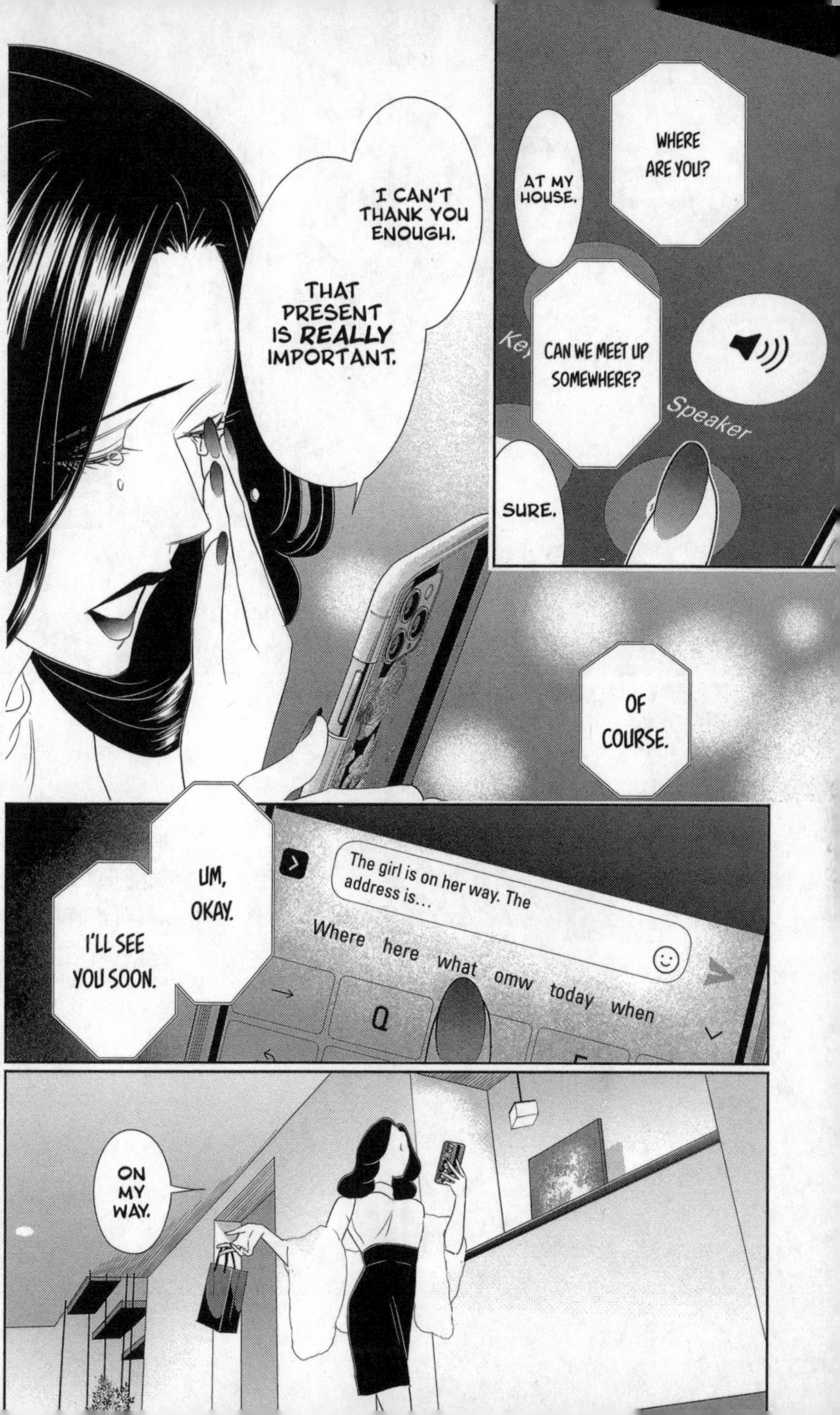
WHERE ARE YOU?
AT MY HOUSE.
Speaker
CAN WE MEET UP SOMEWHERE?
SURE.
I CAN'T THANK YOU ENOUGH.
THAT PRESENT IS **REALLY** IMPORTANT.
OF COURSE.
The girl is on her way. The address is...
Where here what omw today when
Q
UM, OKAY.
I'LL SEE YOU SOON.
ON MY WAY.

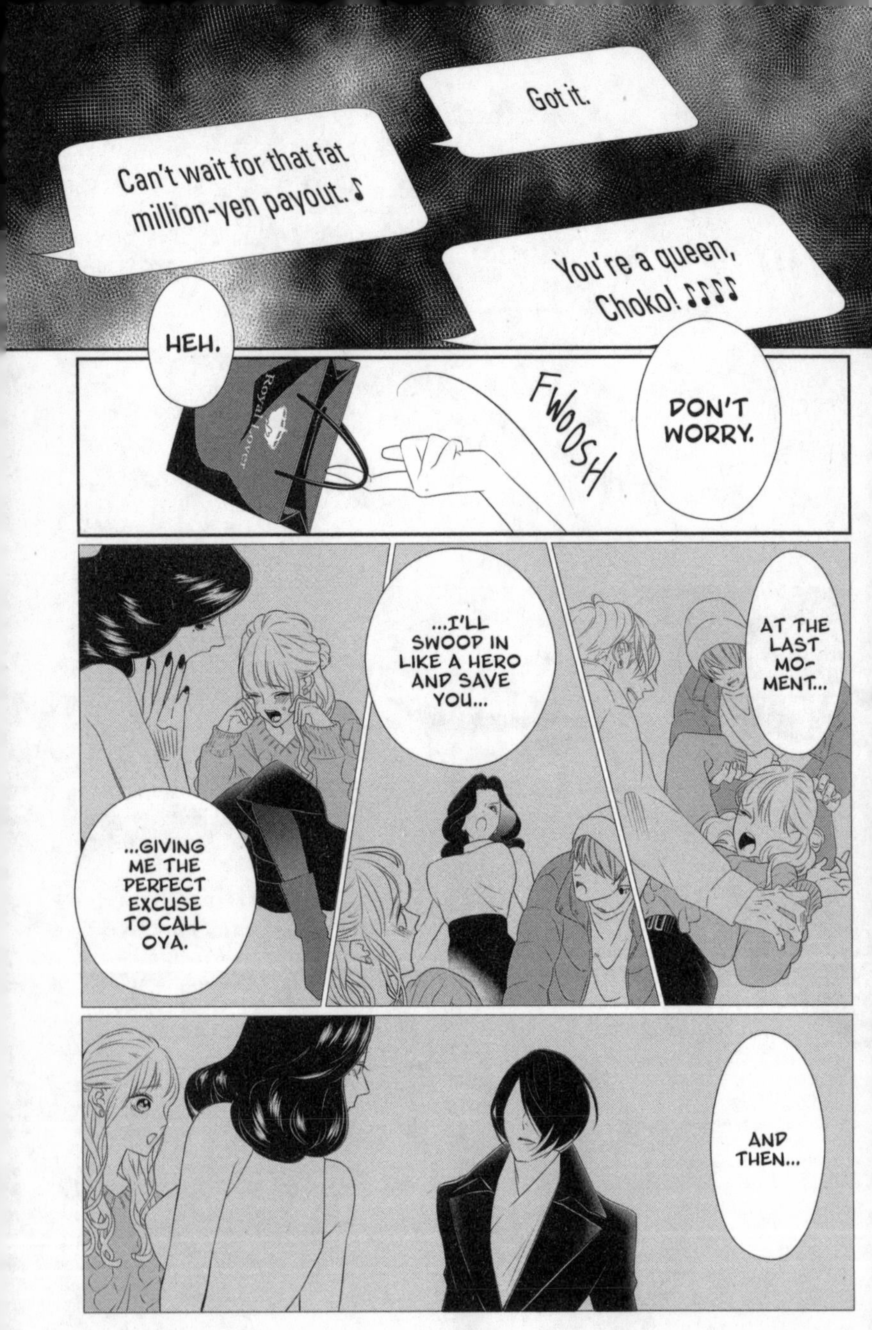
Got it.
Can't wait for that fat million-yen payout. ♪
You're a queen, Choko! ♪♪♪♪
HEH.
DON'T WORRY.
FWOOSH
AT THE LAST MO-MENT...
...I'LL SWOOP IN LIKE A HERO AND SAVE YOU...
...GIVING ME THE PERFECT EXCUSE TO CALL OYA.
AND THEN...

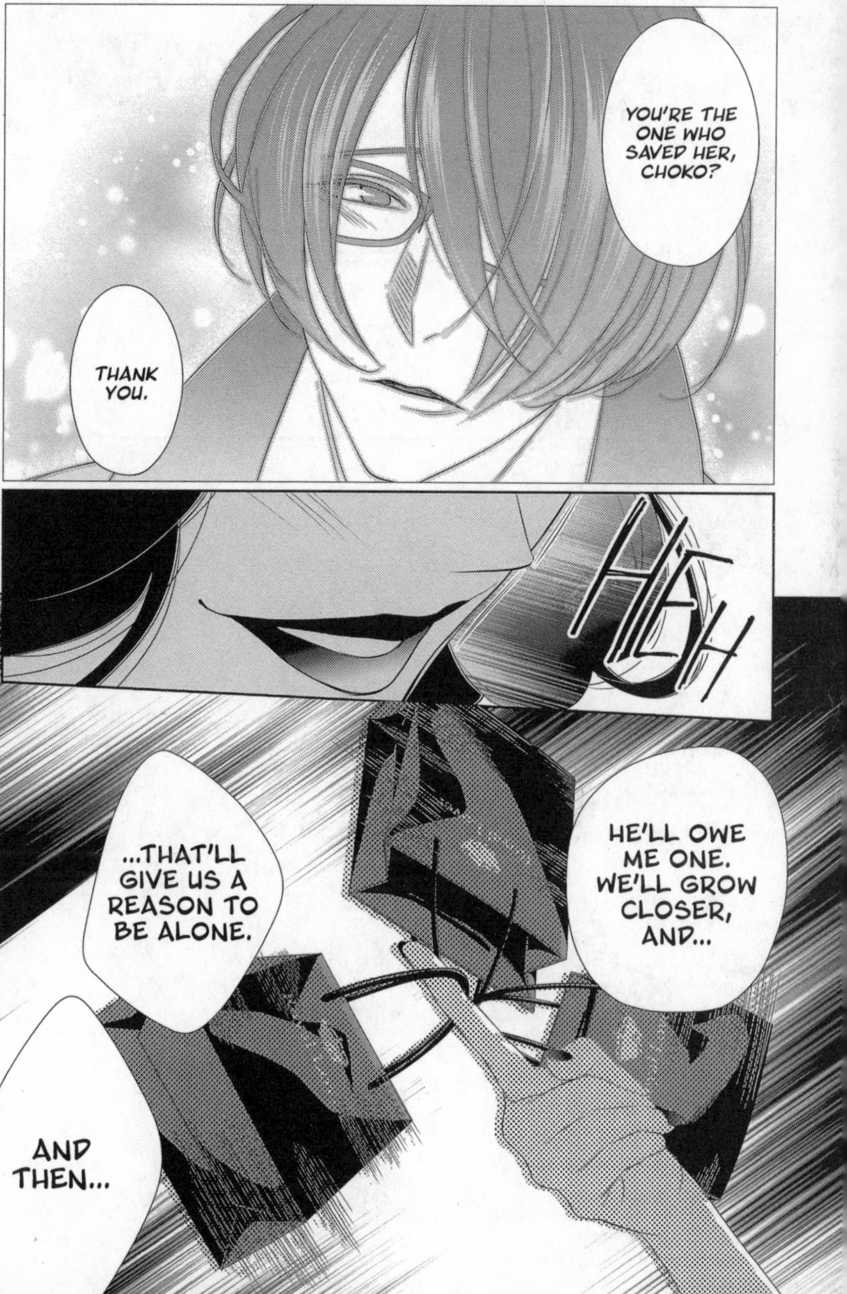
YOU'RE THE ONE WHO SAVED HER, CHOKO?
THANK YOU.
HEH
HE'LL OWE ME ONE. WE'LL GROW CLOSER, AND...
...THAT'LL GIVE US A REASON TO BE ALONE.
AND THEN...

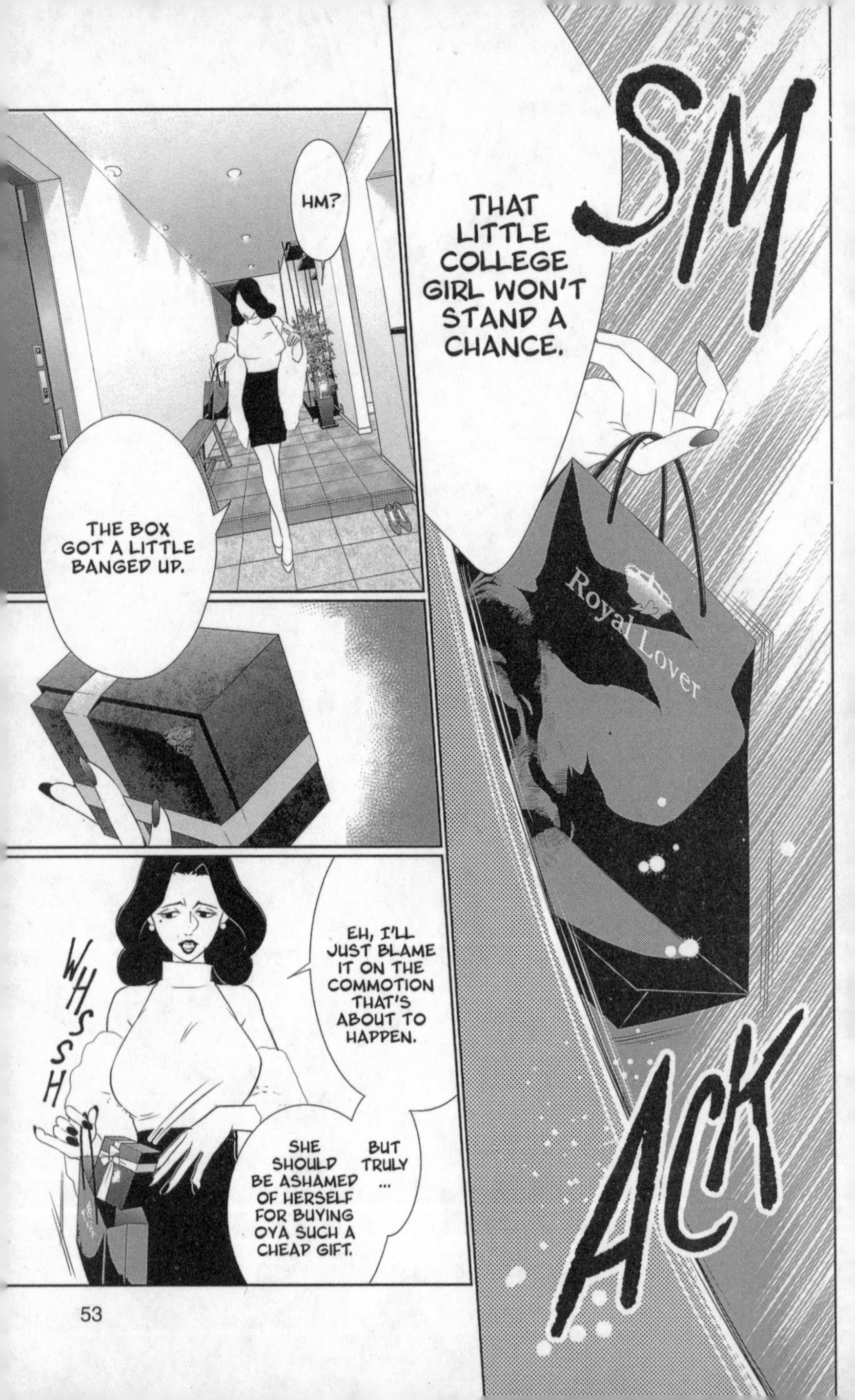

SMACK
THAT LITTLE COLLEGE GIRL WON'T STAND A CHANCE.
Royal Lover
HM?
THE BOX GOT A LITTLE BANGED UP.
WHSSH
EH, I'LL JUST BLAME IT ON THE COMMOTION THAT'S ABOUT TO HAPPEN.
BUT TRULY...
SHE SHOULD BE ASHAMED OF HERSELF FOR BUYING OYA SUCH A CHEAP GIFT.

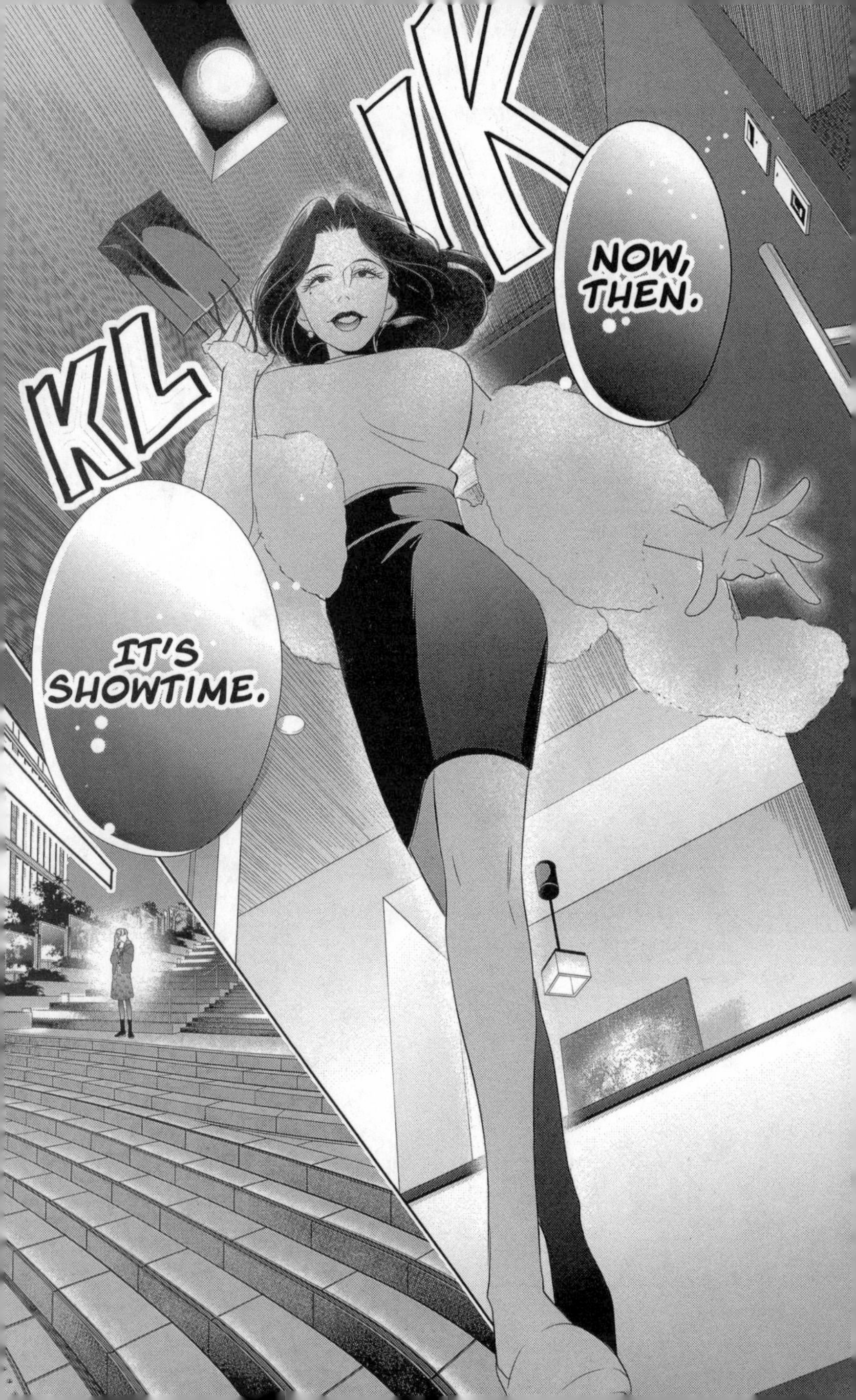
KL IK
NOW, THEN.
IT'S SHOWTIME.

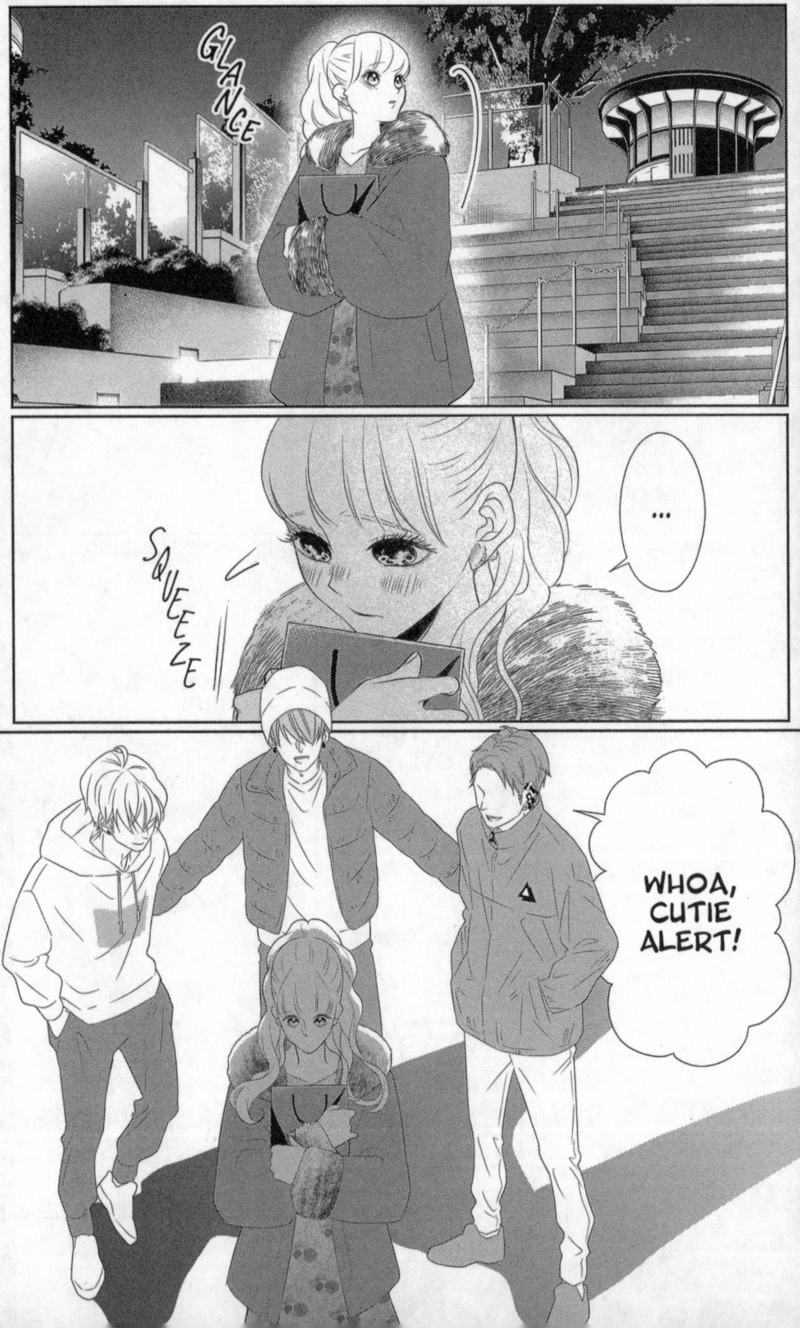
GLANCE
...
SQUEEZE
WHOA, CUTIE ALERT!

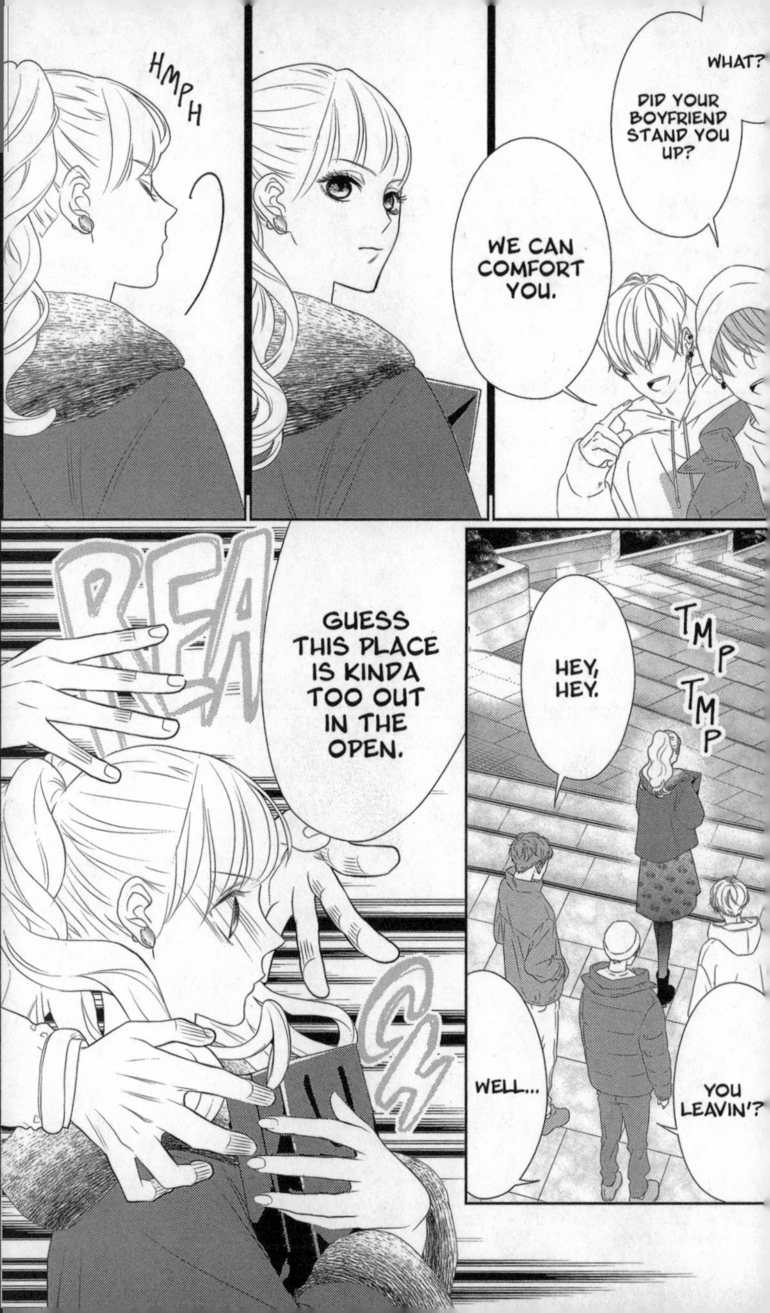
WHAT?
DID YOUR BOYFRIEND STAND YOU UP?
WE CAN COMFORT YOU.
HMPH
TMP TMP
HEY, HEY.
YOU LEAVIN'?
WELL...
GUESS THIS PLACE IS KINDA TOO OUT IN THE OPEN.

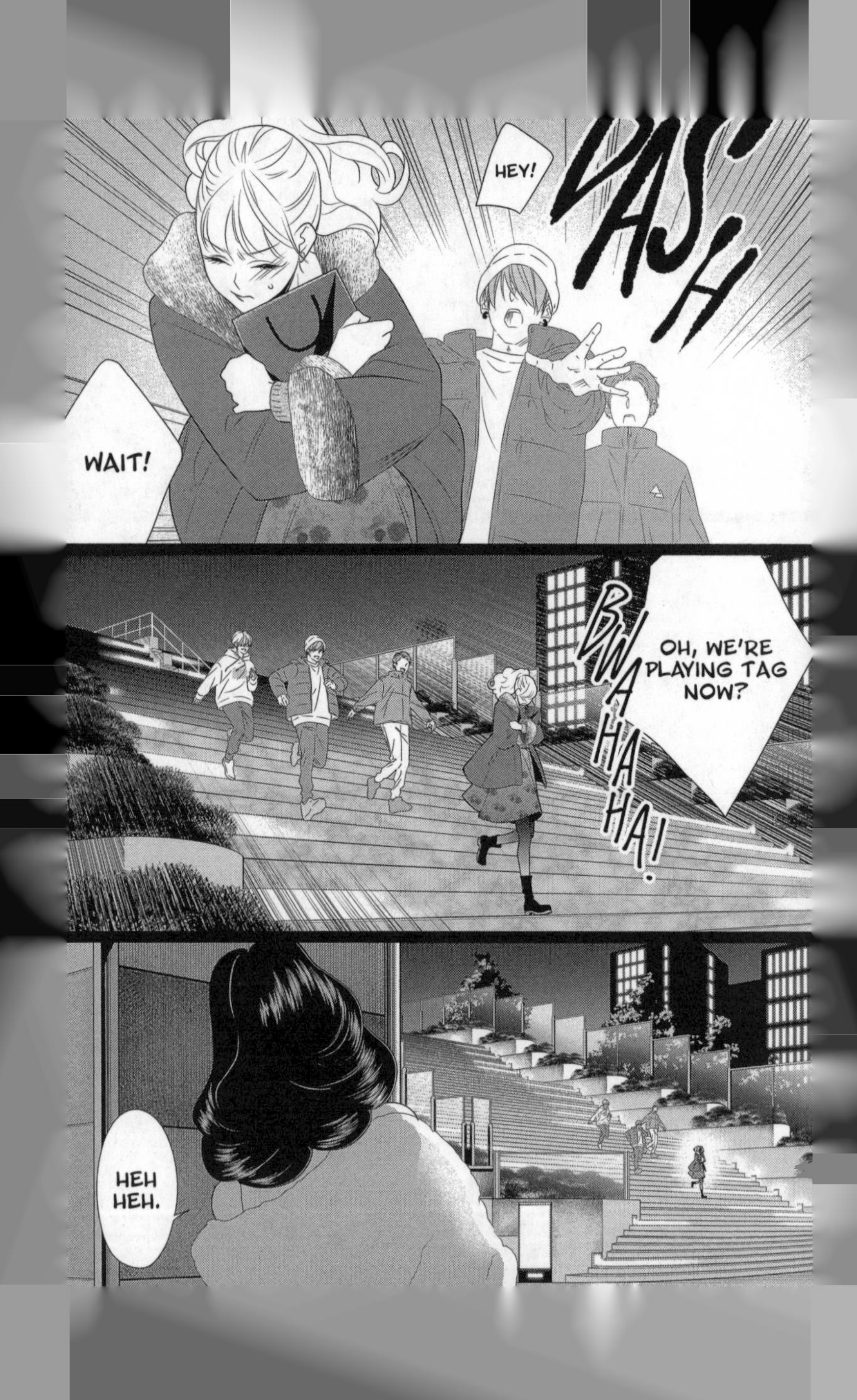
DASH
HEY!
WAIT!
OH, WE'RE PLAYING TAG NOW?
BWAHAHAHA!
HEH HEH.

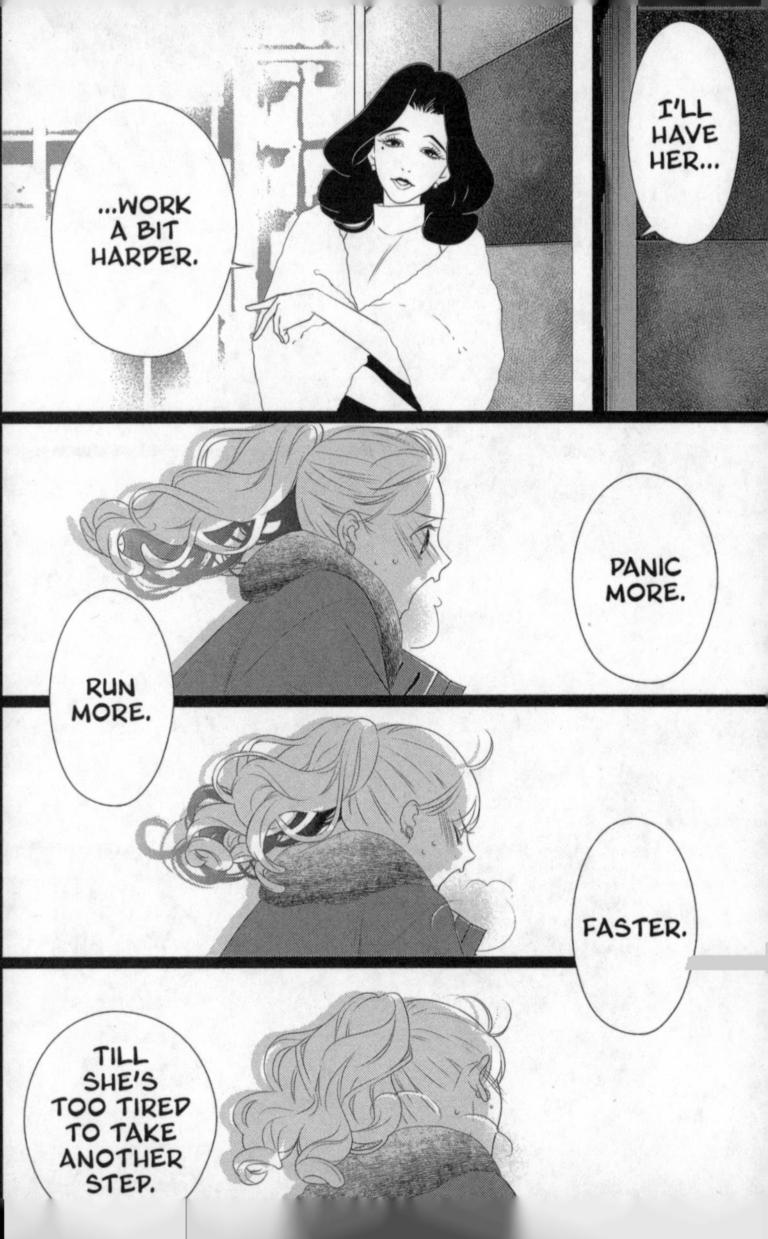
I'LL HAVE HER...
...WORK A BIT HARDER.
PANIC MORE.
RUN MORE.
FASTER.
TILL SHE'S TOO TIRED TO TAKE ANOTHER STEP.

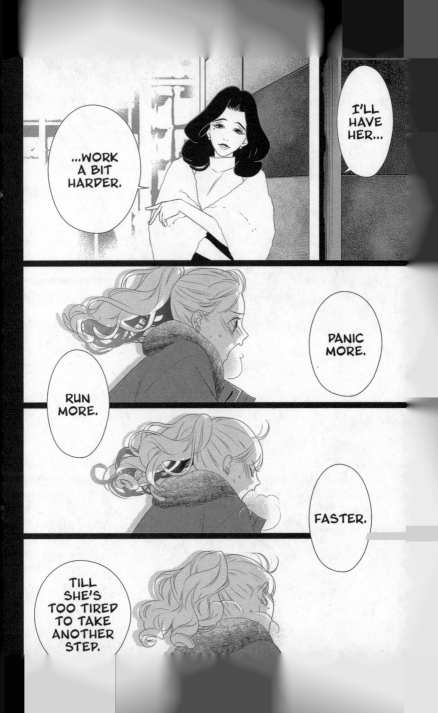

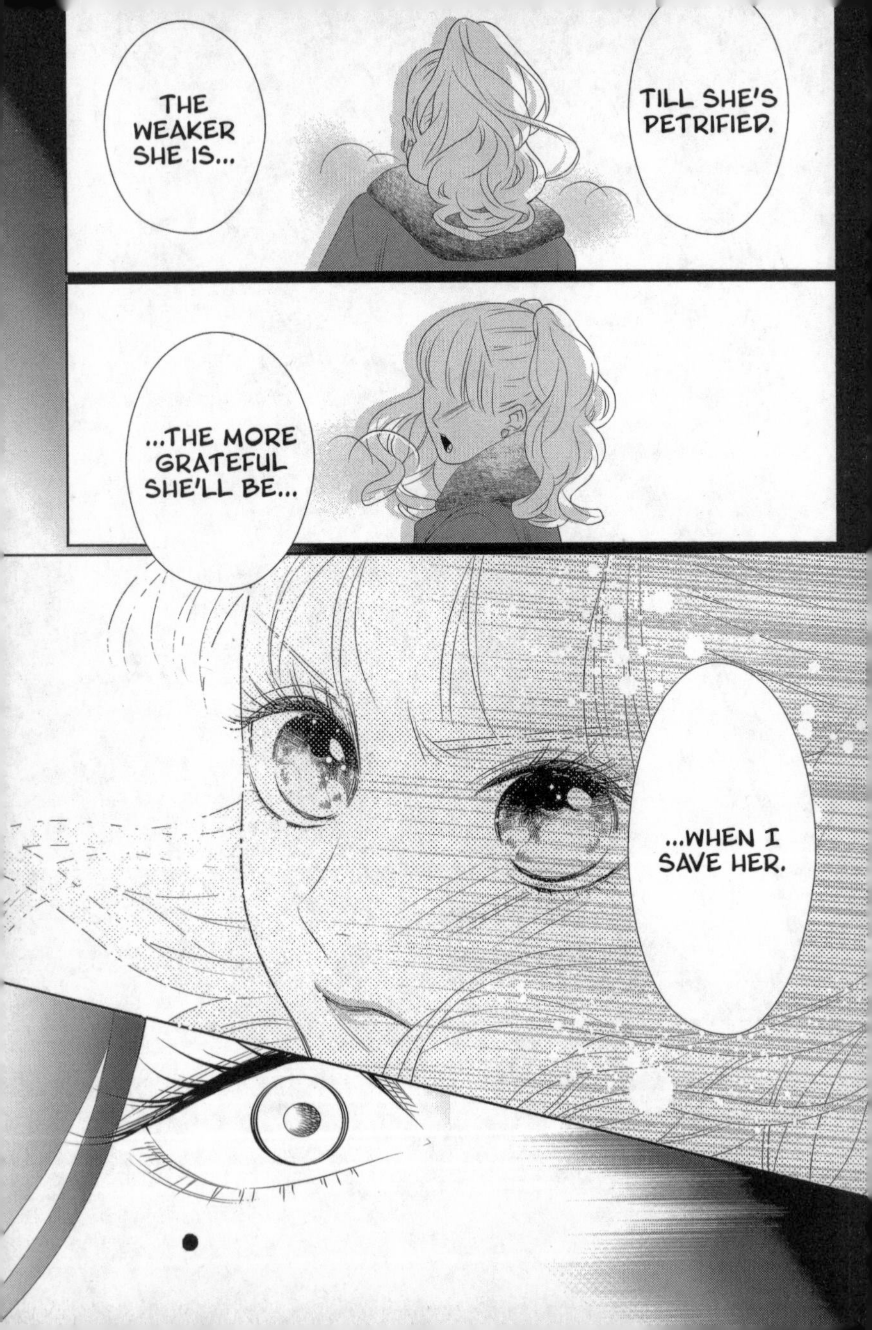
TILL SHE'S PETRIFIED.
THE WEAKER SHE IS...
...THE MORE GRATEFUL SHE'LL BE...
...WHEN I SAVE HER.

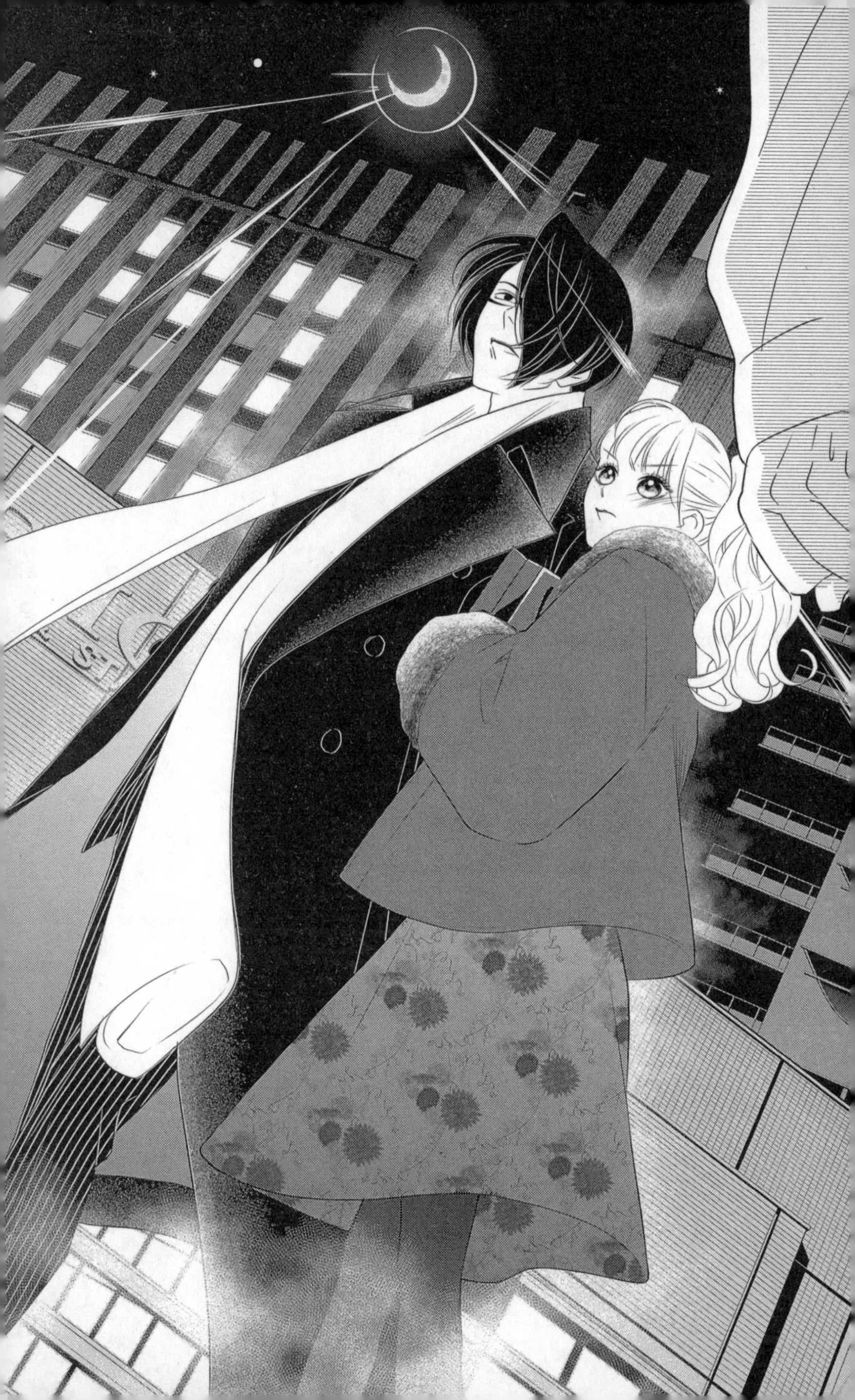

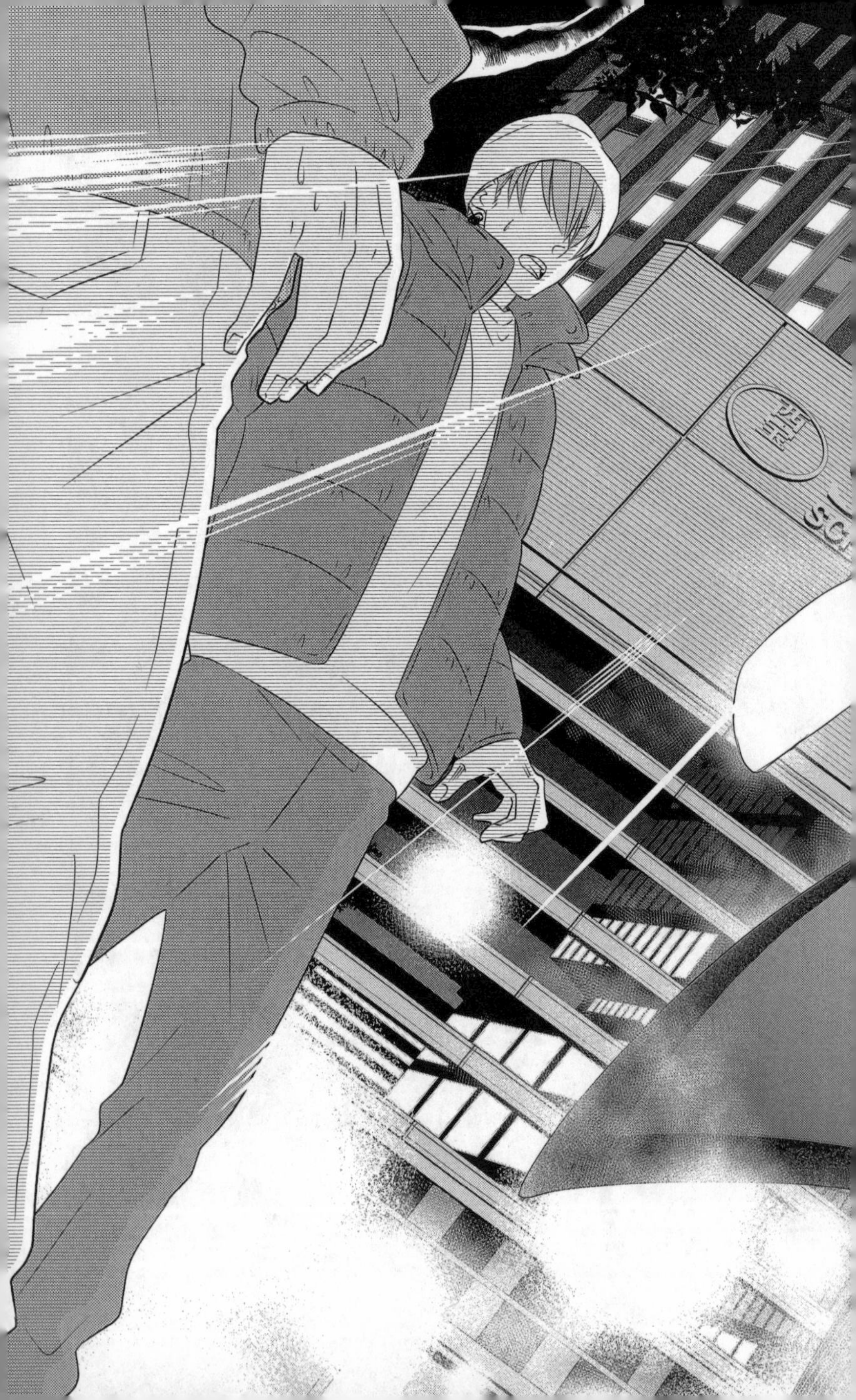

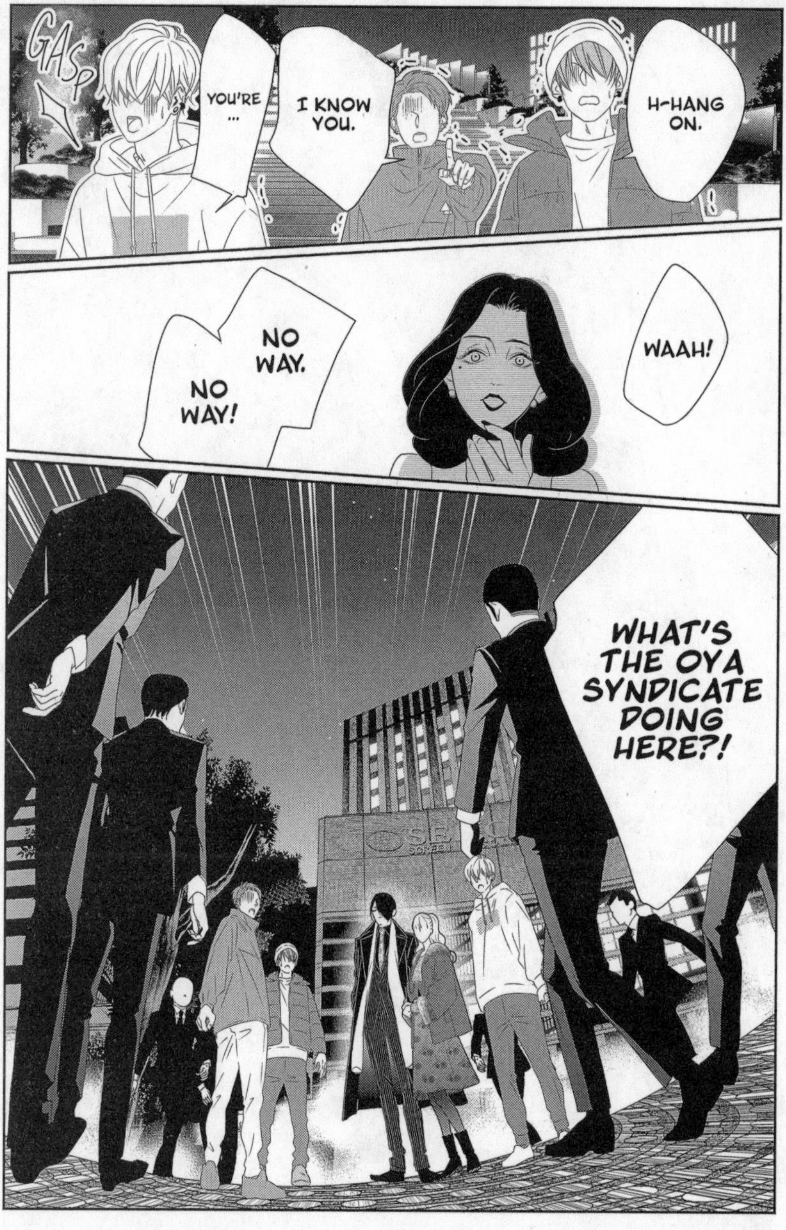
H-HANG ON.
I KNOW YOU.
YOU'RE ...
GASP
WAAH!
NO WAY.
NO WAY!
WHAT'S THE OYA SYNDICATE DOING HERE?!

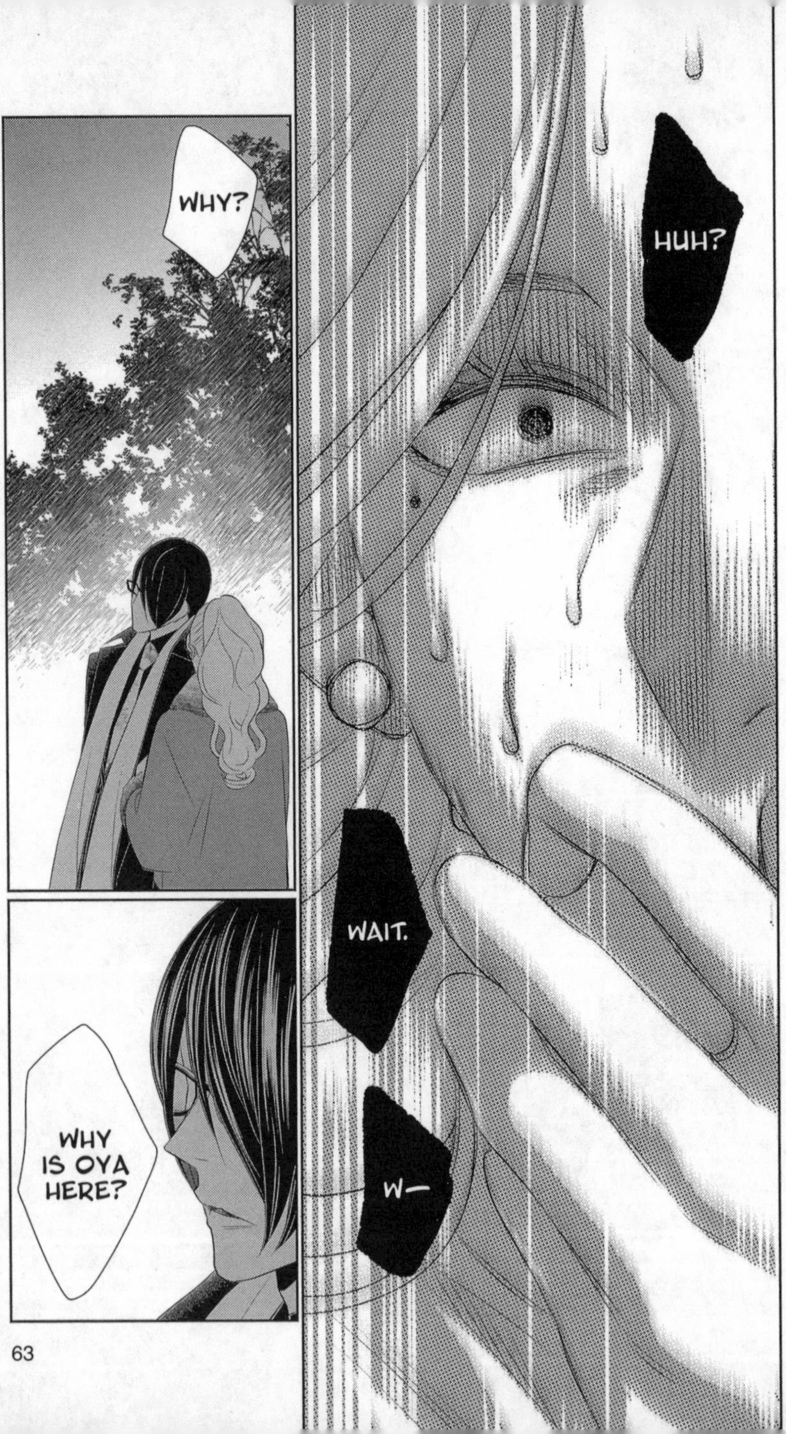
HUH?
WAIT.
W—
WHY?
WHY IS OYA HERE?

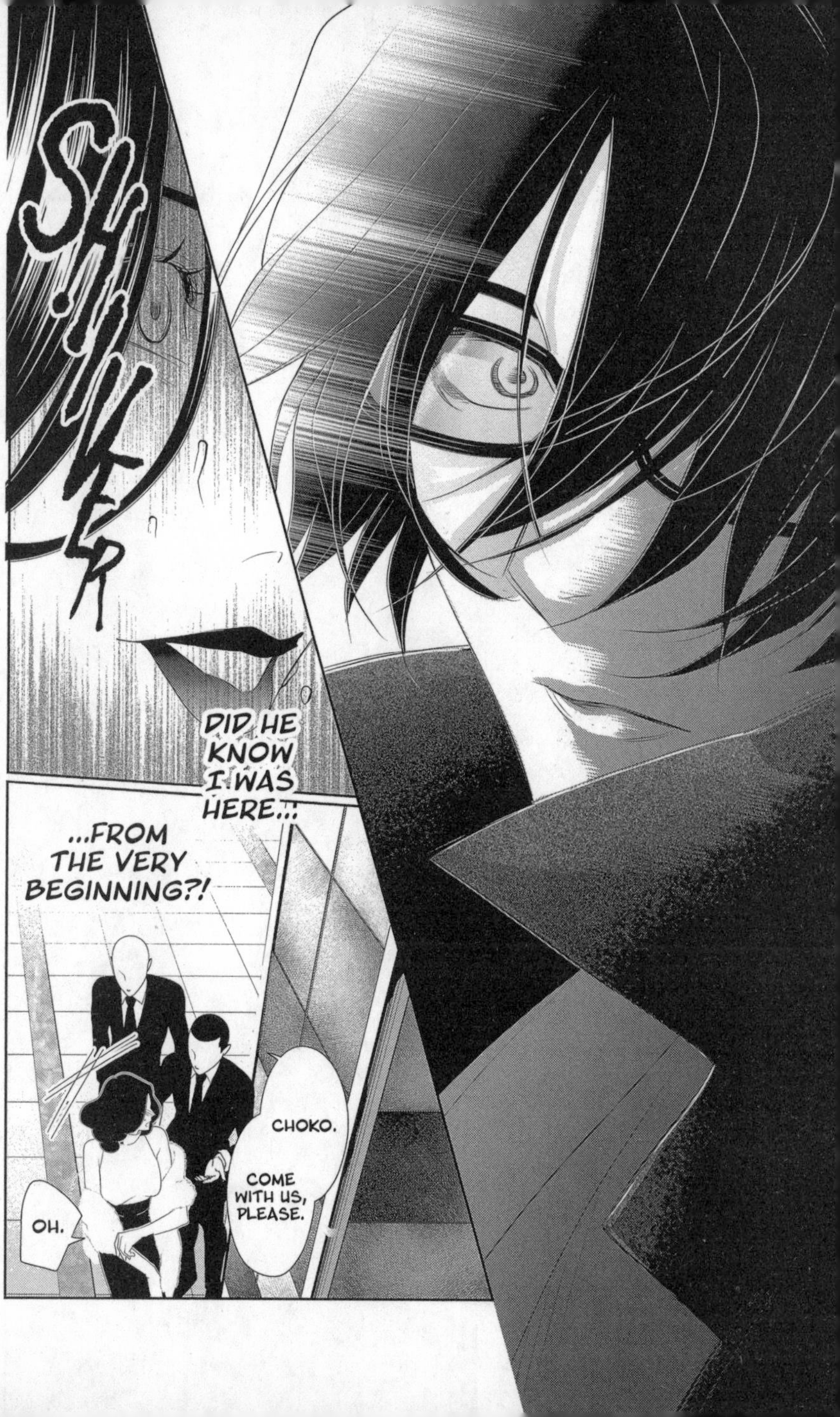
SHIVER
DID HE KNOW I WAS HERE...
...FROM THE VERY BEGINNING?!
CHOKO.
COME WITH US, PLEASE.
OH.

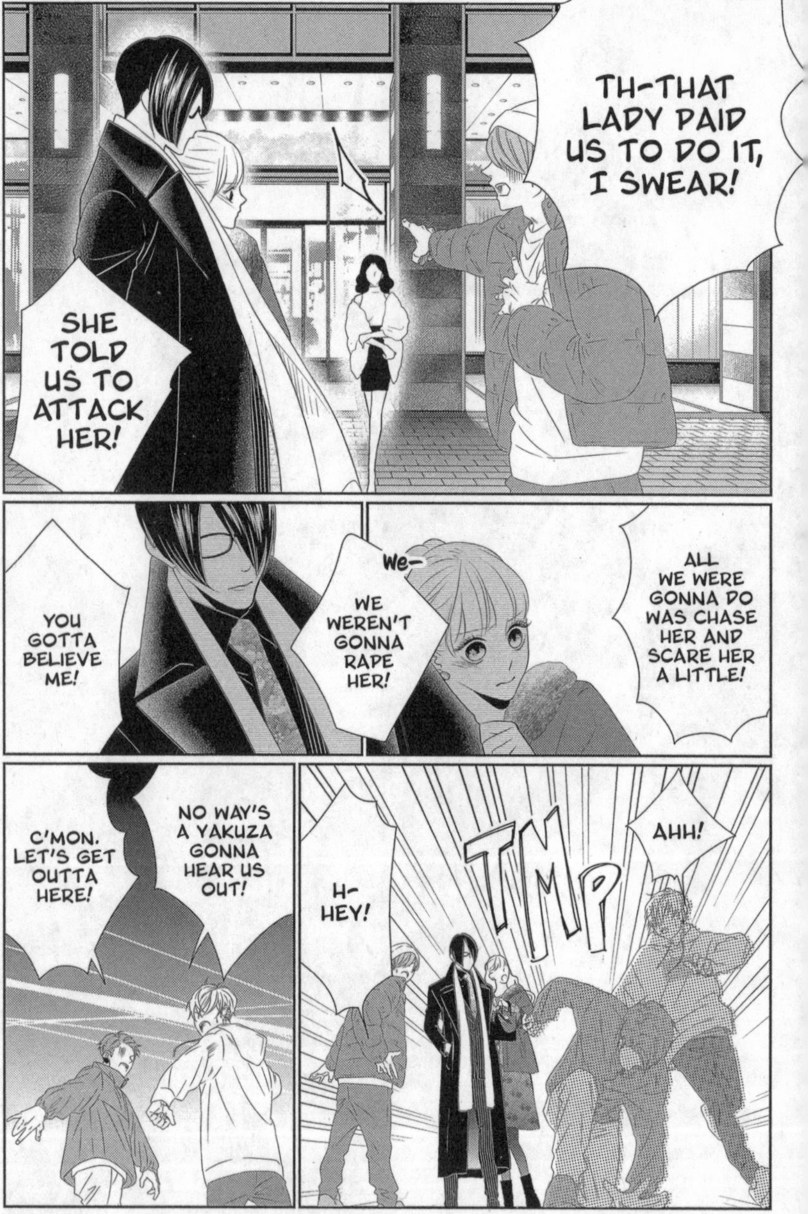
TH-THAT LADY PAID US TO DO IT, I SWEAR!
SHE TOLD US TO ATTACK HER!
ALL WE WERE GONNA DO WAS CHASE HER AND SCARE HER A LITTLE!
We-
WE WEREN'T GONNA RAPE HER!
YOU GOTTA BELIEVE ME!
AHH!
TMP
H-HEY!
NO WAY'S A YAKUZA GONNA HEAR US OUT!
C'MON. LET'S GET OUTTA HERE!

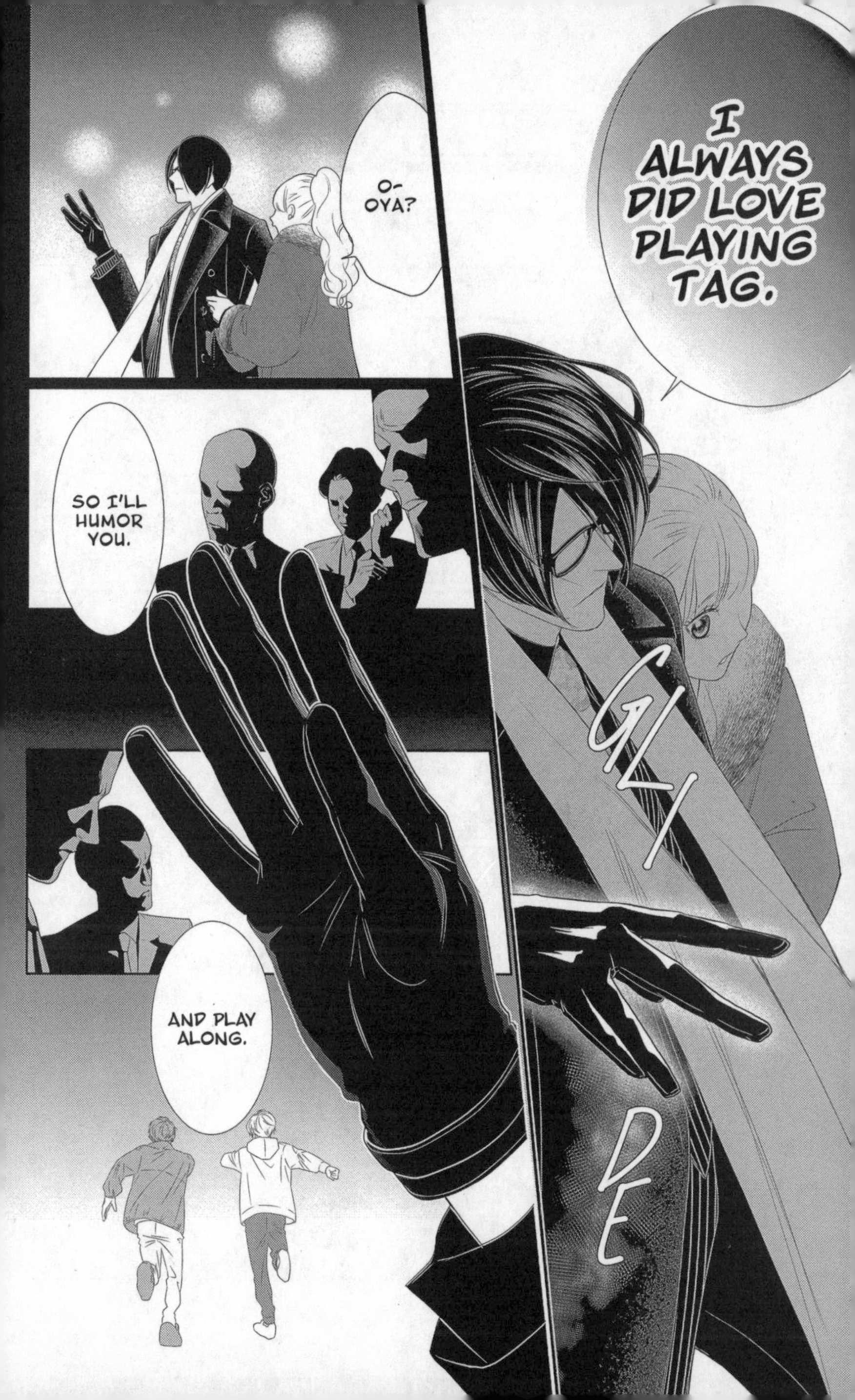
I ALWAYS DID LOVE PLAYING TAG.
GLIDE
O-OYA?
SO I'LL HUMOR YOU.
AND PLAY ALONG.

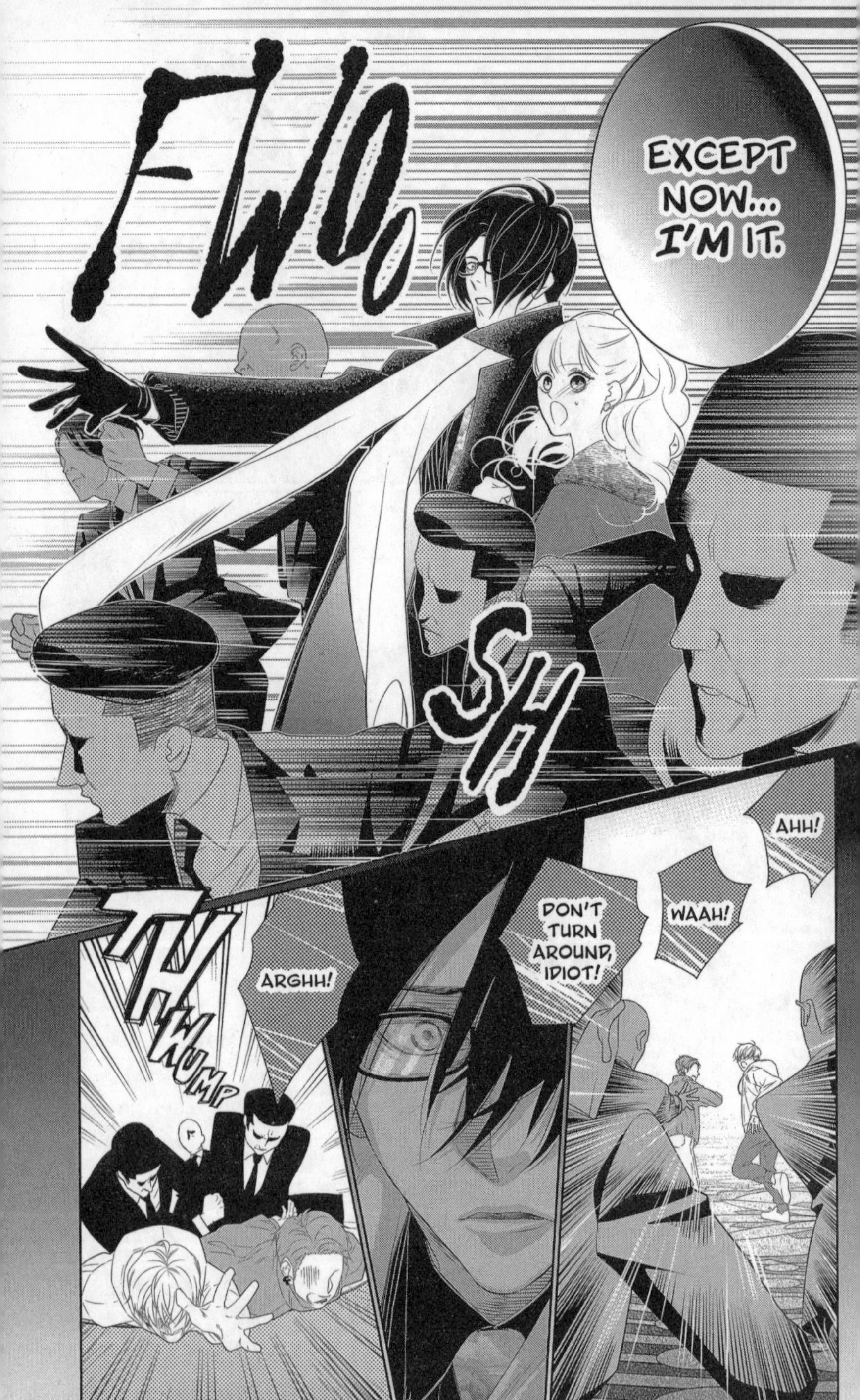
EXCEPT NOW... I'M IT.
FWOO
SH
AHH!
WAAH!
DON'T TURN AROUND, IDIOT!
ARGHH!
THWUMP

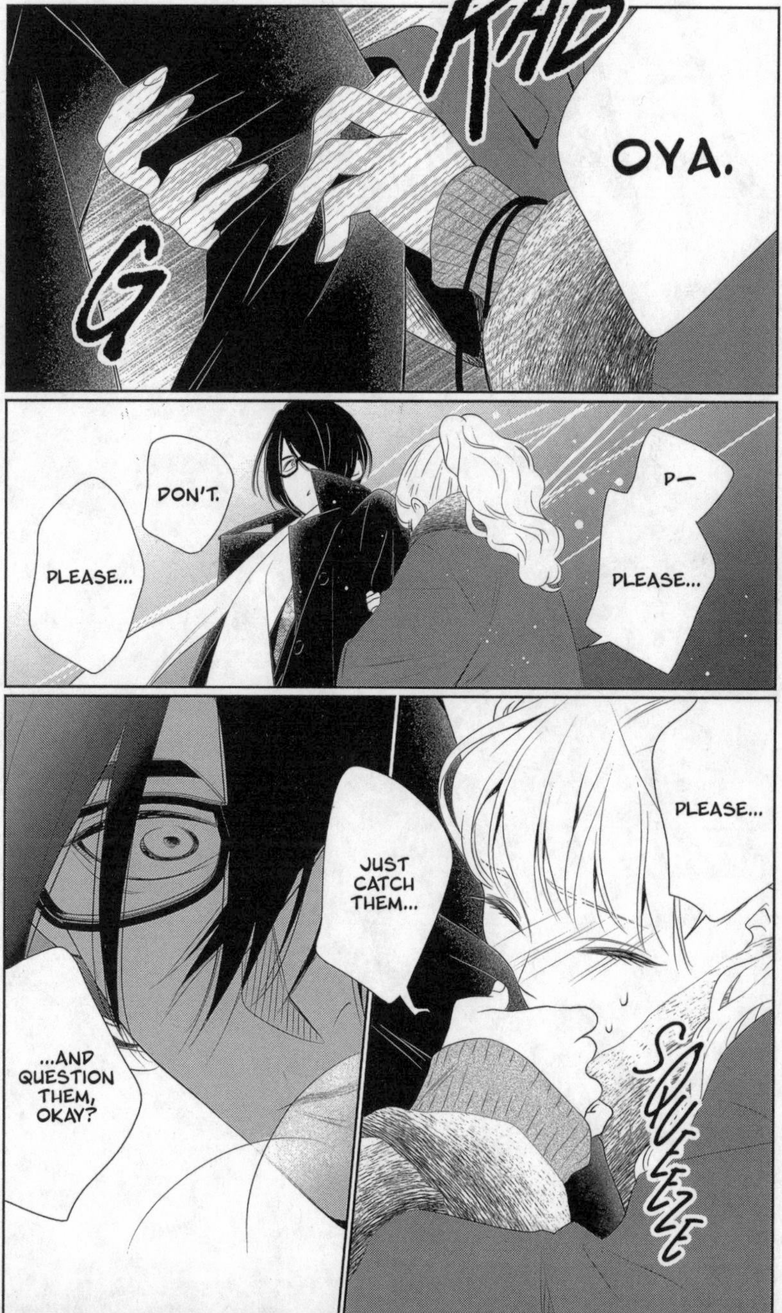
GRAB
OYA.
D—
PLEASE...
DON'T.
PLEASE...
PLEASE...
JUST CATCH THEM...
SQUEEZE
...AND QUESTION THEM, OKAY?

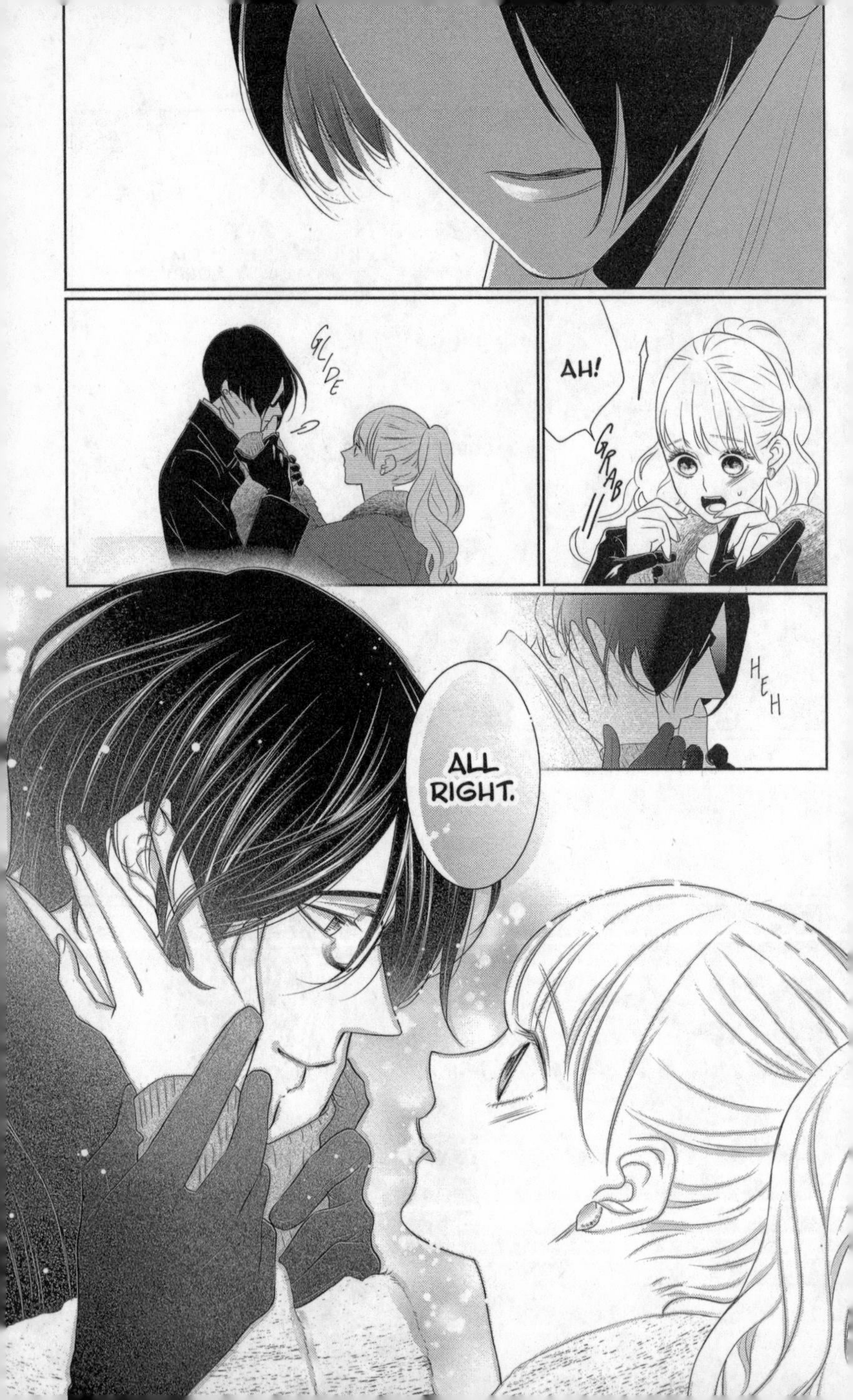
AH!
GRAB
GLIDE
HEH
ALL RIGHT.

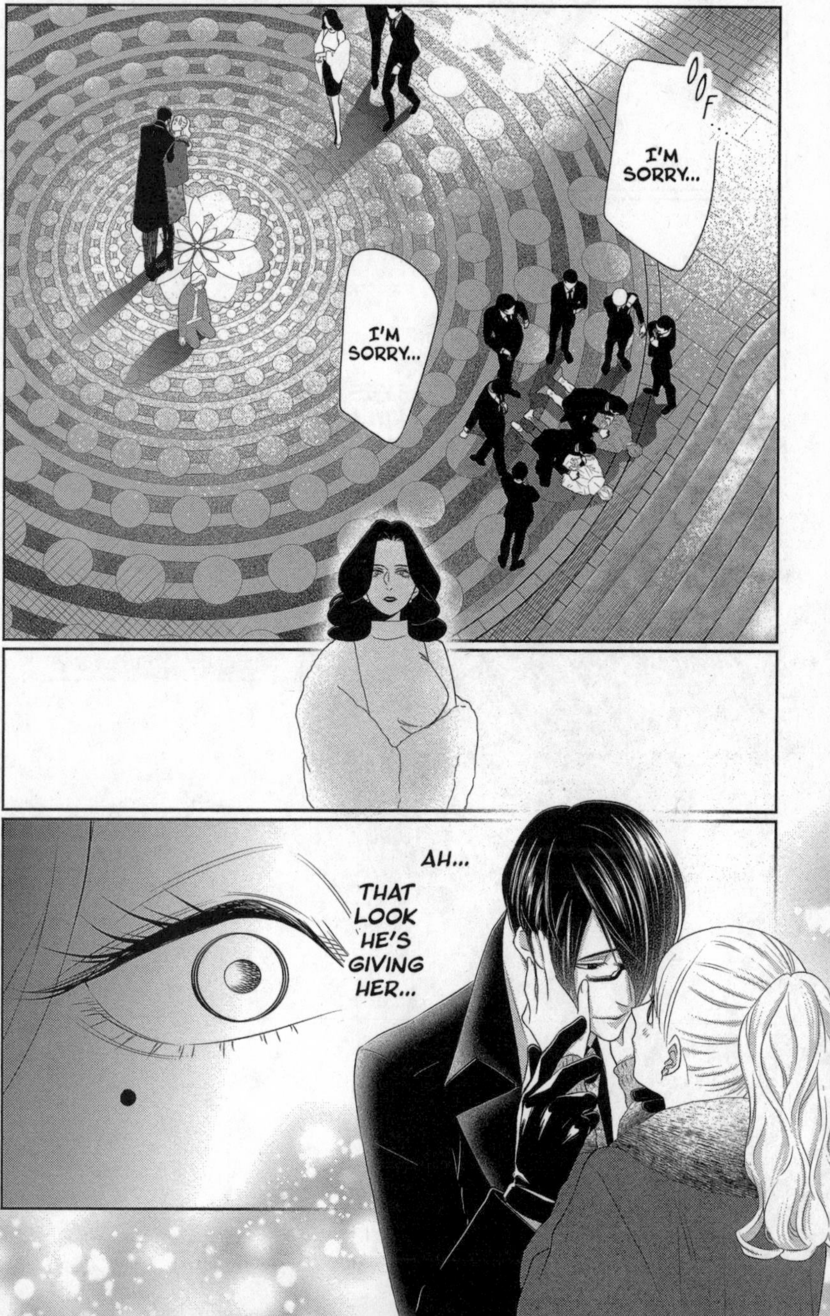
OOF...
I'M SORRY...
I'M SORRY...
AH...
THAT LOOK HE'S GIVING HER...

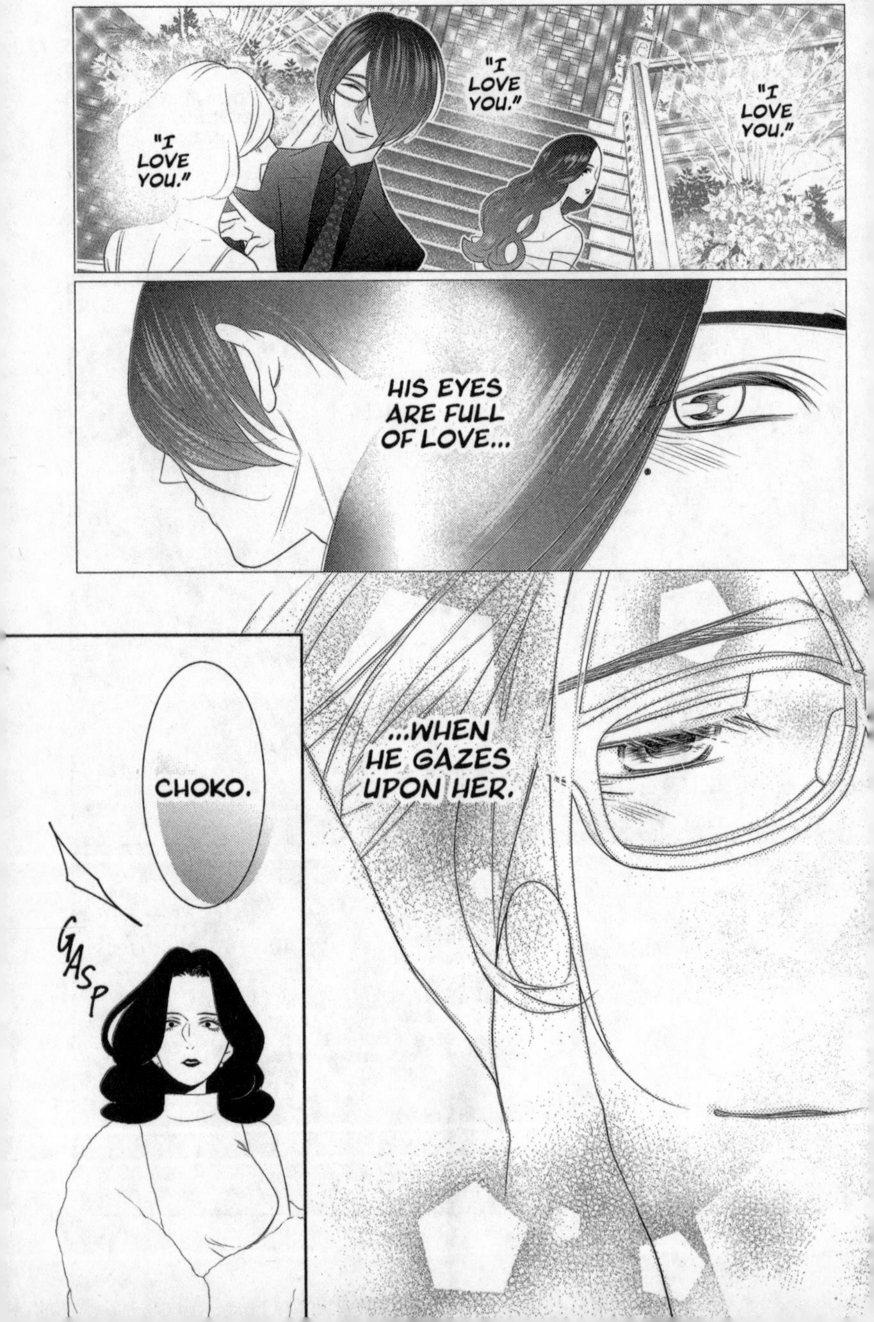
"I LOVE YOU."
"I LOVE YOU."
"I LOVE YOU."
HIS EYES ARE FULL OF LOVE...
...WHEN HE GAZES UPON HER.
CHOKO.
GASP

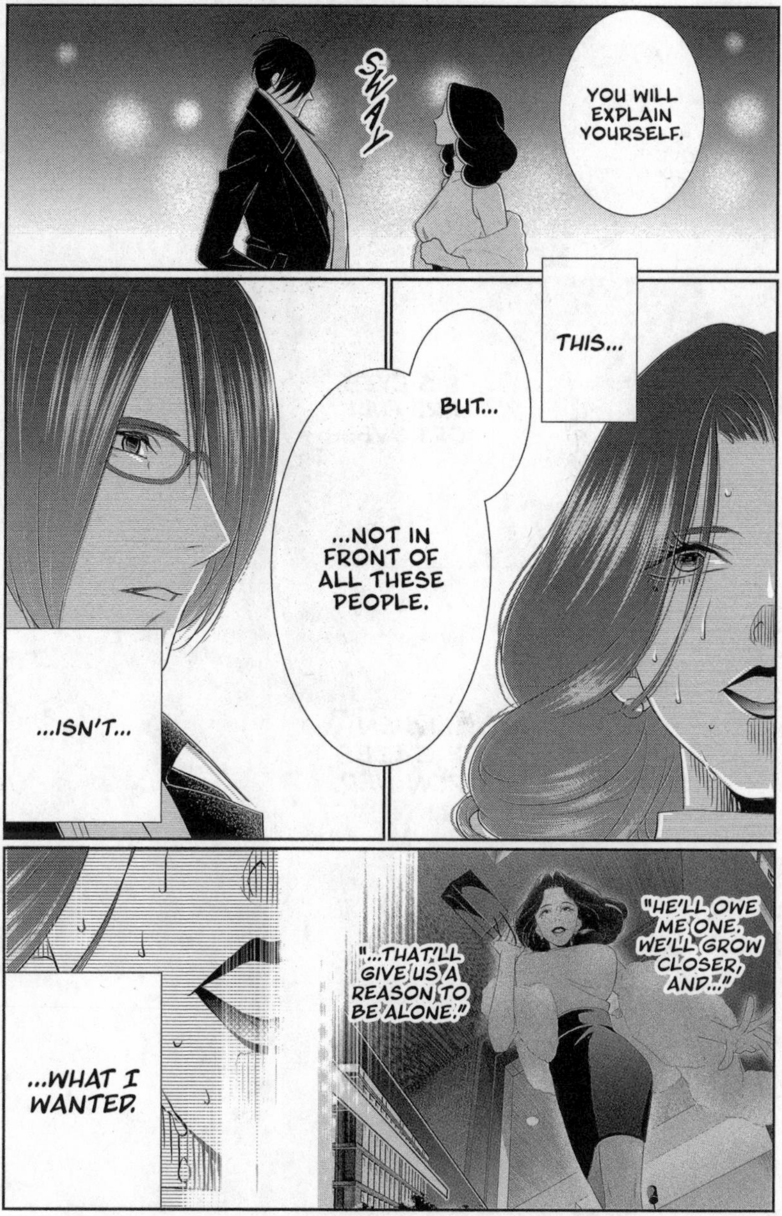
YOU WILL EXPLAIN YOURSELF.
SWAY
THIS...
BUT...
...NOT IN FRONT OF ALL THESE PEOPLE.
...ISN'T...
"HE'LL OWE ME ONE. WE'LL GROW CLOSER, AND..."
"...THAT'LL GIVE US A REASON TO BE ALONE."
...WHAT I WANTED.

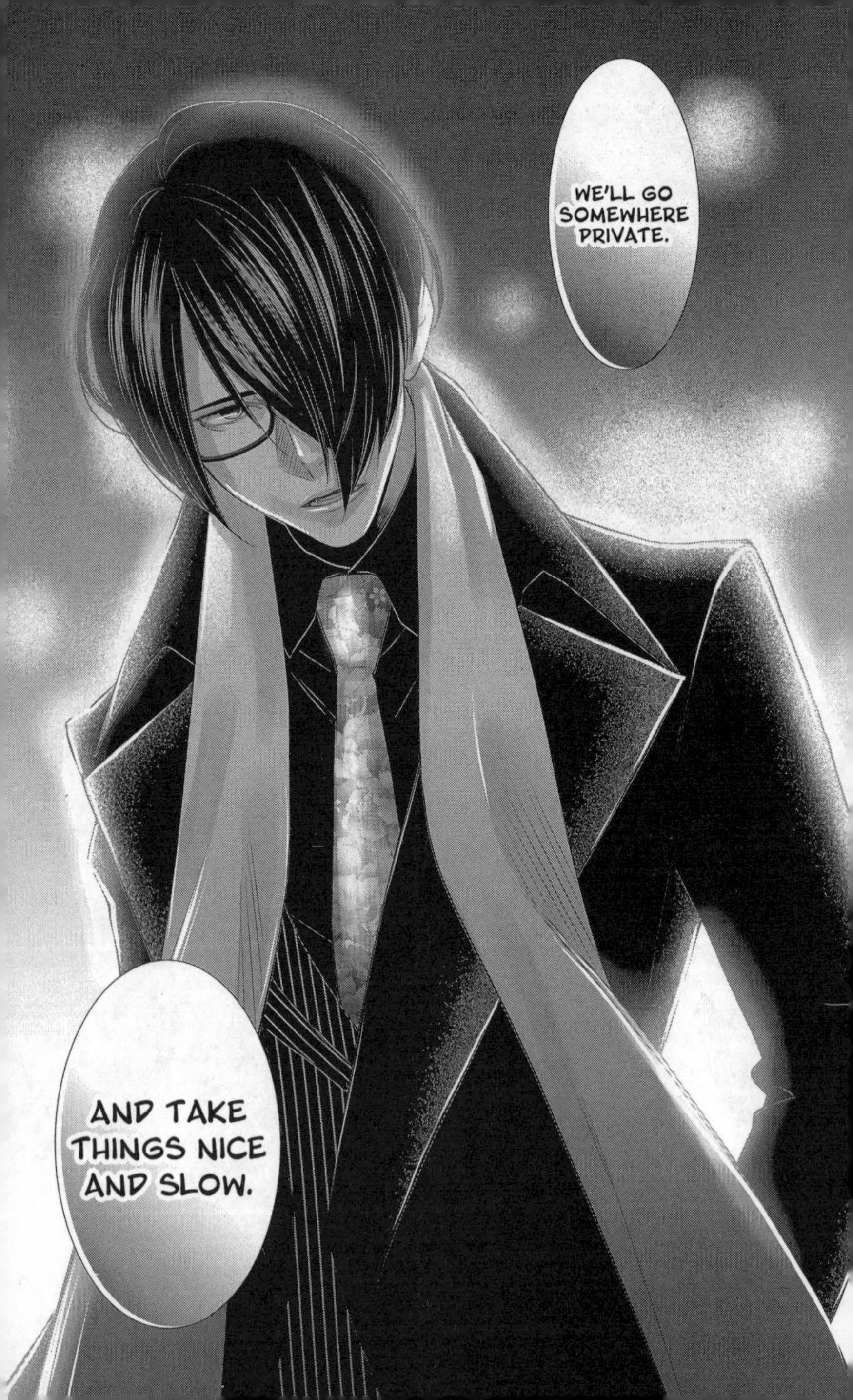
WE'LL GO SOMEWHERE PRIVATE.
AND TAKE THINGS NICE AND SLOW.

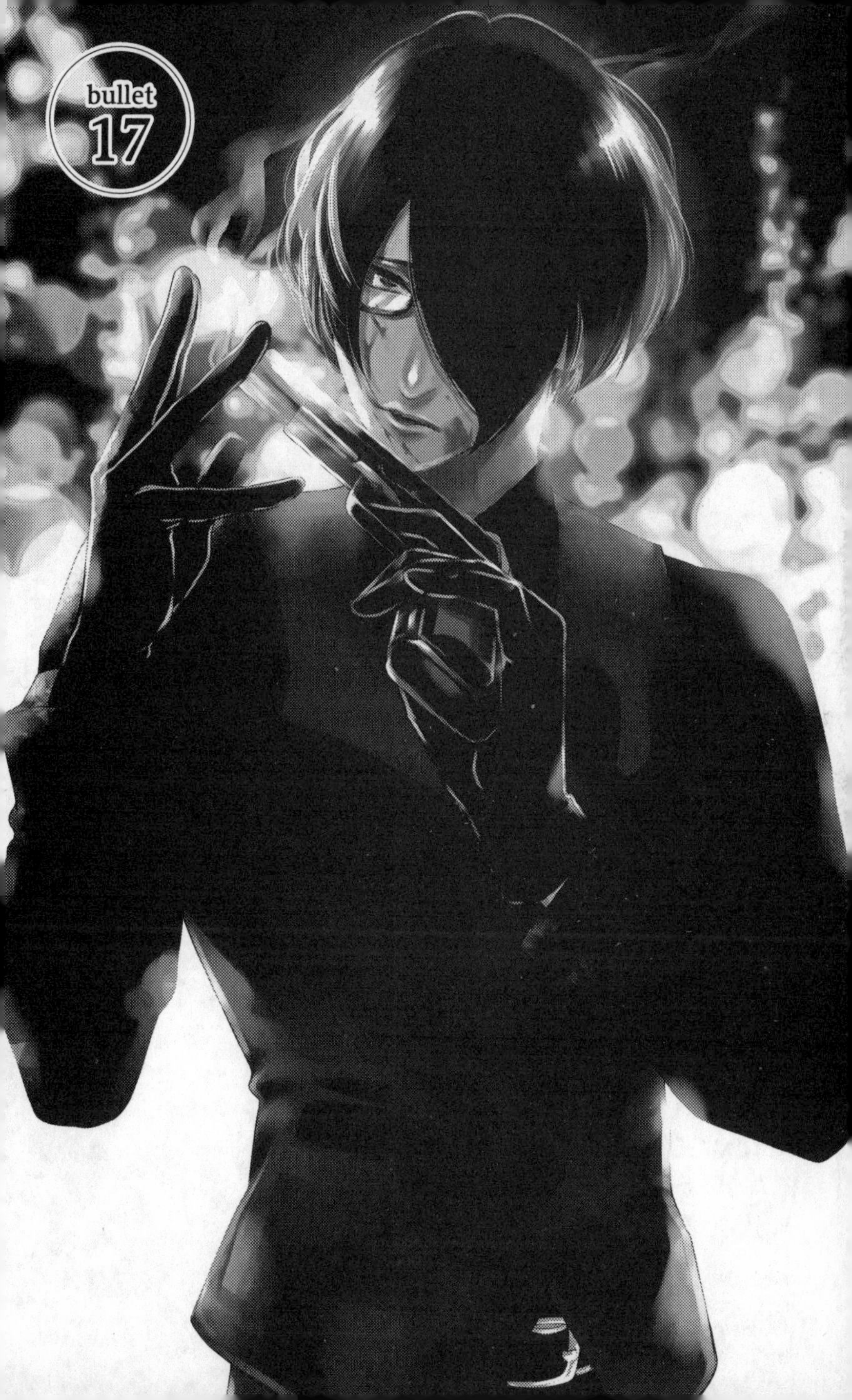
bullet
17

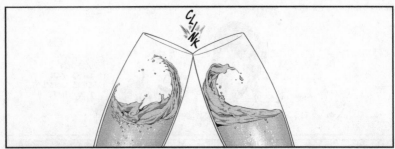

CON-GRATS.

...YOUR CLUB'S FINALLY ABOUT TO OPEN, ISN'T IT?

CHOKO...

I COULDN'T HAVE DONE IT WITHOUT YOUR SUPPORT, PRESIDENT.

75

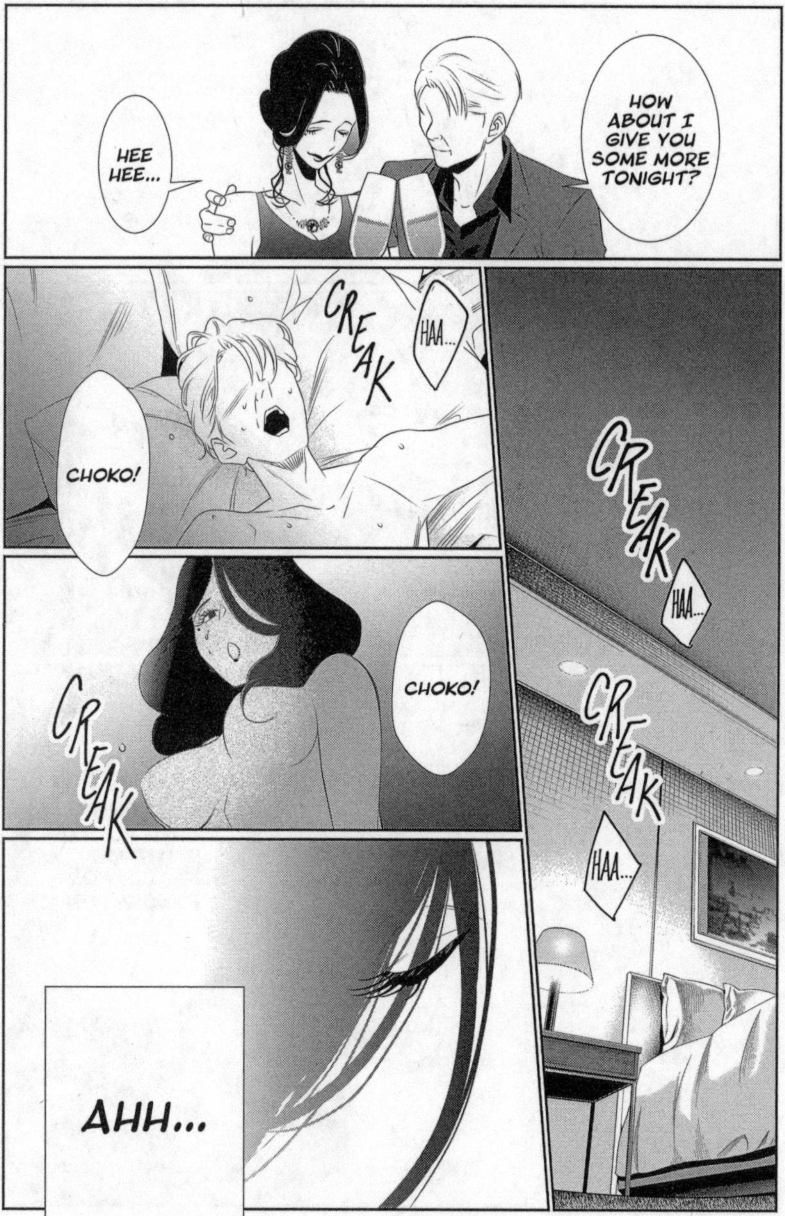
HOW ABOUT I GIVE YOU SOME MORE TONIGHT?
HEE HEE...
CREAK
HAA...
CREAK
HAA...
CREAK
HAA...
CHOKO!
CHOKO!
CREAK
AHH...

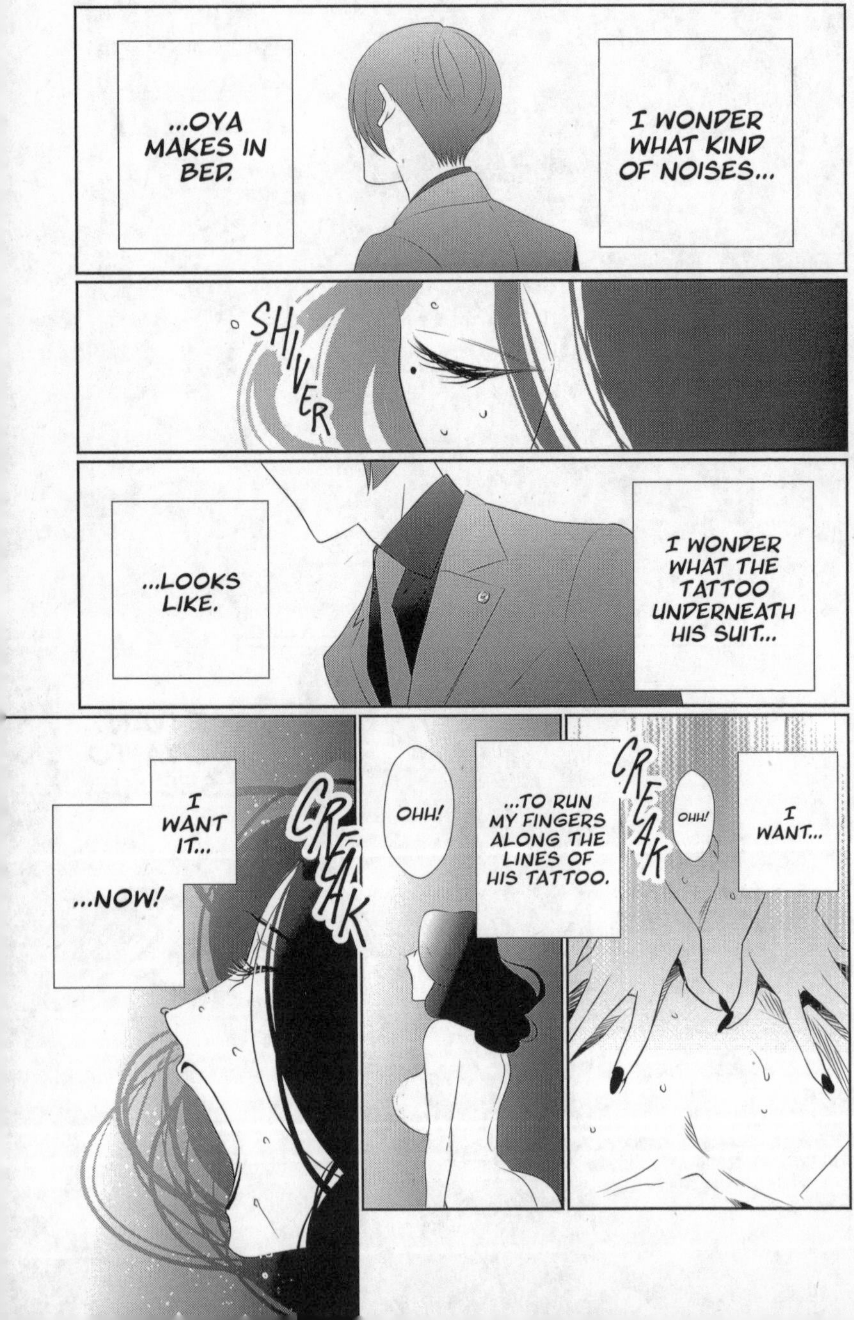
I WONDER WHAT KIND OF NOISES...
...OYA MAKES IN BED.
SHIVER
I WONDER WHAT THE TATTOO UNDERNEATH HIS SUIT...
...LOOKS LIKE.
I WANT...
OHH!
CREAK
...TO RUN MY FINGERS ALONG THE LINES OF HIS TATTOO.
OHH!
CREAK
I WANT IT...
...NOW!

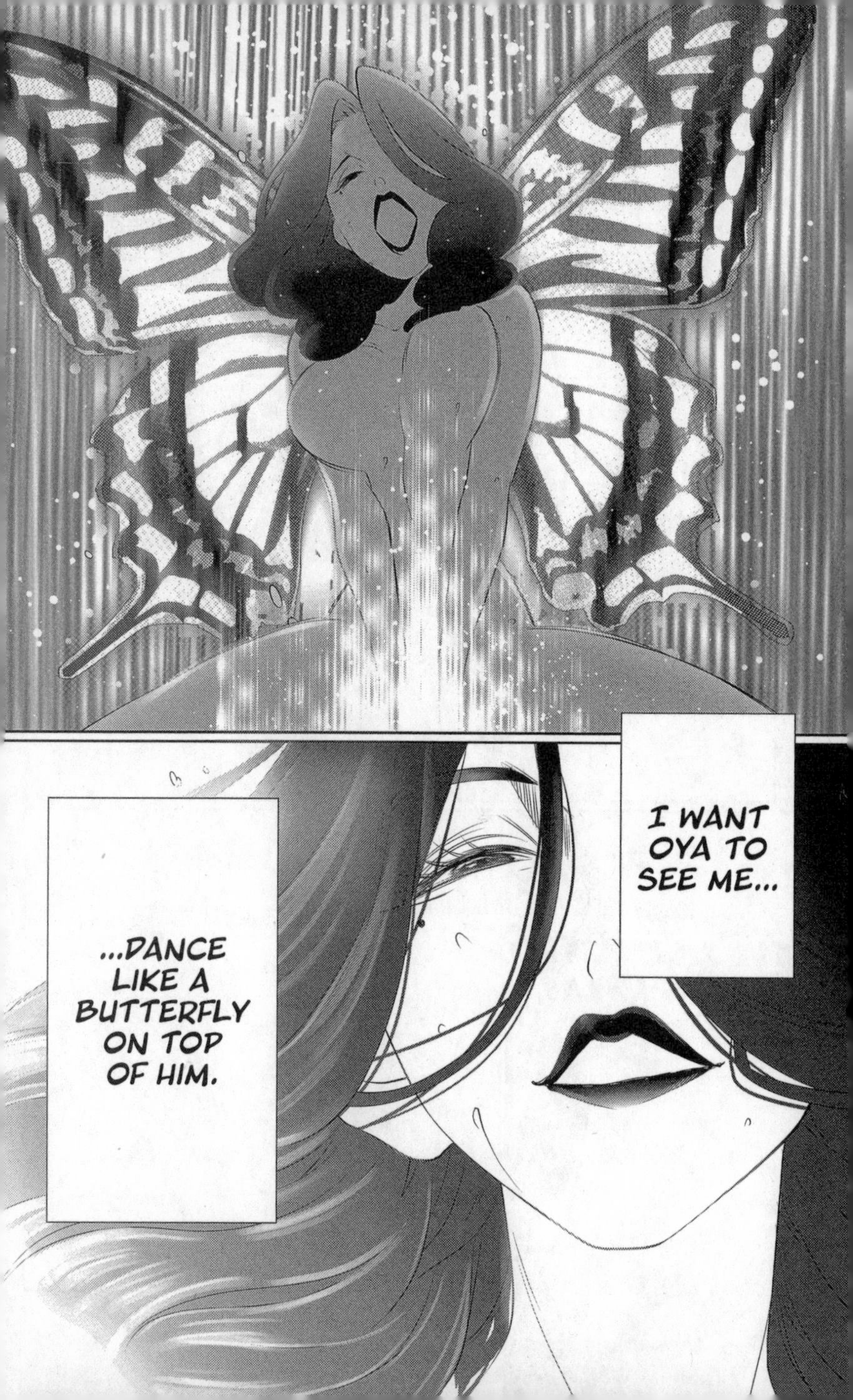
I WANT OYA TO SEE ME...
...DANCE LIKE A BUTTERFLY ON TOP OF HIM.

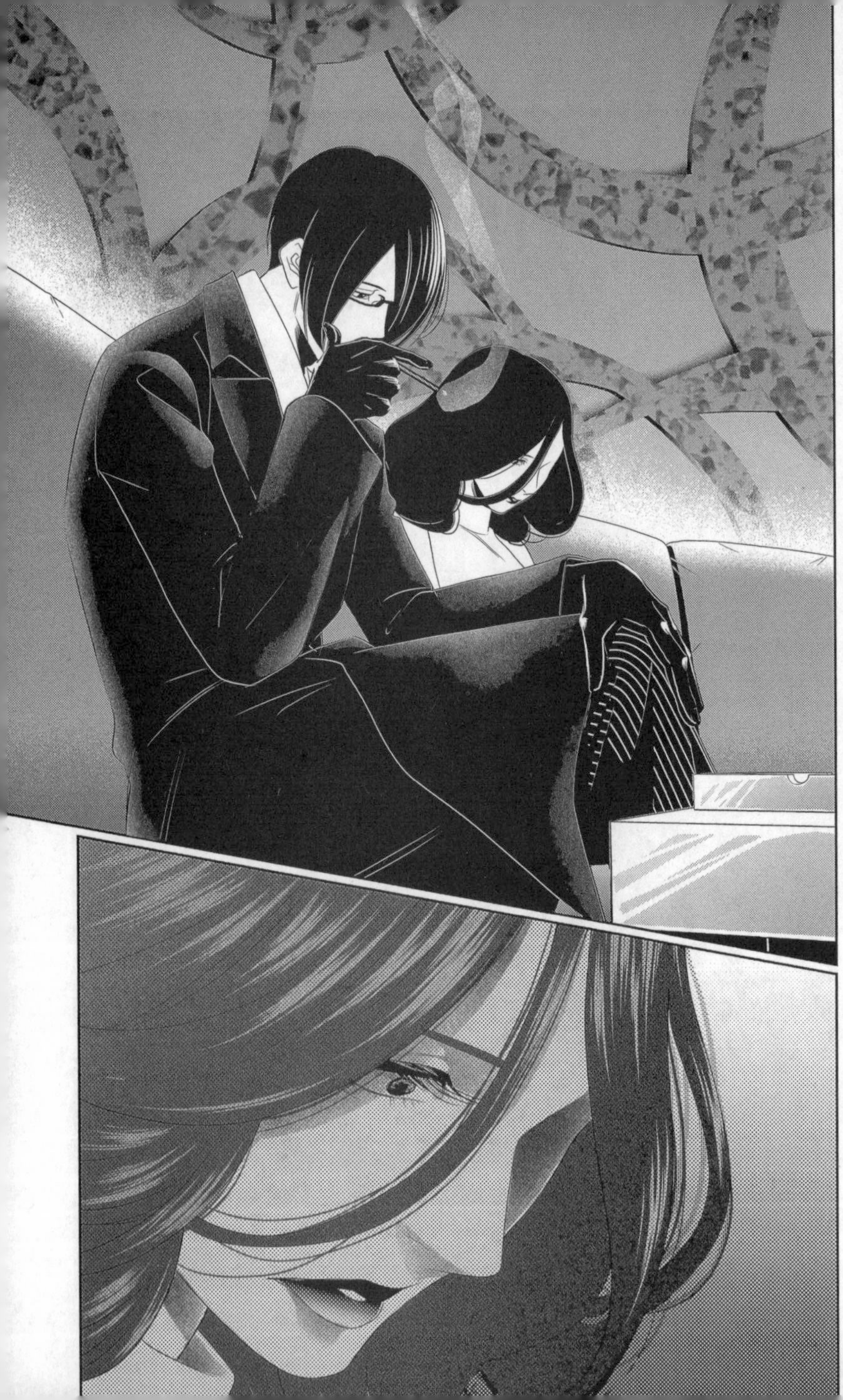

"GO WAIT AT MY CONDO, YURI."

"OKAY."

SHIVER

I'M SO GLAD...

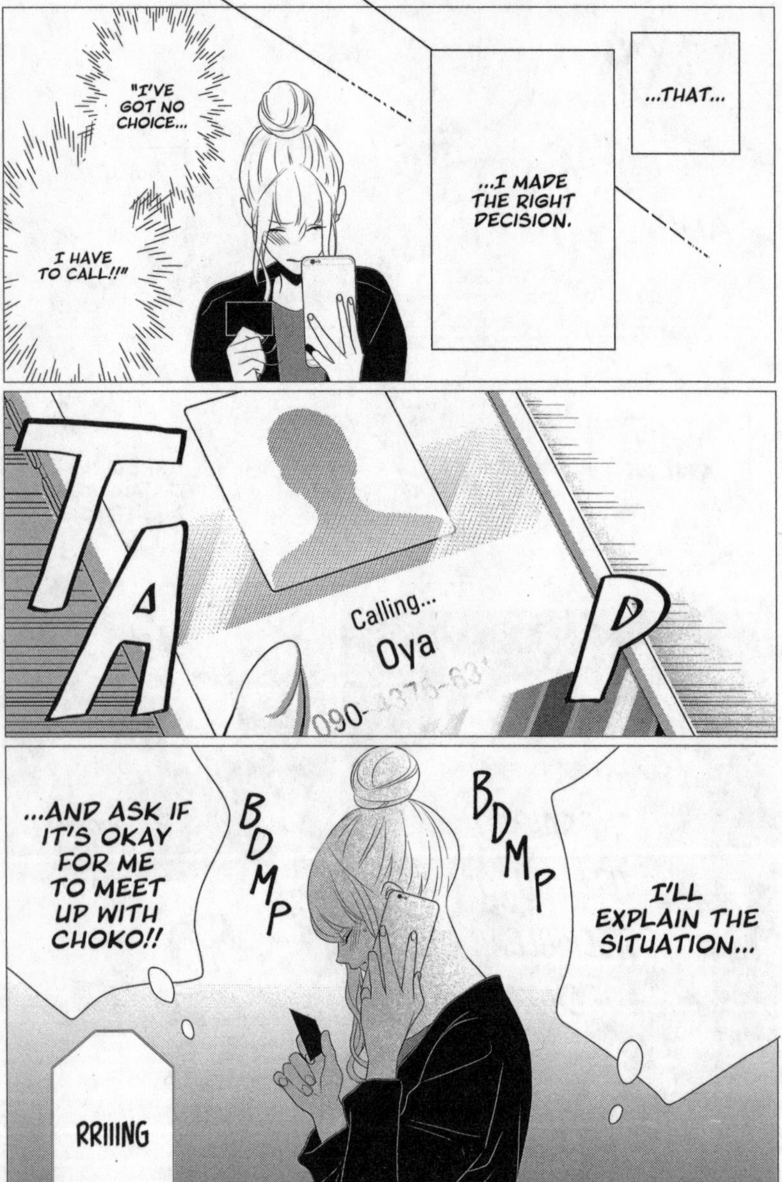
...THAT...
...I MADE THE RIGHT DECISION.
"I'VE GOT NO CHOICE...
I HAVE TO CALL!!"
TAP
Calling...
Oya
090-4376-63
I'LL EXPLAIN THE SITUATION...
BDMP
BDMP
...AND ASK IF IT'S OKAY FOR ME TO MEET UP WITH CHOKO!!
RRIIING

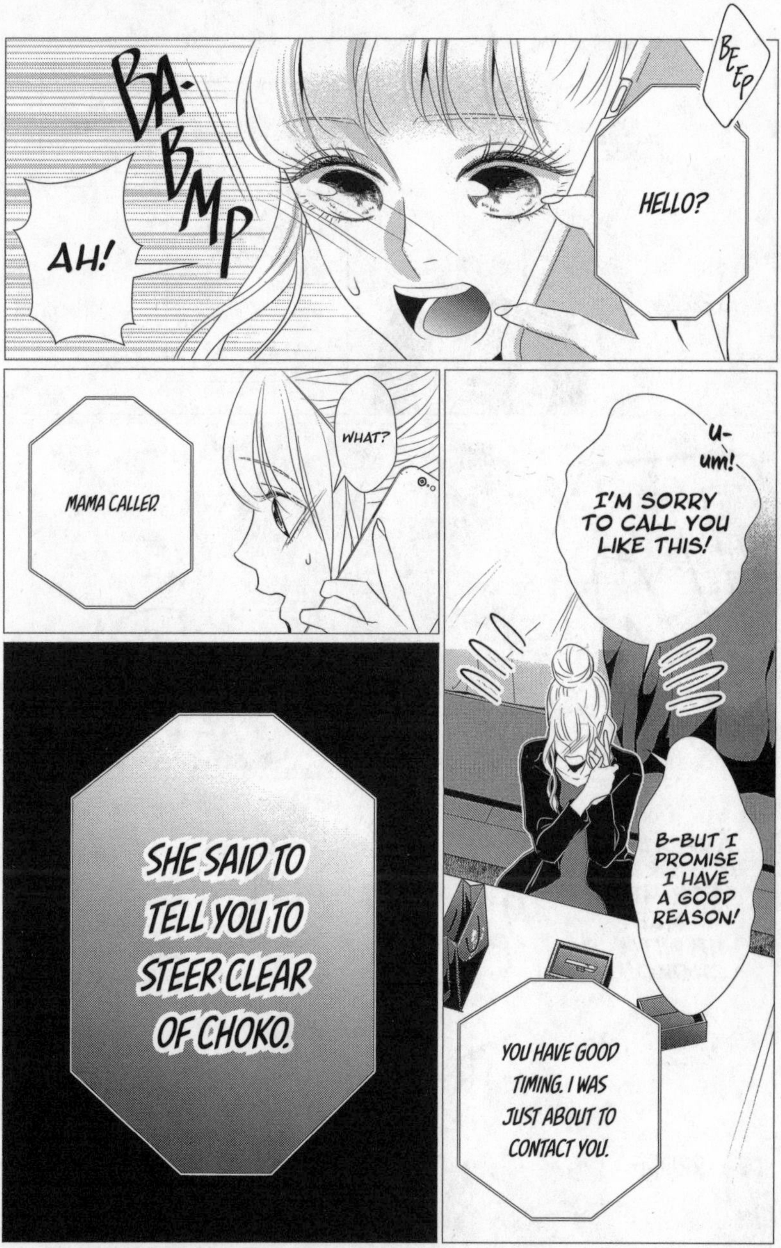
BEEP
HELLO?
BA-BMP
AH!
U-UM!
I'M SORRY TO CALL YOU LIKE THIS!
B-BUT I PROMISE I HAVE A GOOD REASON!
YOU HAVE GOOD TIMING. I WAS JUST ABOUT TO CONTACT YOU.
WHAT?
MAMA CALLED.
SHE SAID TO TELL YOU TO STEER CLEAR OF CHOKO.

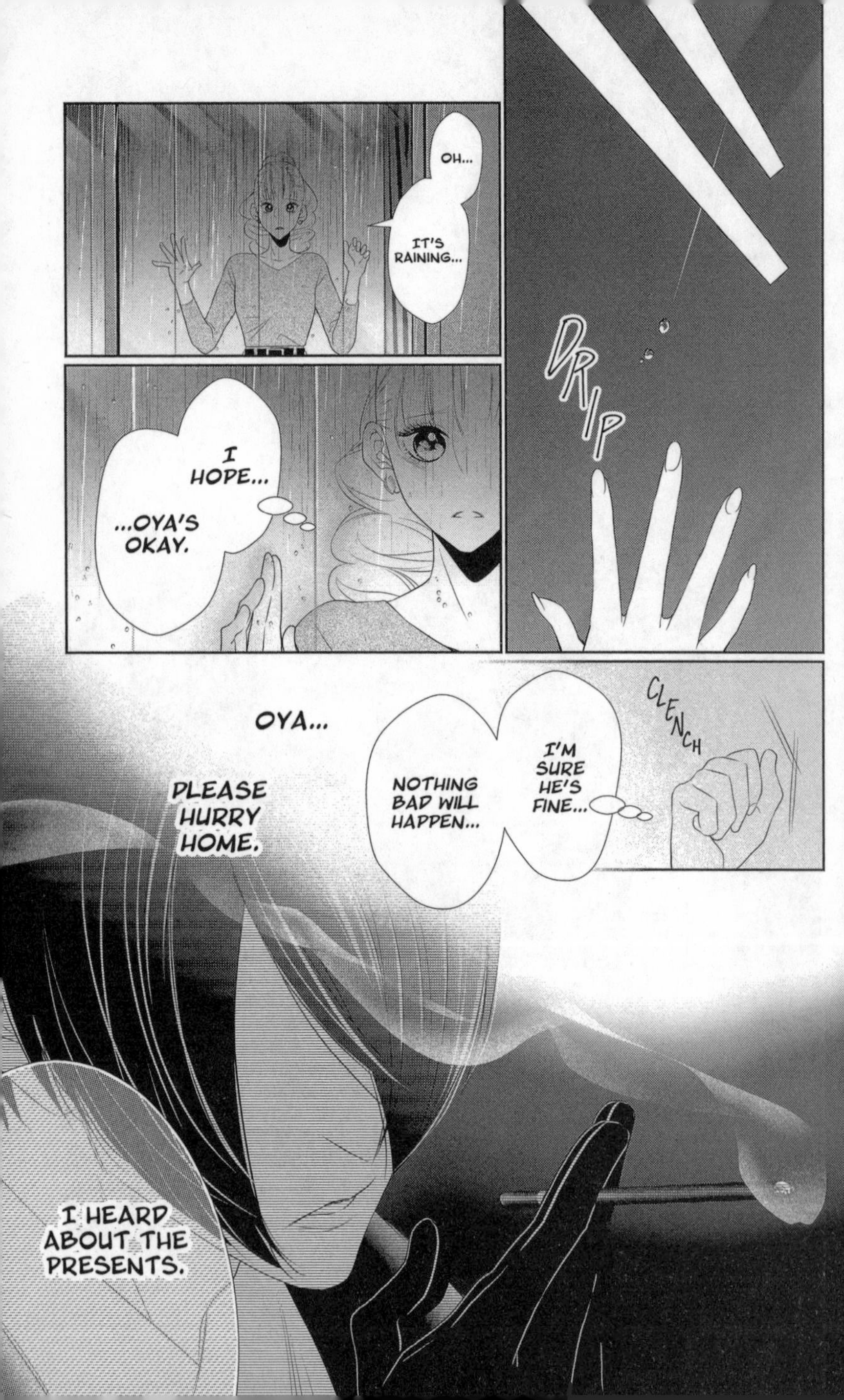
DRIP
OH...
IT'S RAINING...
I HOPE...
...OYA'S OKAY.
CLENCH
I'M SURE HE'S FINE...
NOTHING BAD WILL HAPPEN...
OYA...
PLEASE HURRY HOME.
I HEARD ABOUT THE PRESENTS.

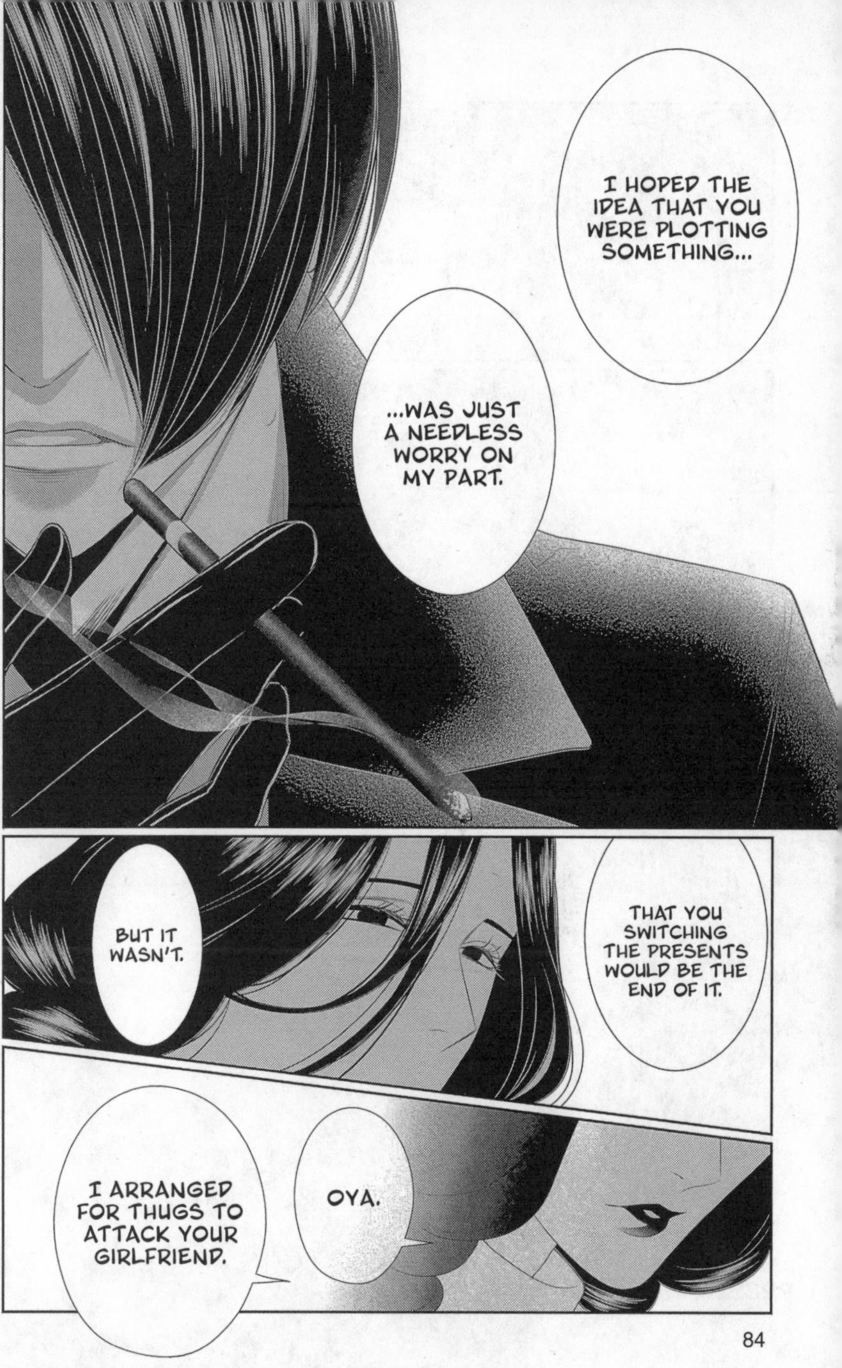
I HOPED THE IDEA THAT YOU WERE PLOTTING SOMETHING...
...WAS JUST A NEEDLESS WORRY ON MY PART.
THAT YOU SWITCHING THE PRESENTS WOULD BE THE END OF IT.
BUT IT WASN'T.
OYA.
I ARRANGED FOR THUGS TO ATTACK YOUR GIRLFRIEND.

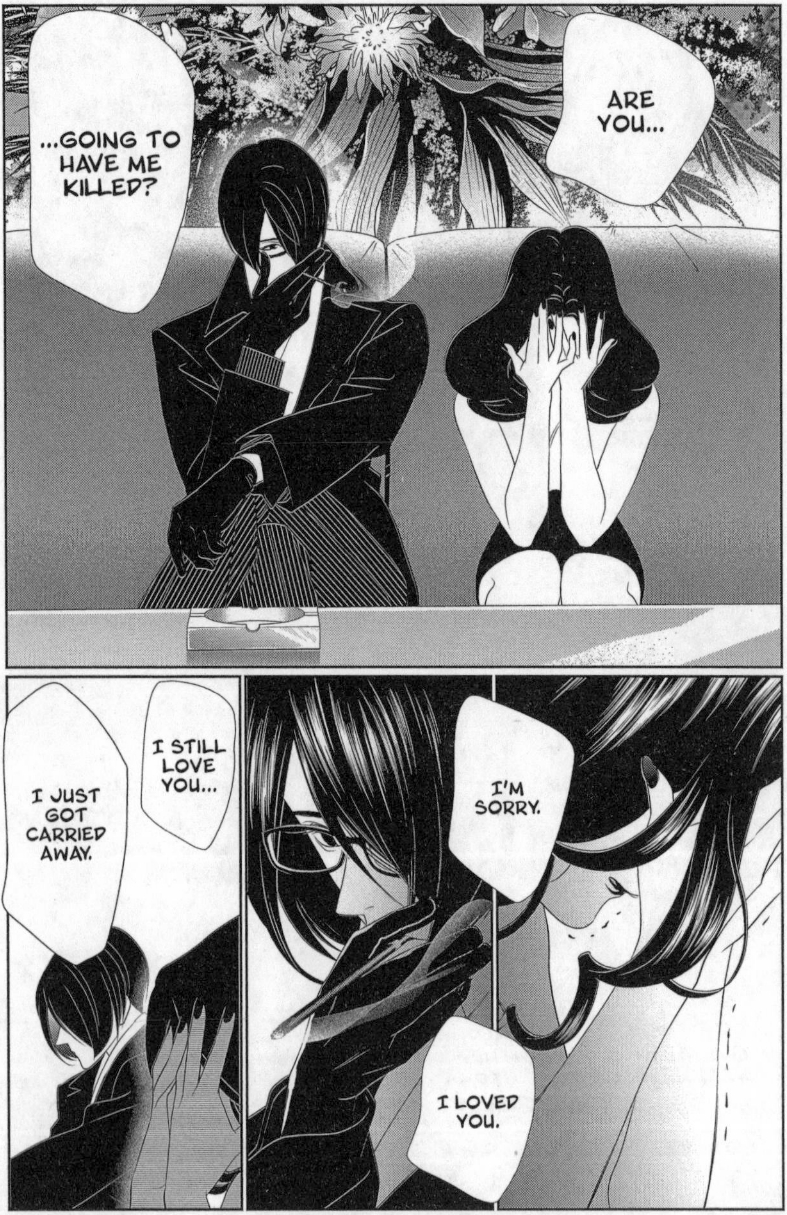
ARE YOU...
...GOING TO HAVE ME KILLED?
I'M SORRY.
I LOVED YOU.
I STILL LOVE YOU...
I JUST GOT CARRIED AWAY.

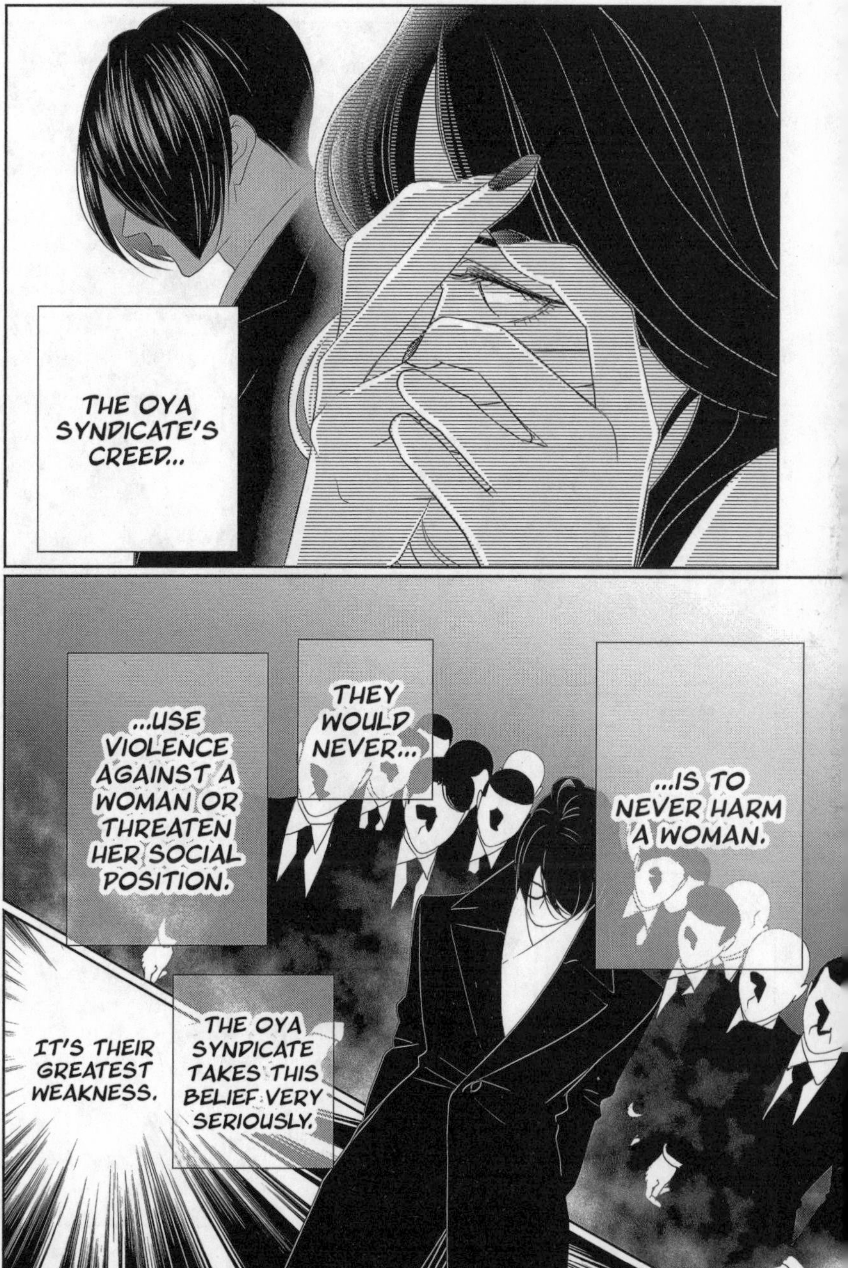
THE OYA SYNDICATE'S CREED...
...IS TO NEVER HARM A WOMAN.
THEY WOULD NEVER...
...USE VIOLENCE AGAINST A WOMAN OR THREATEN HER SOCIAL POSITION.
THE OYA SYNDICATE TAKES THIS BELIEF VERY SERIOUSLY.
IT'S THEIR GREATEST WEAKNESS.

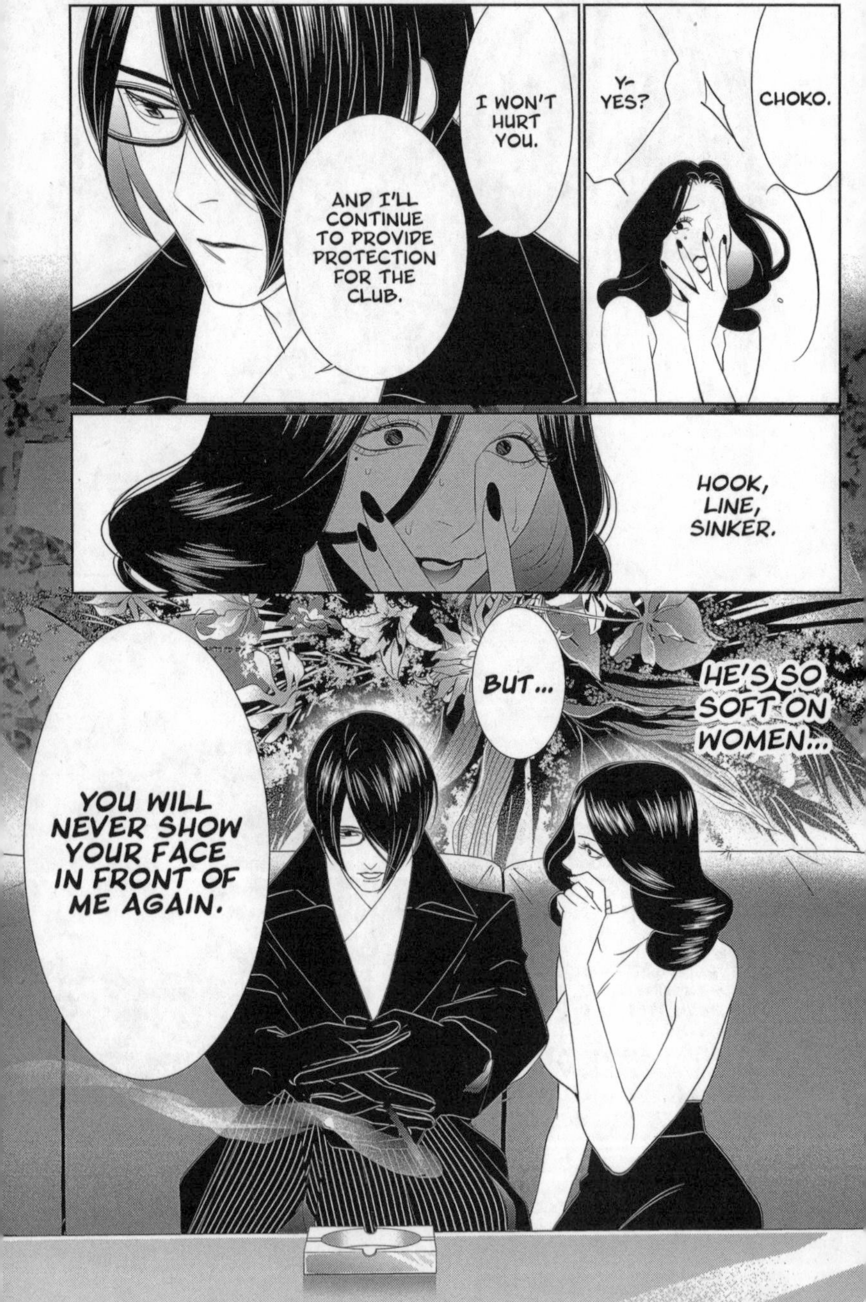
CHOKO.
Y-YES?
I WON'T HURT YOU.
AND I'LL CONTINUE TO PROVIDE PROTECTION FOR THE CLUB.
HOOK, LINE, SINKER.
HE'S SO SOFT ON WOMEN...
BUT...
YOU WILL NEVER SHOW YOUR FACE IN FRONT OF ME AGAIN.

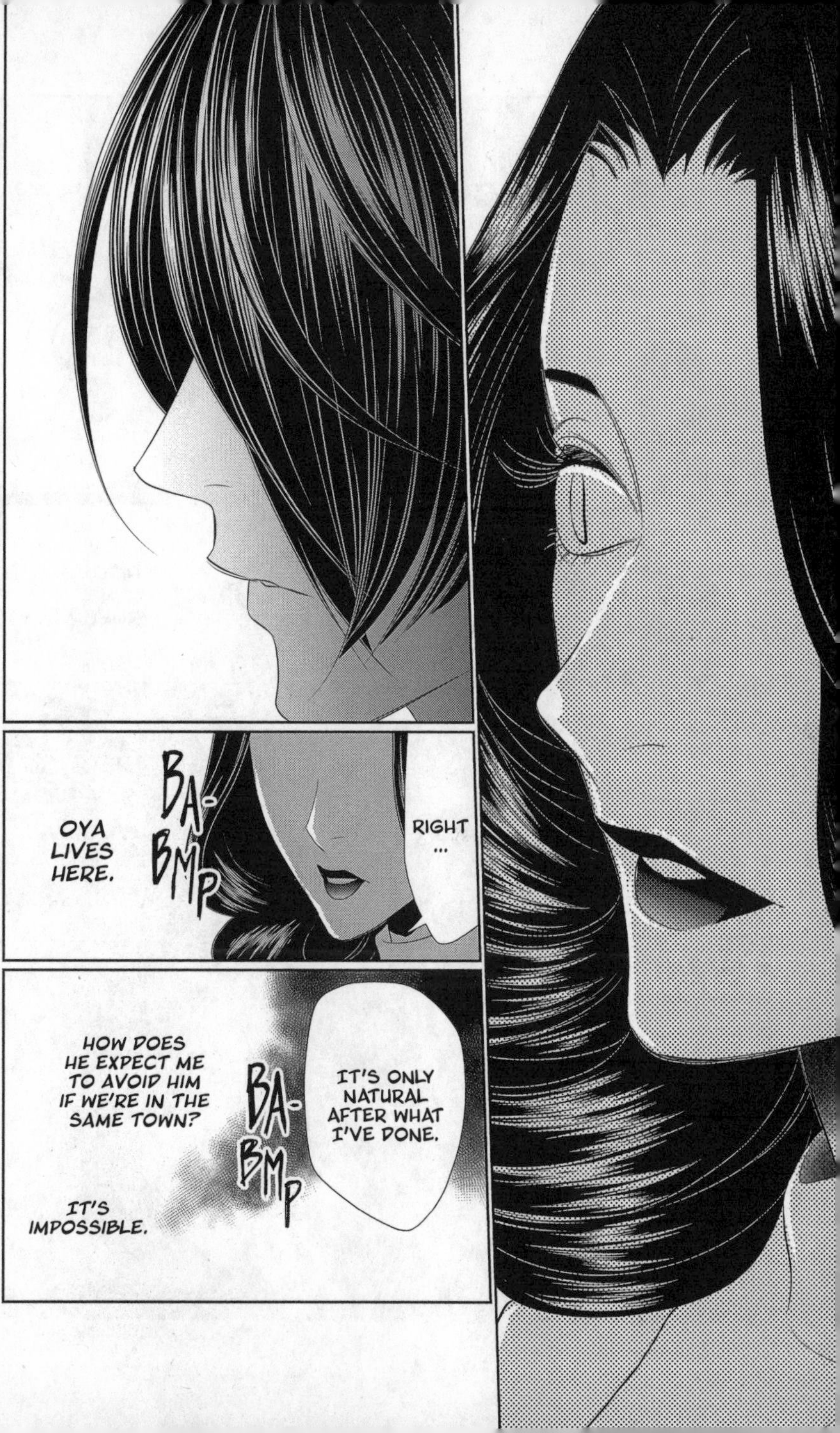
RIGHT ...
BA-BMP
OYA LIVES HERE.
IT'S ONLY NATURAL AFTER WHAT I'VE DONE.
BA-BMP
HOW DOES HE EXPECT ME TO AVOID HIM IF WE'RE IN THE SAME TOWN?
IT'S IMPOSSIBLE.

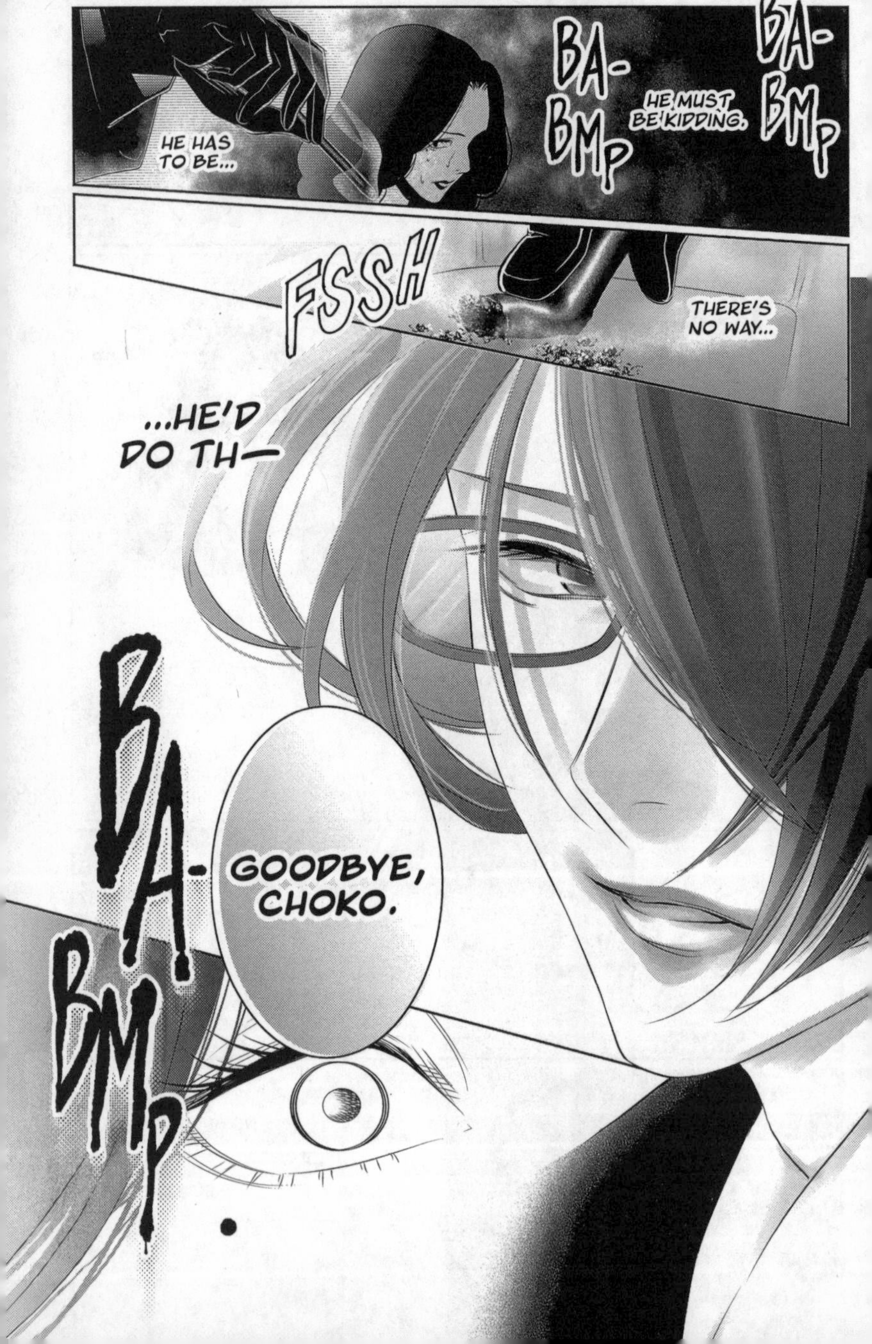
BA-BMP
HE MUST BE KIDDING.
BA-BMP
HE HAS TO BE...
FSSH
THERE'S NO WAY...
...HE'D DO TH—
GOODBYE, CHOKO.
BA-BMP

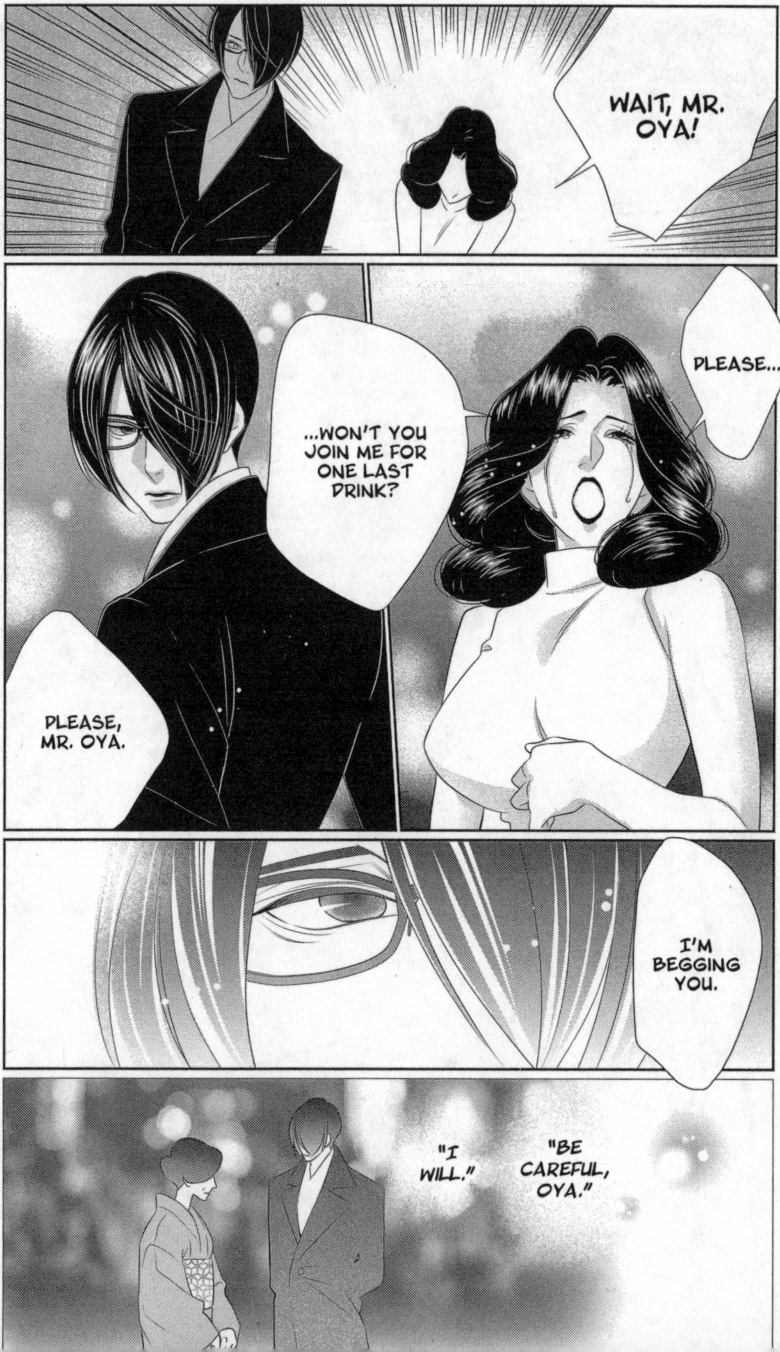
WAIT, MR. OYA!
PLEASE...
...WON'T YOU JOIN ME FOR ONE LAST DRINK?
PLEASE, MR. OYA.
I'M BEGGING YOU.
"BE CAREFUL, OYA."
"I WILL."

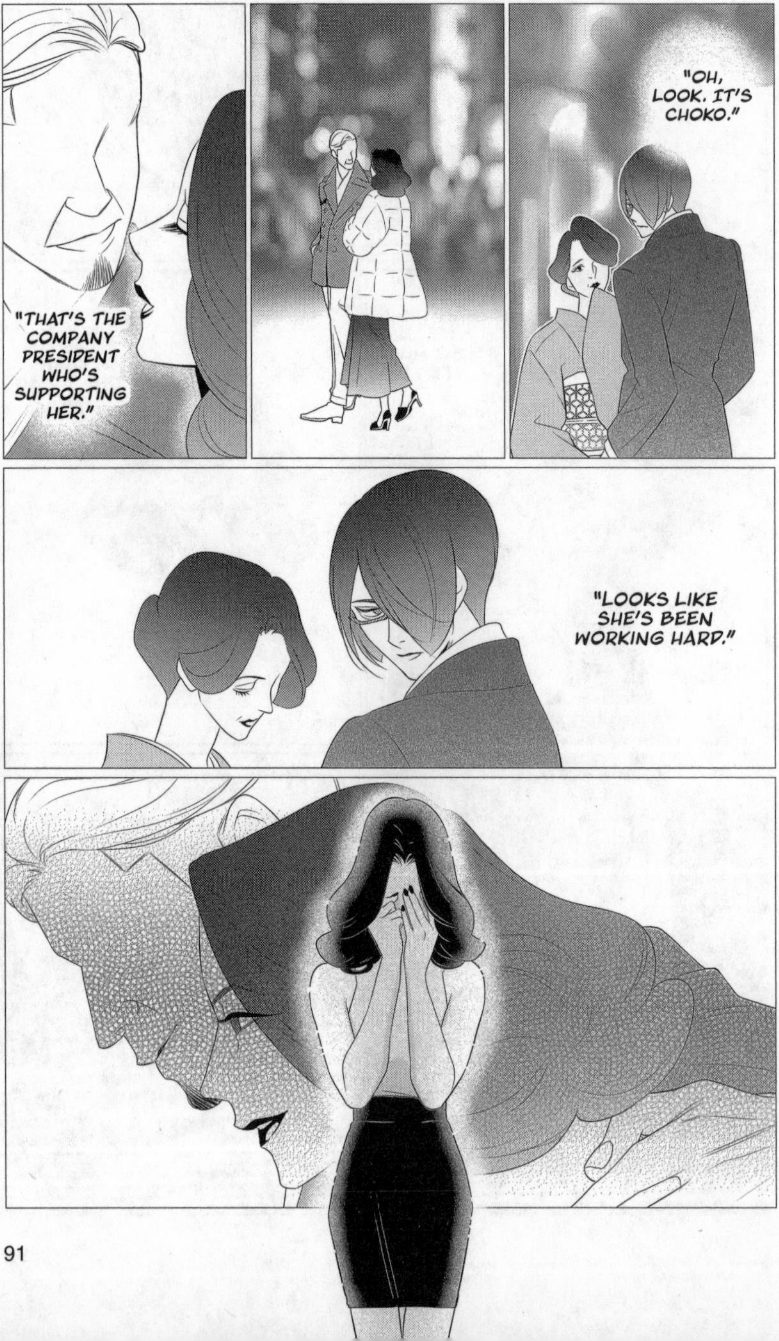
"OH, LOOK. IT'S CHOKO."
"THAT'S THE COMPANY PRESIDENT WHO'S SUPPORTING HER."
"LOOKS LIKE SHE'S BEEN WORKING HARD."

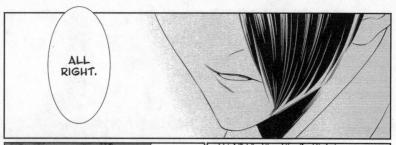

ALL RIGHT.
BUT JUST ONE DRINK.
THIS MEANS SO MUCH TO ME!
TRULY, THANK YOU!
I'LL GO GET IT READY RIGHT NOW.

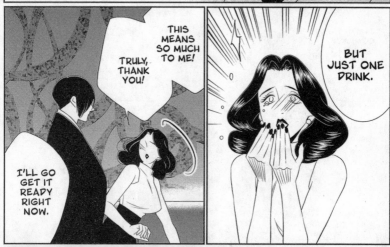

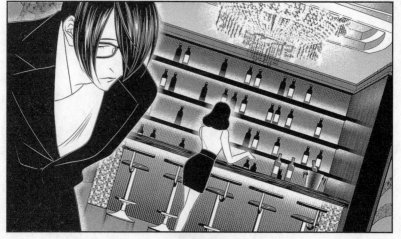

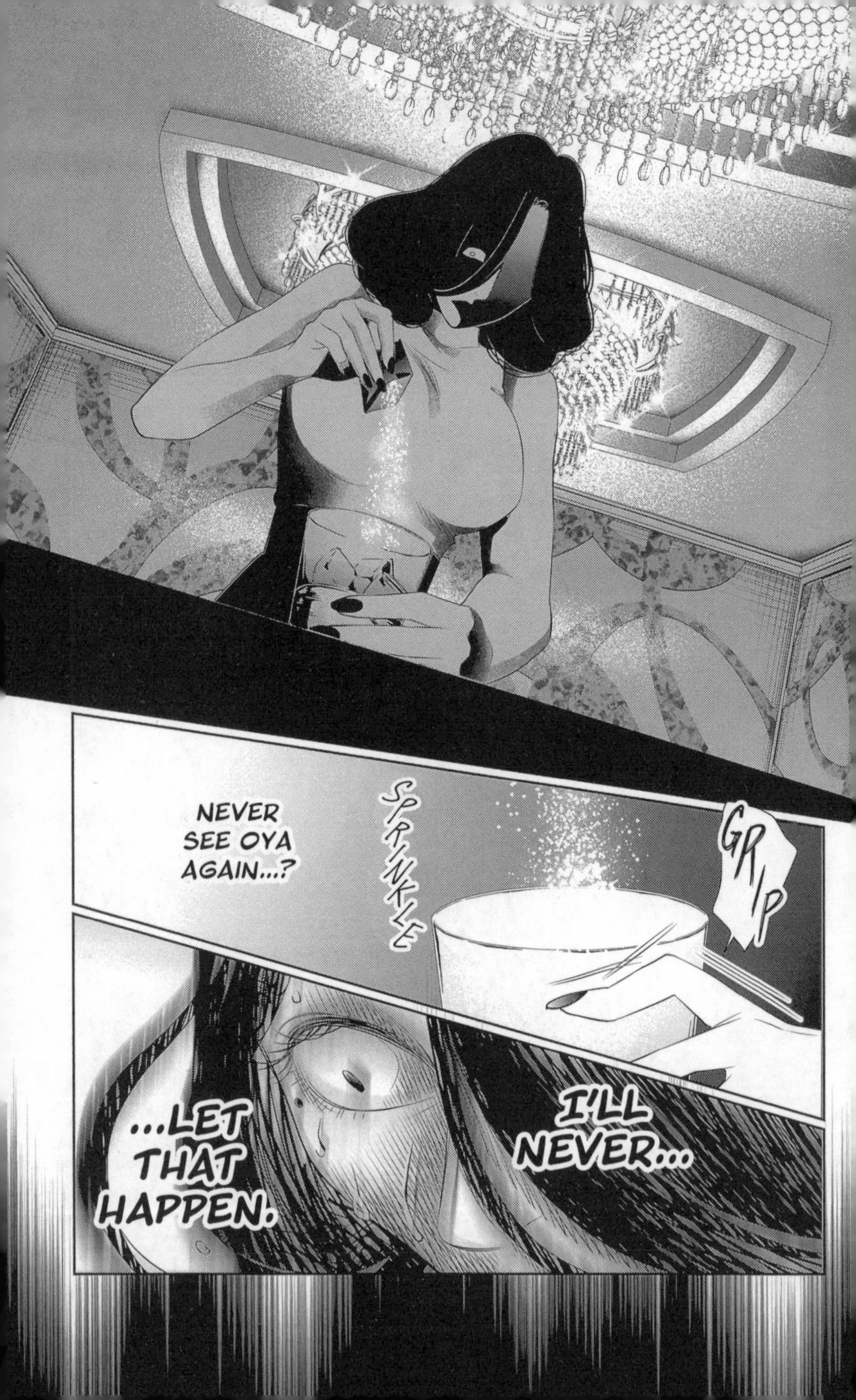
GRIP
SPRINKLE
NEVER SEE OYA AGAIN...?
I'LL NEVER...
...LET THAT HAPPEN.

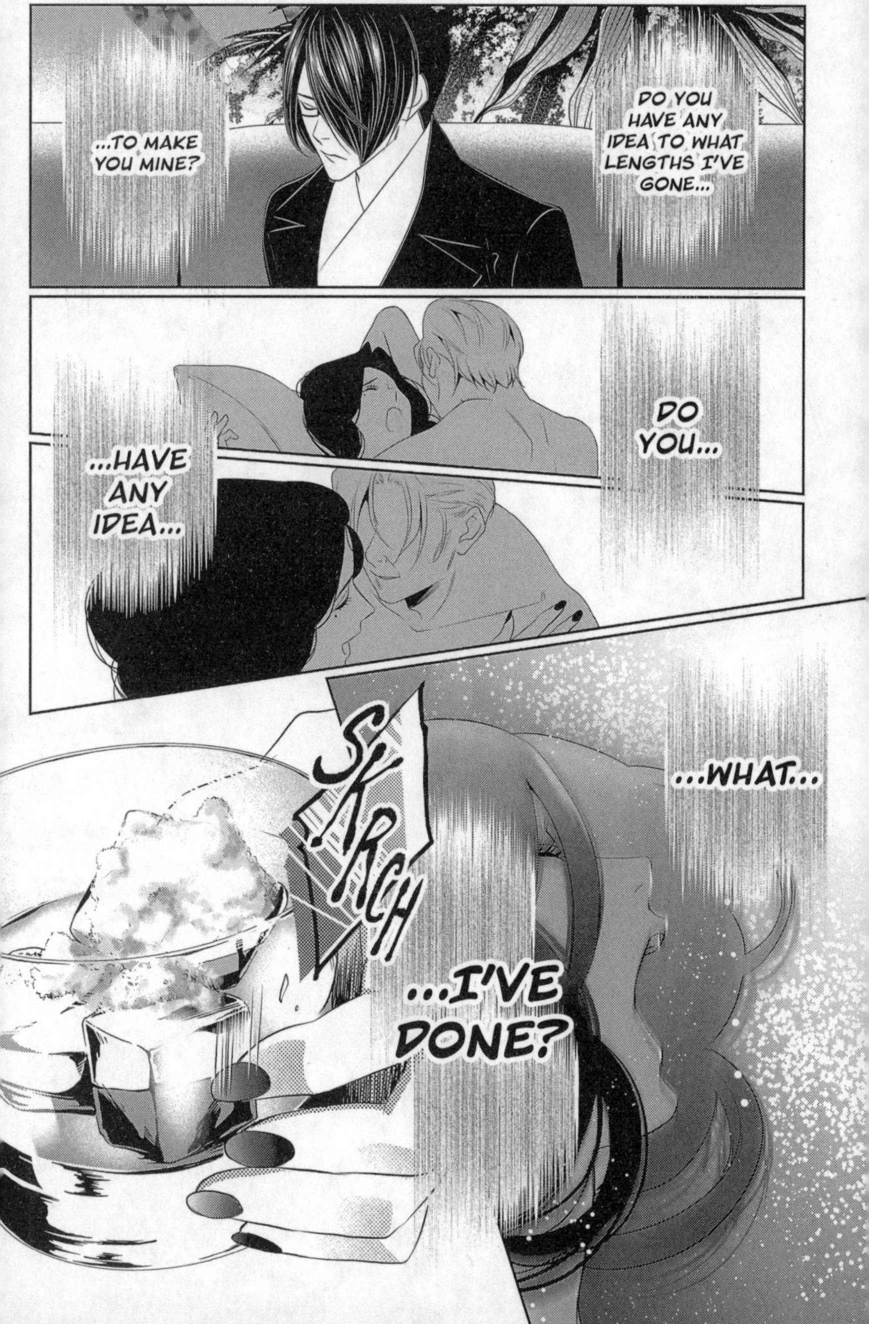
DO YOU HAVE ANY IDEA TO WHAT LENGTHS I'VE GONE...
...TO MAKE YOU MINE?
DO YOU...
...HAVE ANY IDEA...
...WHAT...
SKRCH
...I'VE DONE?

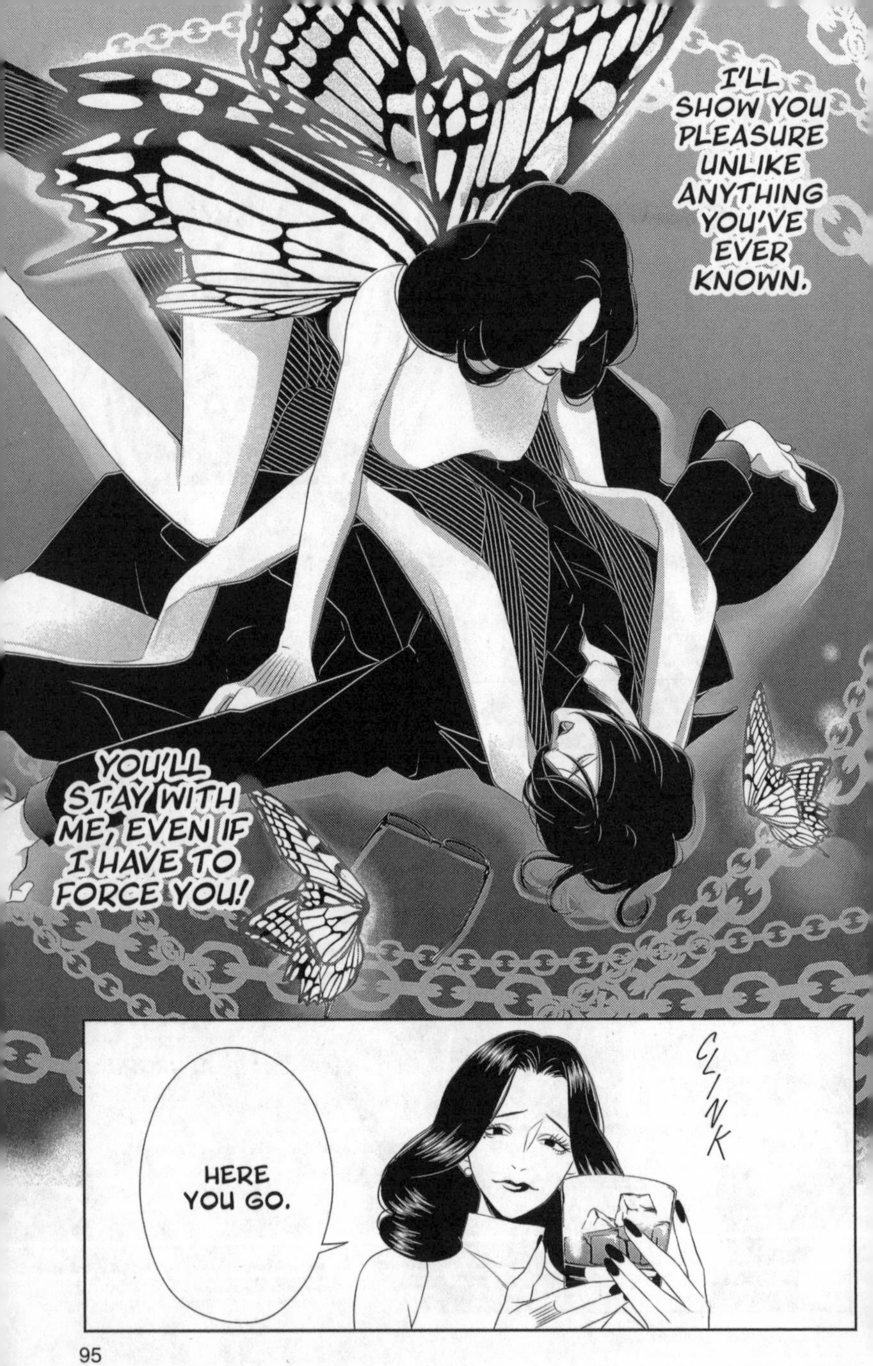
I'LL SHOW YOU PLEASURE UNLIKE ANYTHING YOU'VE EVER KNOWN.
YOU'LL STAY WITH ME, EVEN IF I HAVE TO FORCE YOU!
CLINK
HERE YOU GO.

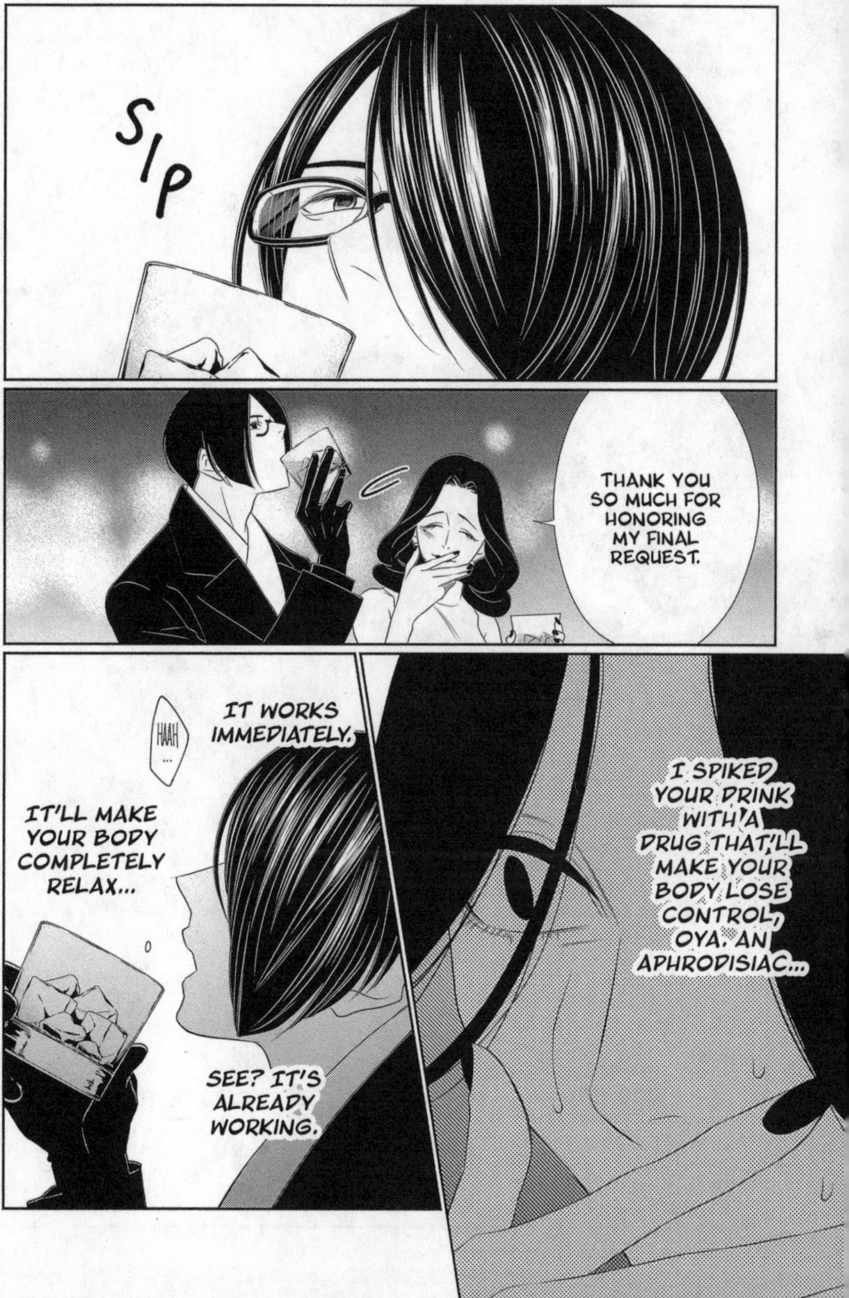
SIP
THANK YOU SO MUCH FOR HONORING MY FINAL REQUEST.
I SPIKED YOUR DRINK WITH A DRUG THAT'LL MAKE YOUR BODY LOSE CONTROL, OYA. AN APHRODISIAC...
IT WORKS IMMEDIATELY.
HAAH...
IT'LL MAKE YOUR BODY COMPLETELY RELAX...
SEE? IT'S ALREADY WORKING.

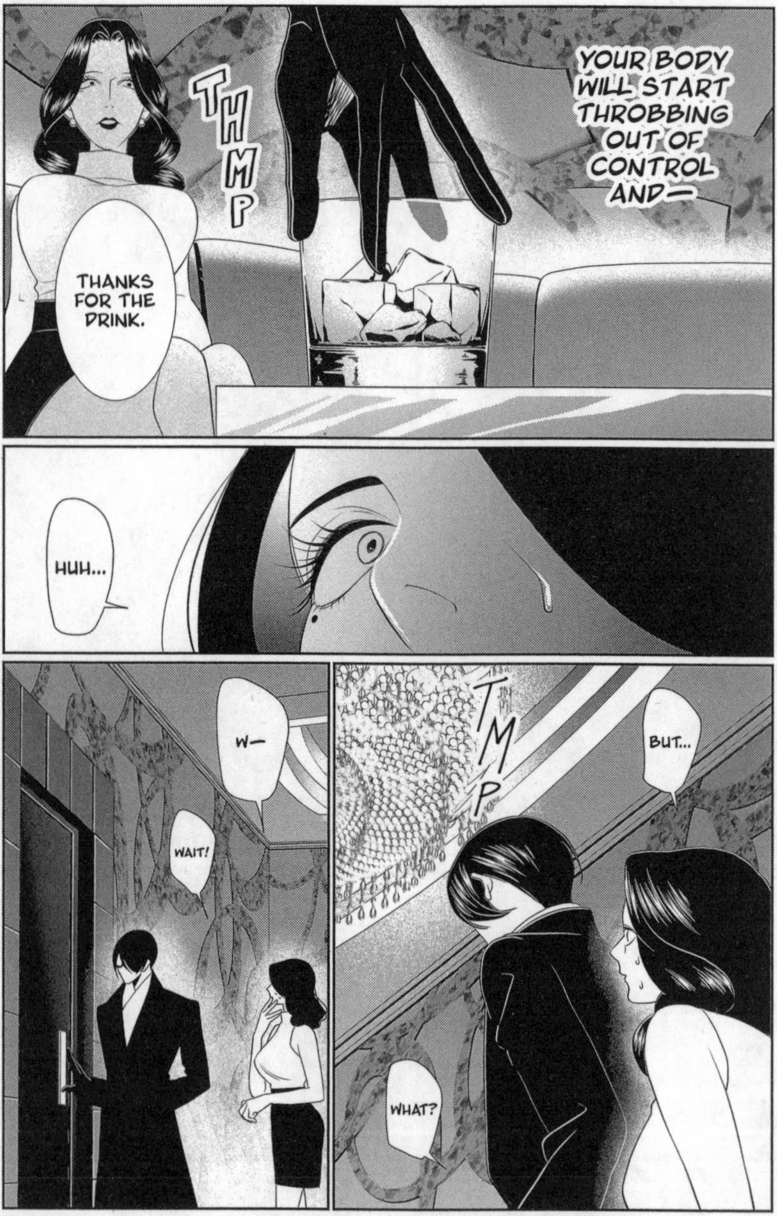
YOUR BODY WILL START THROBBING OUT OF CONTROL AND—
THMP
THANKS FOR THE DRINK.
HUH...
TMP
BUT...
WHAT?
W—
WAIT!

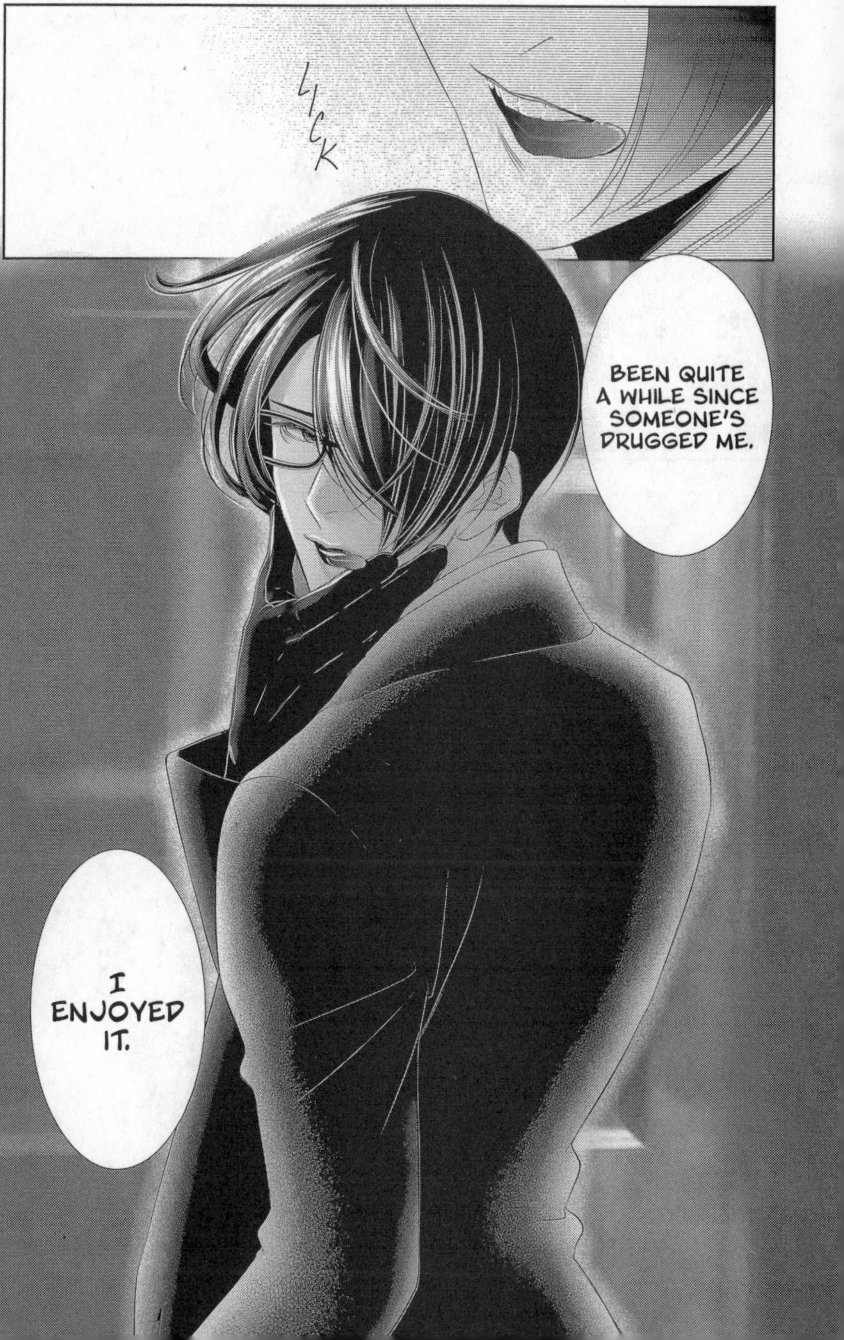
LICK
BEEN QUITE A WHILE SINCE SOMEONE'S DRUGGED ME.
I ENJOYED IT.

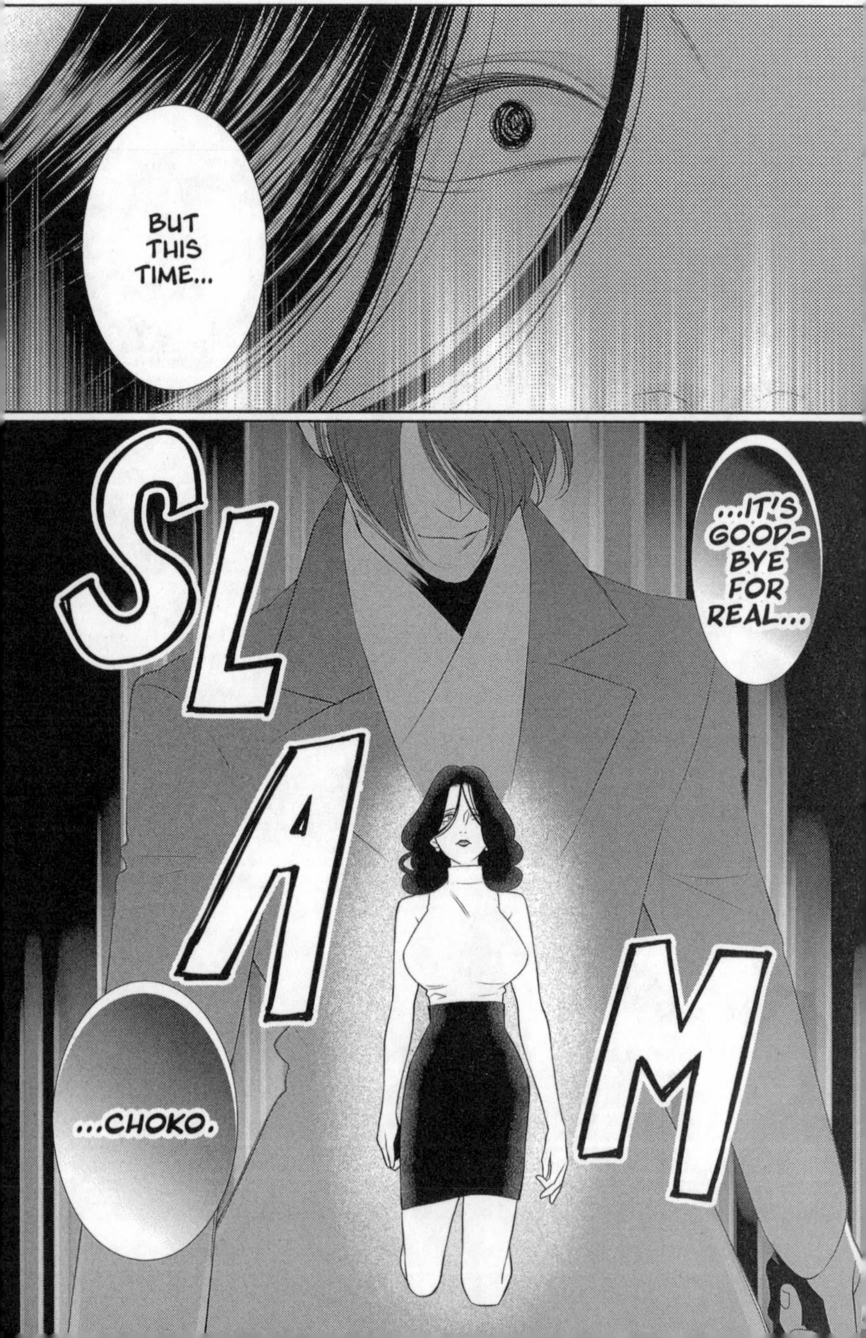
BUT THIS TIME...
...IT'S GOOD-BYE FOR REAL...
SLAM
...CHOKO.

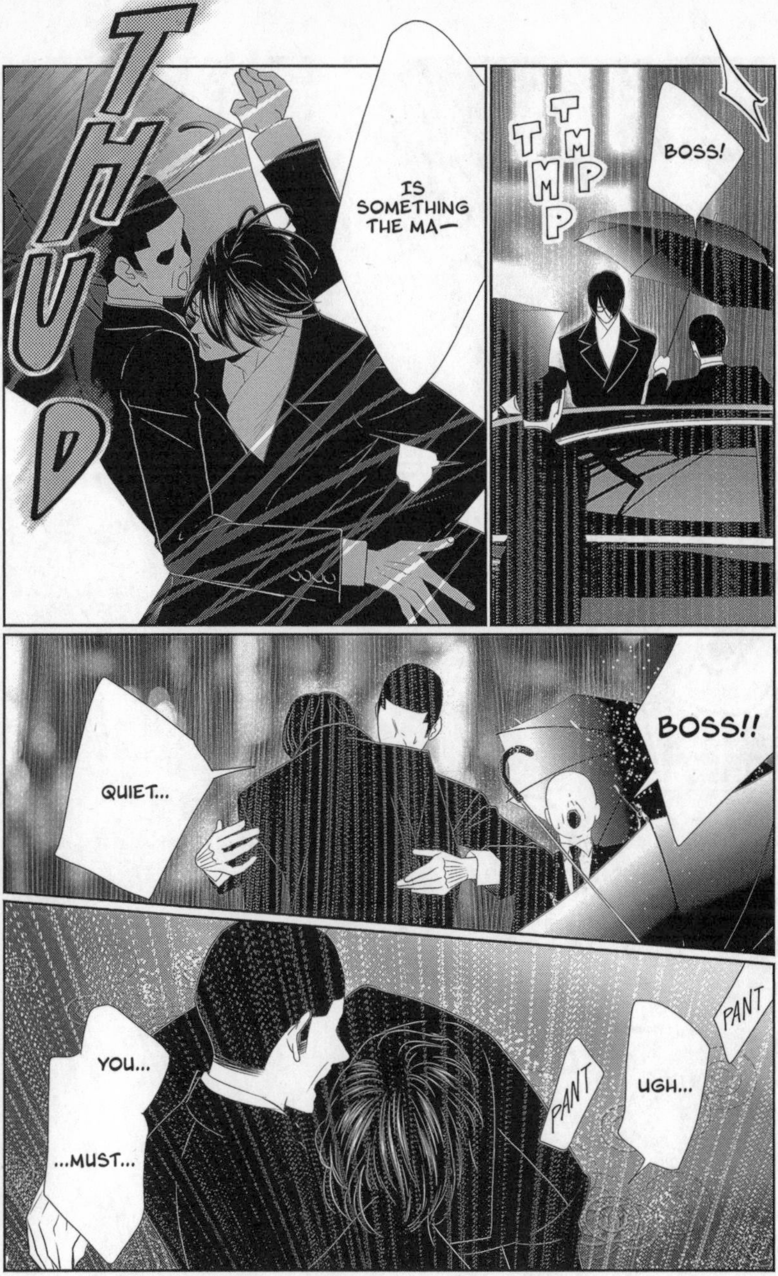
TMP TMP
BOSS!
IS SOMETHING THE MA—
THUD
BOSS!!
QUIET...
PANT
UGH...
PANT
YOU...
...MUST...

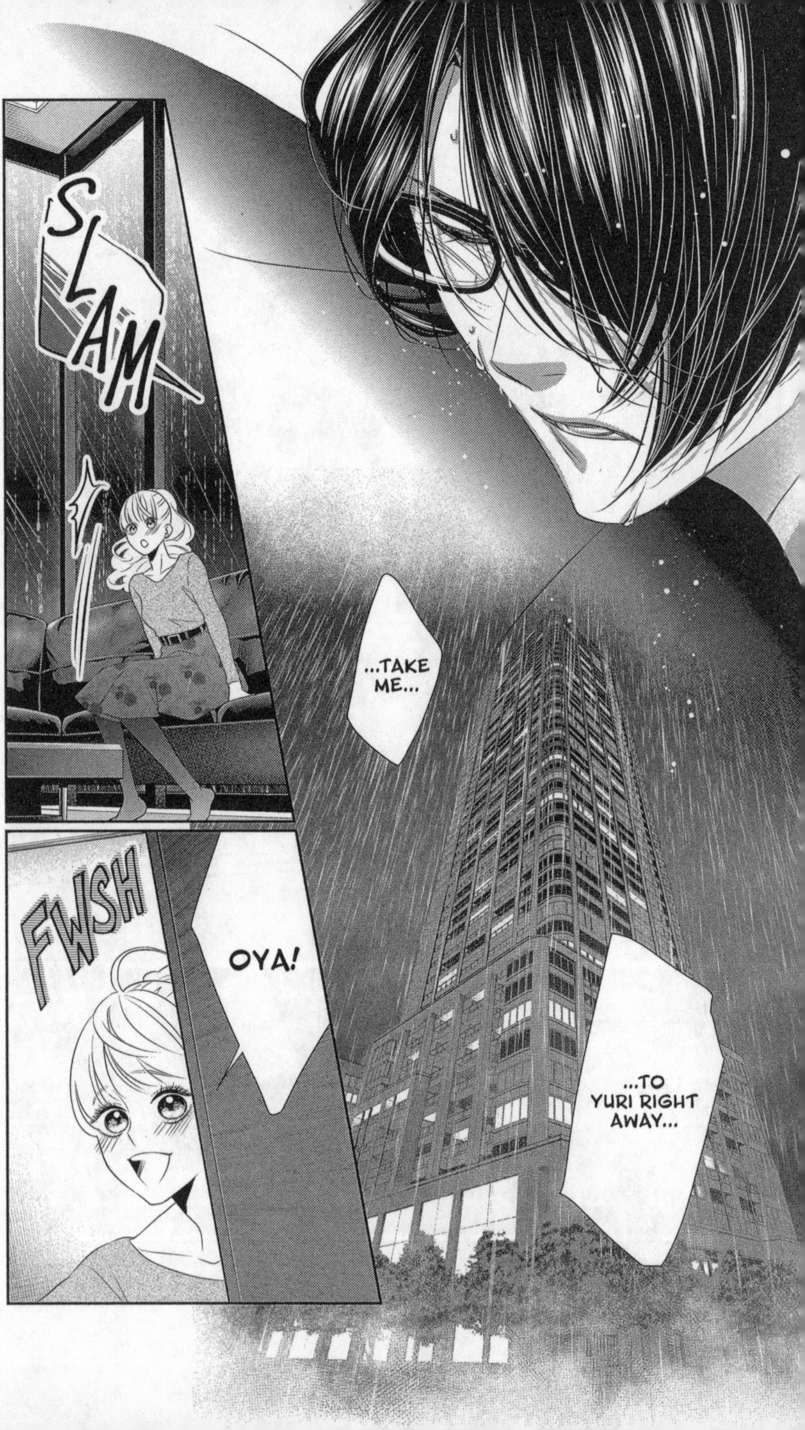
...TAKE ME...
...TO YURI RIGHT AWAY...
SLAM
FWSH
OYA!

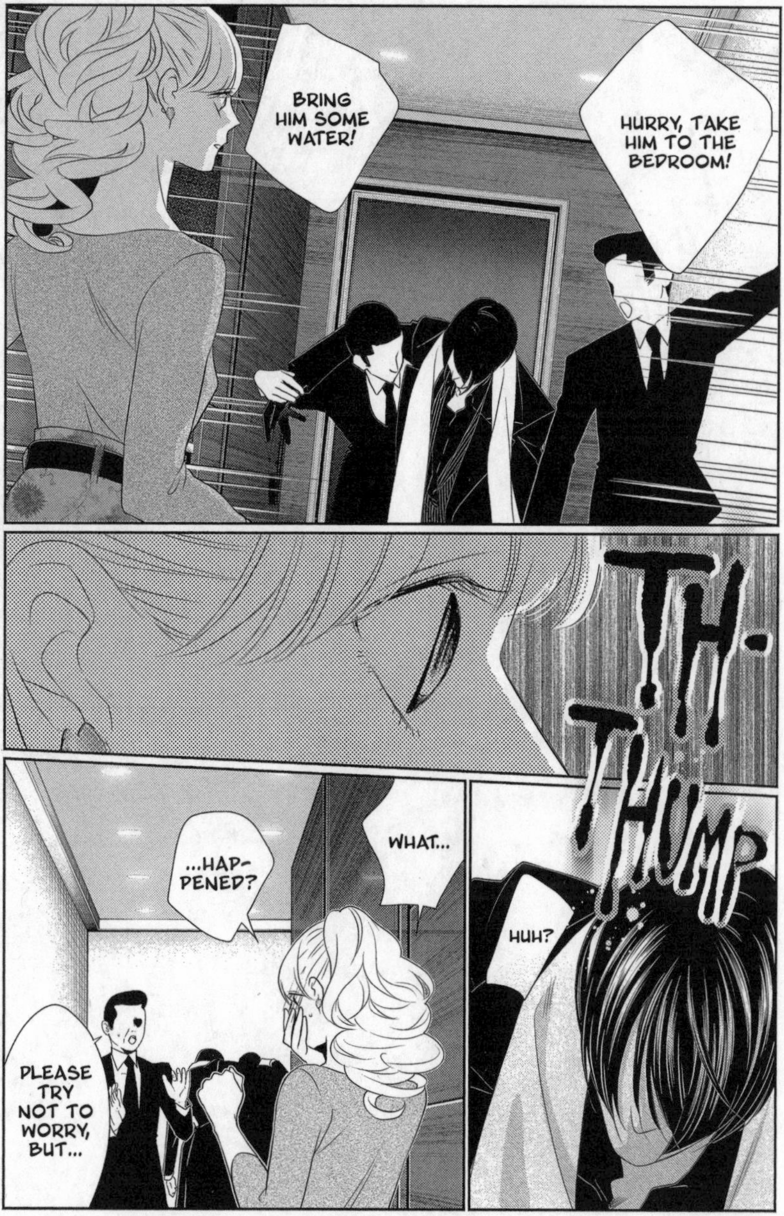
HURRY, TAKE HIM TO THE BEDROOM!
BRING HIM SOME WATER!
TH-THUMP
HUH?
WHAT...
...HAPPENED?
PLEASE TRY NOT TO WORRY, BUT...

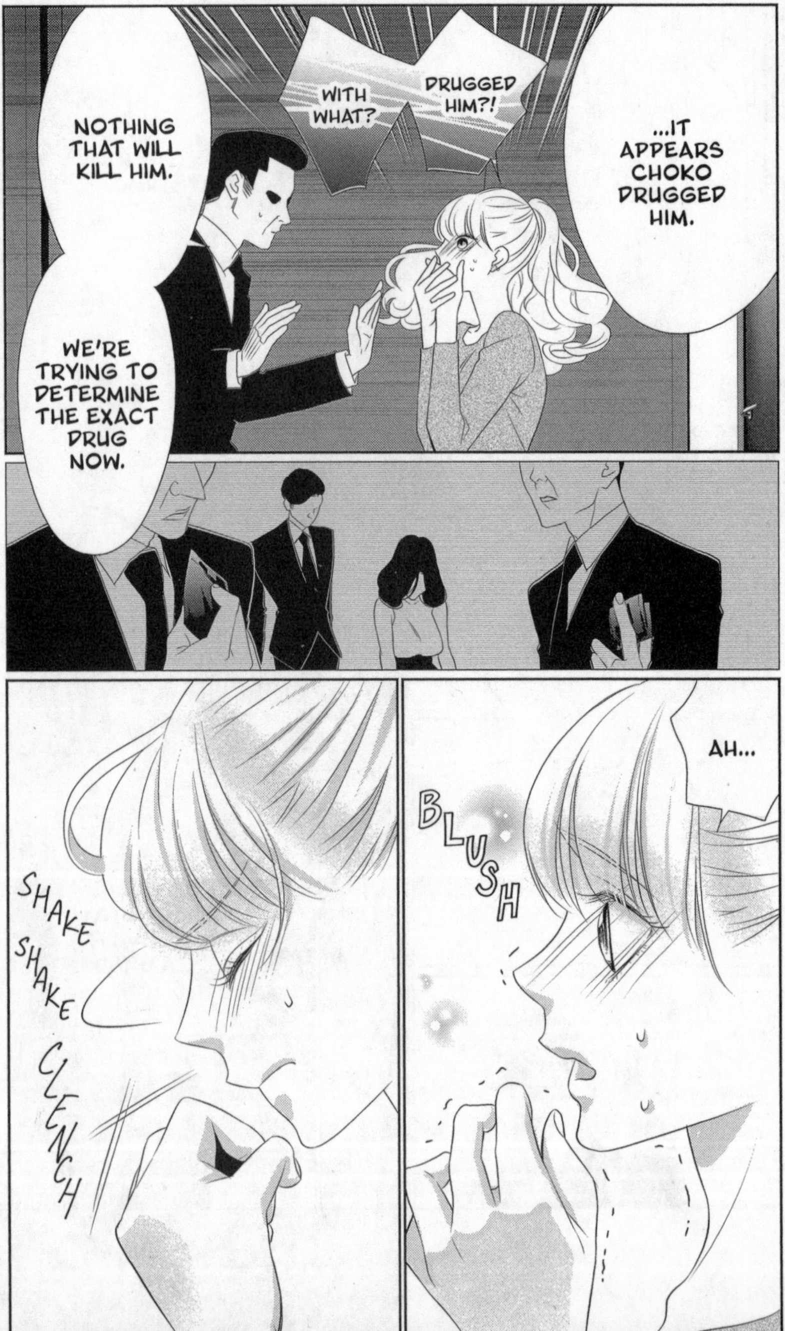
...IT APPEARS CHOKO DRUGGED HIM.
DRUGGED HIM?!
WITH WHAT?
NOTHING THAT WILL KILL HIM.
WE'RE TRYING TO DETERMINE THE EXACT DRUG NOW.
AH...
BLUSH
SHAKE
SHAKE
CLENCH

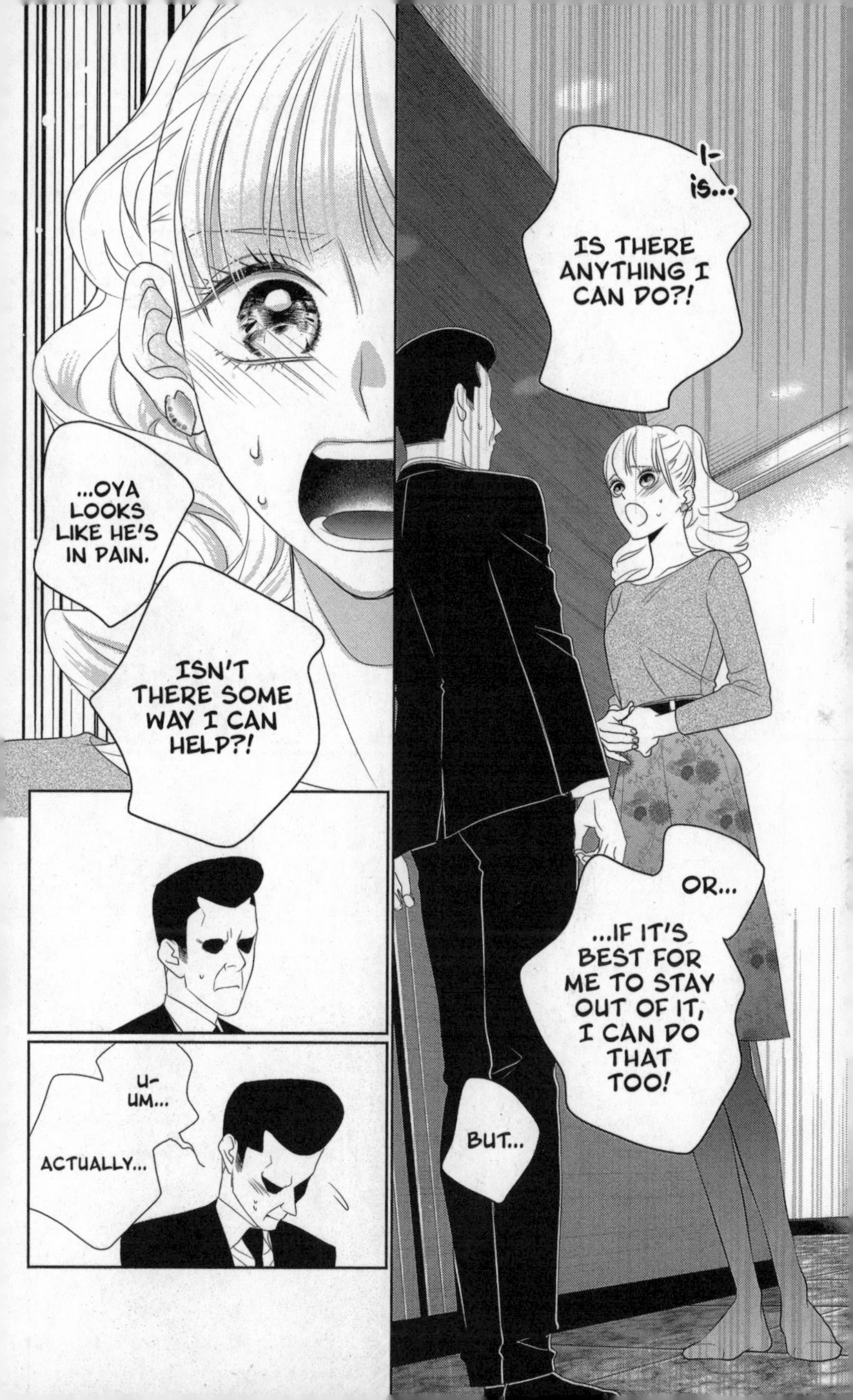
I-
IS...
IS THERE ANYTHING I CAN DO?!
OR...
...IF IT'S BEST FOR ME TO STAY OUT OF IT, I CAN DO THAT TOO!
BUT...
...OYA LOOKS LIKE HE'S IN PAIN.
ISN'T THERE SOME WAY I CAN HELP?!
U-UM...
ACTUALLY...

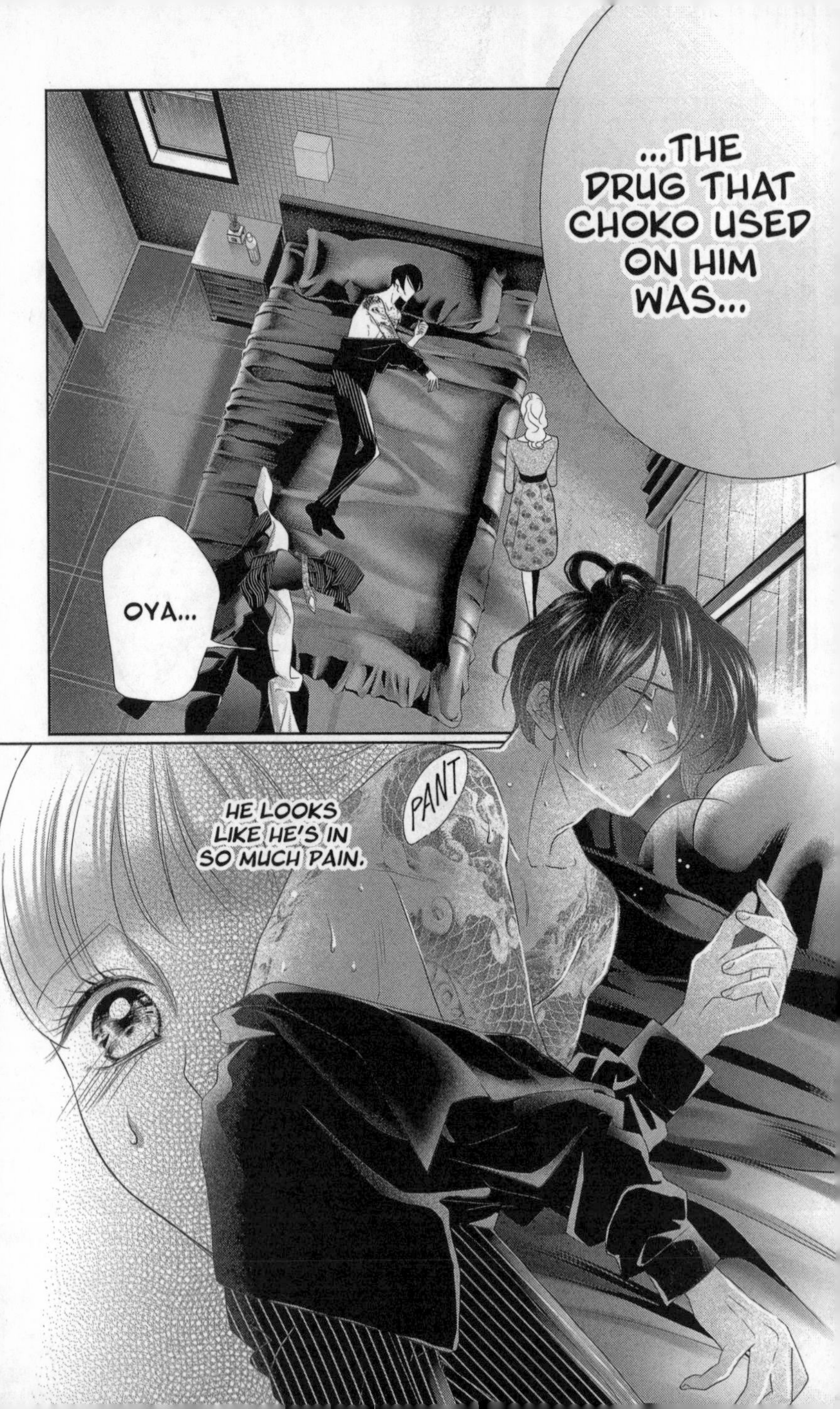
...THE DRUG THAT CHOKO USED ON HIM WAS...
OYA...
PANT
HE LOOKS LIKE HE'S IN SO MUCH PAIN.

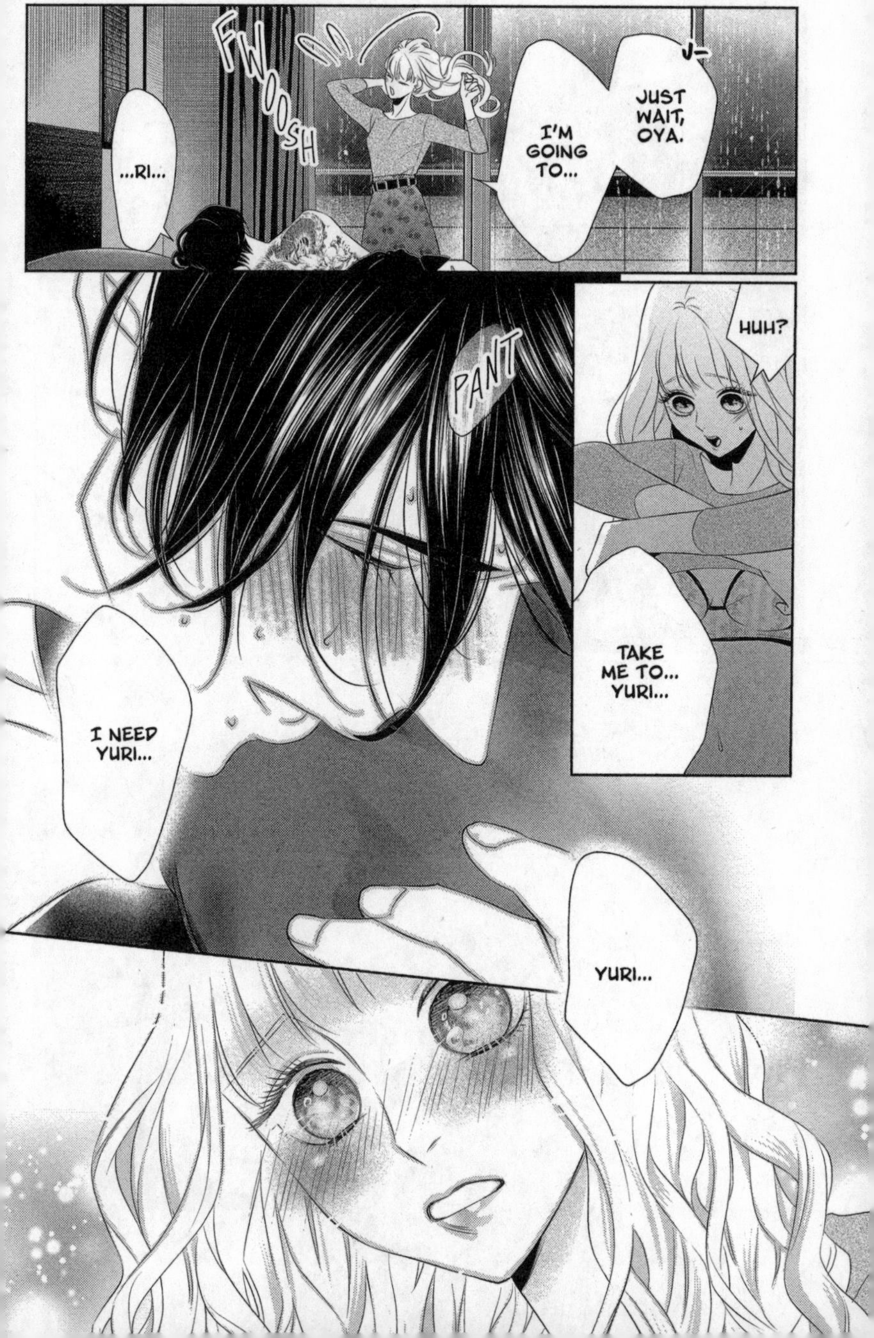
J—
JUST WAIT, OYA.
I'M GOING TO...
FWOOSH
...RI...
HUH?
TAKE ME TO... YURI...
PANT
I NEED YURI...
YURI...

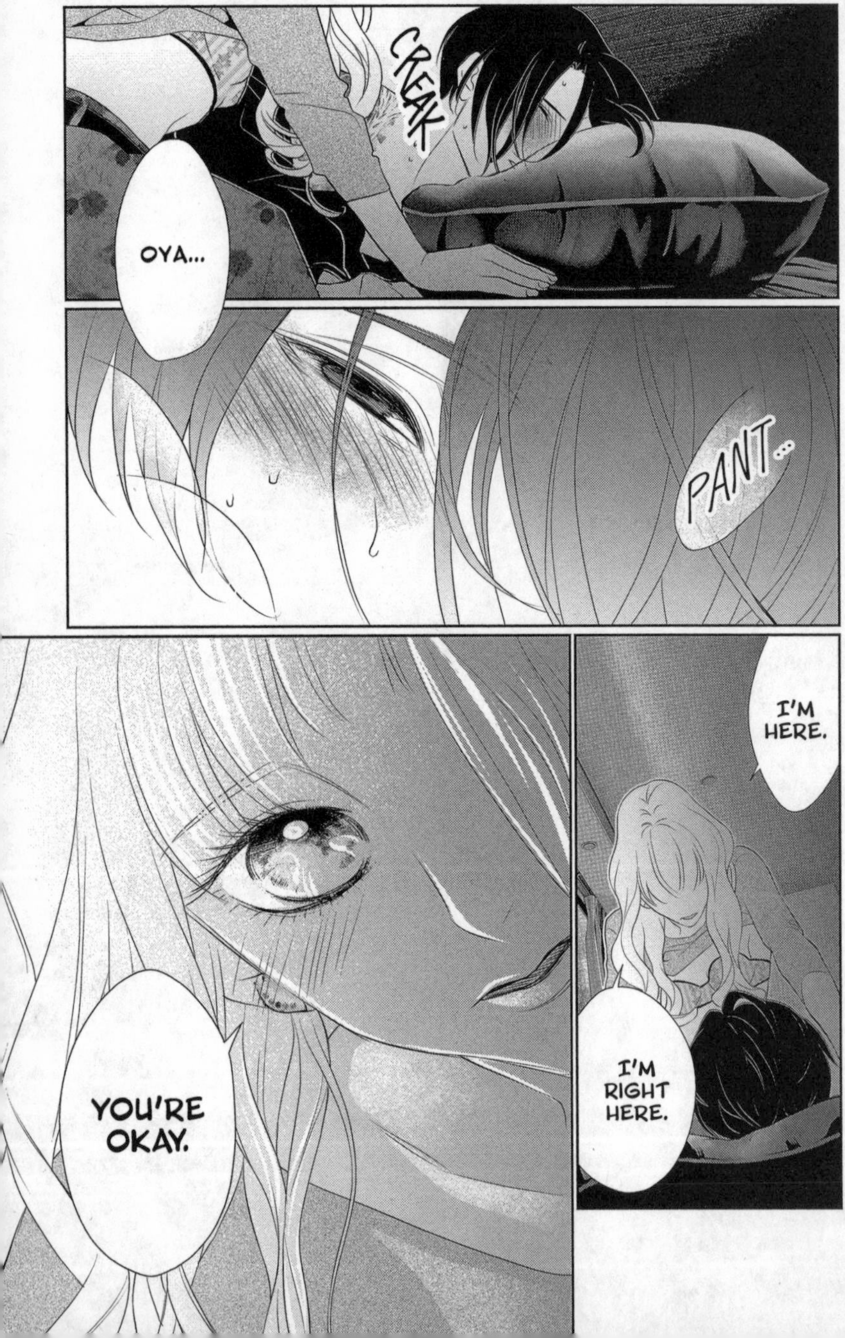
CREAK
OYA...
PANT...
I'M HERE.
I'M RIGHT HERE.
YOU'RE OKAY.

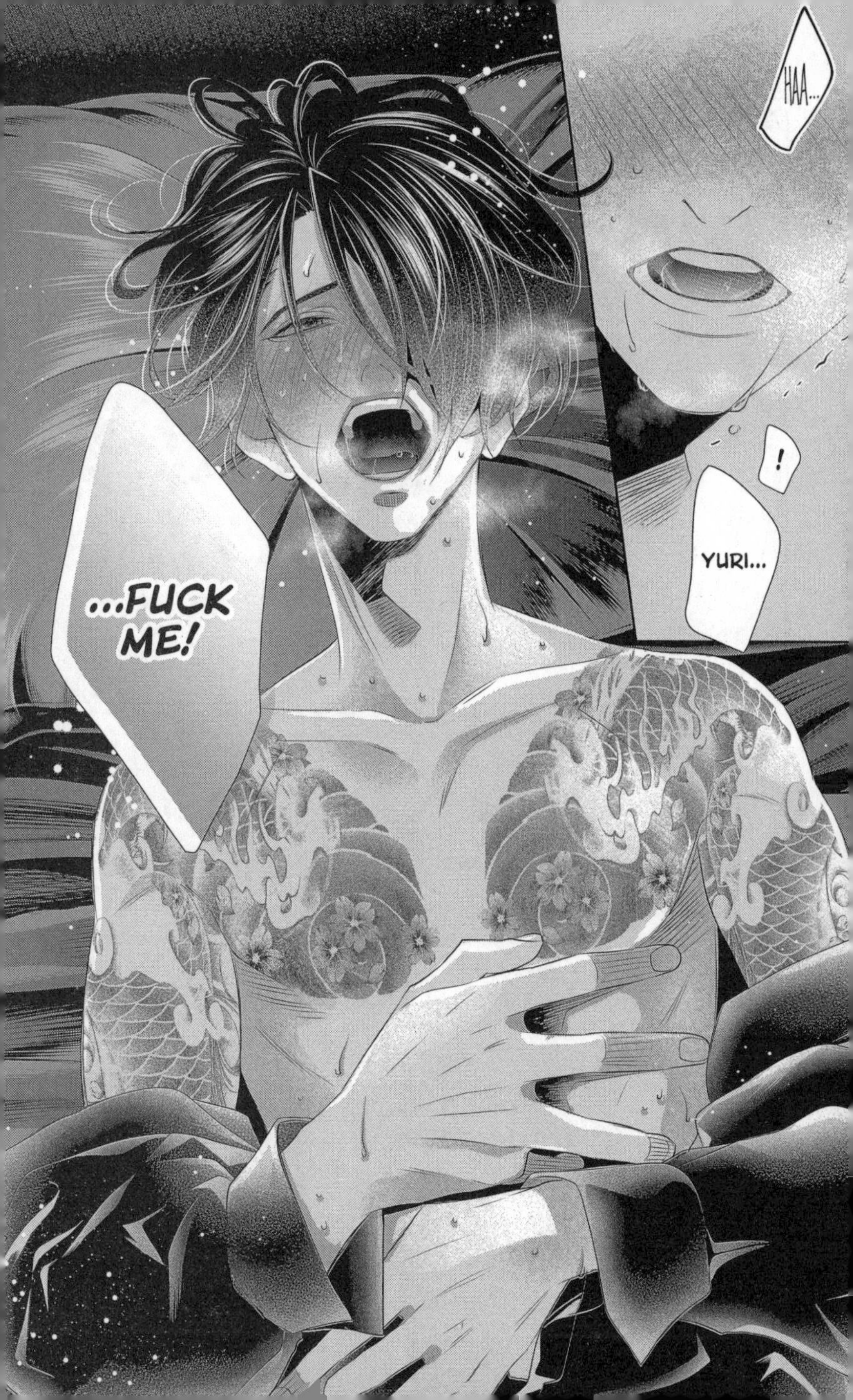
HAA...
!
YURI...
...FUCK ME!

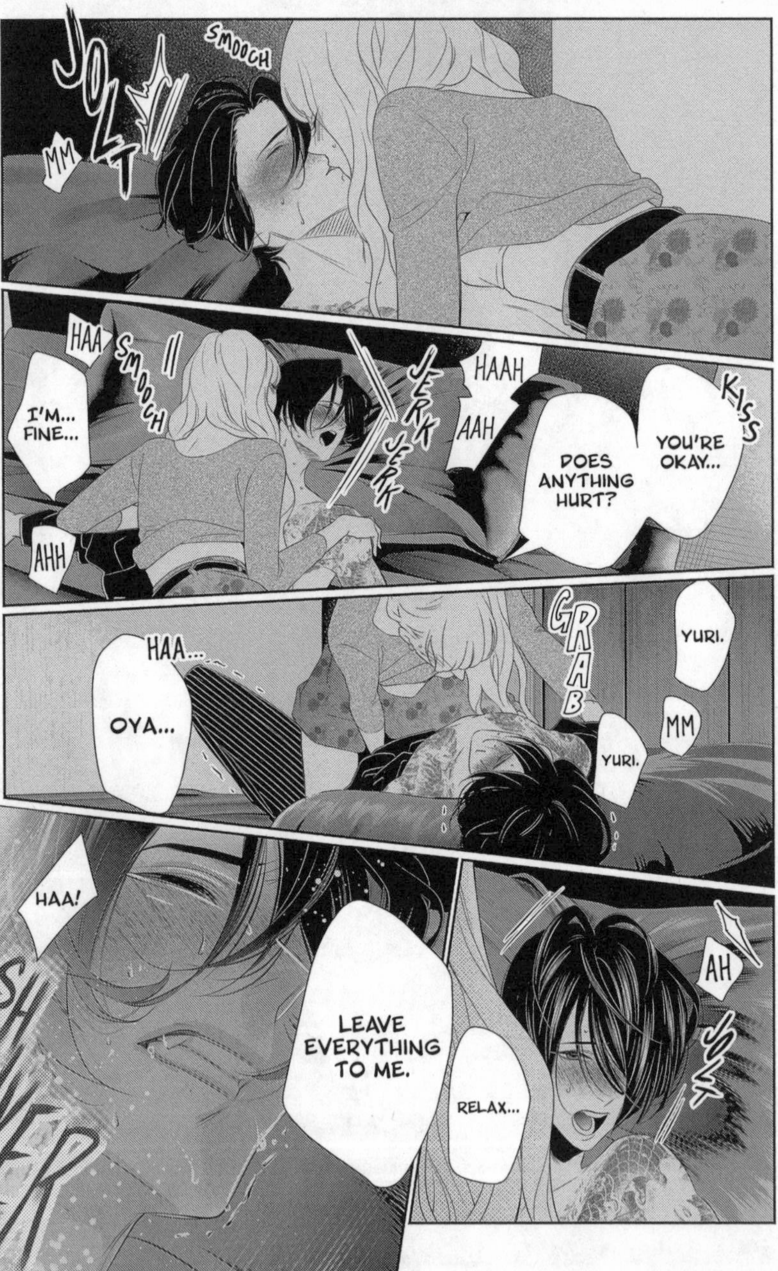
SMOOCH
JOLT
MM
KISS
YOU'RE OKAY...
DOES ANYTHING HURT?
HAAH
AAH
JERK JERK
SMOOCH
HAA
I'M... FINE...
AHH
GRAB
YURI.
MM
YURI.
HAA...
OYA...
AH
JOLT
RELAX...
LEAVE EVERYTHING TO ME.
HAA!
SHIVER

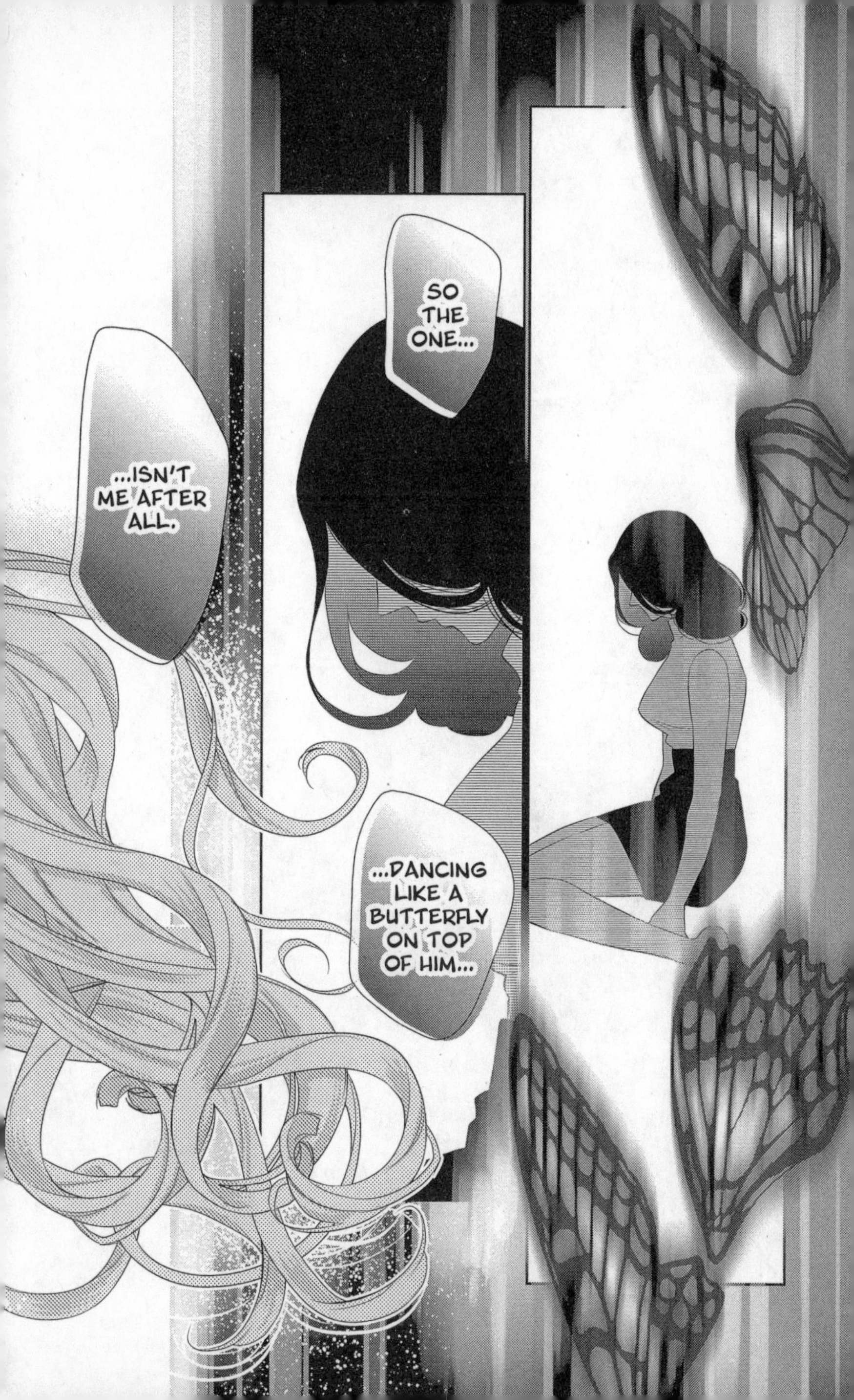
SO THE ONE...
...DANCING LIKE A BUTTERFLY ON TOP OF HIM...
...ISN'T ME AFTER ALL.

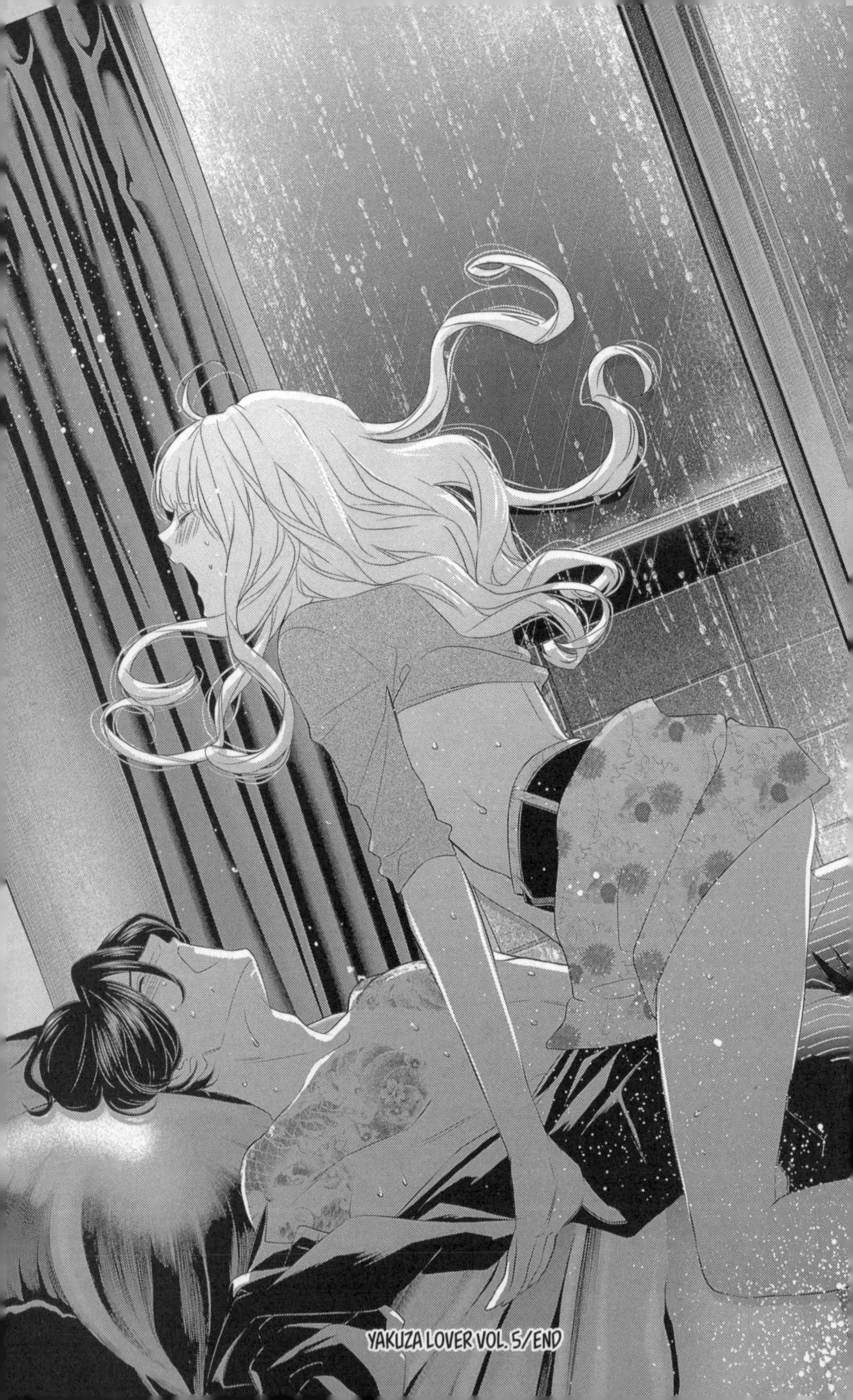
YAKUZA LOVER VOL. 5/END

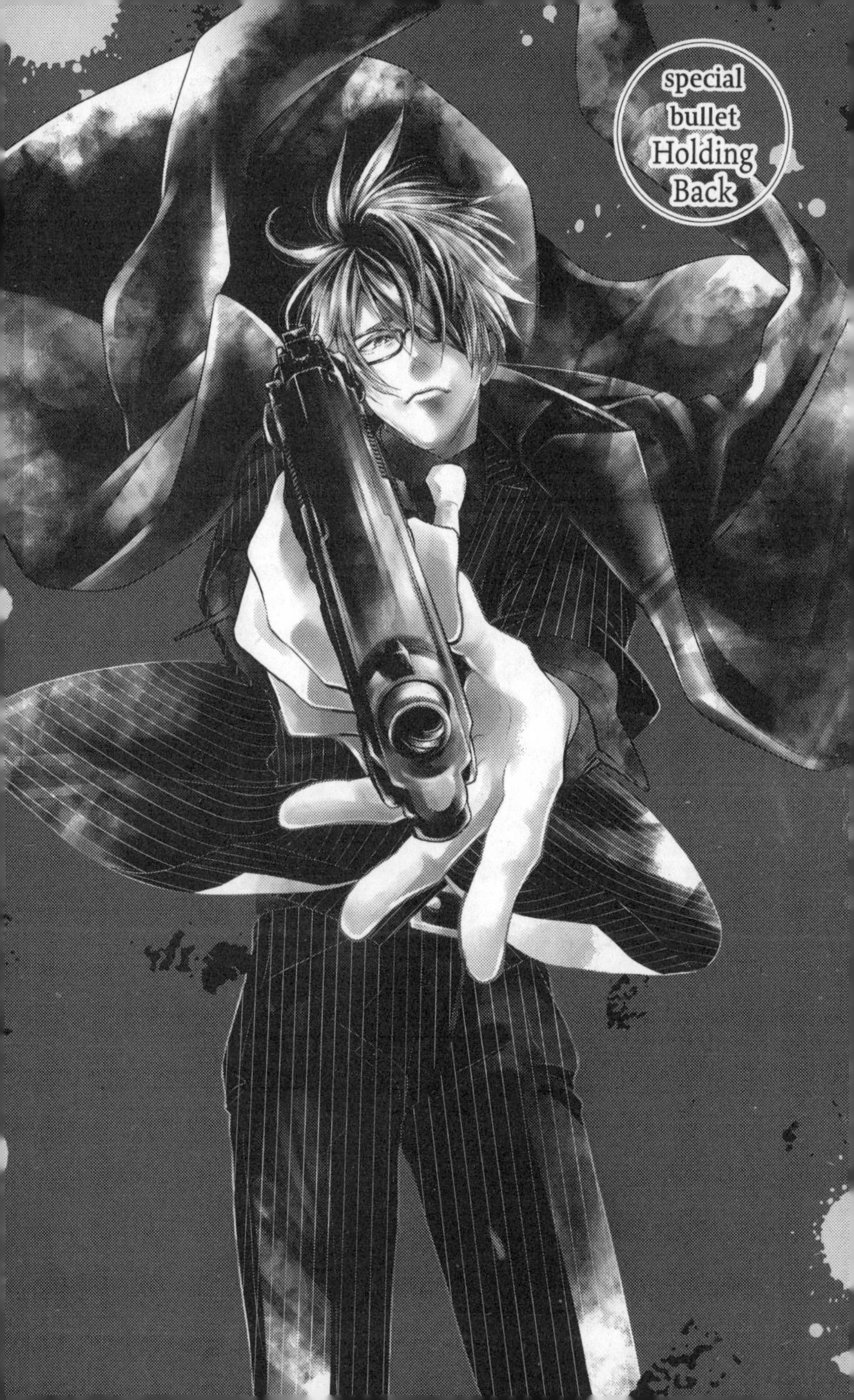
special
bullet
Holding
Back

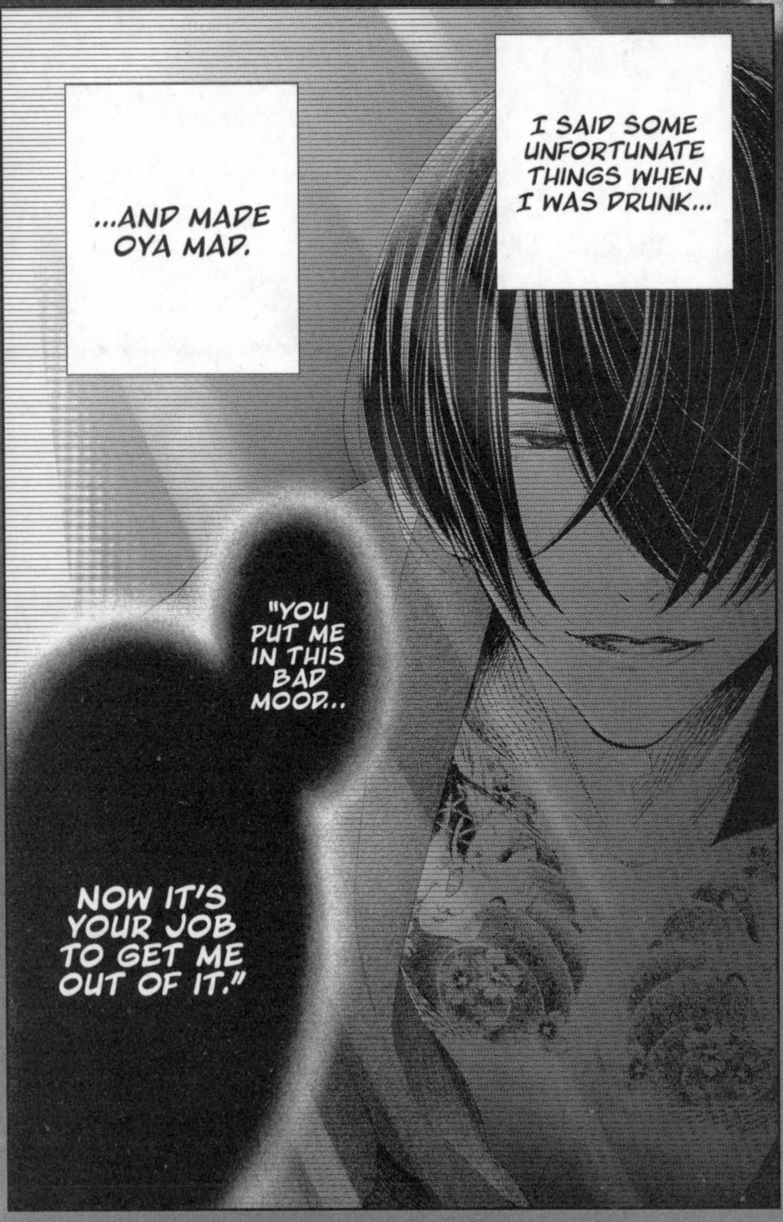
I SAID SOME UNFORTUNATE THINGS WHEN I WAS DRUNK...
...AND MADE OYA MAD.
"YOU PUT ME IN THIS BAD MOOD...
NOW IT'S YOUR JOB TO GET ME OUT OF IT."

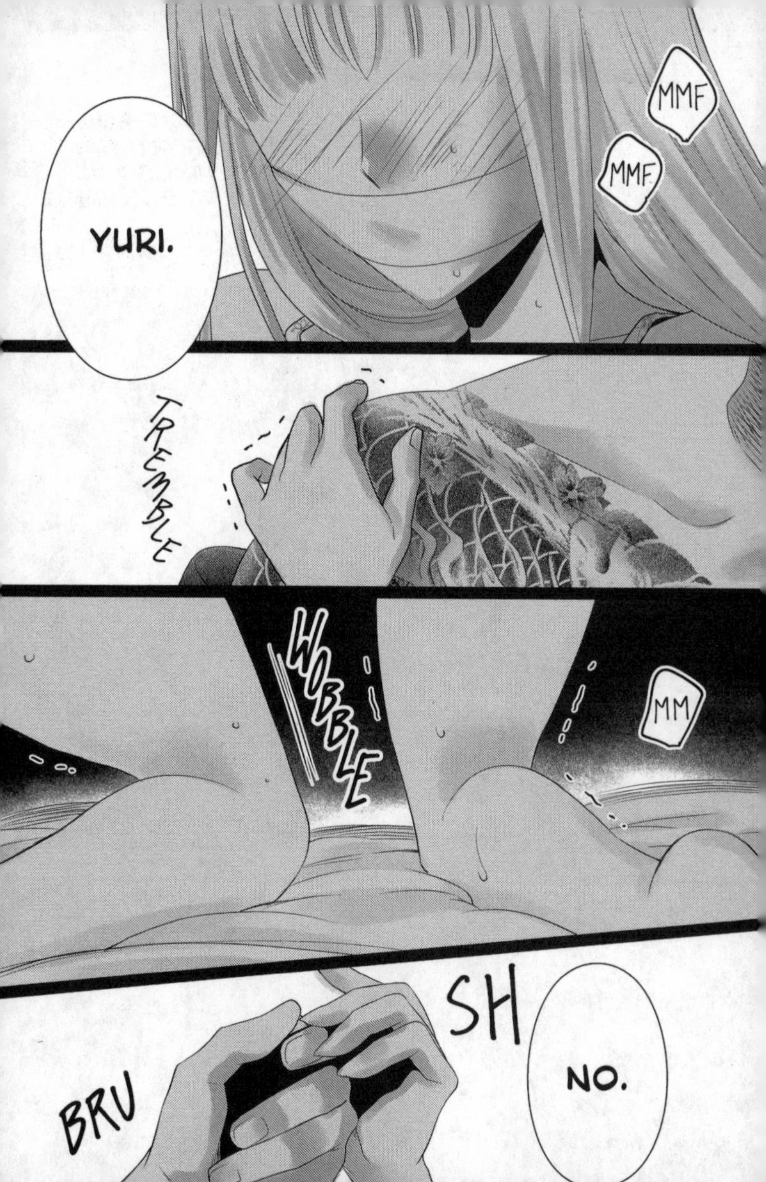
MMF
MMF
YURI.
TREMBLE
MM
WOBBLE
NO.
SH
BRU

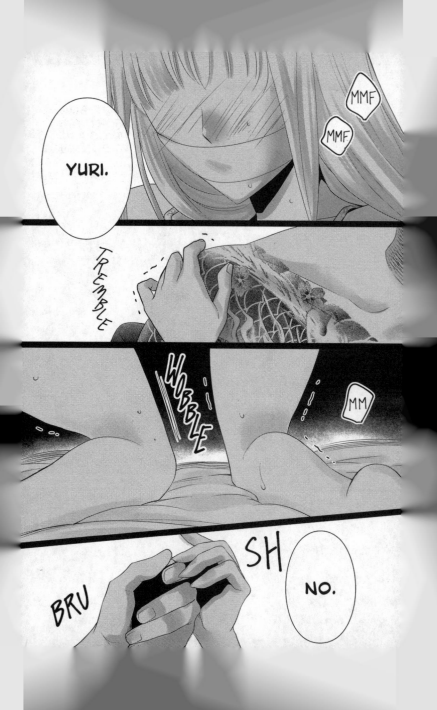

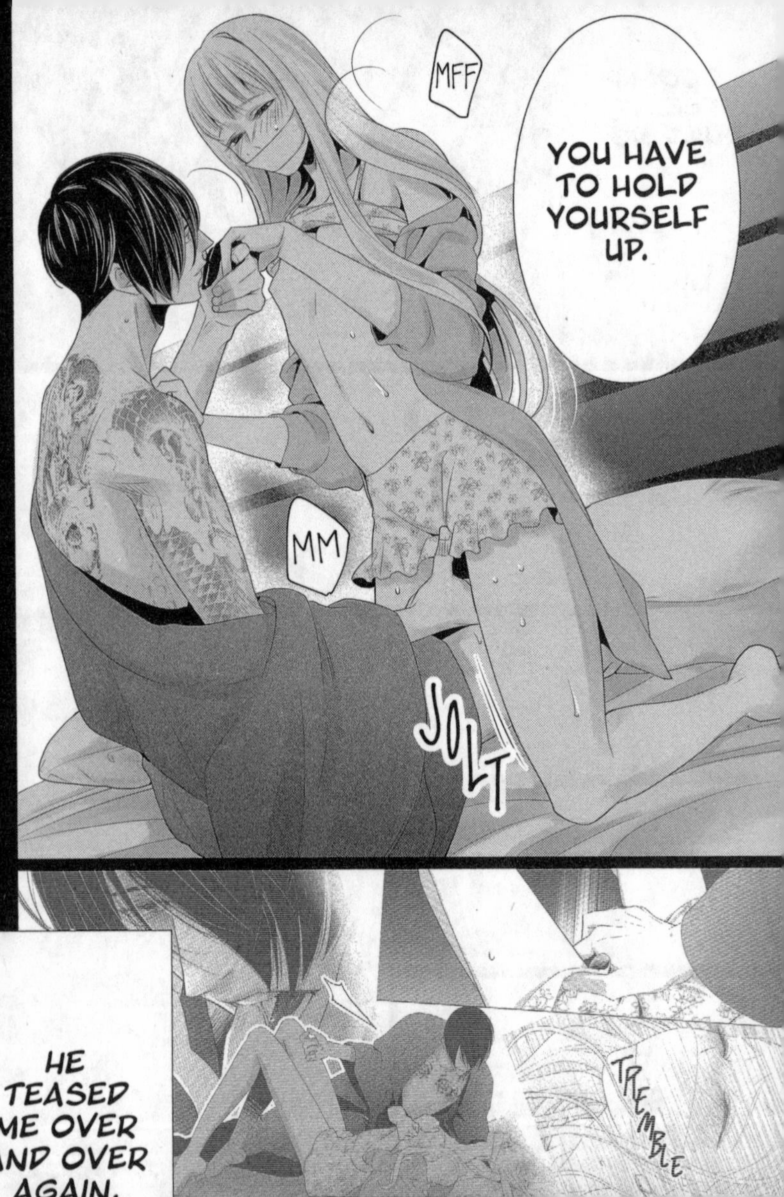
YOU HAVE TO HOLD YOURSELF UP.
MFF
MM
JOLT
TREMBLE
HE TEASED ME OVER ND OVER AGAIN.

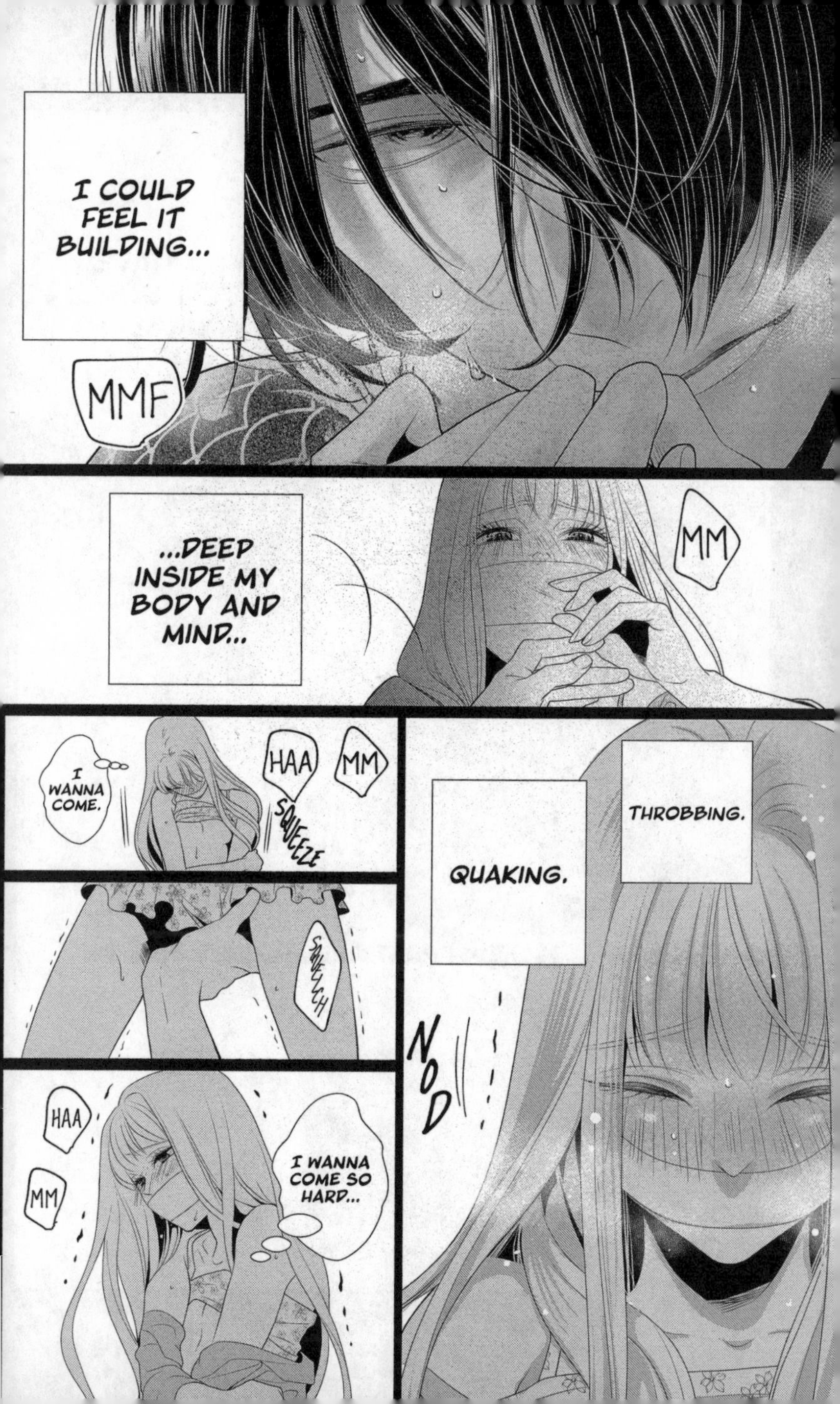
I COULD FEEL IT BUILDING...
MMF
MM
...DEEP INSIDE MY BODY AND MIND...
THROBBING.
QUAKING.
NOD
MM
HAA
I WANNA COME.
SQUEEZE
SQUELCH
I WANNA COME SO HARD...
HAA
MM

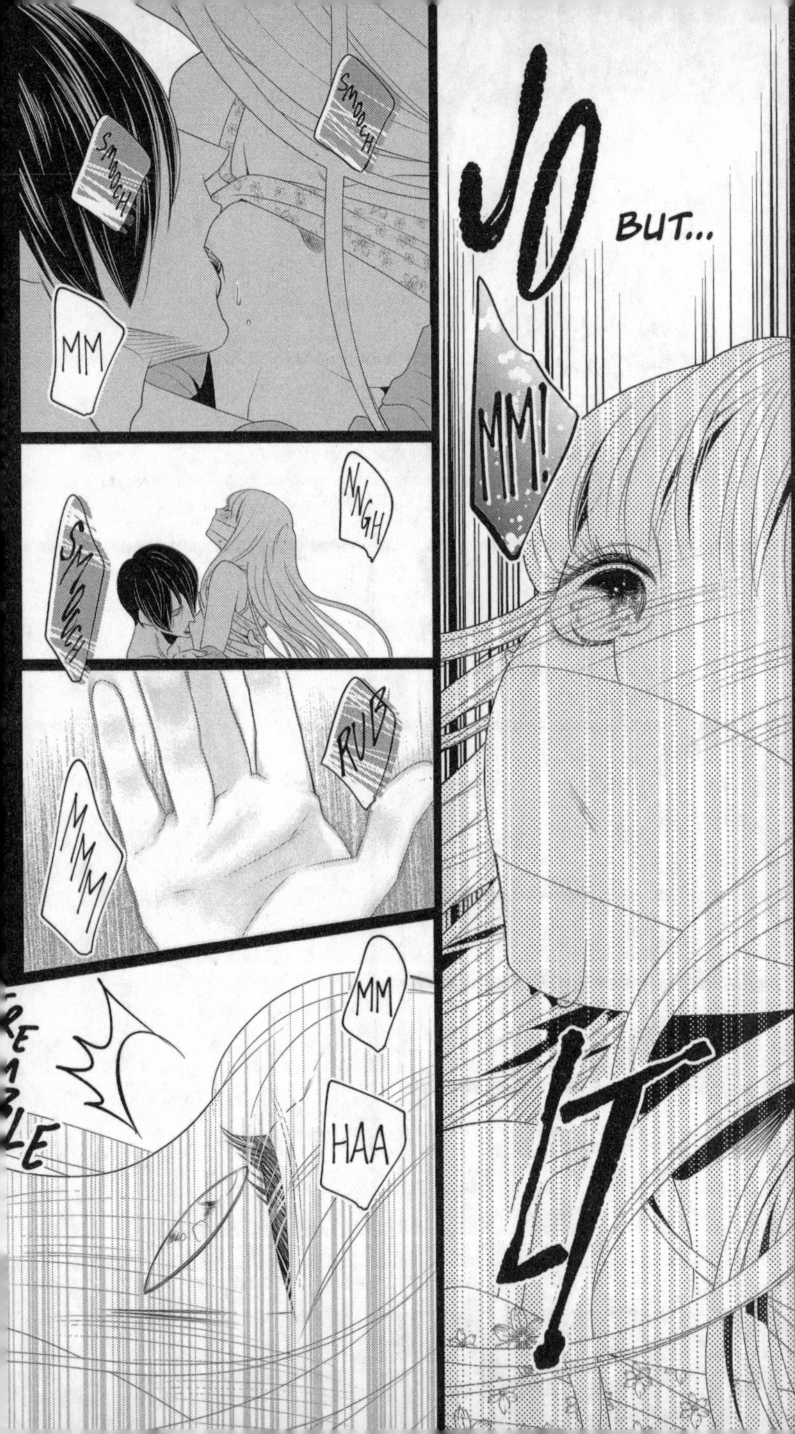
BUT...
MM!
IT
SMOOCH
SMOOCH
MM
NNGH
SMOOCH
RUB
MMM
MM
HAA

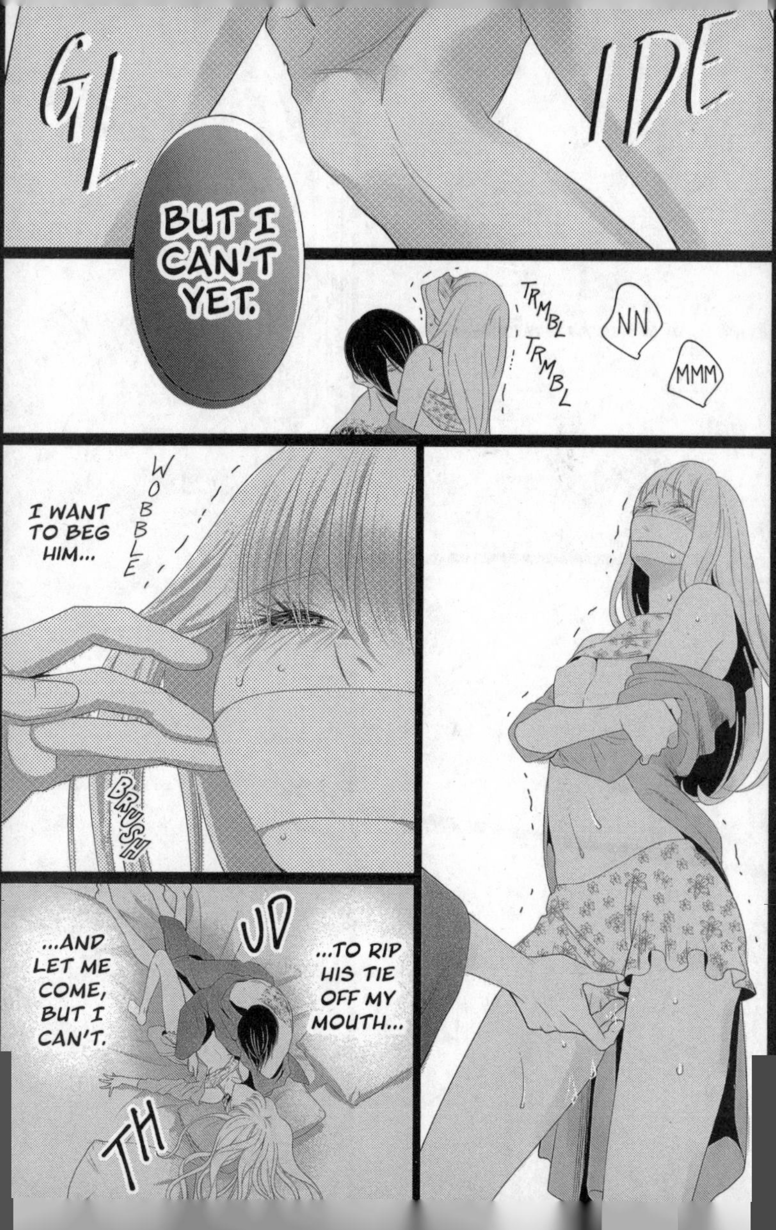
GL
IDE
BUT I CAN'T YET.
NN
MMM
TRMBL TRMBL
WOBBLE
I WANT TO BEG HIM...
BRUSH
UD
...TO RIP HIS TIE OFF MY MOUTH...
...AND LET ME COME, BUT I CAN'T.
TH

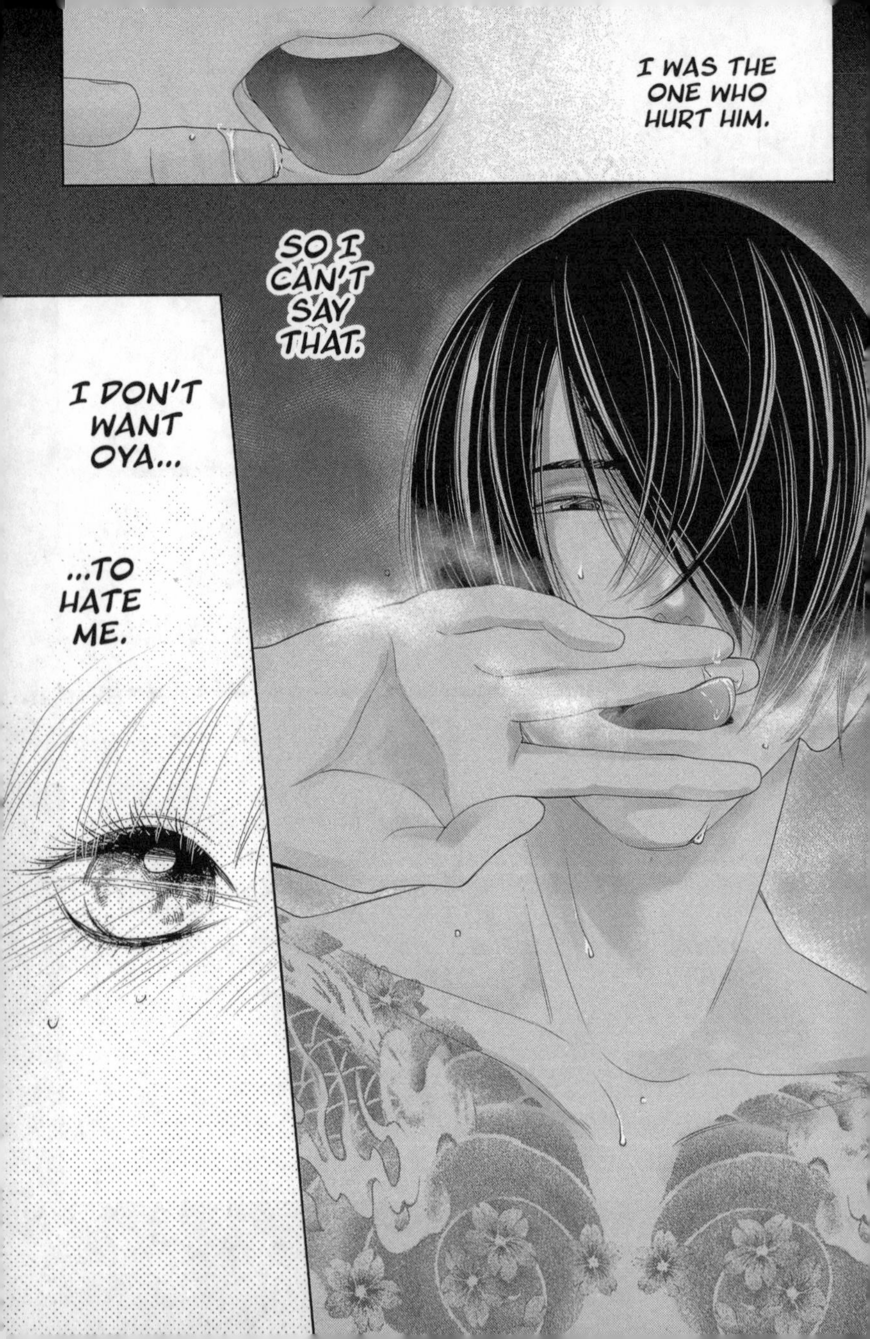
I WAS THE ONE WHO HURT HIM.
SO I CAN'T SAY THAT.
I DON'T WANT OYA...
...TO HATE ME.

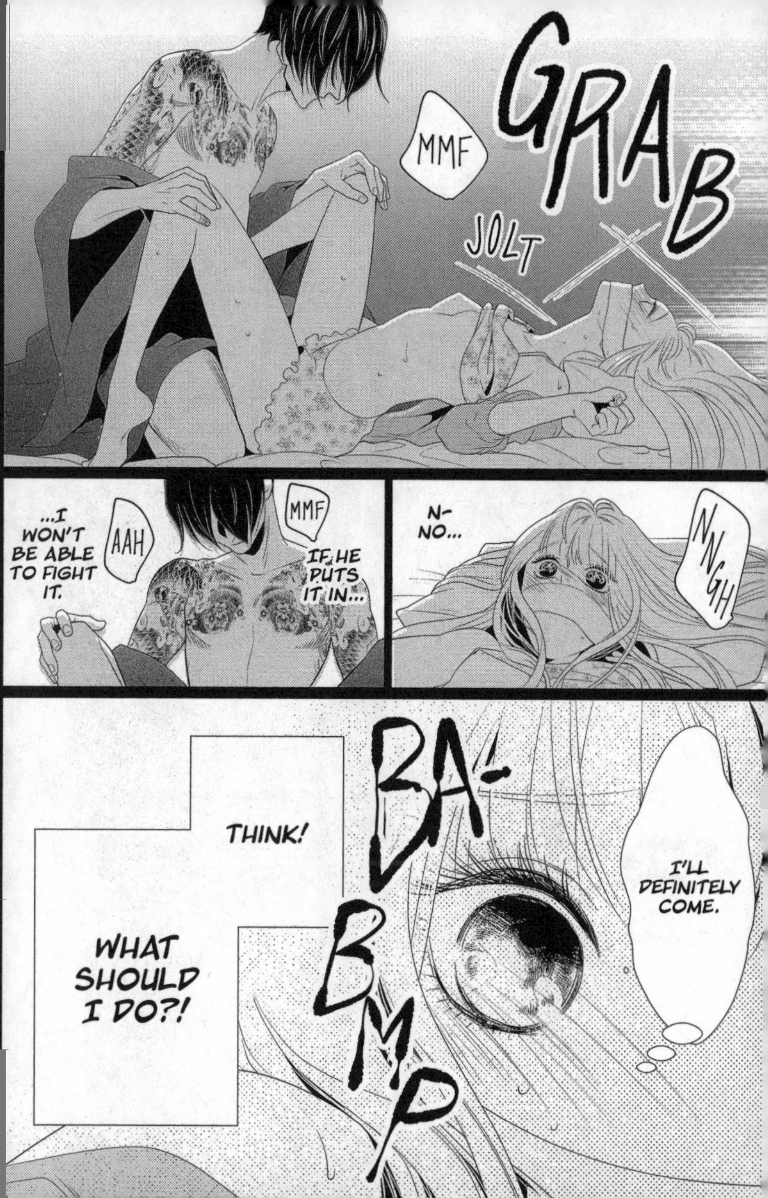
GRAB
MMF
JOLT
NNGH
N-NO...
IF HE PUTS IT IN...
MMF
AAH
...I WON'T BE ABLE TO FIGHT IT.
I'LL DEFINITELY COME.
BA-DUMP
THINK!
WHAT SHOULD I DO?!

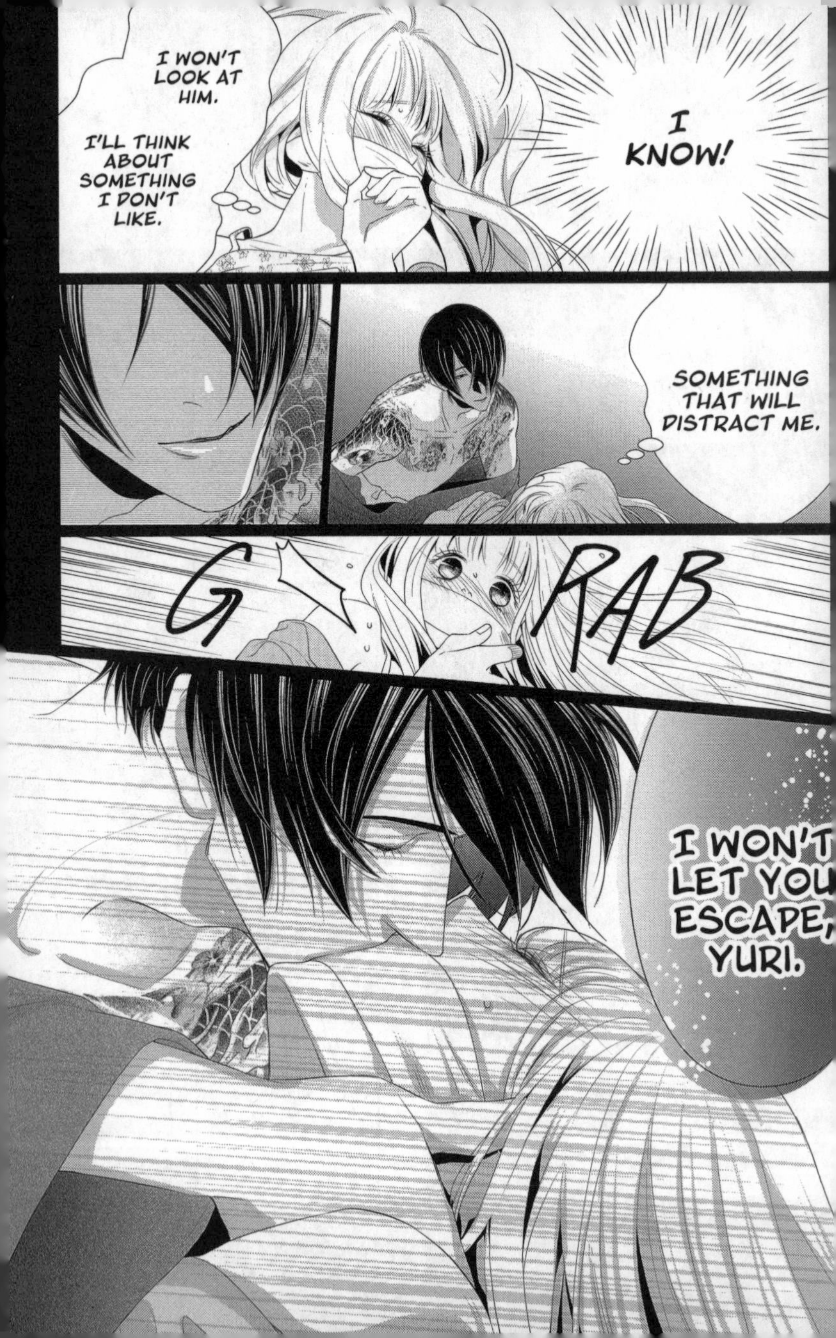
I KNOW!
I WON'T LOOK AT HIM.
I'LL THINK ABOUT SOMETHING I DON'T LIKE.
SOMETHING THAT WILL DISTRACT ME.
GRAB
I WON'T LET YOU ESCAPE, YURI.

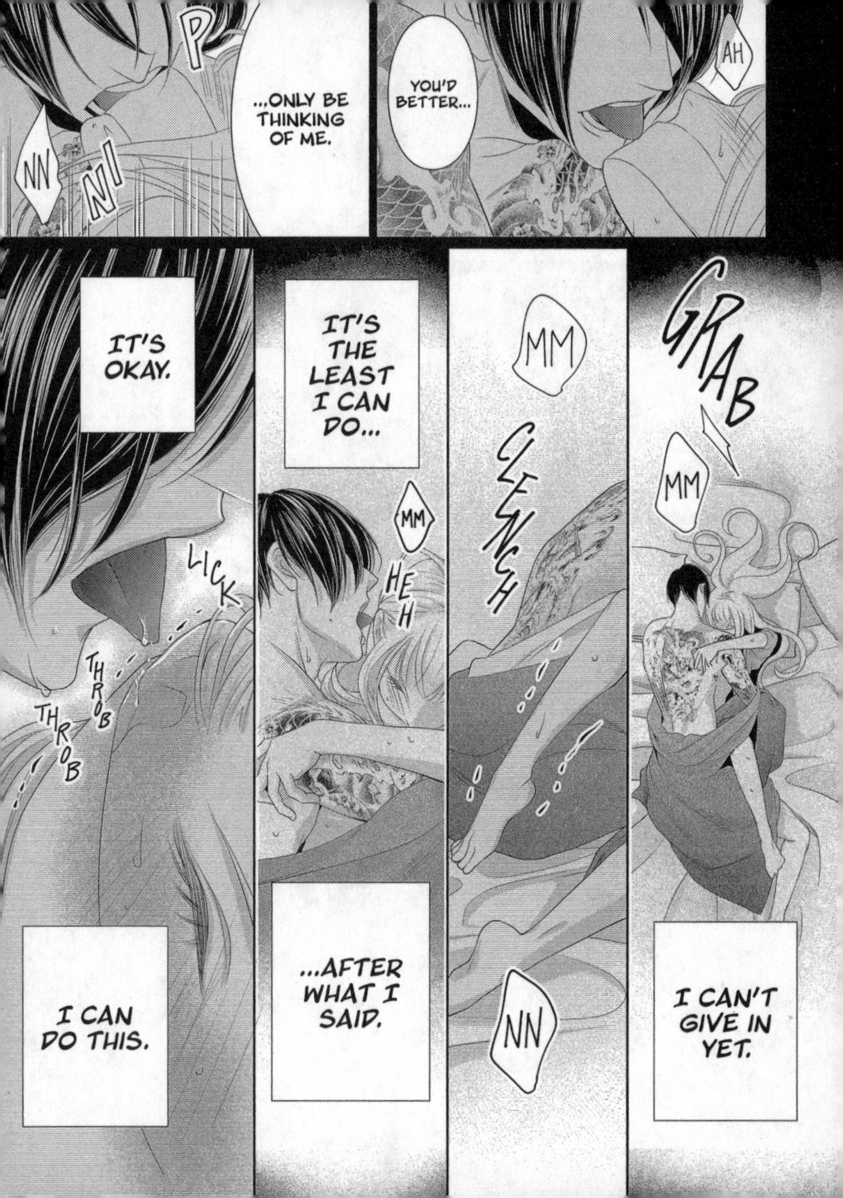
AH
YOU'D BETTER...
...ONLY BE THINKING OF ME.
P
NN
NI
GRAB
MM
I CAN'T GIVE IN YET.
MM
CLENCH
NN
IT'S THE LEAST I CAN DO...
MM
HEH
...AFTER WHAT I SAID.
IT'S OKAY.
LICK
THROB
THROB
I CAN DO THIS.

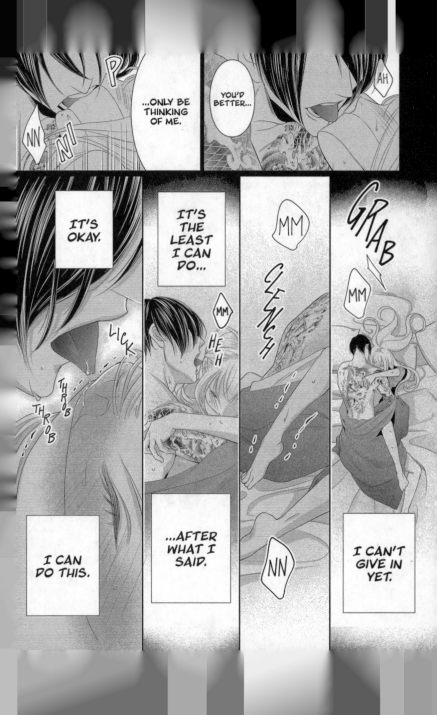

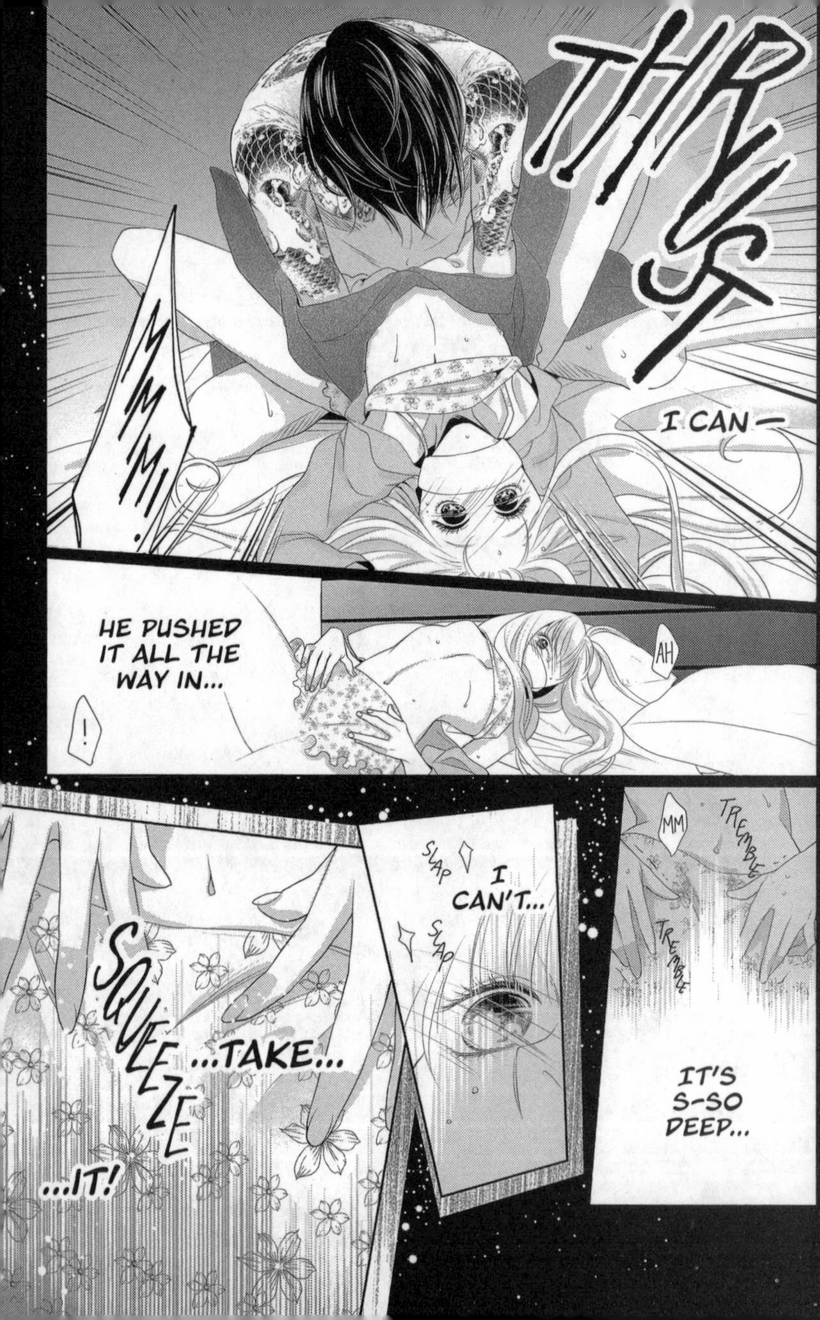
THRUST
I CAN—
MMMM!
AH
HE PUSHED IT ALL THE WAY IN...
!
MM
TREMBLE
TREMBLE
IT'S S-SO DEEP...
SLAP
I CAN'T...
SLAP
...TAKE...
SQUEEZE
...IT!

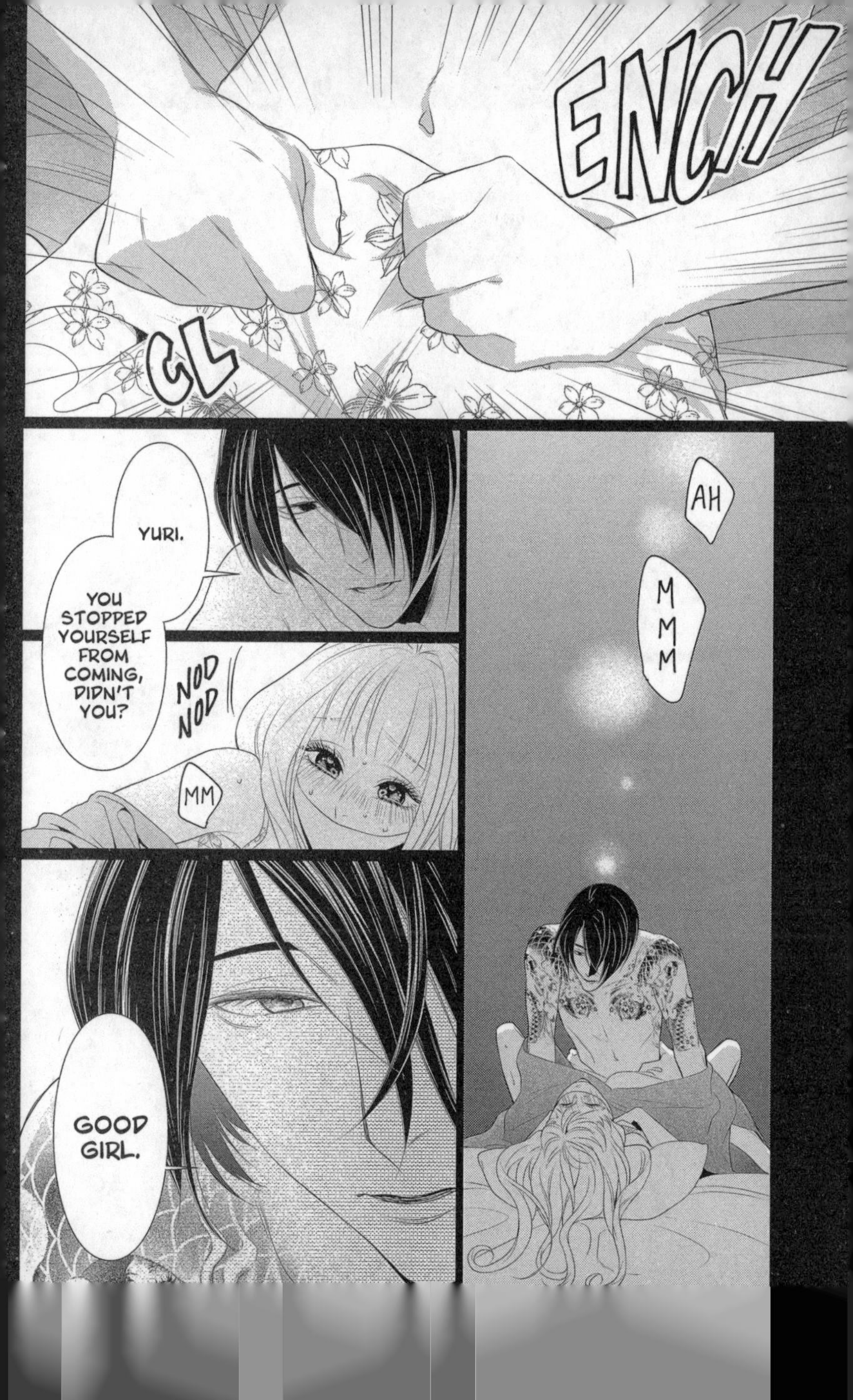
CL
ENCH
AH
MMM
YURI.
YOU STOPPED YOURSELF FROM COMING, DIDN'T YOU?
NOD NOD
MM
GOOD GIRL.

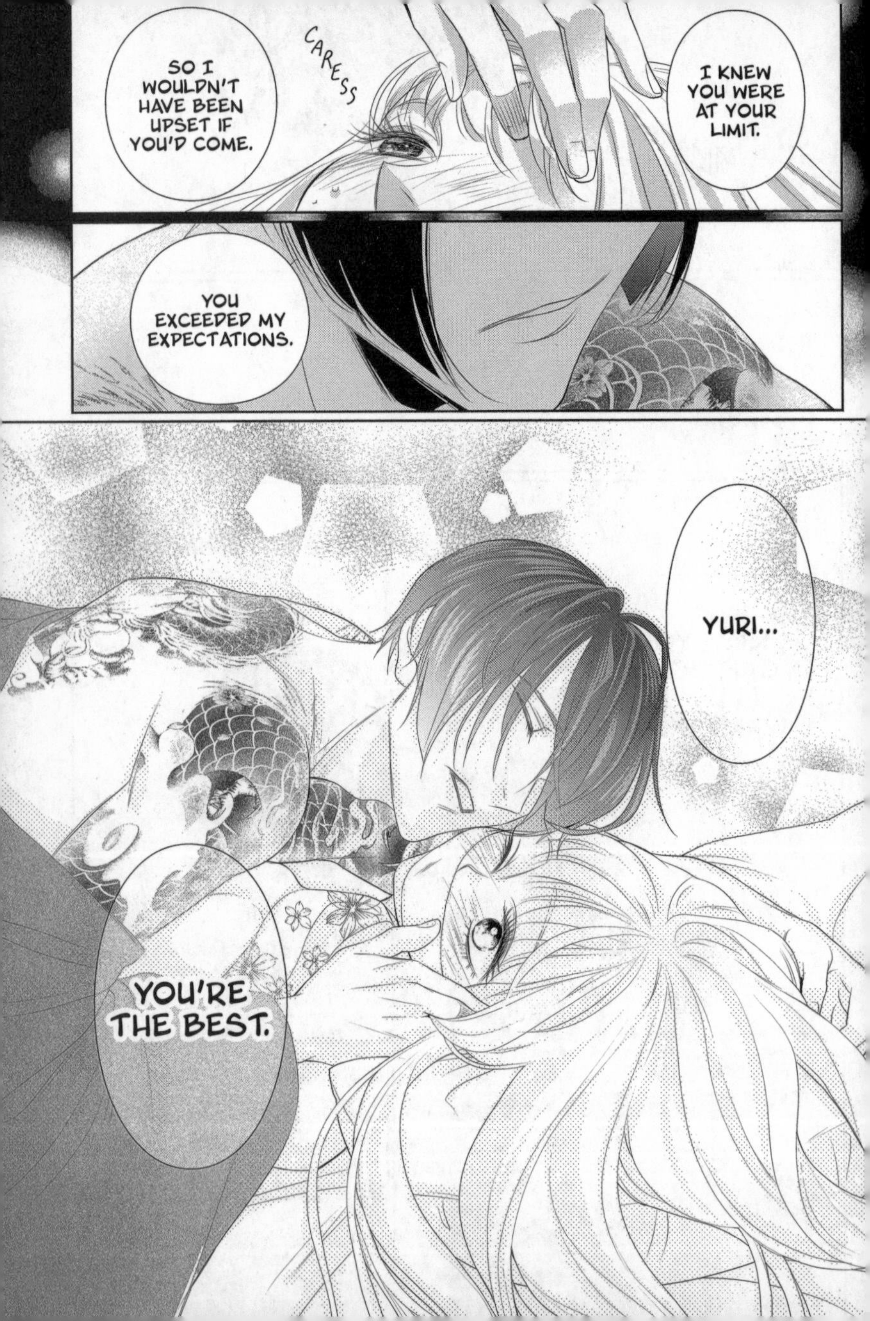
I KNEW YOU WERE AT YOUR LIMIT.
CARESS
SO I WOULDN'T HAVE BEEN UPSET IF YOU'D COME.
YOU EXCEEDED MY EXPECTATIONS.
YURI...
YOU'RE THE BEST.

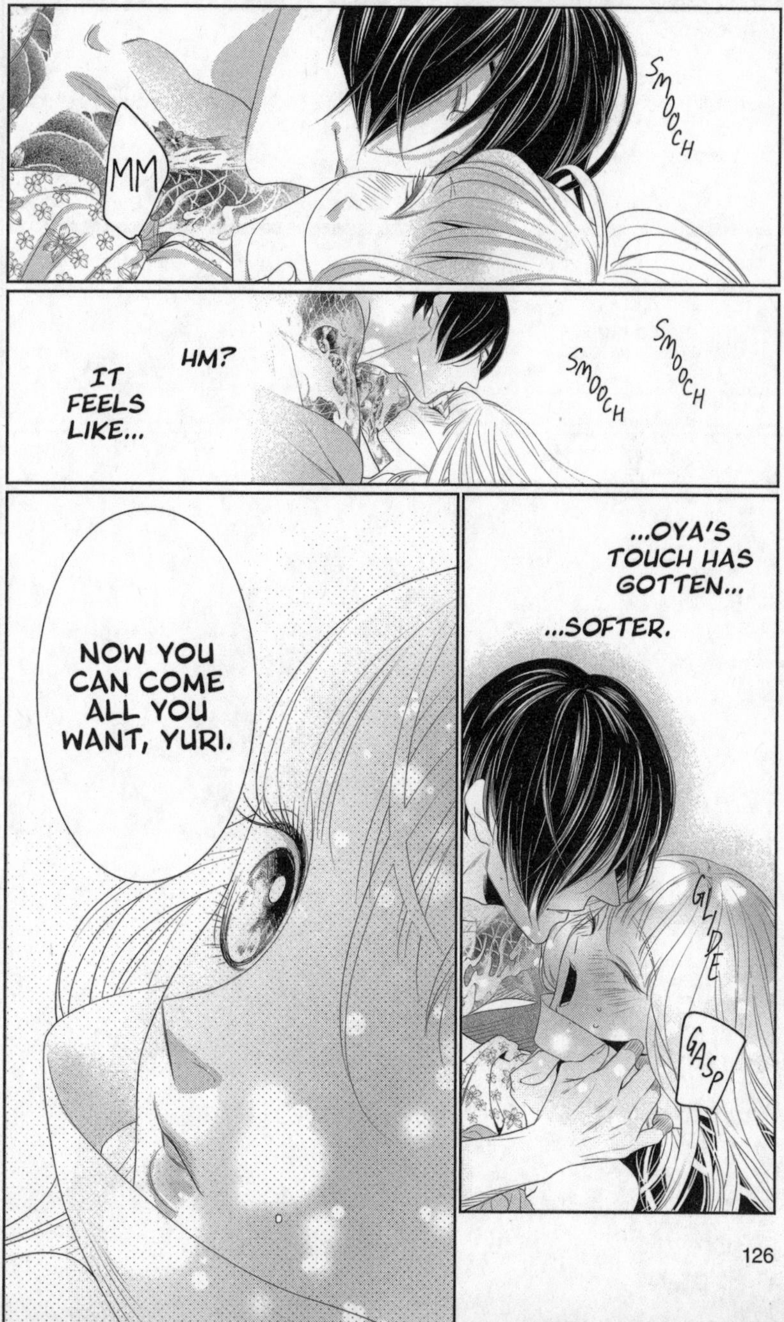
SMOOCH
MM
SMOOCH
SMOOCH
HM?
IT FEELS LIKE...
...OYA'S TOUCH HAS GOTTEN...
...SOFTER.
GLIDE
GASP
NOW YOU CAN COME ALL YOU WANT, YURI.

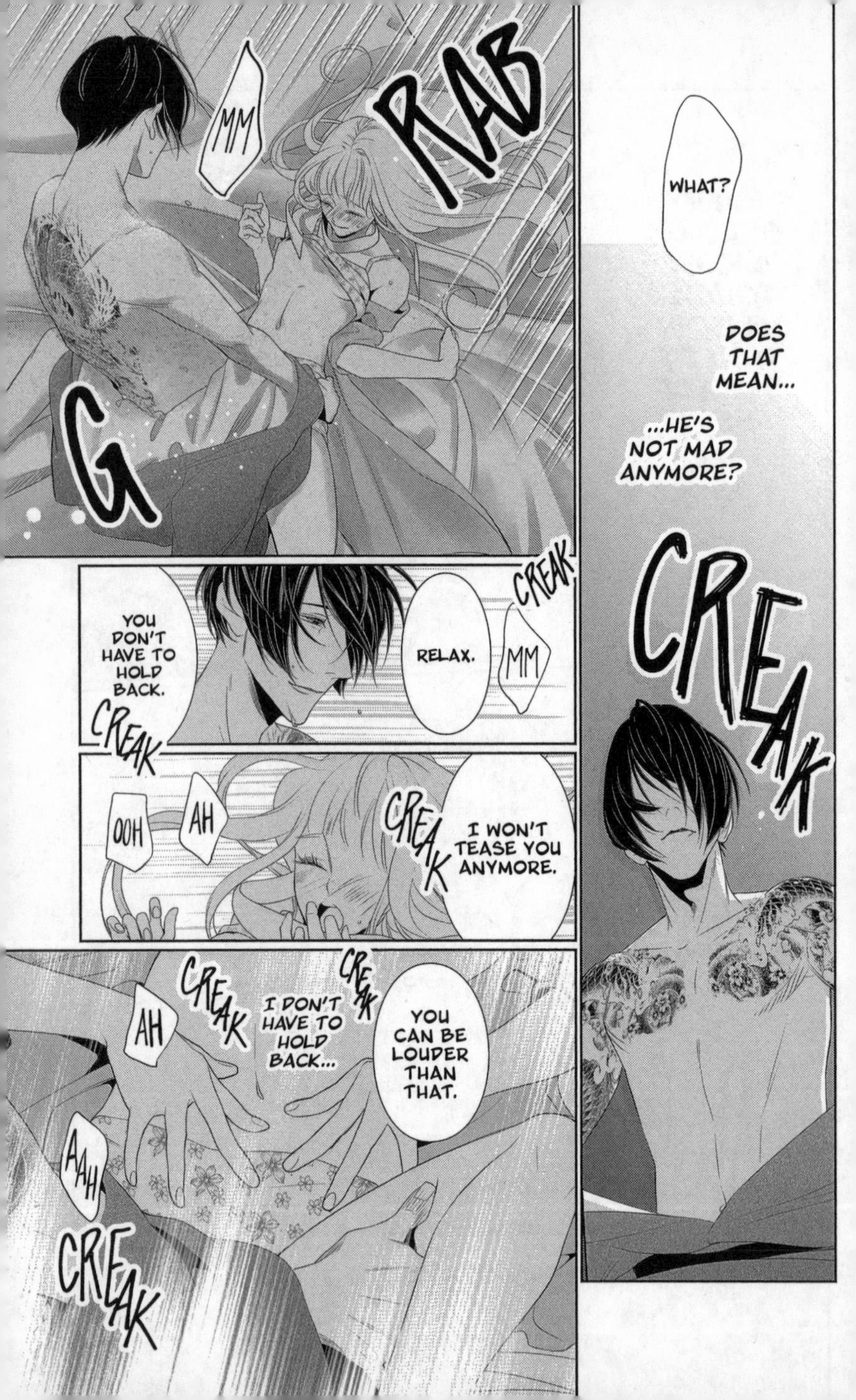

WHAT?
DOES THAT MEAN...
...HE'S NOT MAD ANYMORE?
CREAK
RAB
MM
G
CREAK
MM
RELAX.
YOU DON'T HAVE TO HOLD BACK.
CREAK
I WON'T TEASE YOU ANYMORE.
CREAK
AH
OOH
CREAK
YOU CAN BE LOUDER THAN THAT.
I DON'T HAVE TO HOLD BACK...
CREAK
AH
AAH
CREAK

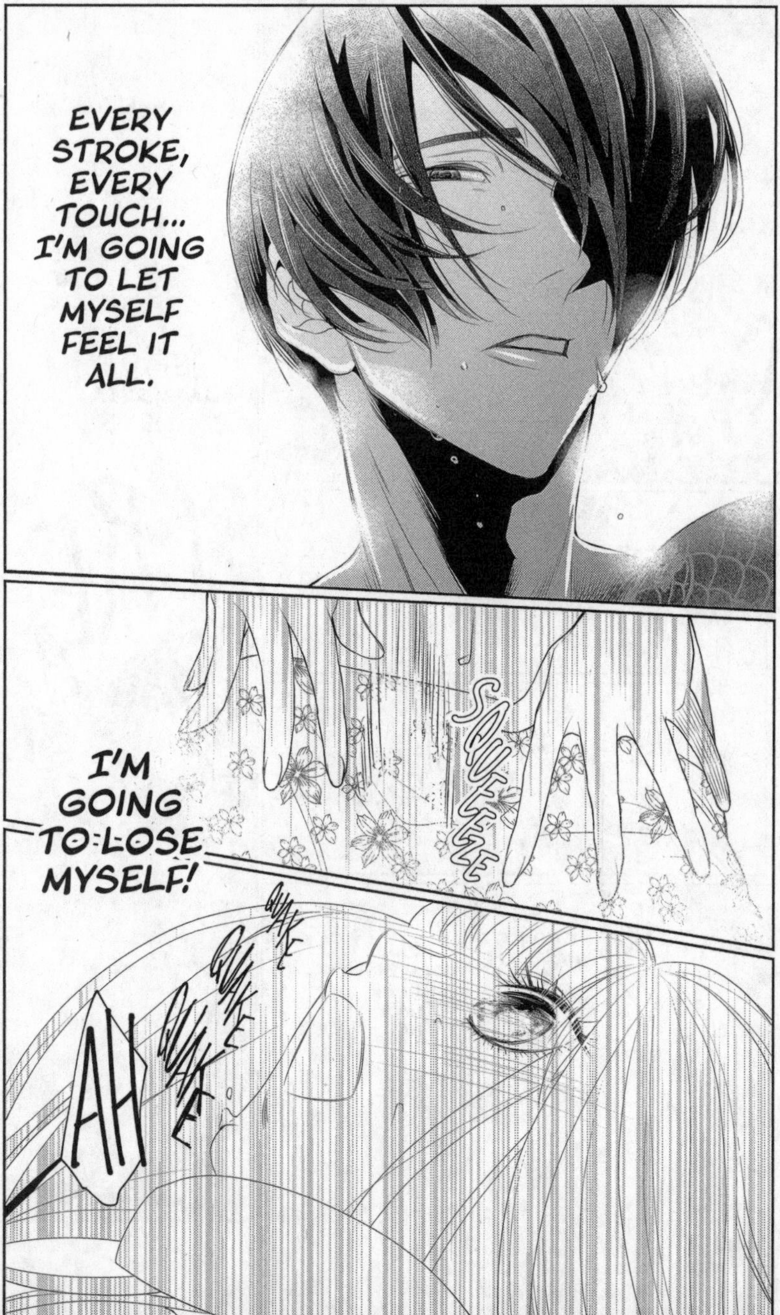
EVERY STROKE, EVERY TOUCH... I'M GOING TO LET MYSELF FEEL IT ALL.
SQUEEZE
I'M GOING TO LOSE MYSELF!
QUAKE
QUAKE
QUAKE
AH

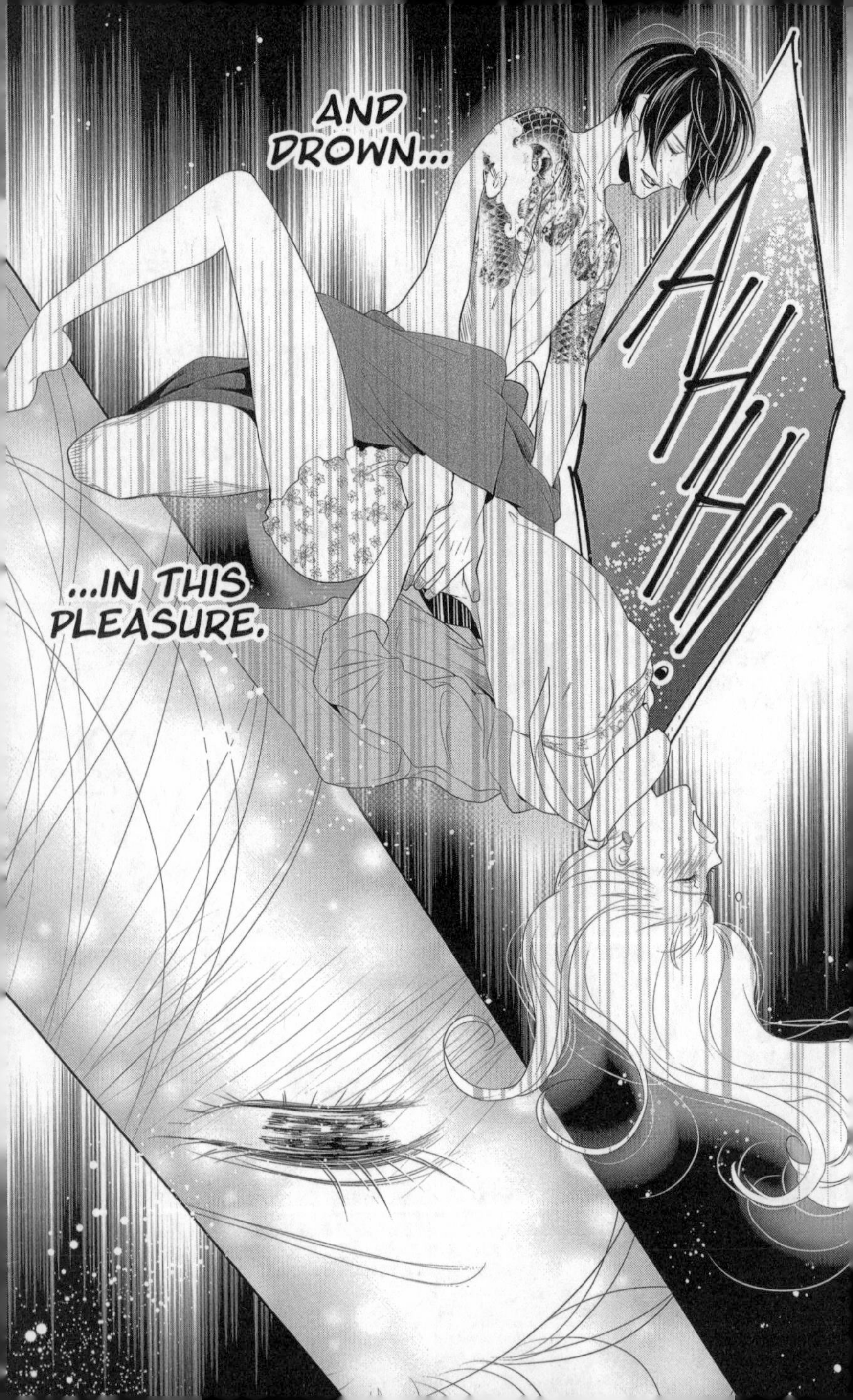
AND DROWN...
AAHH!
...IN THIS PLEASURE.

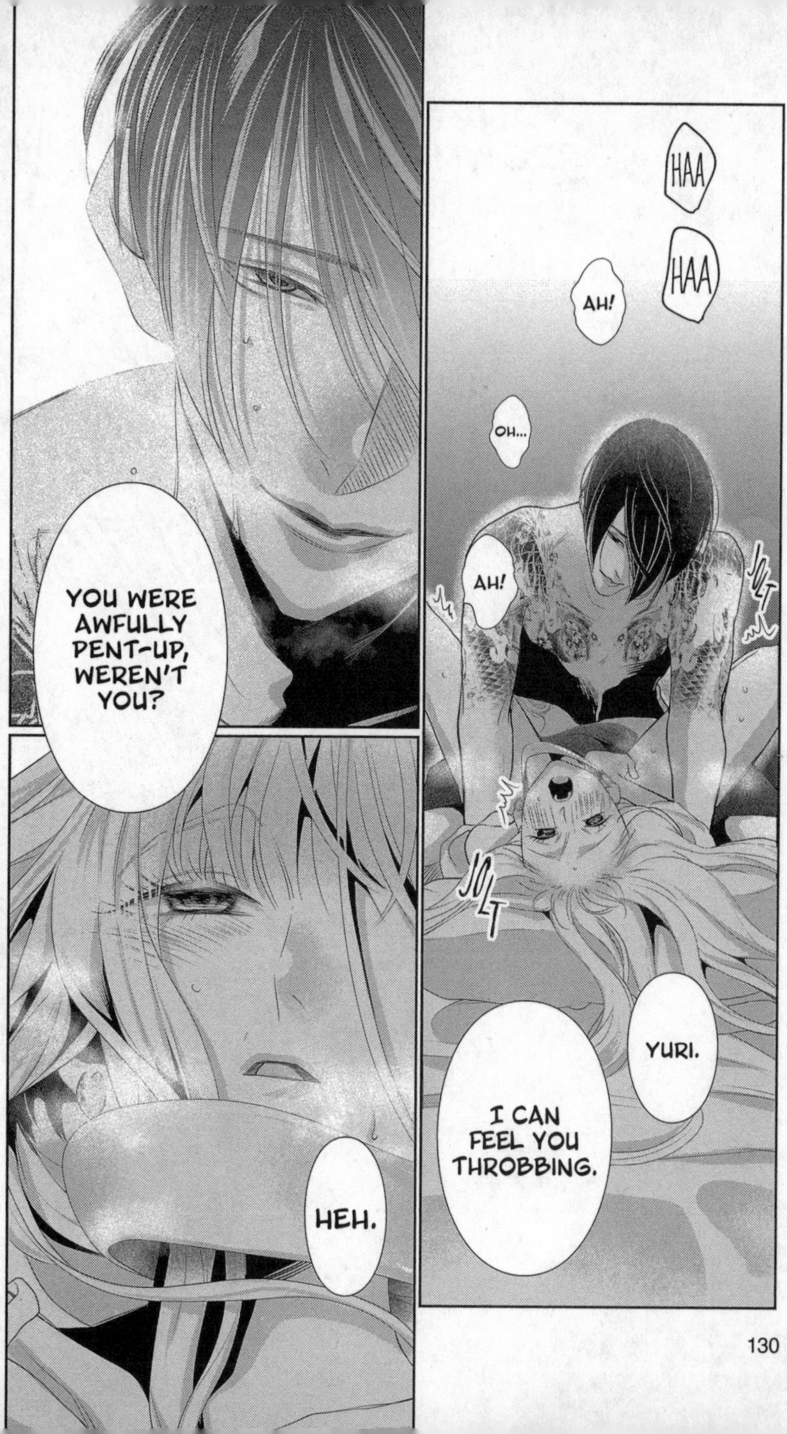
HAA
HAA
AH!
OH...
AH!
JOLT
JOLT
YURI.
I CAN FEEL YOU THROBBING.
YOU WERE AWFULLY PENT-UP, WEREN'T YOU?
HEH.

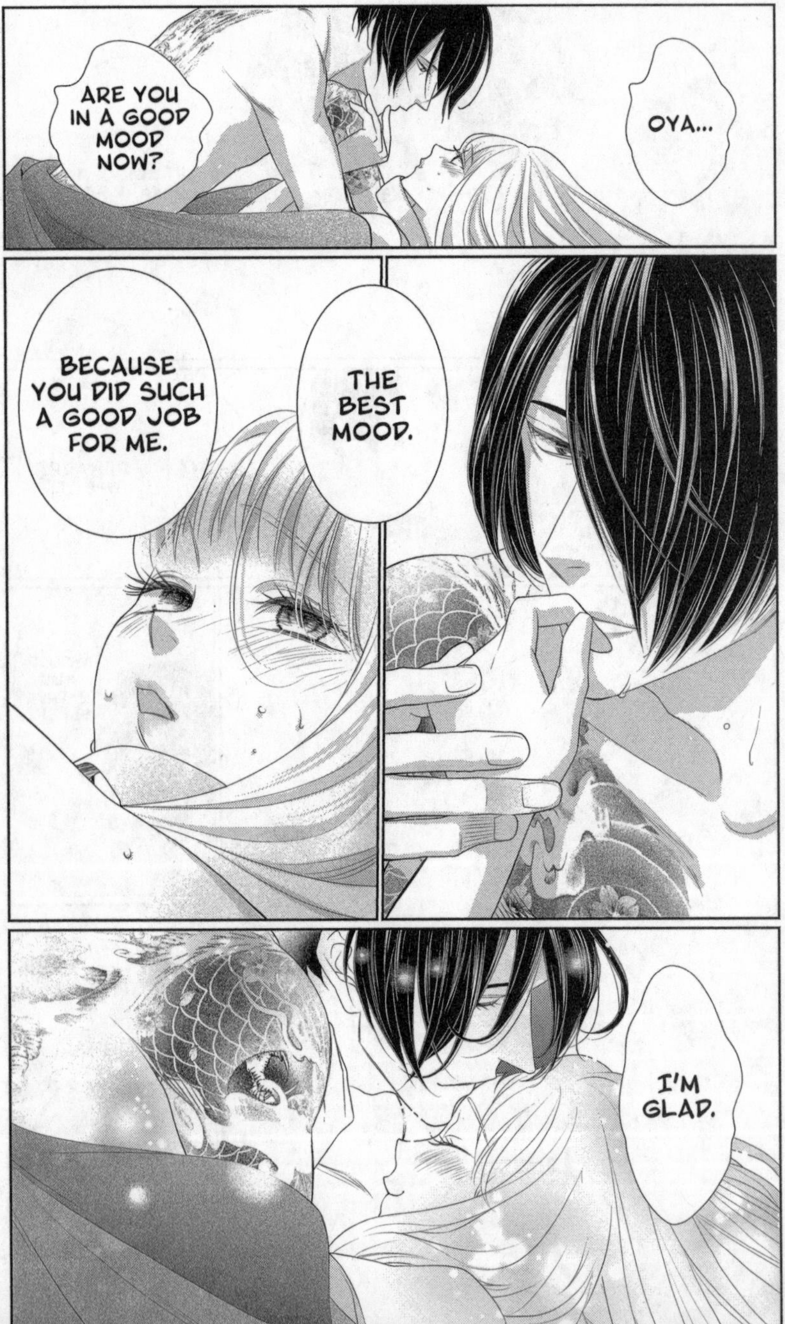
OYA...
ARE YOU IN A GOOD MOOD NOW?
THE BEST MOOD.
BECAUSE YOU DID SUCH A GOOD JOB FOR ME.
I'M GLAD.

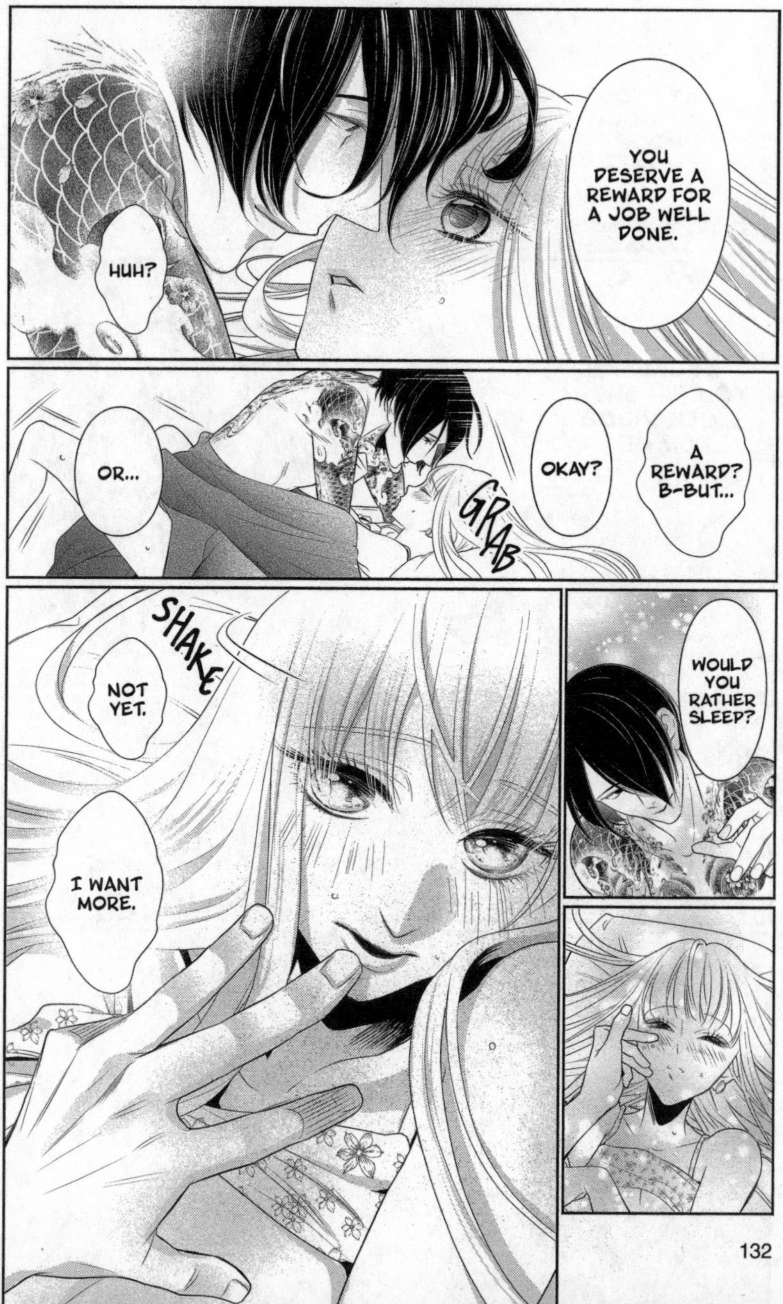
YOU DESERVE A REWARD FOR A JOB WELL DONE.
HUH?
A REWARD? B-BUT...
OKAY?
GRAB
OR...
WOULD YOU RATHER SLEEP?
SHAKE
NOT YET.
I WANT MORE.

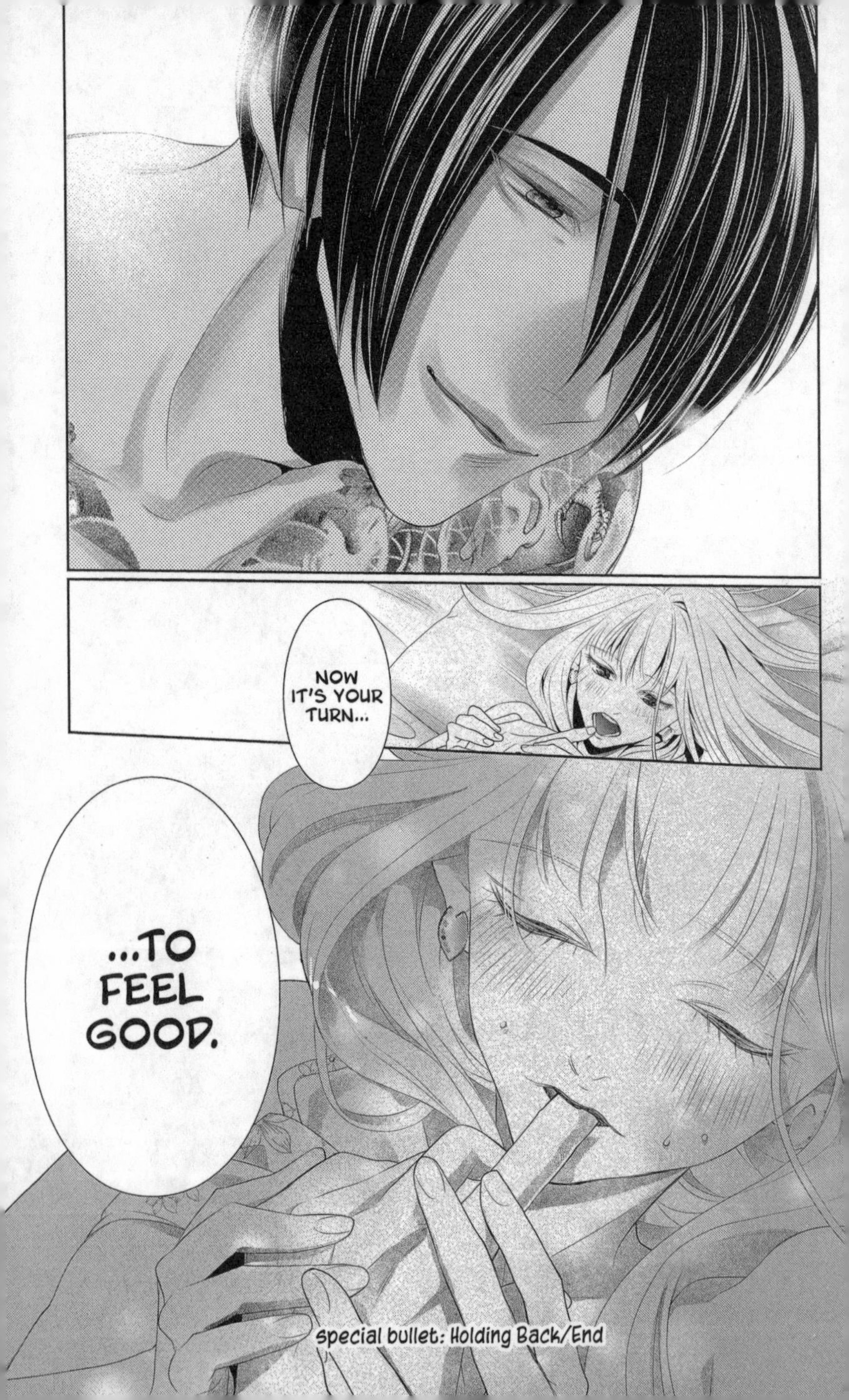
NOW IT'S YOUR TURN...
...TO FEEL GOOD.
Special bullet: Holding Back/End

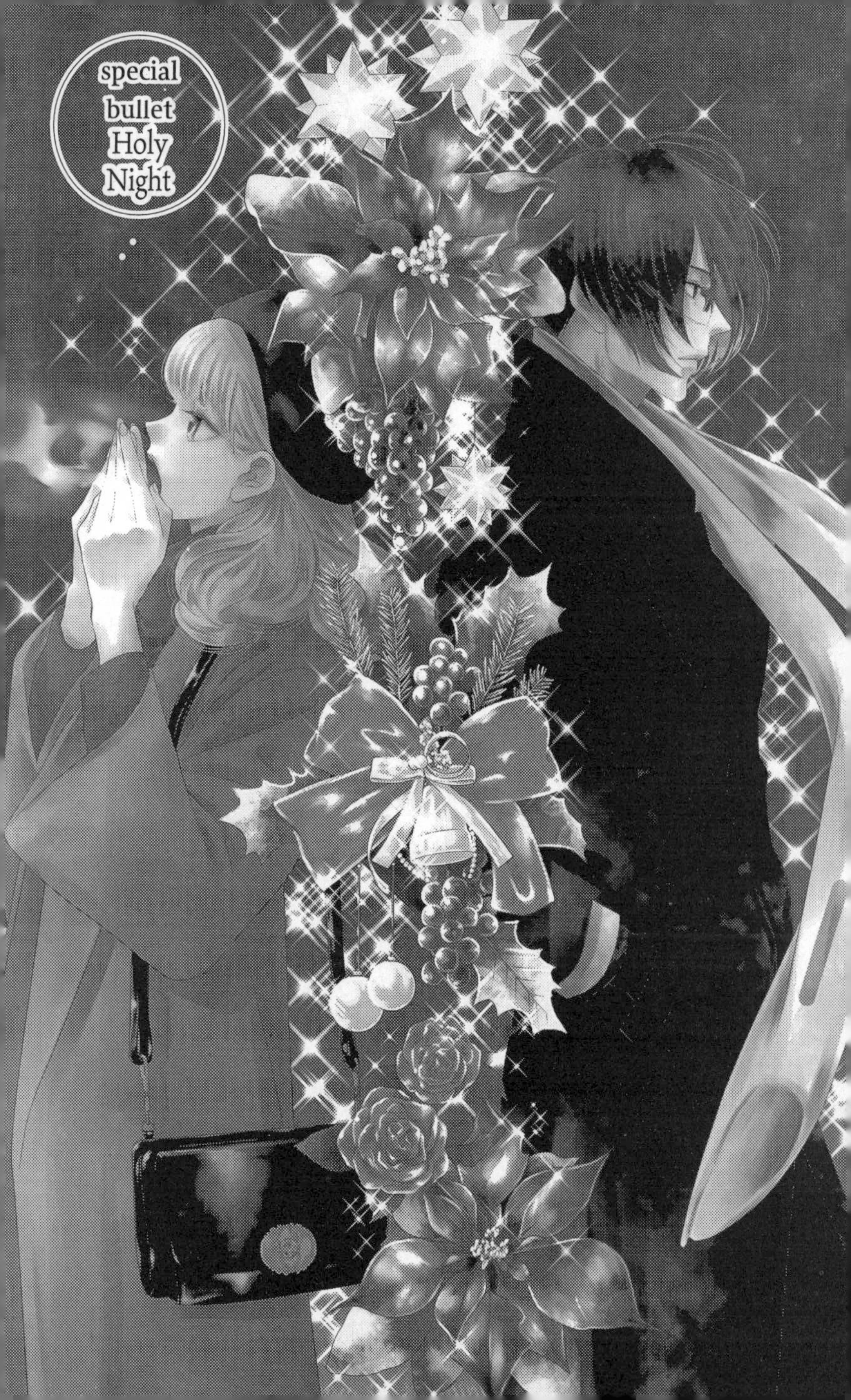
special bullet Holy Night

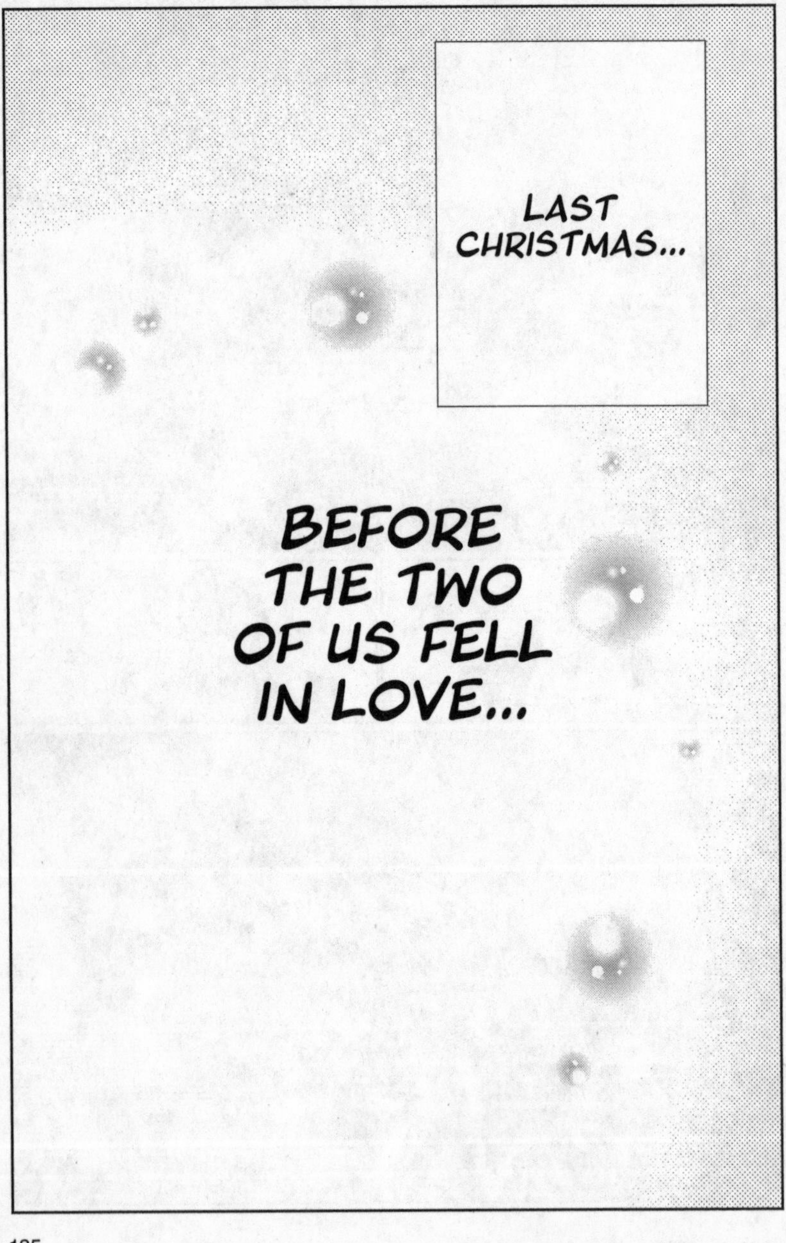
LAST CHRISTMAS...
BEFORE THE TWO OF US FELL IN LOVE...

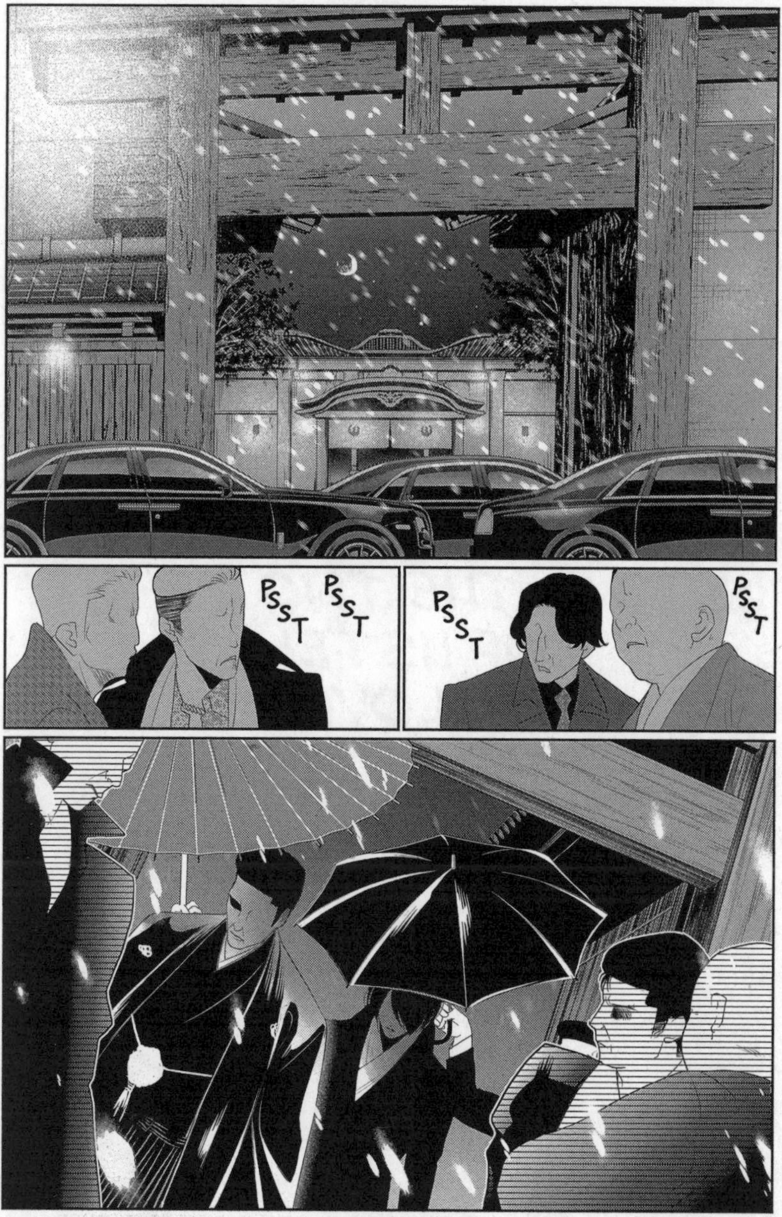
PSSST
PSSST
PSSST
PSSST

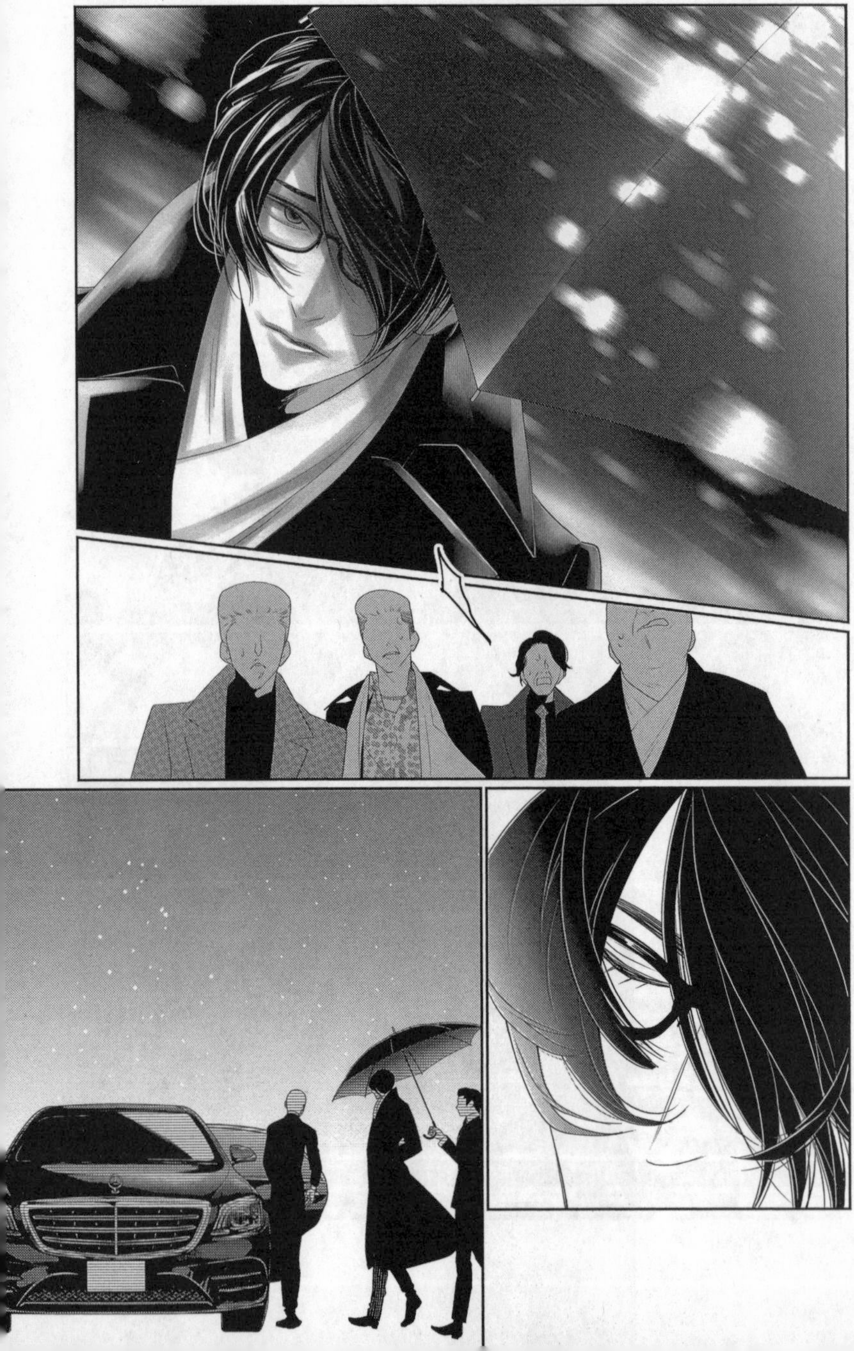

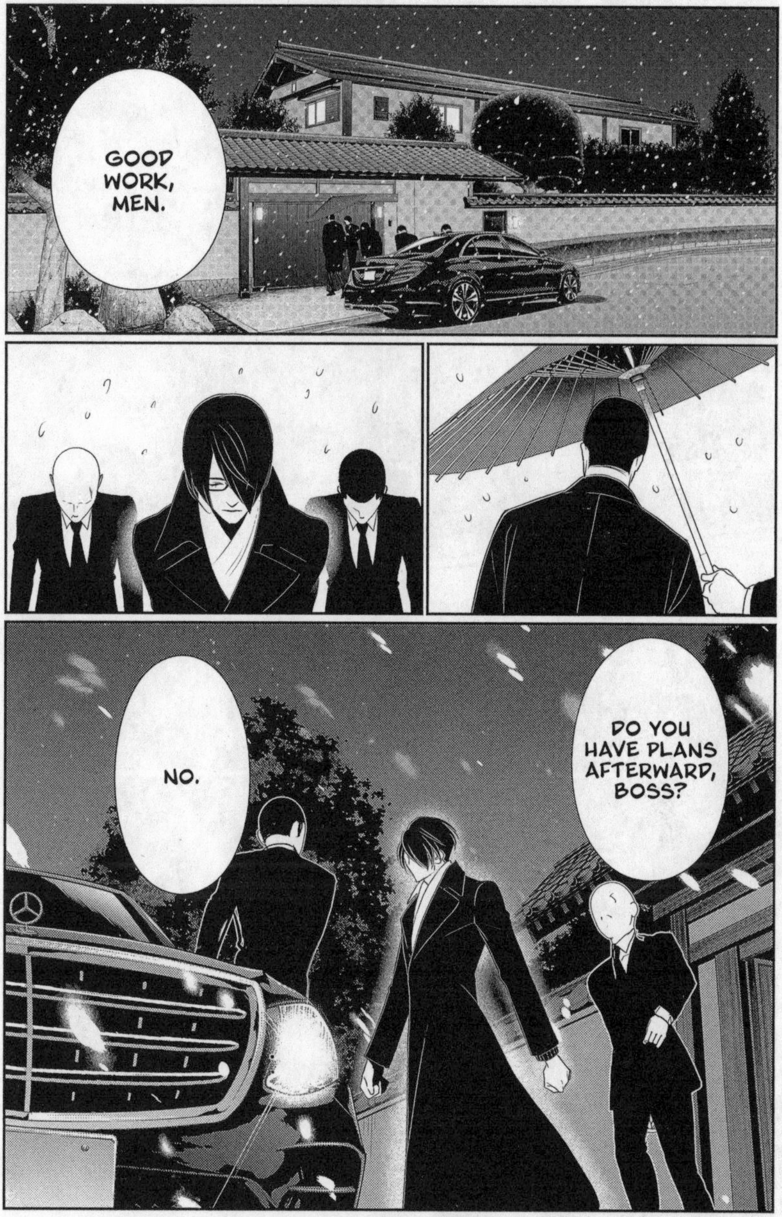
GOOD WORK, MEN.
DO YOU HAVE PLANS AFTERWARD, BOSS?
NO.

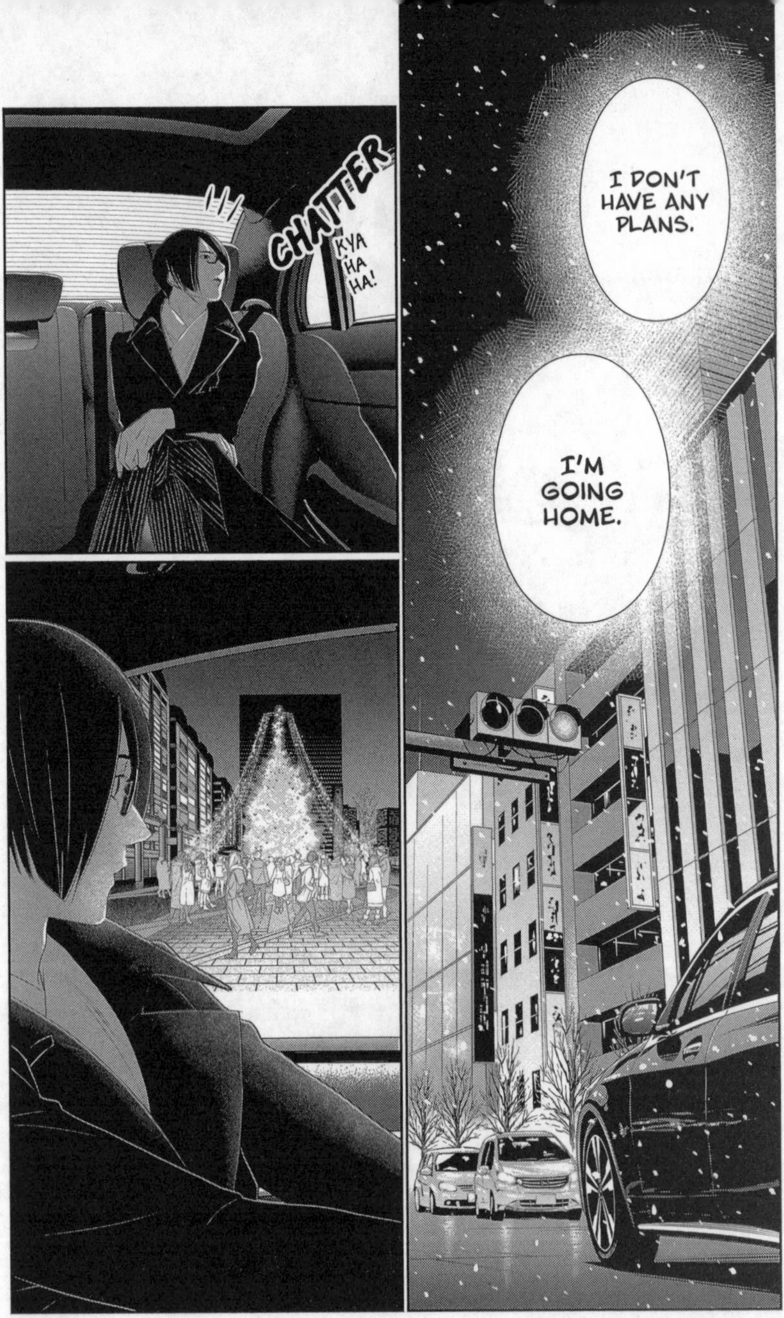
I DON'T HAVE ANY PLANS.
I'M GOING HOME.
CHATTER
KYA HA HA!

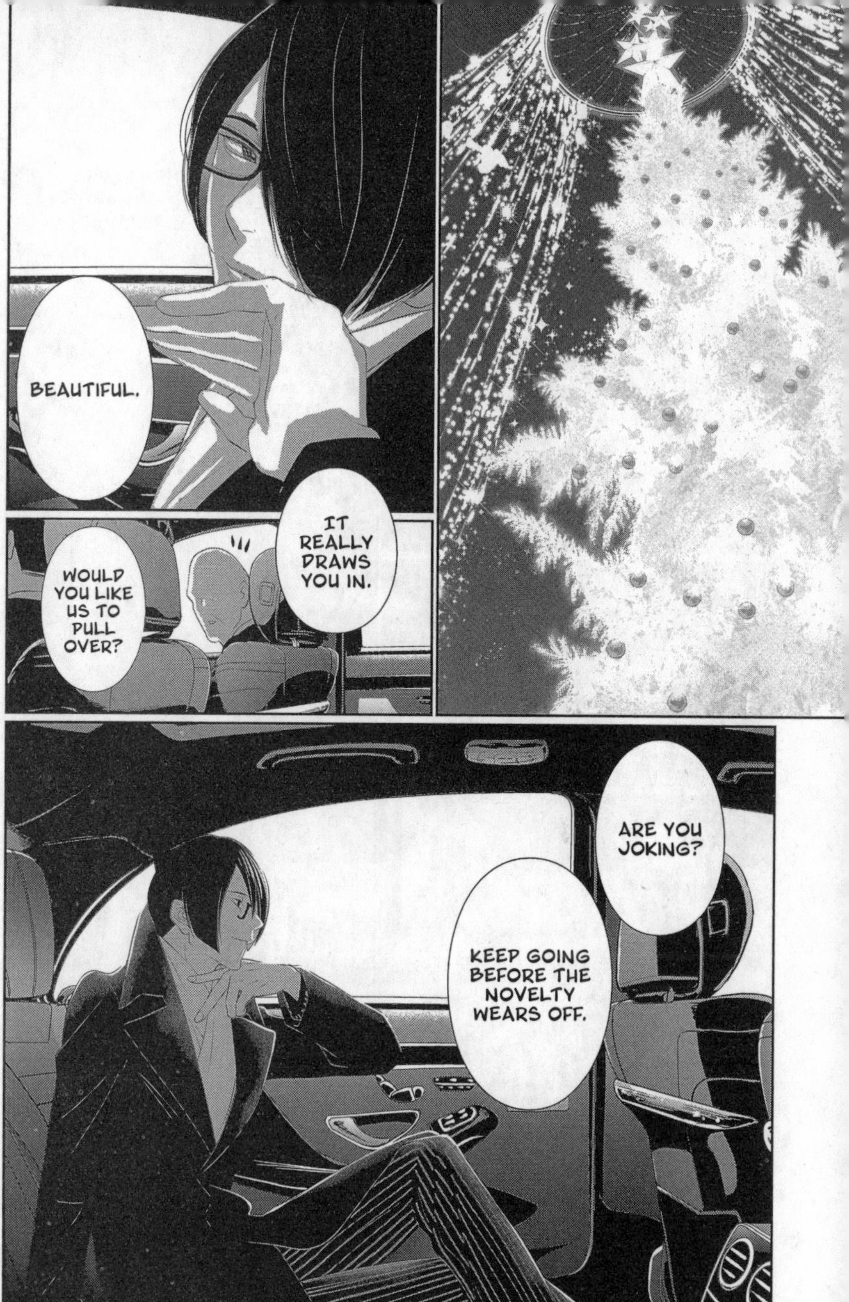
BEAUTIFUL.
IT REALLY DRAWS YOU IN.
WOULD YOU LIKE US TO PULL OVER?
ARE YOU JOKING?
KEEP GOING BEFORE THE NOVELTY WEARS OFF.

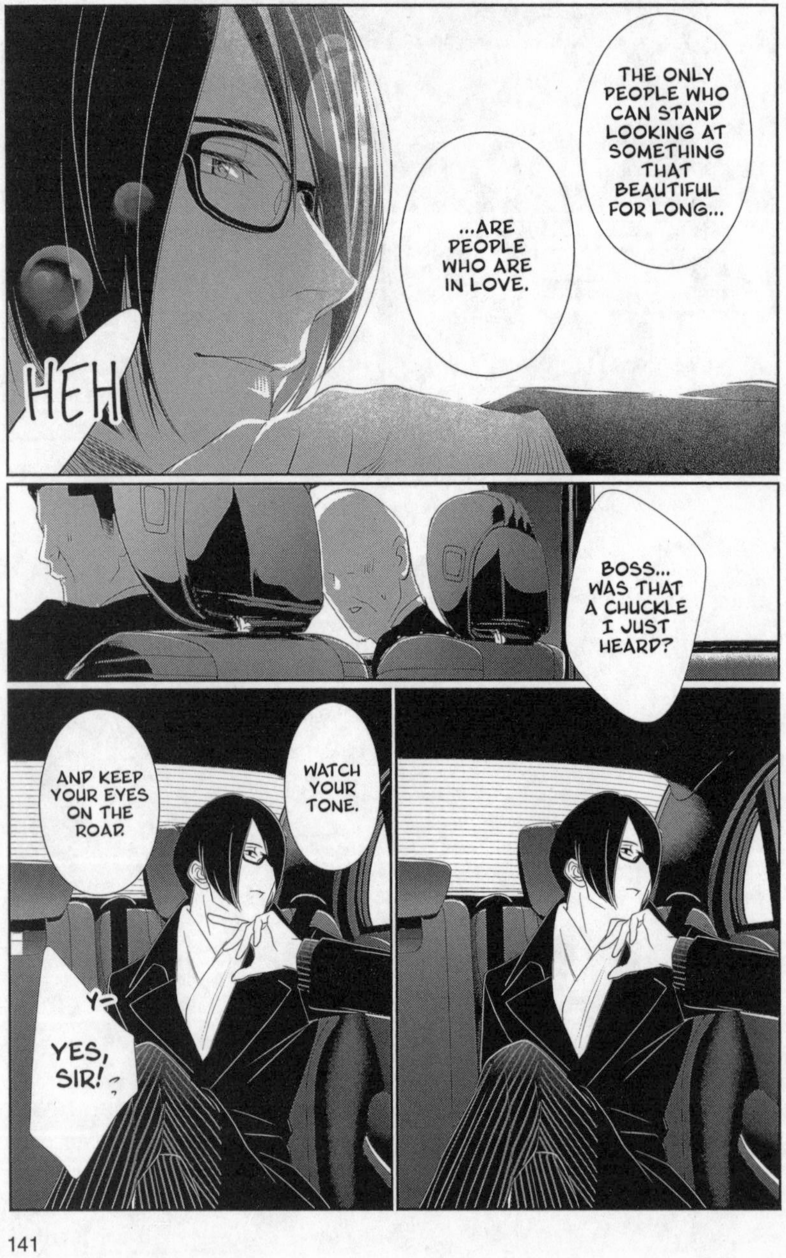
THE ONLY PEOPLE WHO CAN STAND LOOKING AT SOMETHING THAT BEAUTIFUL FOR LONG...
...ARE PEOPLE WHO ARE IN LOVE.
HEH
BOSS... WAS THAT A CHUCKLE I JUST HEARD?
WATCH YOUR TONE.
AND KEEP YOUR EYES ON THE ROAD.
Y-
YES, SIR!

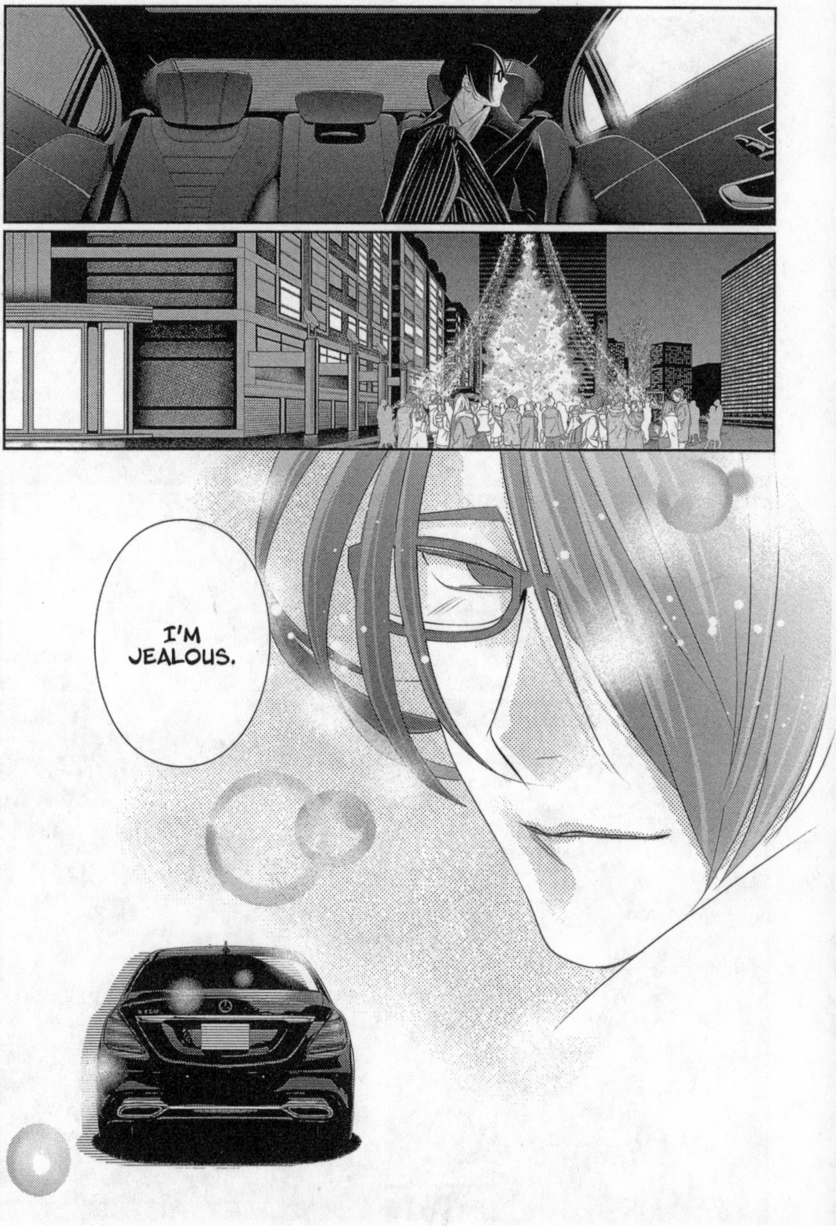
I'M JEALOUS.

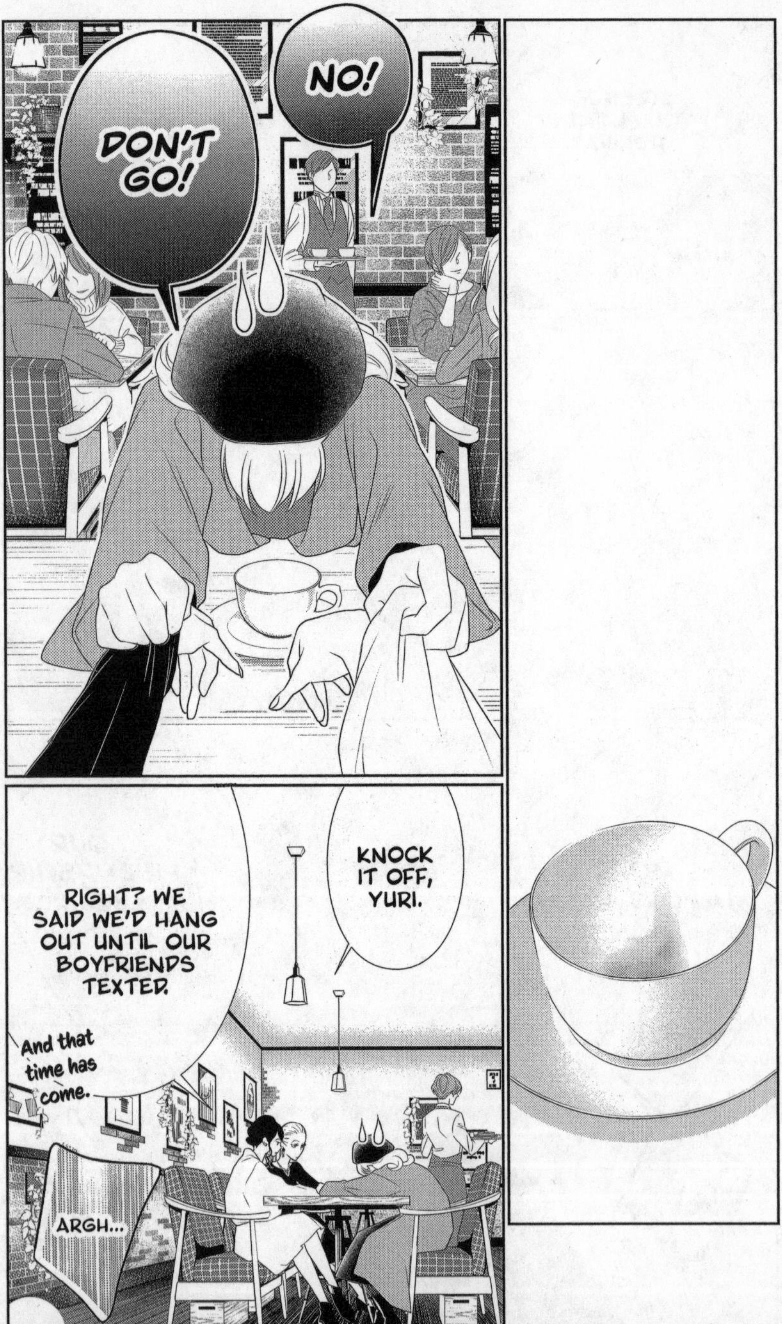
NO!
DON'T GO!
KNOCK IT OFF, YURI.
RIGHT? WE SAID WE'D HANG OUT UNTIL OUR BOYFRIENDS TEXTED.
And that time has come.
ARGH...

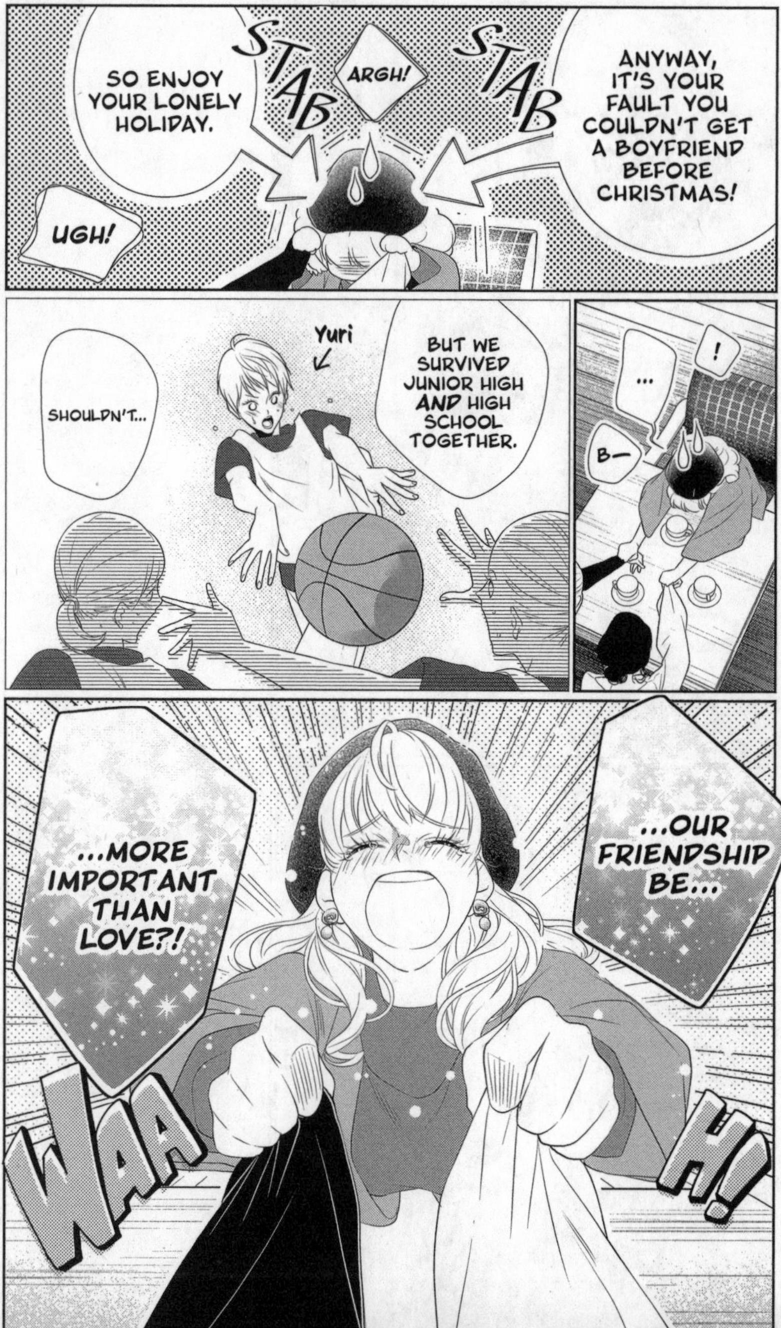
ANYWAY, IT'S YOUR FAULT YOU COULDN'T GET A BOYFRIEND BEFORE CHRISTMAS!
STAB
ARGH!
STAB
SO ENJOY YOUR LONELY HOLIDAY.
UGH!
!
...
B—
BUT WE SURVIVED JUNIOR HIGH AND HIGH SCHOOL TOGETHER.
Yuri
SHOULDN'T...
...OUR FRIENDSHIP BE...
...MORE IMPORTANT THAN LOVE?!
WAAH!

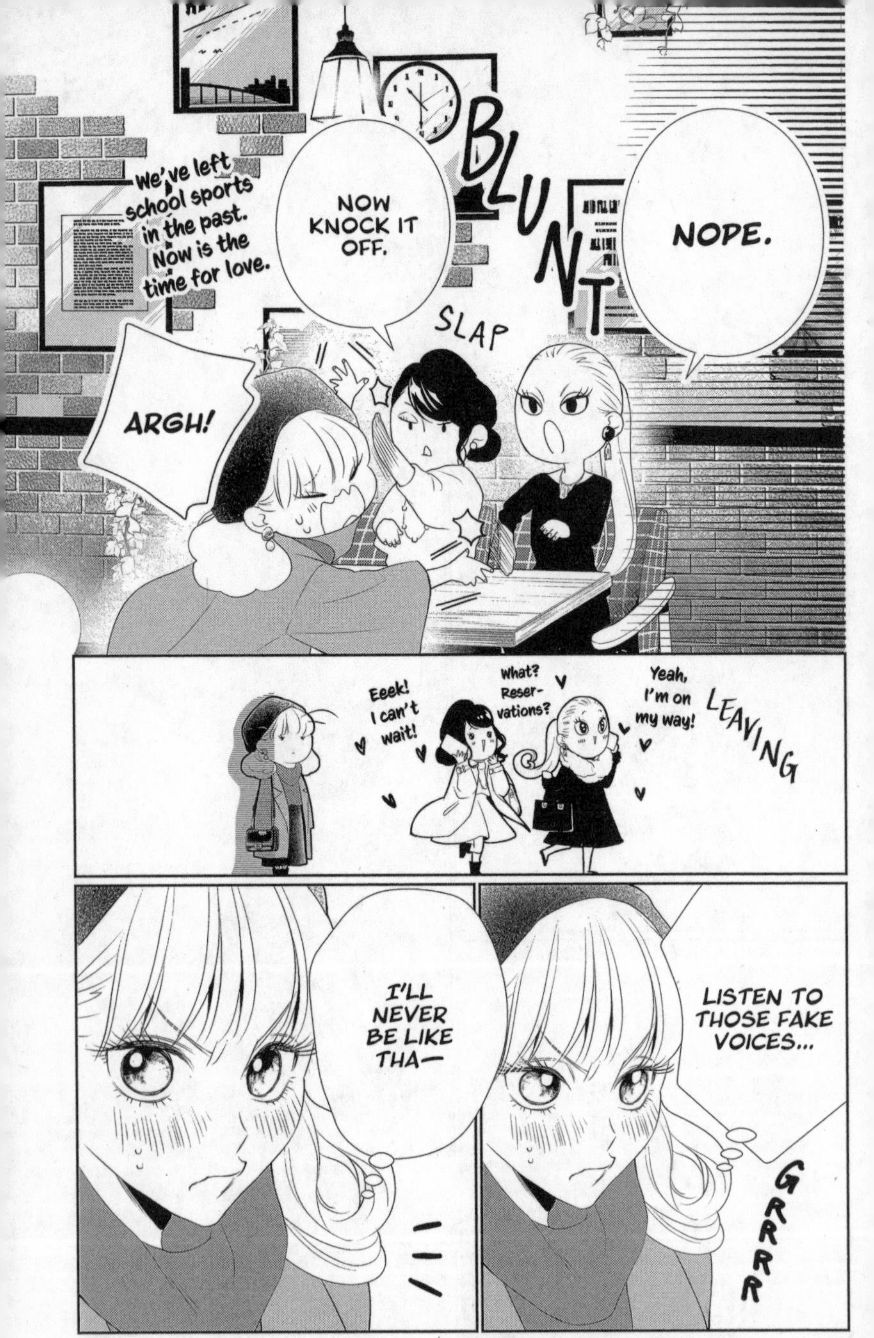
NOPE.
BLUNT
NOW KNOCK IT OFF.
SLAP
We've left school sports in the past. Now is the time for love.
ARGH!
LEAVING
Yeah, I'm on my way!
What? Reser-vations?
Eeek! I can't wait!
LISTEN TO THOSE FAKE VOICES...
GRRRR
I'LL NEVER BE LIKE THA—

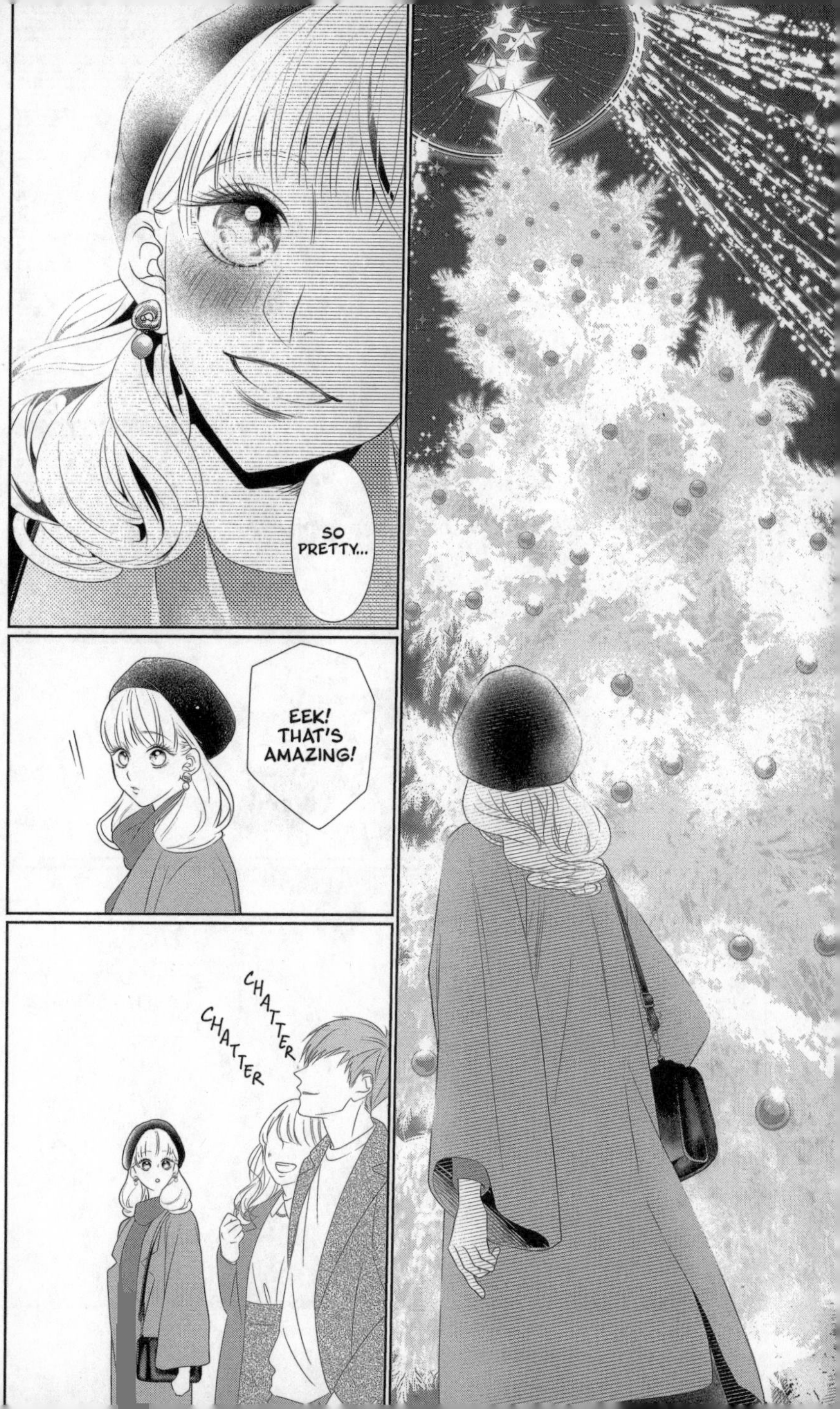
SO PRETTY...
EEK! THAT'S AMAZING!
CHATTER
CHATTER

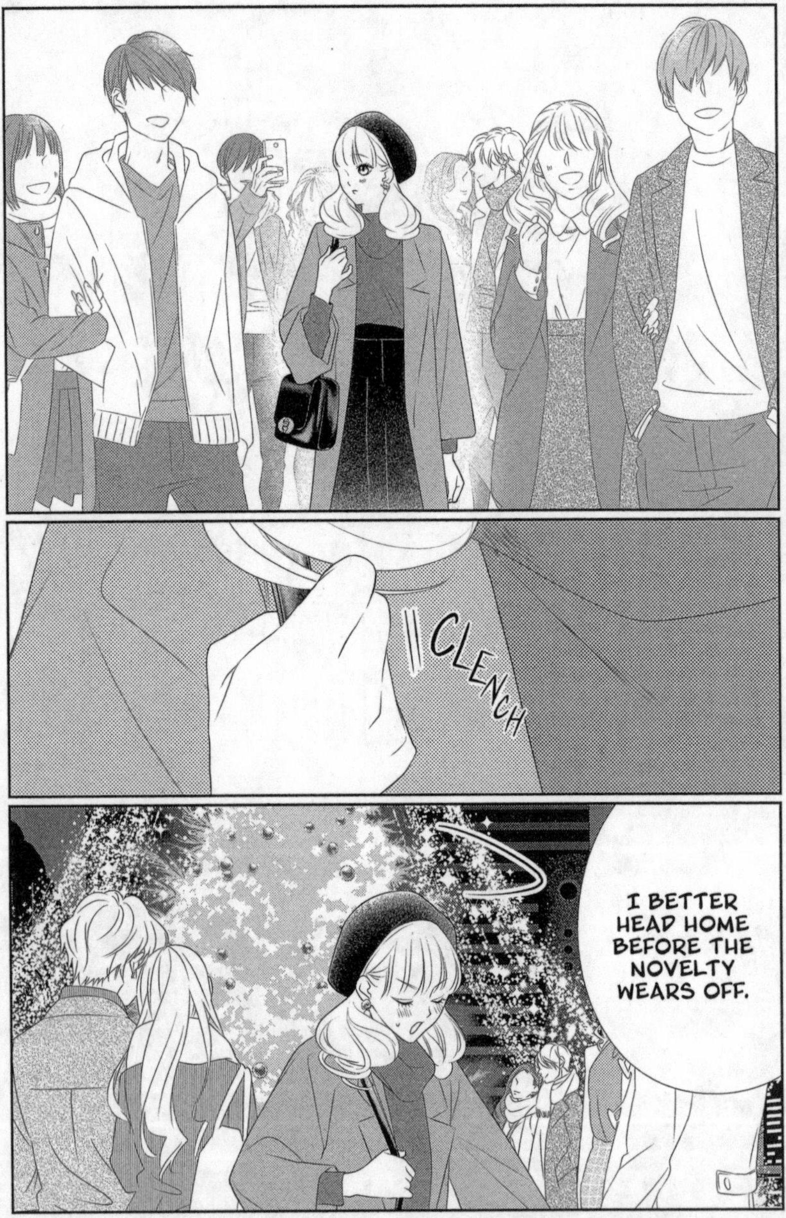
CLENCH
I BETTER HEAD HOME BEFORE THE NOVELTY WEARS OFF.

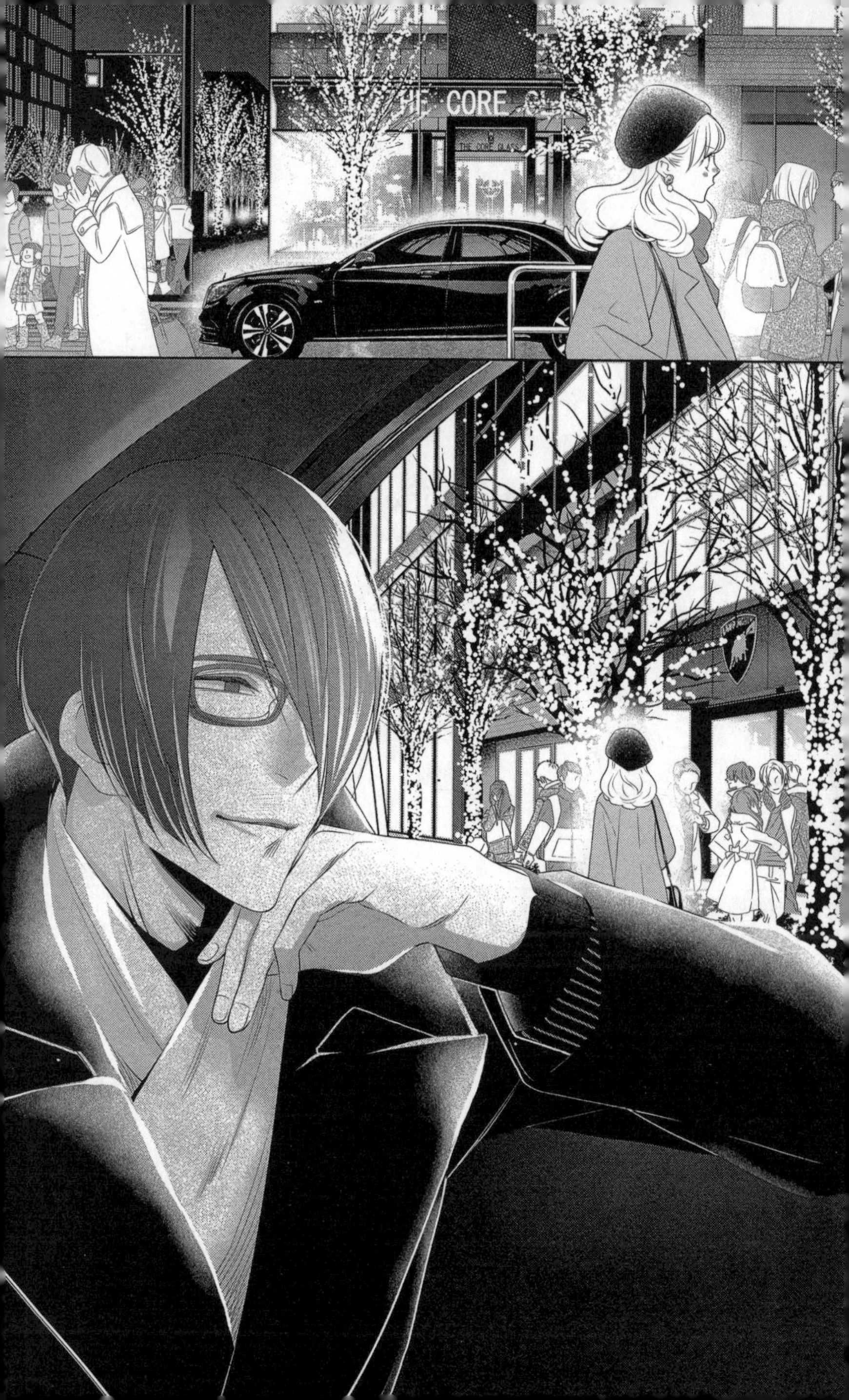
HE CORE

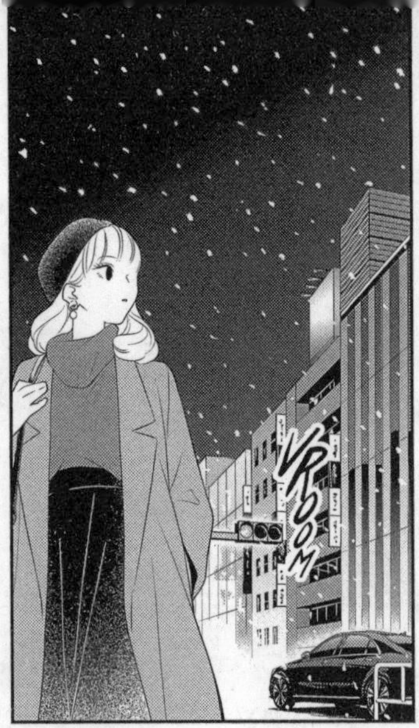
VROOM
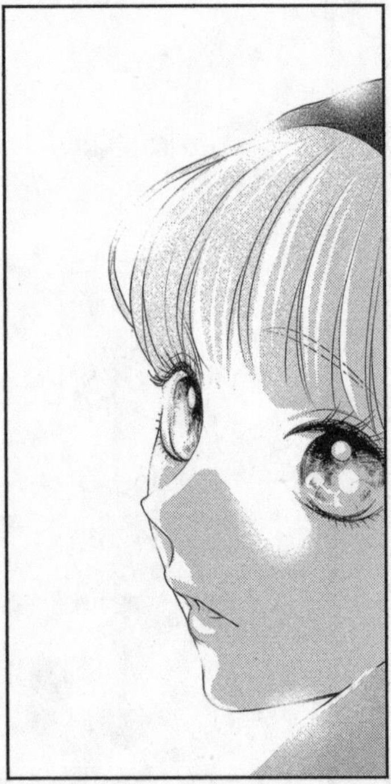
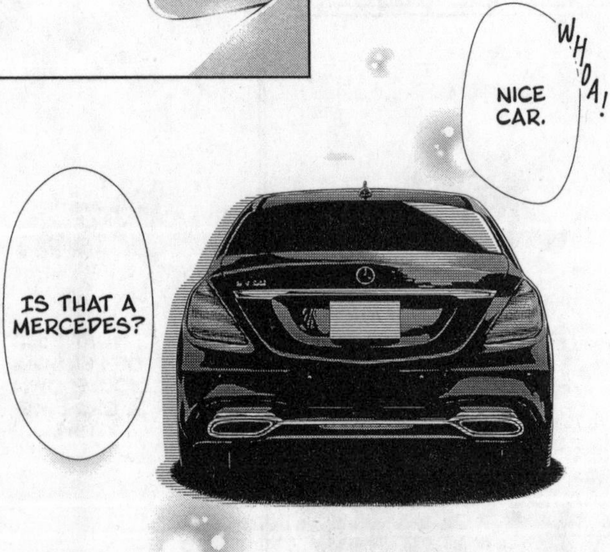
WHOA!
NICE CAR.
IS THAT A MERCEDES?

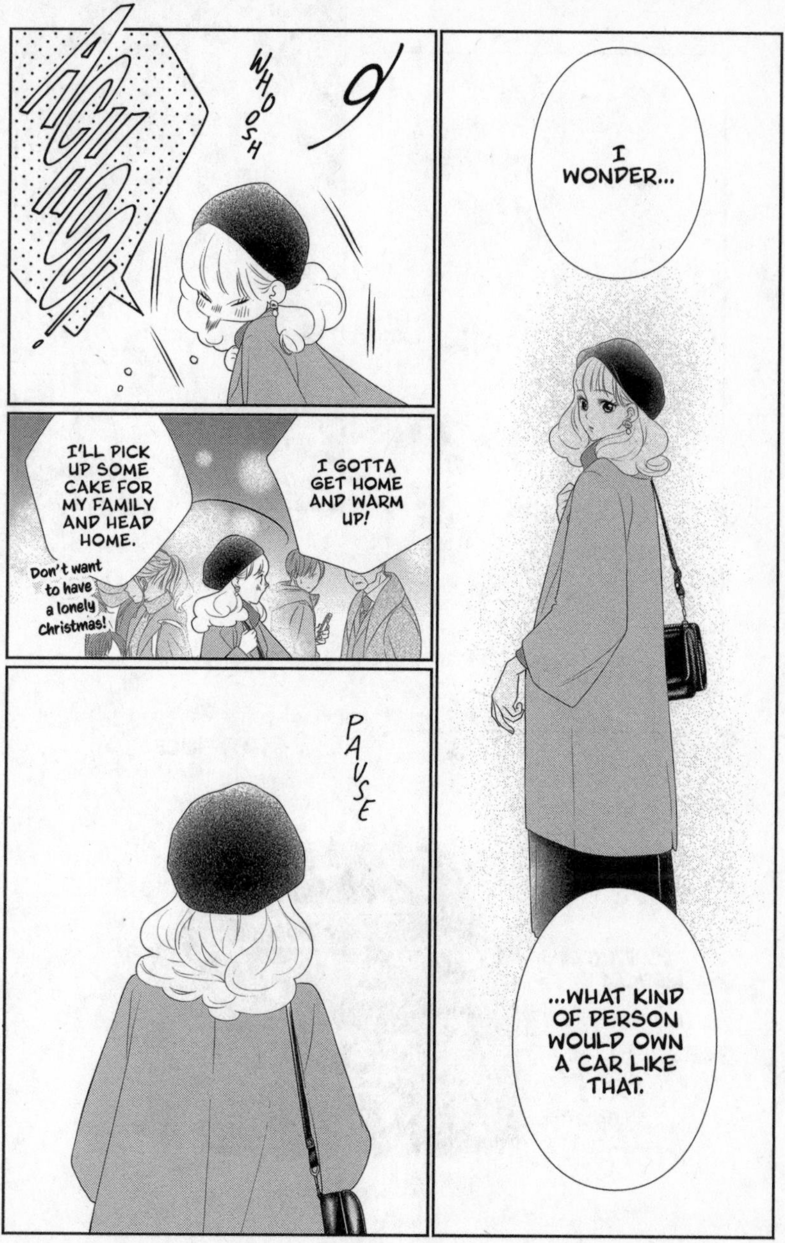
I WONDER...
...WHAT KIND OF PERSON WOULD OWN A CAR LIKE THAT.
WHOOSH
ACHOO!
I GOTTA GET HOME AND WARM UP!
I'LL PICK UP SOME CAKE FOR MY FAMILY AND HEAD HOME.
Don't want to have a lonely Christmas!
PAUSE

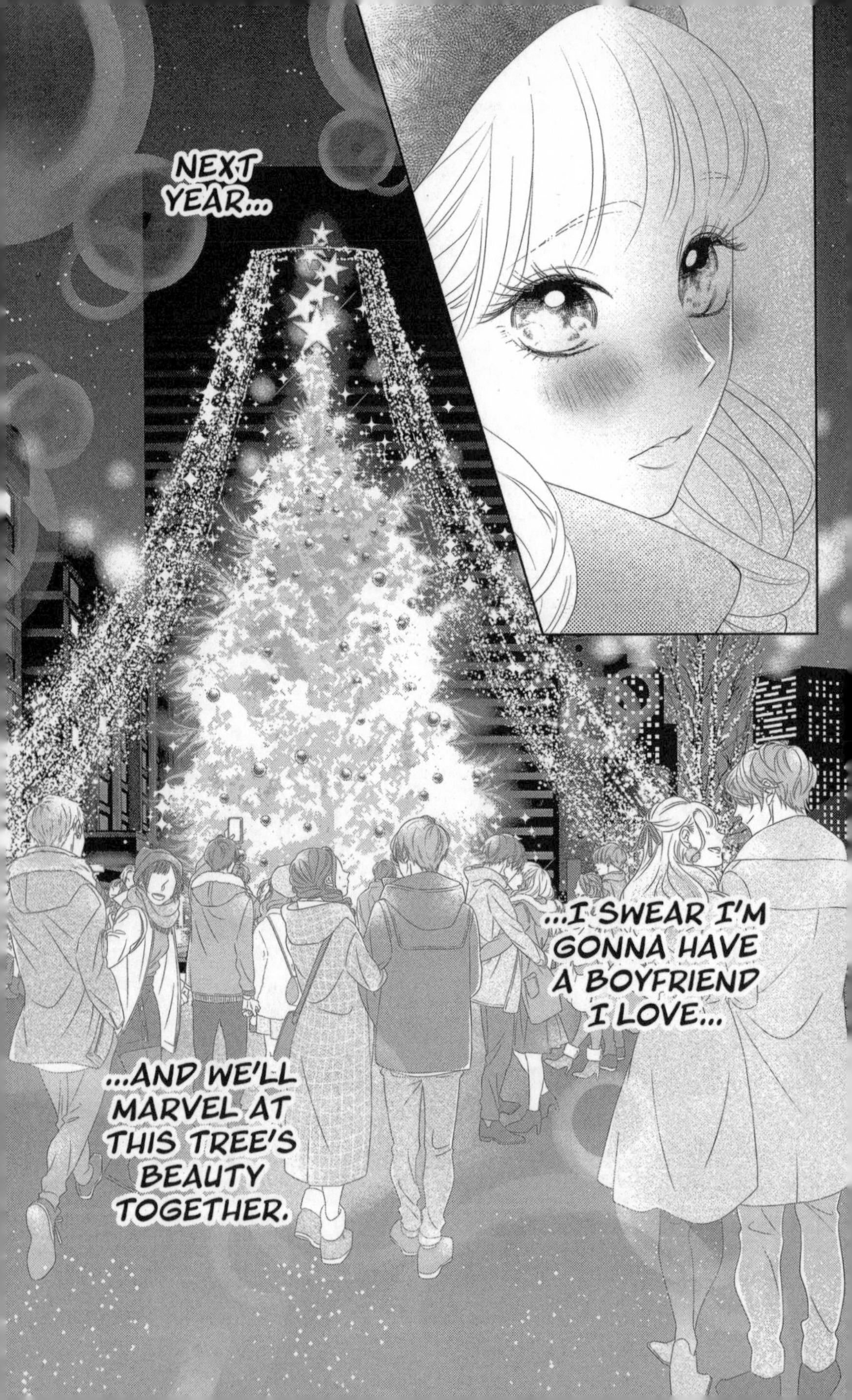
NEXT YEAR...
...I SWEAR I'M GONNA HAVE A BOYFRIEND I LOVE...
...AND WE'LL MARVEL AT THIS TREE'S BEAUTY TOGETHER.

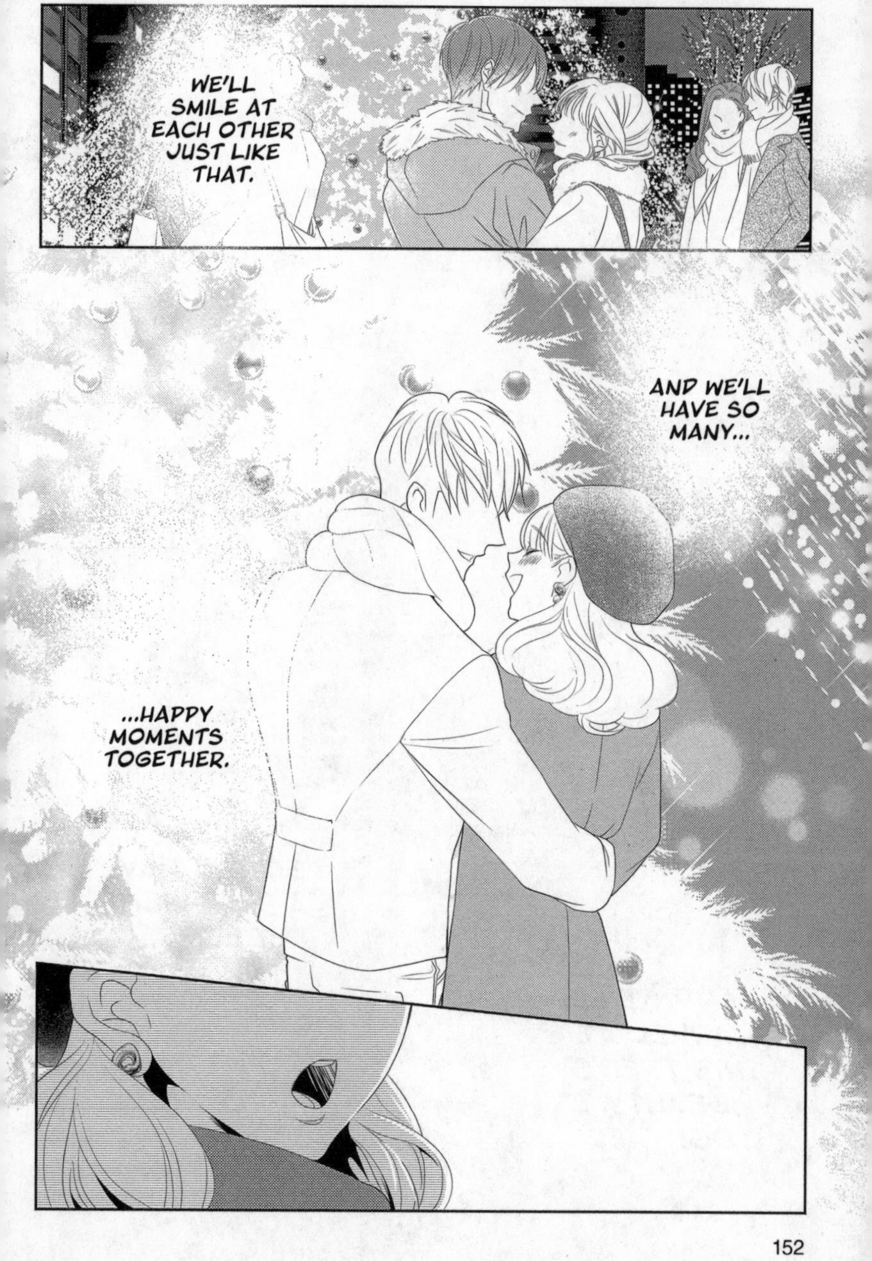
WE'LL SMILE AT EACH OTHER JUST LIKE THAT.
AND WE'LL HAVE SO MANY...
...HAPPY MOMENTS TOGETHER.

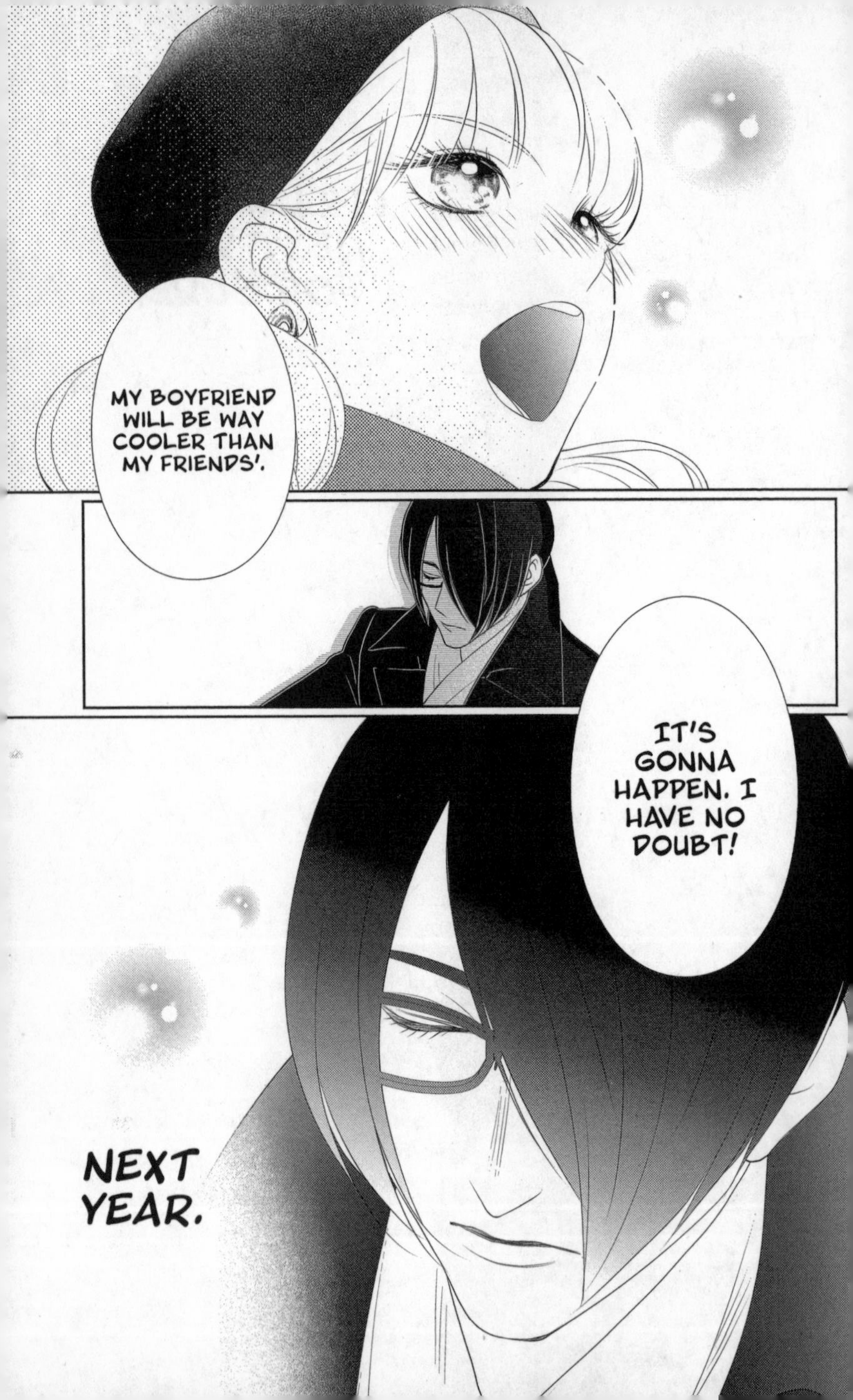
MY BOYFRIEND WILL BE WAY COOLER THAN MY FRIENDS'.
IT'S GONNA HAPPEN. I HAVE NO DOUBT!
NEXT YEAR.

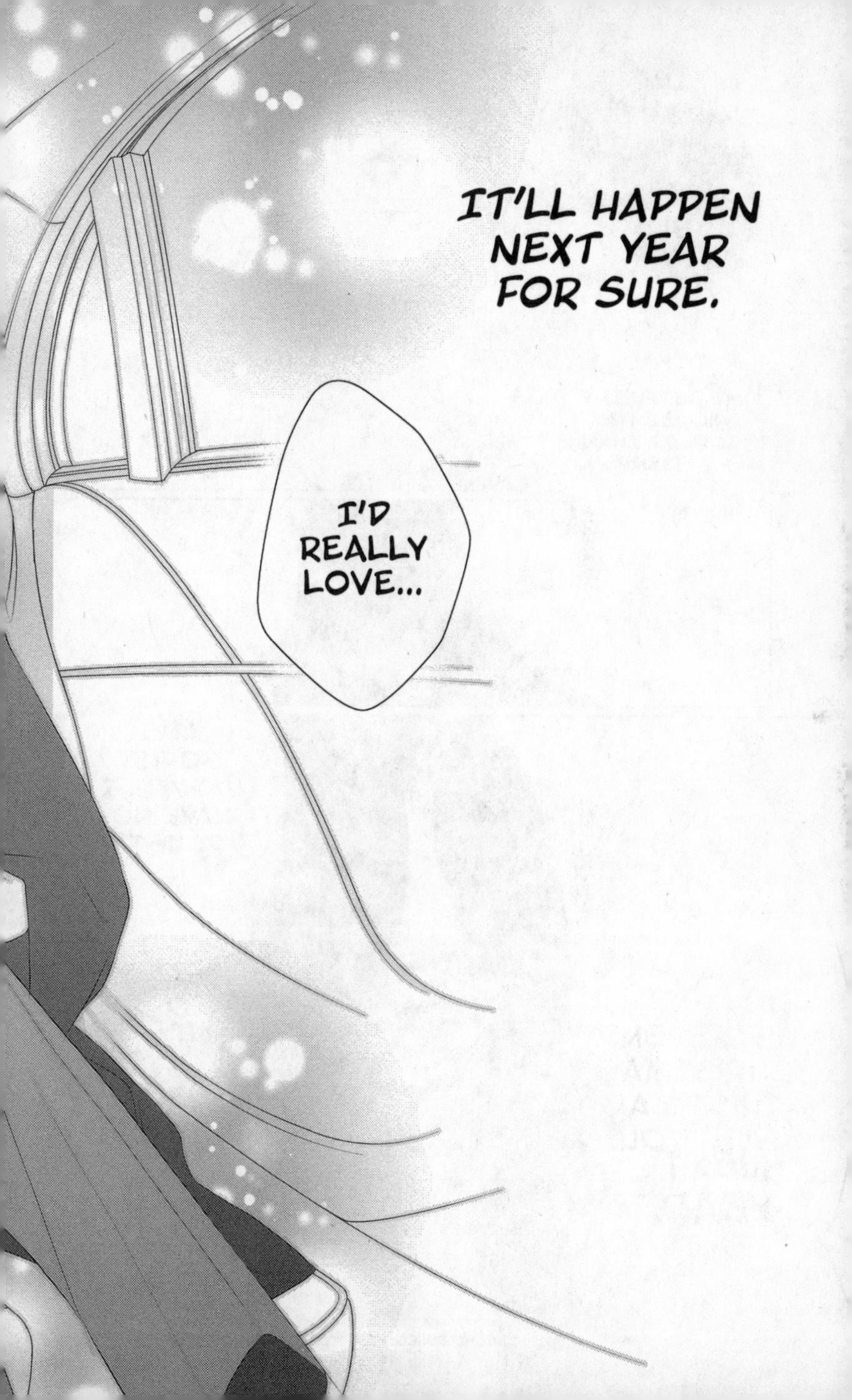
IT'LL HAPPEN NEXT YEAR FOR SURE.
I'D REALLY LOVE...

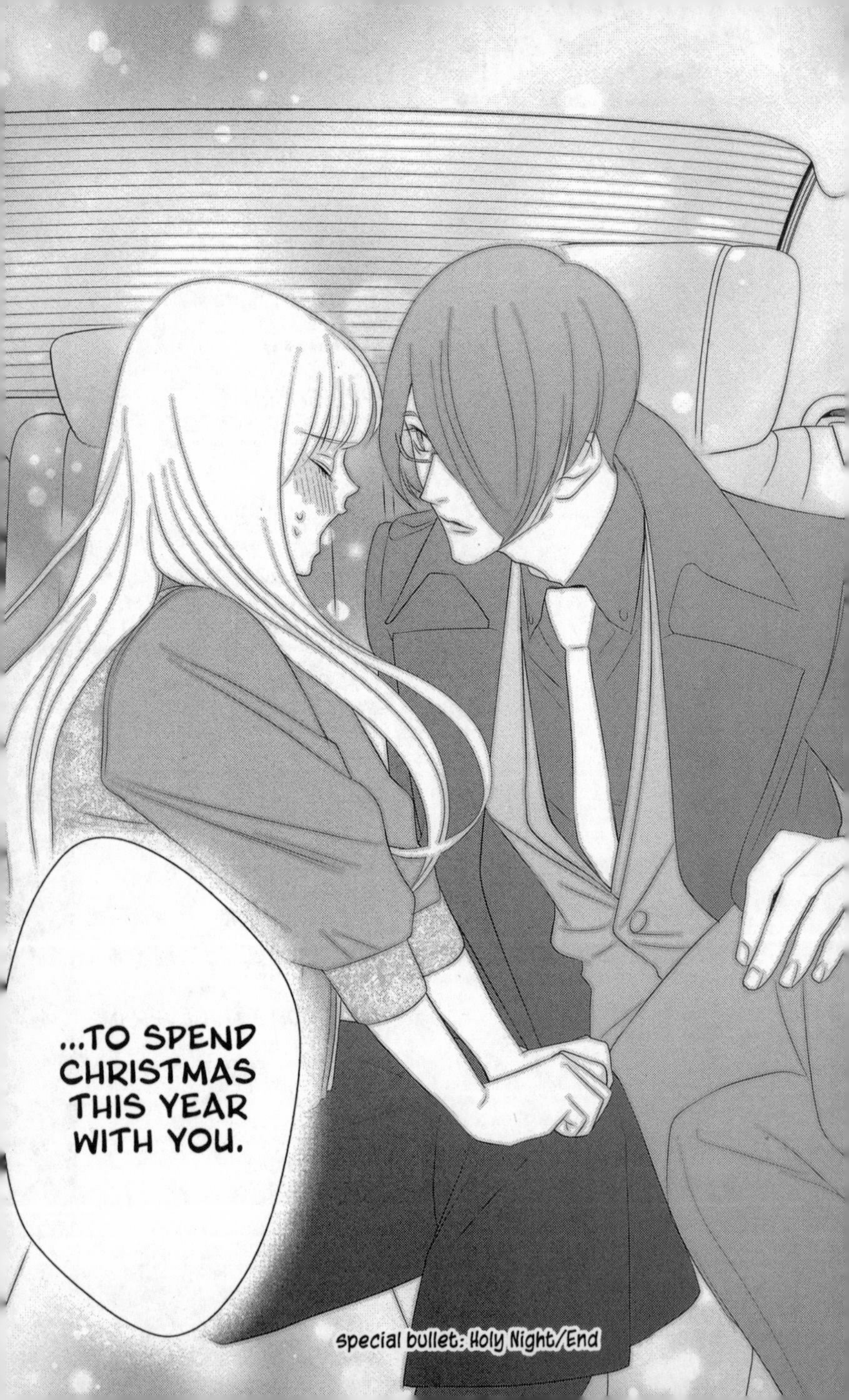
...TO SPEND CHRISTMAS THIS YEAR WITH YOU.
special bullet: Holy Night/End

Special Thanks

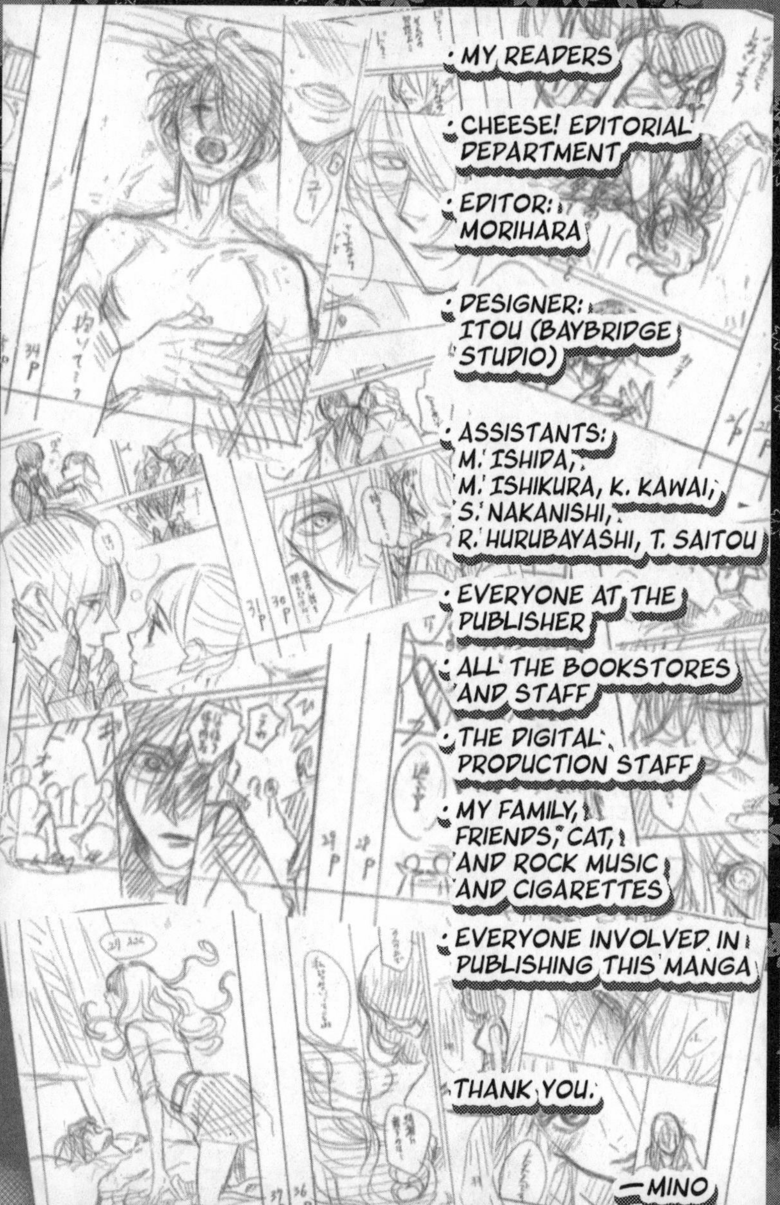

- MY READERS
- CHEESE! EDITORIAL DEPARTMENT
- EDITOR: MORIHARA
- DESIGNER: ITOU (BAYBRIDGE STUDIO)
- ASSISTANTS: M. ISHIDA, M. ISHIKURA, K. KAWAI, S. NAKANISHI, R. HURUBAYASHI, T. SAITOU
- EVERYONE AT THE PUBLISHER
- ALL THE BOOKSTORES AND STAFF
- THE DIGITAL PRODUCTION STAFF
- MY FAMILY, FRIENDS, CAT, AND ROCK MUSIC AND CIGARETTES
- EVERYONE INVOLVED IN PUBLISHING THIS MANGA

THANK YOU.

—MINO

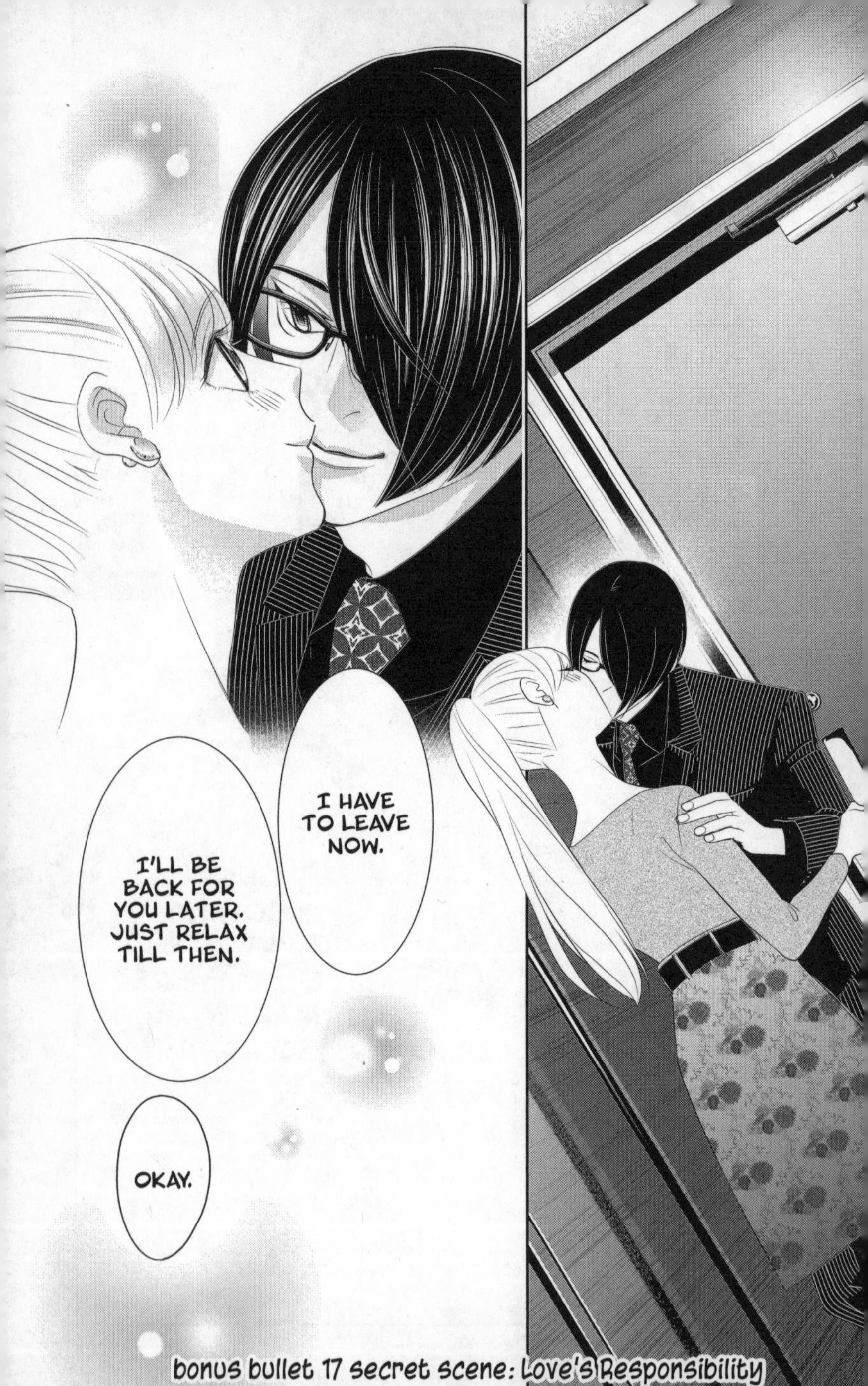
I HAVE TO LEAVE NOW.
I'LL BE BACK FOR YOU LATER. JUST RELAX TILL THEN.
OKAY.

bonus bullet 17 secret scene: Love's Responsibility

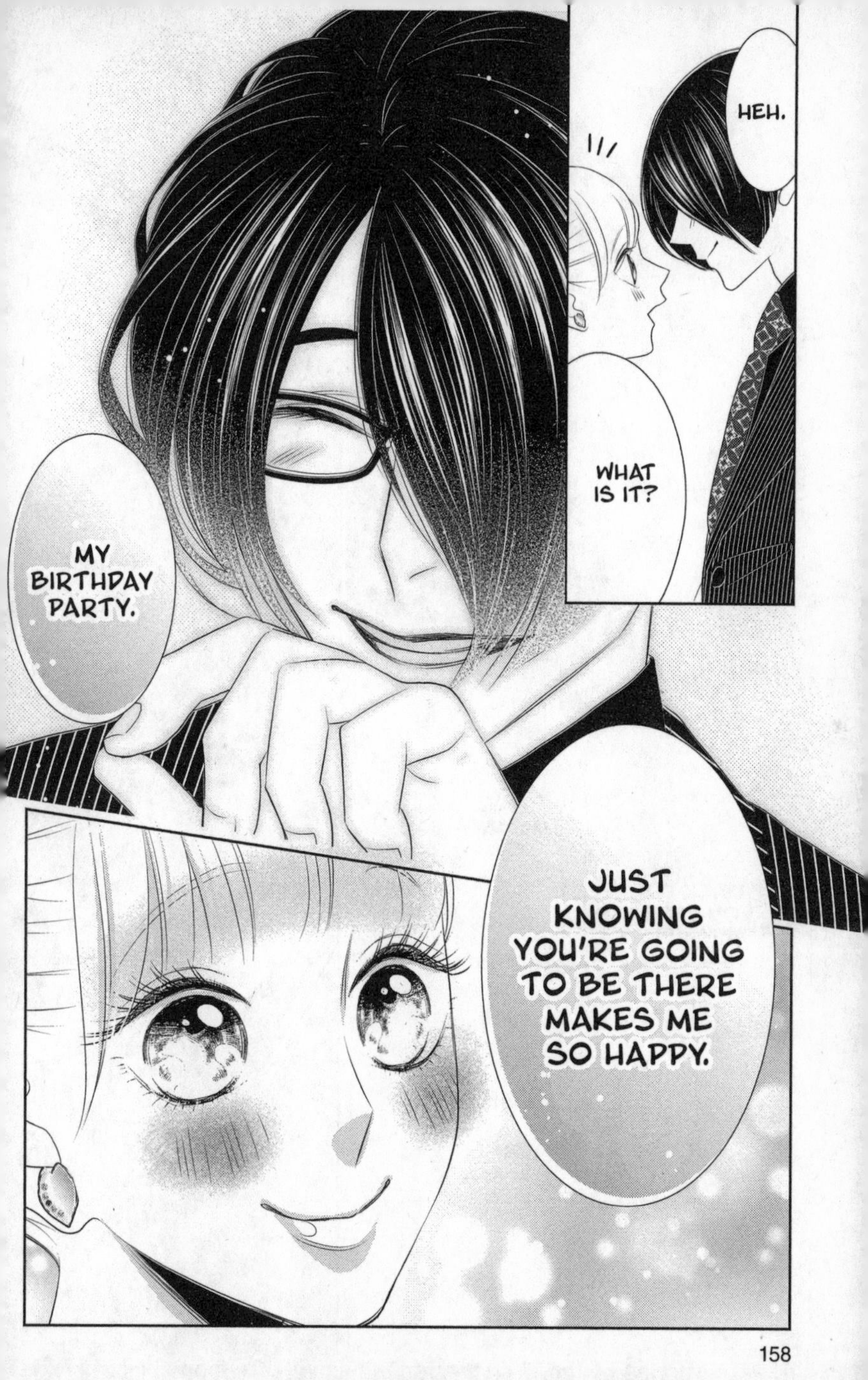
HEH.
WHAT IS IT?
MY BIRTHDAY PARTY.
JUST KNOWING YOU'RE GOING TO BE THERE MAKES ME SO HAPPY.

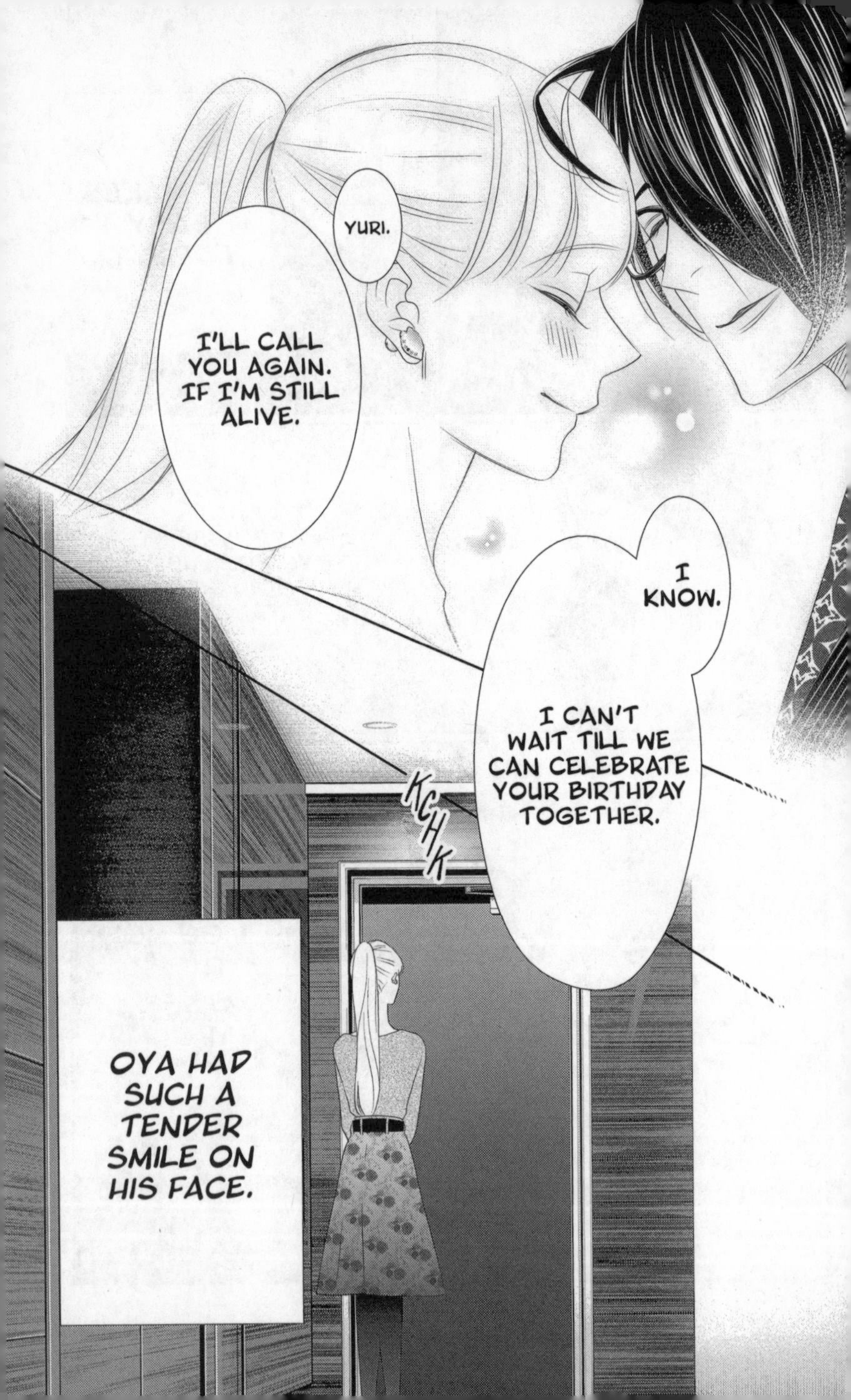
YURI.
I'LL CALL YOU AGAIN. IF I'M STILL ALIVE.
I KNOW.
I CAN'T WAIT TILL WE CAN CELEBRATE YOUR BIRTHDAY TOGETHER.
KCHK
OYA HAD SUCH A TENDER SMILE ON HIS FACE.

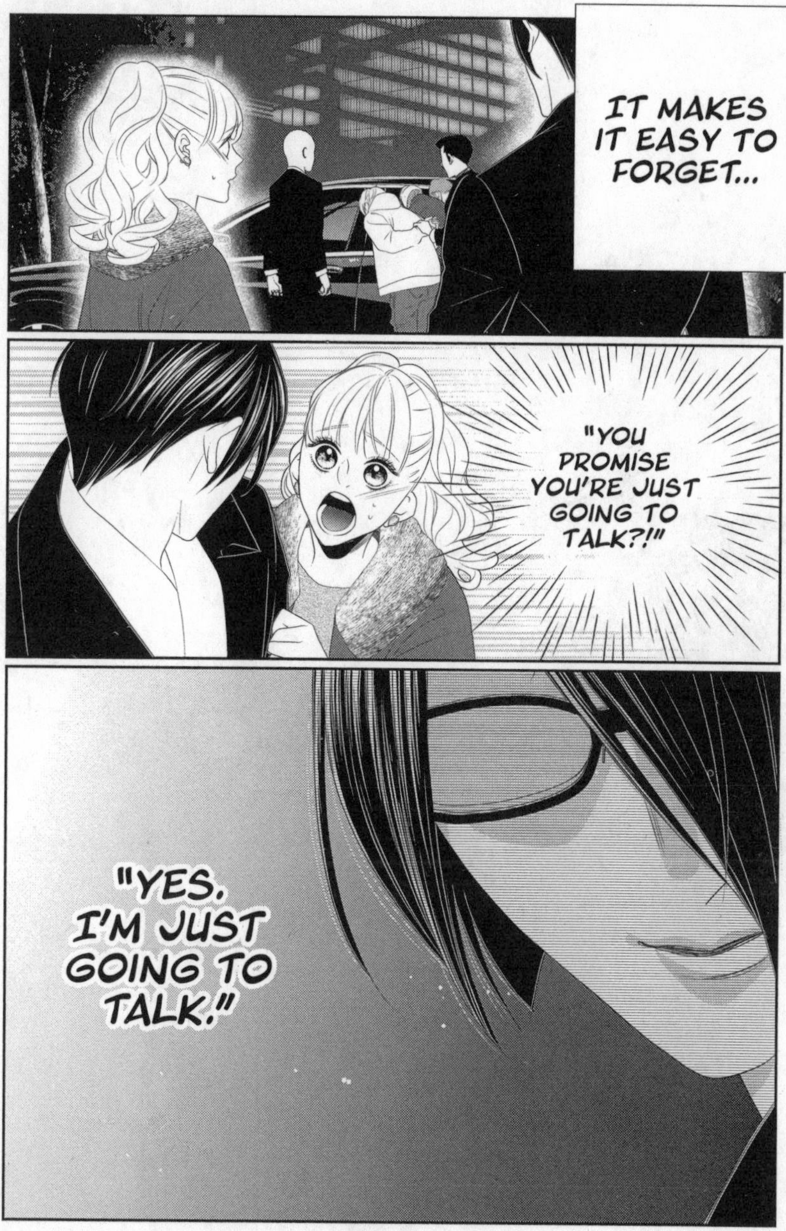
IT MAKES IT EASY TO FORGET...
"YOU PROMISE YOU'RE JUST GOING TO TALK?!"
"YES. I'M JUST GOING TO TALK."

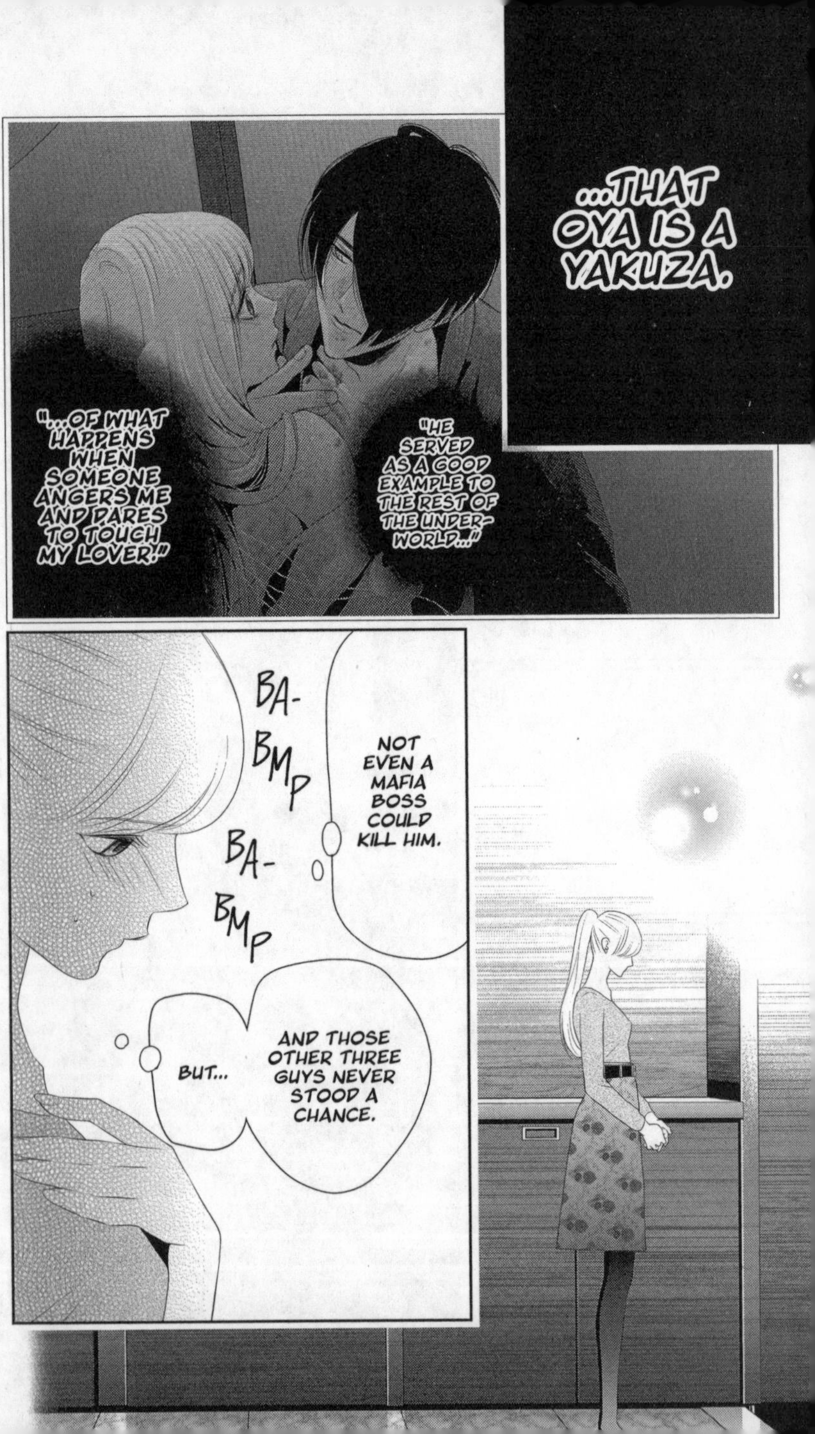
...THAT OYA IS A YAKUZA.
"HE SERVED AS A GOOD EXAMPLE TO THE REST OF THE UNDER-WORLD..."
"...OF WHAT HAPPENS WHEN SOMEONE ANGERS ME AND DARES TO TOUCH MY LOVER!"
NOT EVEN A MAFIA BOSS COULD KILL HIM.
BA-BMP
BA-BMP
AND THOSE OTHER THREE GUYS NEVER STOOD A CHANCE.
BUT...

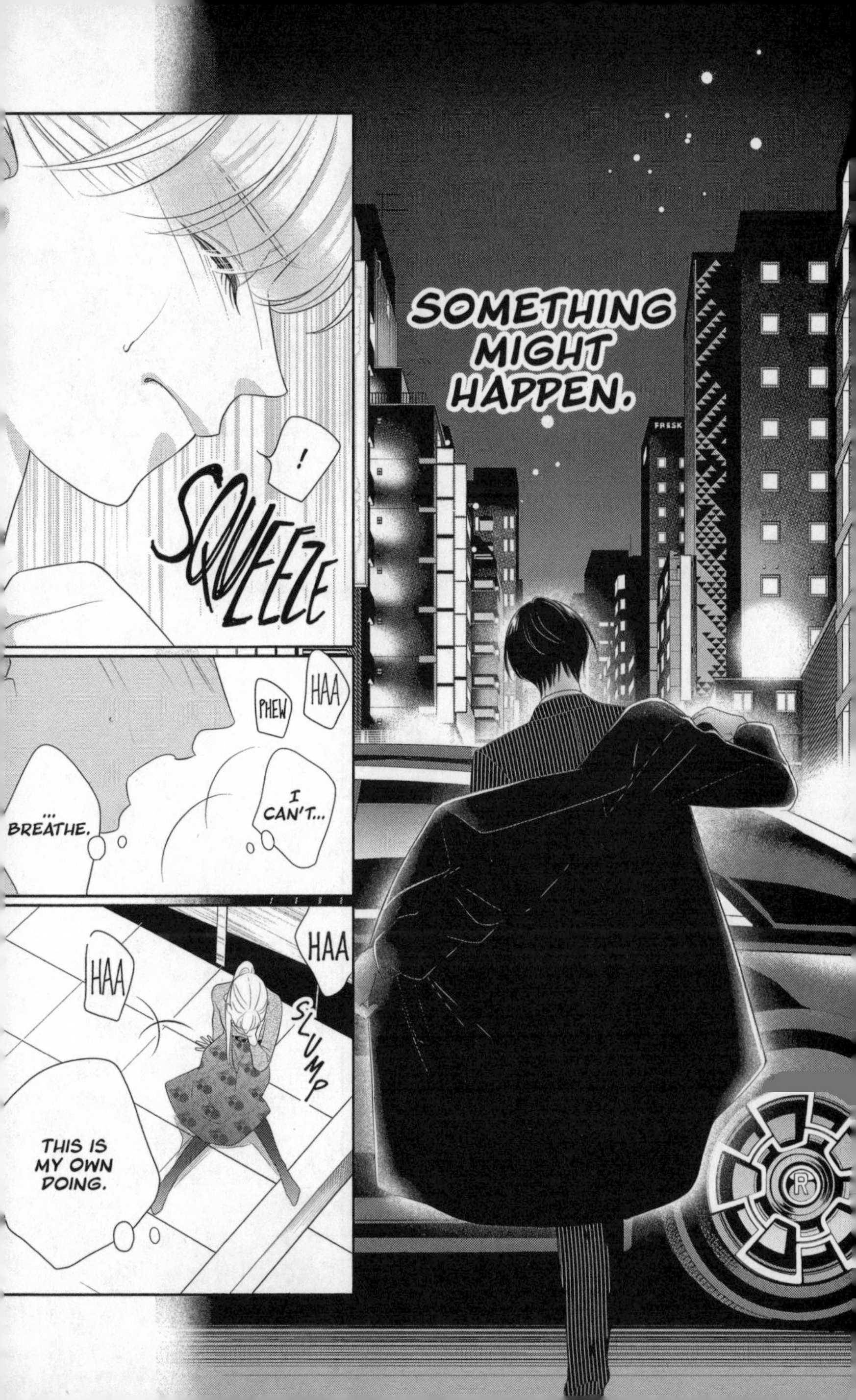
SOMETHING MIGHT HAPPEN.
!
SQUEEZE
HAA
PHEW
I CAN'T...
... BREATHE.
HAA
HAA
SLUMP
THIS IS MY OWN DOING.

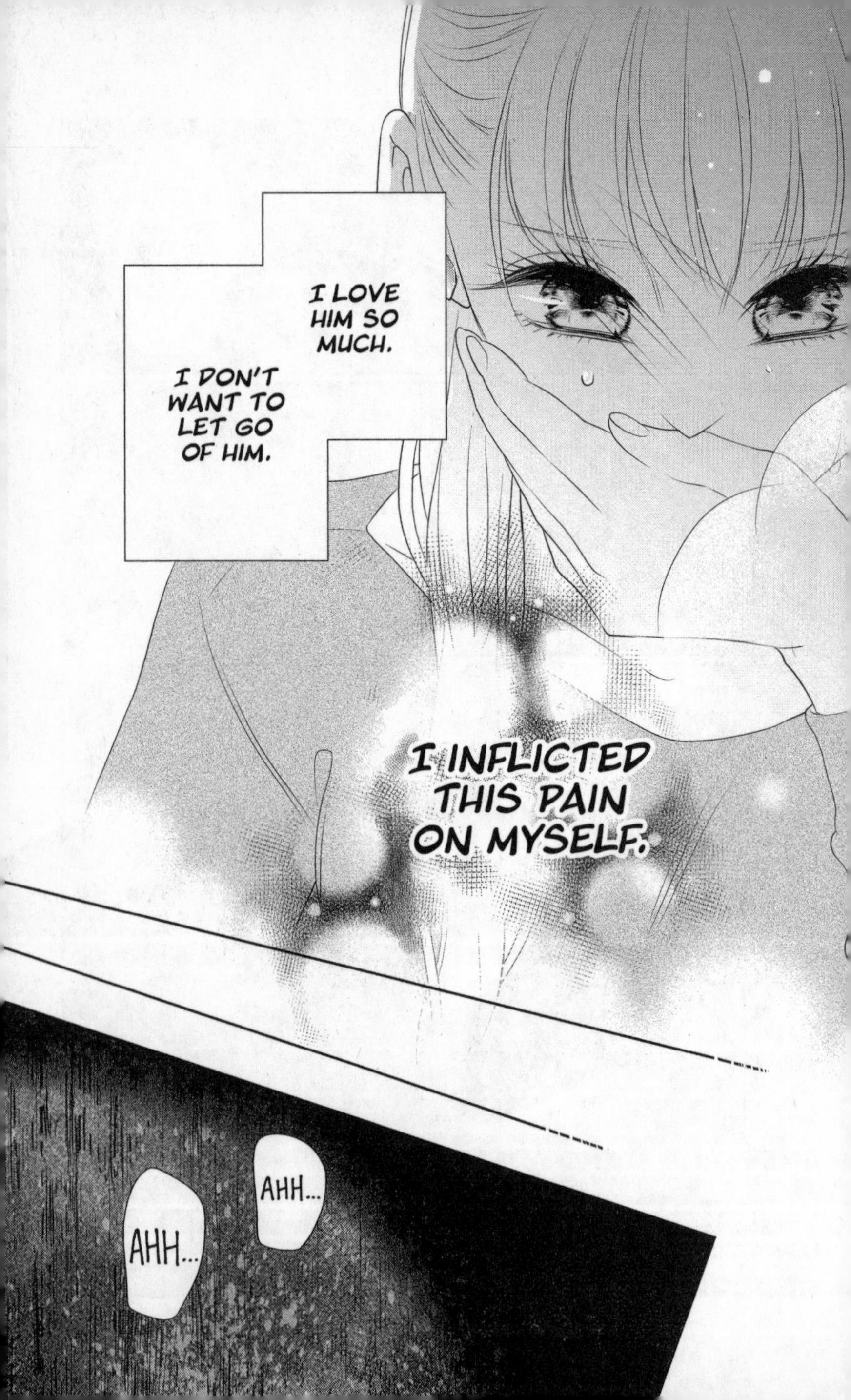
I LOVE HIM SO MUCH.
I DON'T WANT TO LET GO OF HIM.
I INFLICTED THIS PAIN ON MYSELF.
AHH...
AHH...

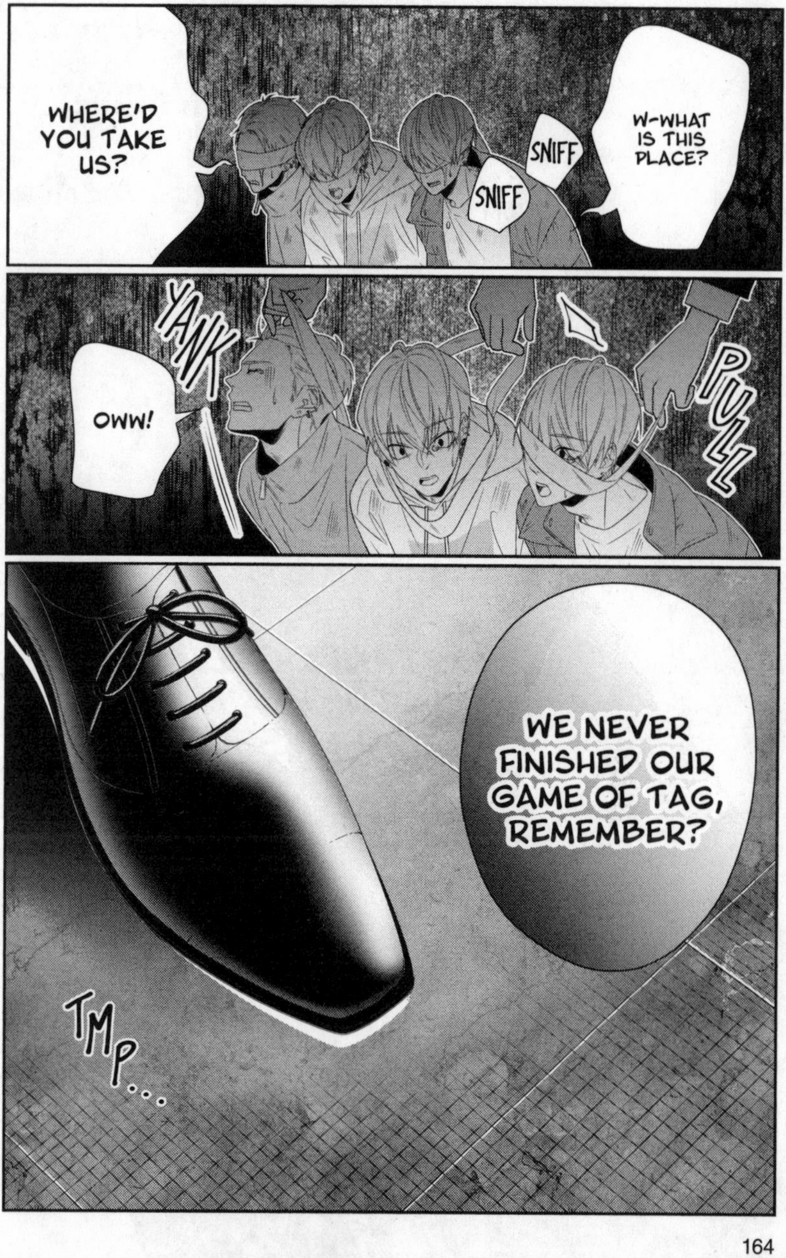
W-WHAT IS THIS PLACE?
SNIFF
SNIFF
WHERE'D YOU TAKE US?
PULL
YANK
OWW!
WE NEVER FINISHED OUR GAME OF TAG, REMEMBER?
TMP...

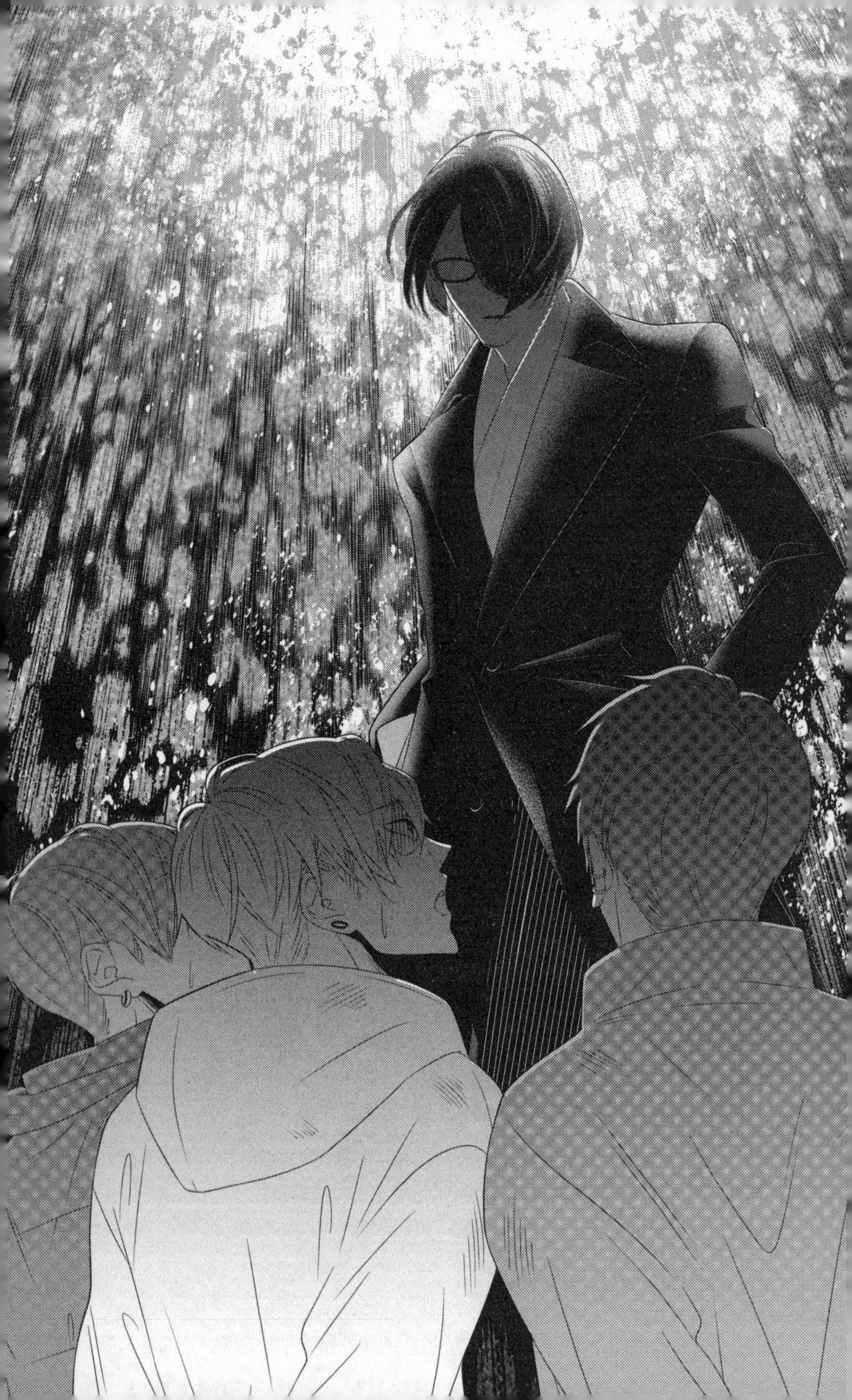

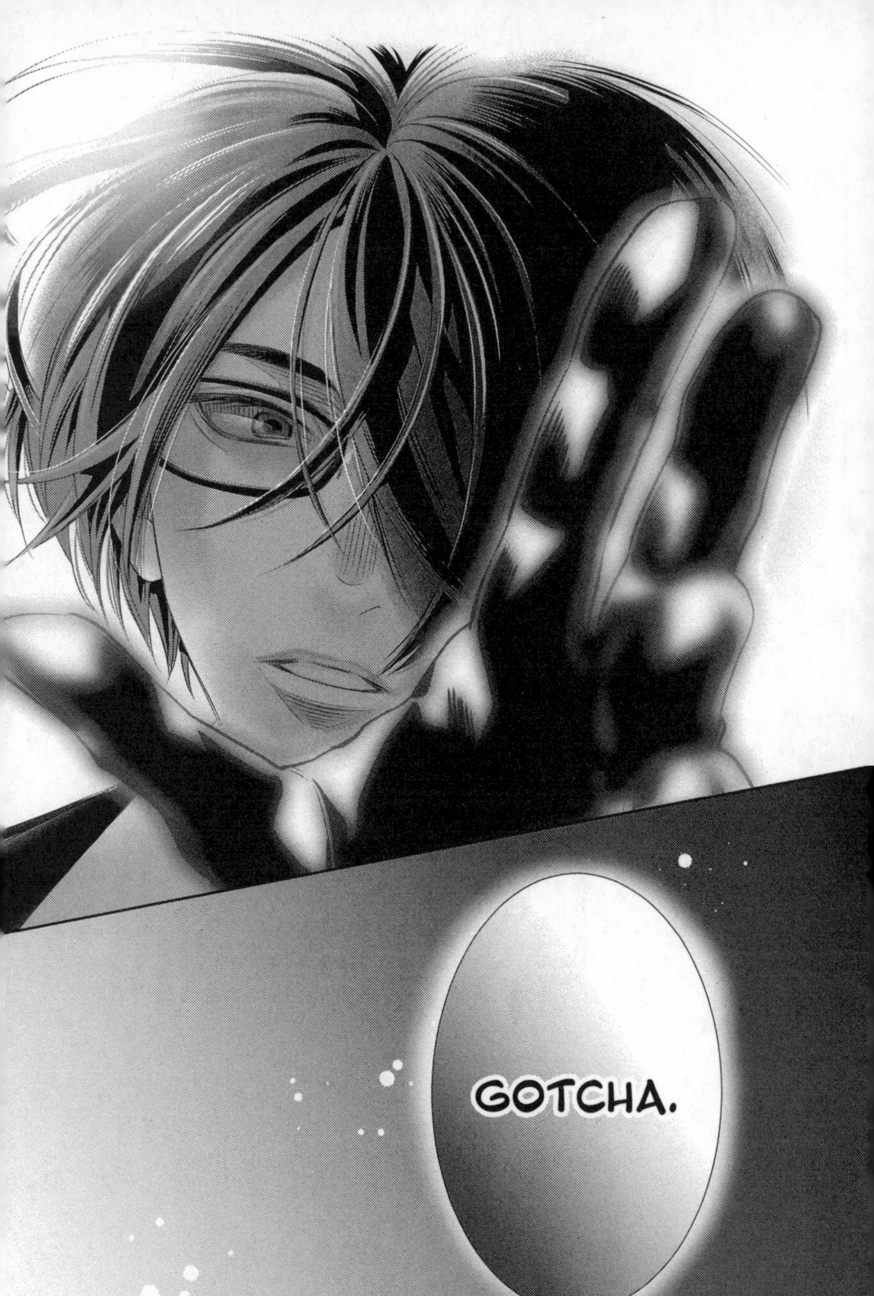
GOTCHA.

bonus bullet 17 secret scene: Love's Responsibility/End

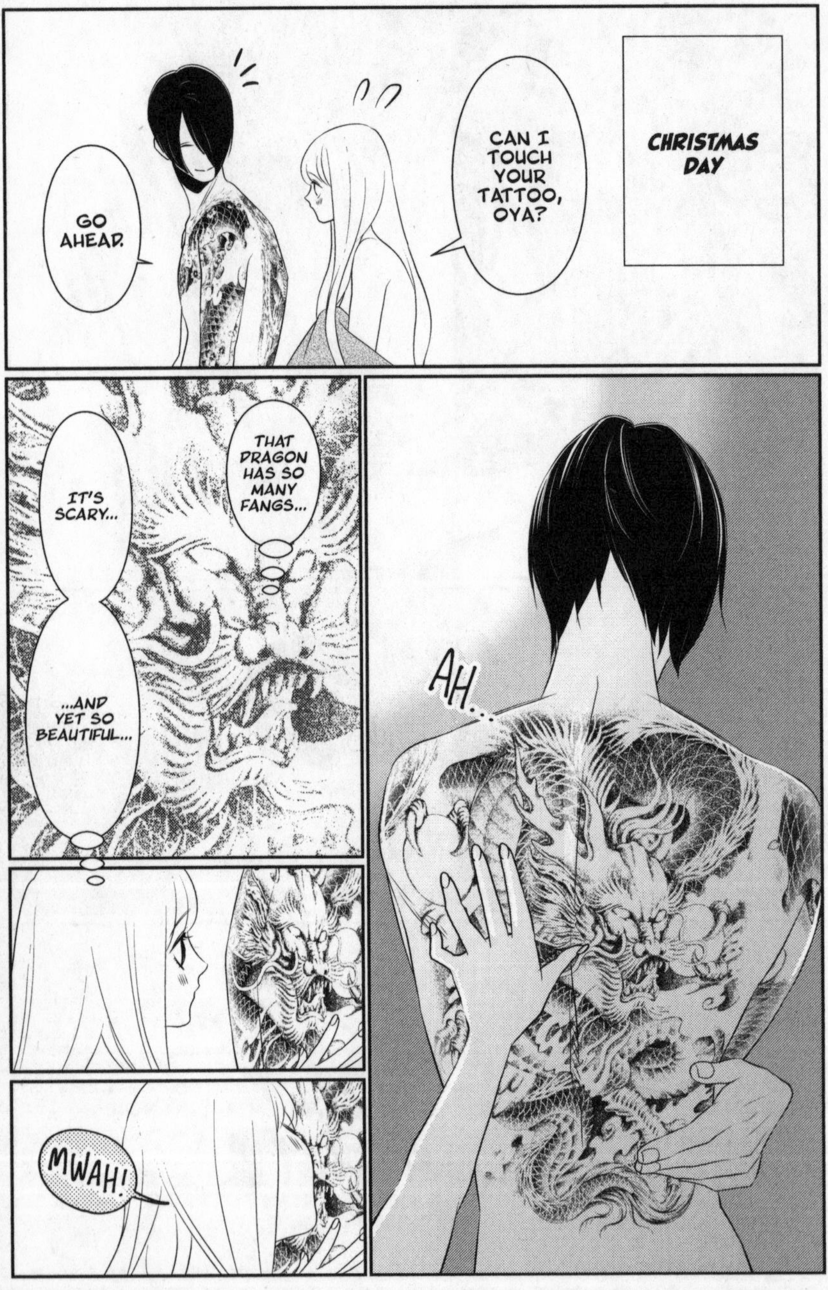
CHRISTMAS DAY
CAN I TOUCH YOUR TATTOO, OYA?
GO AHEAD.
AH...
THAT DRAGON HAS SO MANY FANGS...
IT'S SCARY...
...AND YET SO BEAUTIFUL...
MWAH!

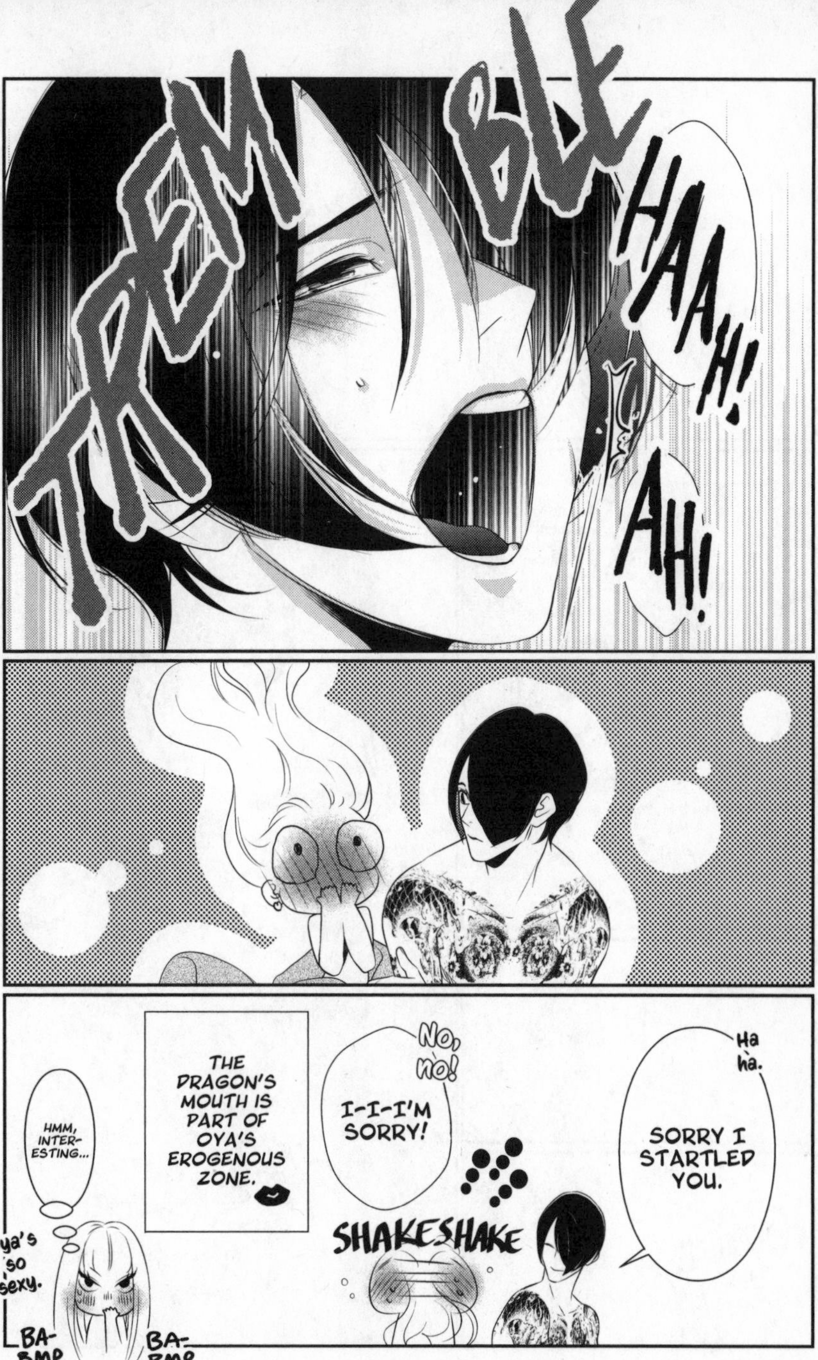
HAAAH!
AH!
TREMBLE
Ha ha.
SORRY I STARTLED YOU.
No, no!
I-I-I'M SORRY!
SHAKESHAKE
THE DRAGON'S MOUTH IS PART OF OYA'S EROGENOUS ZONE.
HMM, INTERESTING...
Oya's so sexy.
BA-BMP
BA-BMP

I want to make an announcement animation just for Twitter.
I'm also planning on making Oya and Yuri dolls this year.

❀ They won't be for sale, but I'll upload pics to Twitter.

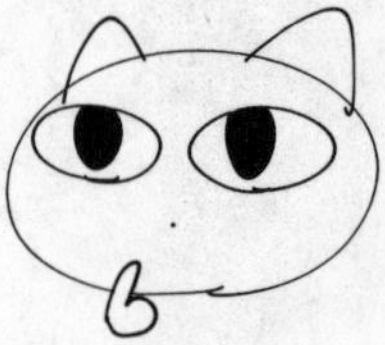

Thank you so much for reading. I call this volume the Yacho (Oya + Choko) volume. I also call it the Choko volume! Will Choko the butterfly dance beautifully when faced with Oya and Yuri's intense love? I hope you enjoy this story.

—Nozomi Mino

Nozomi Mino was born on February 12 in Himeji, Hyogo Prefecture, in Japan, making her an Aquarius. She made her shojo manga debut in the May 2006 issue of *Cheese!* with "LOVE MANTEN" (Love Perfect Score). Since then, she has gone on to publish numerous works, including *Sweet Marriage*, *Wagamama Otoko wa Ichizu ni Koisuru* (Selfish Guys Love Hard), and *LOVE x PLACE.fam*. Her hobbies include going on drives and visiting cafes.

YAKUZA LOVER

Vol. 5
Shojo Beat Edition

STORY AND ART BY
Nozomi Mino

Translation: Andria Cheng
Touch-Up Art & Lettering: Michelle Pang
Design: Yukiko Whitley
Editor: Karla Clark

KOI TO DANGAN Vol. 5
by Nozomi MINO
© 2019 Nozomi MINO
All rights reserved.
Original Japanese edition published by SHOGAKUKAN.
English translation rights in the United States of America, Canada, the United
Kingdom, Ireland, Australia and New Zealand arranged with SHOGAKUKAN.

Printed in the U.S.A.

Published by VIZ Media, LLC
P.O. Box 77010
San Francisco, CA 94107

10 9 8 7 6 5 4 3 2 1
First printing, June 2022

 MEDIA

viz.com   shojobeat.com

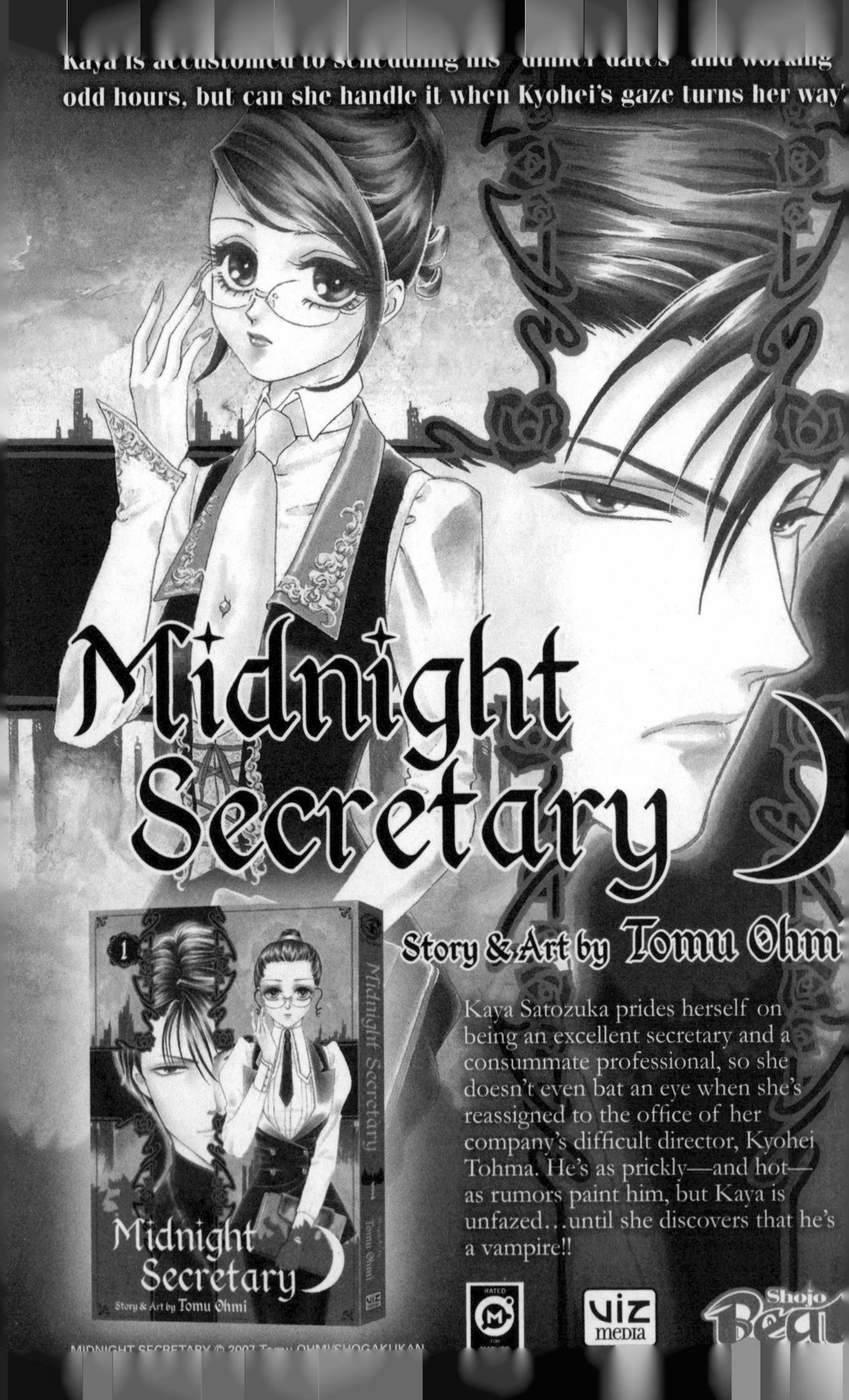
Kaya is accustomed to scheduling his "dinner dates" and working
odd hours, but can she handle it when Kyohei's gaze turns her way?
Midnight Secretary
Story & Art by Tomu Ohmi
Kaya Satozuka prides herself on being an excellent secretary and a consummate professional, so she doesn't even bat an eye when she's reassigned to the office of her company's difficult director, Kyohei Tohma. He's as prickly—and hot—as rumors paint him, but Kaya is unfazed…until she discovers that he's a vampire!!
Midnight Secretary
Story & Art by Tomu Ohmi
RATED M
VIZ media
Shojo Beat
MIDNIGHT SECRETARY © 2007 Tomu OHMI/SHOGAKUKAN

Happy Marriage?!

Story & Art by **Maki Enjoji**

Can two strangers living together find their way to a happy marriage?!

In order to help her father, Chiwa Takanashi agrees to an arranged marriage with the company president, Hokuto Mamiya—a man she doesn't know—at the request of Hokuto's grandfather. Chiwa believes the arrangement isn't binding, but her new partner seems to think otherwise...

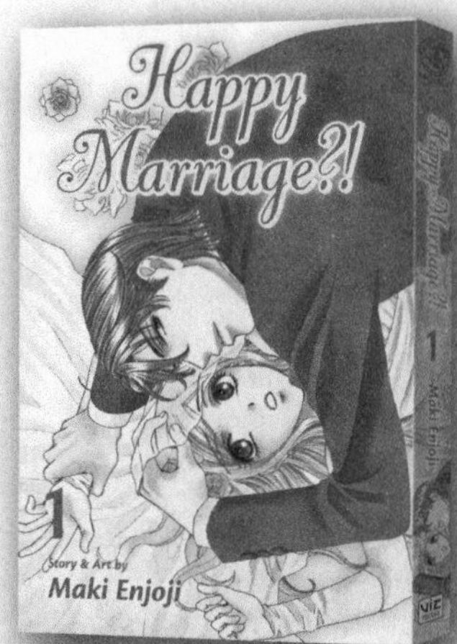

Happy Marriage?!
1
Story & Art by
Maki Enjoji

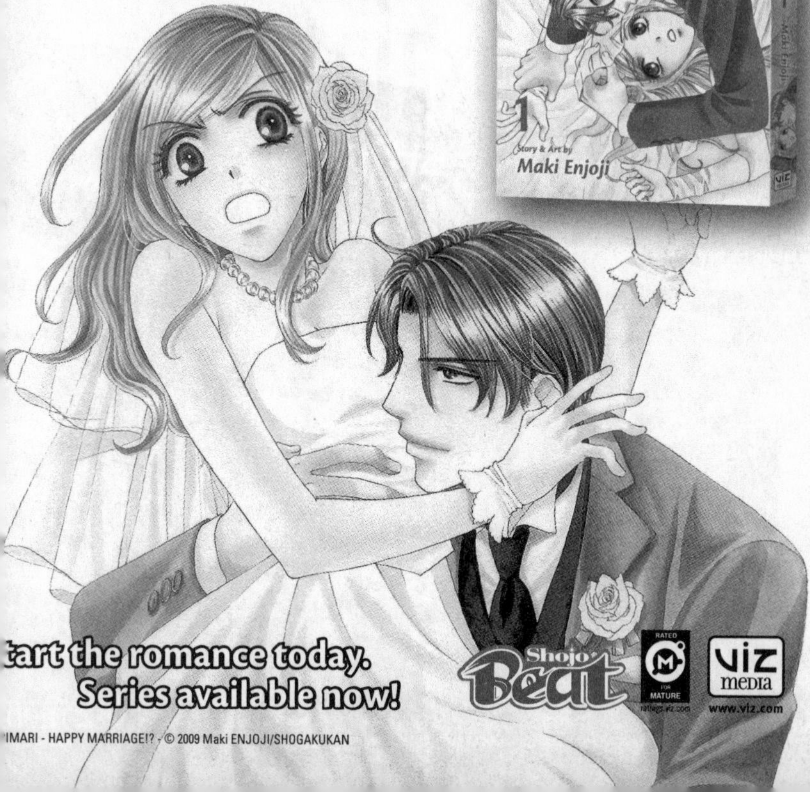

tart the romance today.
Series available now!

Shojo Beat

RATED M FOR MATURE ratings.viz.com

VIZ media
www.viz.com

Everyone's Getting Married

STORY AND ART BY IZUMI MIYAZONO

Successful career woman Asuka Takana has an old-fashioned dream of getting married and becoming a housewife.

After her long-term boyfriend breaks up with her to pursue his own career goals, she encounters popu newscaster Ryu Nanami. Asuka and Ryu get along well, but the last thing he wants is to ever get mar This levelheaded pair who want the opposite thin in life should never get involved, except...

RATED M MATURE

Shojo**Beat**
shojobeat.com

viz me
viz.co

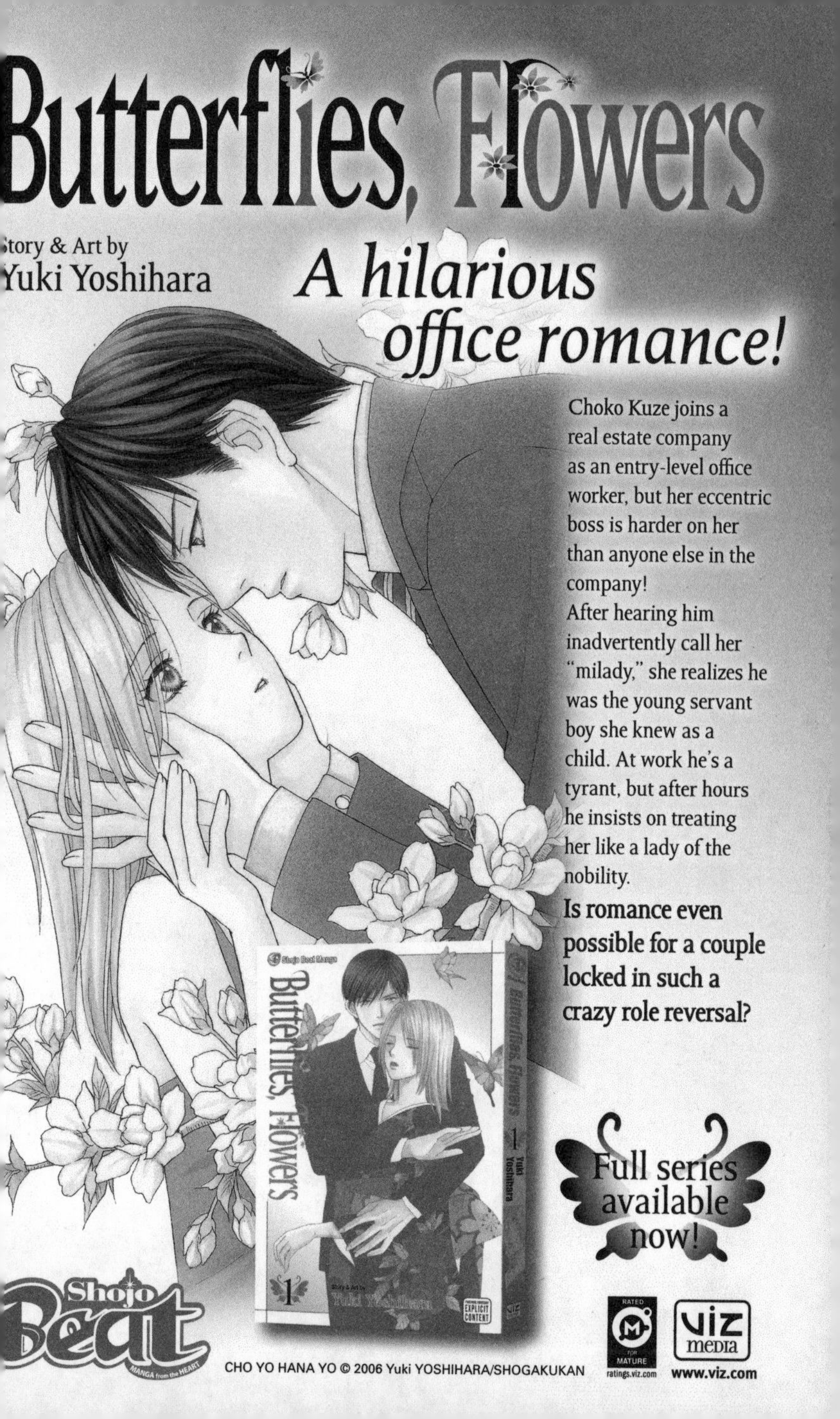
Butterflies, Flowers
Story & Art by Yuki Yoshihara
A hilarious office romance!
Choko Kuze joins a real estate company as an entry-level office worker, but her eccentric boss is harder on her than anyone else in the company!
After hearing him inadvertently call her "milady," she realizes he was the young servant boy she knew as a child. At work he's a tyrant, but after hours he insists on treating her like a lady of the nobility.
Is romance even possible for a couple locked in such a crazy role reversal?
Shojo Beat Manga
Butterflies, Flowers
1
Yuki Yoshihara
EXPLICIT CONTENT
Full series available now!
Shojo Beat
MANGA from the HEART
CHO YO HANA YO © 2006 Yuki YOSHIHARA/SHOGAKUKAN
RATED M FOR MATURE
ratings.viz.com
VIZ media
www.viz.com

lolololol

So Cute It Hurts!!

Story and Art by Go Ikeyamada

The Kobayashi twins, Megumu and Mitsuru, were named after historical figures, but only Megumu has grown up with a taste for history. So when Mitsuru is in danger of losing his weekends to extra history classes, he convinces his sister to swap clothes with him and ace his tests! After all, how hard can it be for them to play each other?

But Megumu can't rely on just her book smarts in Mitsuru's all-boys, delinquents' paradise of a high school. And Mitsuru finds life as a high school girl to be much more complicated than he expected!

lolololol

So Cute It Hurts!!

Story and Art by Go Ikeyamada

KOBAYASHI GA KAWAISUGITE TSURAI!! © 2012 Go IKEYAMADA/SHOGAKUKAN

STOP RIGHT THERE!

You're reading the wrong way!

In keeping with the original Japanese comic format, *Yakuza Lover* reads from right to left, starting in the upper-right corner—so action, sound effects, and word-balloon order are completely reversed to preserve the orientation of the original artwork.

So go ahead and flip the book over. You wouldn't want to spoil the ending for yourself now, would you?

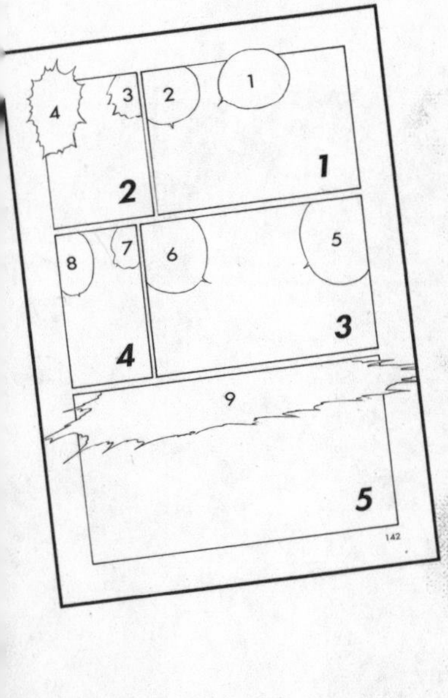
1
2
3
4
1
2
5
6
7
8
3
4
9
5
142

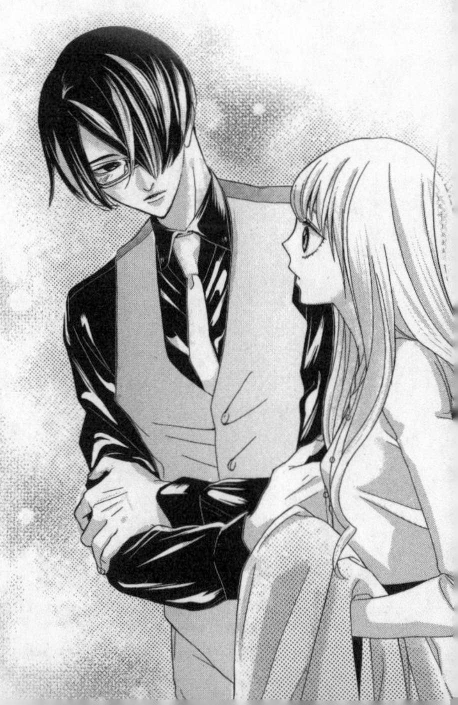